RECENT ADVANCES IN INDIAN MEDICAL ANTHROPOLOGY

Editors

P. C. Joshi is the acting Vice-Chancellor of the University of Delhi. He has been the Head of the Department in Anthropology in the University of Delhi. He served as Head of the Department in various institutions like HNB Garhwal University and Institute of Human Behaviour and Allied Sciences. He is the current president of the Society for Indian Medical Anthropology, Mysore and specializes in the fields of Medical Anthropology, Himalayan Anthropology, Antibiotic Resistance and Qualitative Research Methods. His scientific publications are in the field of Medical Anthropology, Traditional Medicines, Shamanism, Impact of Disasters, Life Style Diseases and Antibiotic Resistance. Besides nine books, his papers numbering more than 150 have appeared in various professional journals of international repute. (pcjoshi@anthro.du.ac.in)

Chakraverti Mahajan is Assistant Professor in Anthropology at the University of Delhi. His research has focused on Western Himalayas (especially Jammu & Kashmir and Himachal Pradesh) and Delhi, and has engaged a broad range of ethnographic and theoretical issues. These include the politics of militarization, state-society relations, communalism and Hindu-Muslim relations, shifting practices of food, Sufism and shared sacred spaces, Islamic Law and property inheritance, visibility/invisibility of Muslims in urban spaces and Devta institutions. He has published research papers in various journals. (cmahajan@anthro.du.ac.in)

RECENT ADVANCES IN INDIAN MEDICAL ANTHROPOLOGY

Edited by
P. C. JOSHI
CHAKRAVERTI MAHAJAN

CONCEPT PUBLISHING COMPANY PVT. LTD.
NEW DELHI-110059

ISBN-13: 978-93-5439-064-7

First Published 2021

Published and Printed by

Concept Since 1974

Concept Publishing Company Pvt. Ltd.
A/15-16, Commercial Block, Mohan Garden
New Delhi-110059 (India)
T: 91 11 41101460, 91 11 25351460, 91 11 25351794
E: publishing@conceptpub.com; W : www.conceptpub.com

Cataloging in Publication Data--Courtesy: D.K. Agencies (P) Ltd. <docinfo@dkagencies.com>

Recent advances in Indian medical anthropology / edited by P.C. Joshi, Chakraverti Mahajan.
pages cm
Contributed articles.
Includes bibliographical references and index.
ISBN 9789354390647

1. Medical anthropology--India. I. Joshi, P. C., 1956- editor. II. Mahajan, Chakraverti, editor.

LCC GN296.5.I4R43 2021 | DDC 306.4610954 23

Acknowledgements

In editing this volume of essays, we have incurred a huge debt of gratitude to the contributors, spread across the country and abroad, whose diligence, competency and professionalism have made what is undeniably a challenging task an exhilarating and learning venture. We are also indebted to a number of people, too many to mention individually. However, following deserve special mention: B.V. Sharma, Abhik Ghosh, Prashant Khattri, Gunjan Arora and Nilisha Vashisht for reviewing the essays and providing constructive comments which helped us to shape the book and Rashmi Patel, Subhradeep Pathak and Krishna Kant Yadav for their assistance in preparing the manuscript. We are thankful to Mr. Ashok Mittal and the Concept Publishing Company for working on this volume with utmost care in the difficult times.

Contents

Contributors

A.K. Sinha is Professor of Social Anthropology in the Department of Anthropology, Panjab University, Chandigarh. He was the chairperson of the Department at Chandigarh and Coordinator of its Centre of Advanced Studies (CAS) funded by University Grants Commission (UGC), Delhi. He has carried out many research projects under the Special Assistance Programme (SAP) and CAS programmes. His research areas include anthropology of sweetmeats, pilgrimage studies, Health, Women and Panchayati Raj, Tribal studies and many more. He has published 15 books and 125 research articles in various national and international journals. (aksinha58@gmail.com)

Abhishek Sharma is working as Project Coordinator in the School of Public Health, PGIMER, Chandigarh. He is looking after the project on health vulnerability assessment of urban slums in Haryana. Earlier, he was employed in the same organization as Data Analyst conducting population health research. He has a doctorate degree in Anthropology from Panjab University, specializing in the field of medical anthropology. He is keenly interested in biosocial and ethnographic research. (abhishekanthropu@gmail.com)

Asaf Sharabi is a Senior Lecturer in the School of Behavioural Sciences at Peres Academic Centre, Israel, and an associate member in the Centre for Himalayan Studies (CEH), Aubervilliers, France. His research interests include anthropology of religion and medical anthropology both in India and Israel. His research in the Western Himalaya focuses on the *devi-devta* culture, while his research in Israel focuses on the religious revival movement. Until now he has published 16 articles in peer reviewed journals including *Ethnography, Anthropological Forum, Medical Anthropology, Anthropology and Medicine, Religion, and Journal of Contemporary Religion*. (asafsharabi@gmail.com)

Ashwin Tripathi is a doctoral student at the Indian Institute of Technology, Gandhi Nagar. She is working on Social Ageing, Intergenerational Relationships and Caring Responsibilities among Indian families. She has received her Bachelor's degree in Anthropology from University of Delhi, where she worked on the socio-cultural aspects of the Bhil community in Udaipur. She has earned her MA in Social Anthropology from Queen's University of Belfast (United Kingdom). Her MA research focused on the Indian Immigrants in the UK and she worked on developing care models within the community. She has also worked as an independent researcher with the Indian Community Centre (Belfast) and ArtsEkta. Her research interests include areas of Social Anthropology, Sociology of Ageing and Population studies. (tripathi.ashwin05@gmail.com)

Avanee Khatri is ICSSR Post-Doctoral Fellow in the Department of Anthropology, Panjab University, Chandigarh. Her current research deals with the nature of medical pluralism and evolution of AYUSH in India. Her earlier work focused on anthropological discourses on information and communication technologies. She has published in many reputed journals including *The Eastern Anthropologist, The Oriental Anthropologist* and the *Journal of Anthropological Survey of India*. (khatriavni@gmail.com)

Bamdev Subedi is a medical anthropologist with an interest in public health issues. He holds an MA in Anthropology from Tribhuvan University, Kathmandu and MPhil and Ph.D. from Centre of Social Medicine and Community Health, Jawaharlal Nehru University, New Delhi. He has more than a decade of working experience in health and community development programmes. His research interests include traditional medicine, medical pluralism and political economy of health. (bamdevsubedi@gmail.com)

Drabita Dutta is a Doctoral student in the Department of Anthropology, University of Delhi. She is working on metal-craft works in Assam. Her interest areas include Labour Studies, Gender Studies and Medical Anthropology. (drabita10arya@gmail.com)

Gunjan Arora is Post-Doctoral Fellow at the Centre of Social Medicine and Community Health, Jawaharlal Nehru University, New Delhi. She has an experience of teaching 'gender studies' and 'social anthropology' at the University of Delhi and Guru Gobind Singh Indraprastha University and has written course content for IGNOU. She is actively engaged with the Anthropos India Foundation (AIF) for more than year now. Her Ph.D. work engages with Anthropology of Body, Body Politics and Medical Anthropology. Her research interests include assisted reproductive technologies and motherhood, gender studies, Feminism, Body and Space, Ethnography and Narrative method. (gunjanedu@yahoo.co.in)

Gurinder Kaur is Assistant Professor at a reputed ICSSR (New Delhi), research institute, Centre for Research in Rural and Industrial Development, Chandigarh, India. She has a Ph.D. in Anthropology from Panjab University, Chandigarh. Her academic training is in social anthropology and her research interests include medical anthropology, particularly critical medical anthropology. Her research focuses on medical pluralism, cultural connotations of health and illness, social biography of drug addiction and structural and institutional factors influencing health and illness. She has published research articles in edited books and journals and has published book on *Religion and Health: Narratives on Faith Healing*. She has been part of the research teams conducting research studies on gender, drug addiction, farmer suicide, childhood immunisation, women self-employment. (ginniesodhi@gmail.com)

Kalyan K. Ganguly superannuated from Indian Council for Medical Research as Scientist G/Sr. Dy. Director General. He has been involved in various socio-behavioral researches all through his research career. Some of the works on Drug de-addiction got published in books and journals in the UK. And on the basis of those publications he was awarded ICMR young scientist award 1996. Subsequently he got NIH fellowship to work on HIV AIDS in the year 2011. He has been chair and member of many Institutional ethics committees across India. (kalyanganguly@hotmail.com)

Khirod Chandra Moharana is an Assistant Professor in the Department of Anthropology, University of Allahabad since 2013. He received his Ph.D. from Indian Institute of Technology, Delhi and the title of his thesis is "Mental Illness among the Hos of Odisha: An Ethnographic Study". Based on six-month anthropological fieldwork in three tribal villages in Odisha he examined how social suffering gets translated into mental illness. His research interest includes mental health/illness, climate change and consumption. In 2012 he attended the "Leadership for Mental Health" course by London School of Hygiene and Tropical Medicine, UK and Sangath, Goa. He has experience of anthropological fieldwork among the Hos and Santhals of Odisha, the Chenchus (a primitive tribal group) of Mehboobnagar district of Andhra Pradesh, and the Bharias and Gonds of Madhya Pradesh. He has also contributed for the Self-Learning Course Material published by IGNOU and for epg-pathshala by MHRD. (khirodmoharana@gmail.com)

Mathew George is Professor with the Centre for Public Health, School of Health Systems Studies, Tata Institute of Social Sciences, Mumbai. He has a basic training in Public Health with a doctorate in Social Medicine and Community Health from Jawaharlal Nehru University (JNU), New Delhi. His background in public health has created a keen interest in developing a social epidemiological approach in public health as it is relevant in Indian context. Currently, he is engaged with research on the scope of restructuring the Indian Health Services System from a public health perspective. As a passion he is also engaged in the field of Sociology of Health and Illness with special emphasis on the sociology of medical practice and medical knowledge in biomedicine and also interaction between multiple systems of medicine. (mathewg@tiss.edu)

Prashant Khattri is currently working as Assistant Professor, Department of Anthropology, University of Allahabad, Prayagraj. He is the Charles Wallace Fellow in Social Anthropology at the Queen's University, Belfast, UK, for the session 2020-21. He has done his MSc and Ph.D. from the Department of Anthropology, University of Delhi. His areas of interest include Anthropology of Disasters, Environmental Anthropology, Anthropology of Health and Well-being and Tribal and National Identity Politics. He has published articles in journals like the *Economic and Political Weekly* and Journals published from Sage. He has also edited (co-editor) a book on *Indian Diaspora* in Hindi, published from Rajkamal Prakashan. (prashantkhattri3@gmail.com)

Priyanka Ghosh is currently pursuing her Ph.D. in Public Health in the School of Health Systems Studies, Tata Institute of Social Sciences, Mumbai. She did her M.Phil. research from the same institute, which focused on various issues related to pregnancy and childbirth in an urban Indian context. She has done her graduation and post-graduation in Anthropology from West Bengal State University and University of Delhi, respectively. Her specialisation has been in Social Anthropology, and her interest areas lie mostly within the domain of Medical Anthropology. (priyankaghosh.tiss@gmail.com)

Ravin Srivastava is a master's graduate from Department of Anthropology, University of Delhi. He has previously worked with the National Centre for Disease Control, Delhi as a Medical Social Worker. His interest areas include anthropology of food, health and languages. (srivastava.ravin@gmail.com)

Ravinder Singh is Associate Professor and Head, Department of Medical Anthropology, Institute of Human Behaviour and Allied Sciences Hospital, Faculty of Medical Sciences, University of

Delhi. He has published more than thirty five papers in reputed international and national journals. Formerly, he had been Assistant Director (Child Care) for more than a decade in National Institute of Public Cooperation and Child Development, Ministry of Women and Child Development, Government of India, New Delhi. (medicalanthropology.ihbas@gmail.com)

Reetinder Kaur is currently a graduate student in Asian Studies at the University of British Columbia, Vancouver. She works as a Research Coordinator at Providence Health Care Research Institute, Vancouver. She has a strong research background in the field of Anthropology and received a Ph.D. degree from Panjab University, Chandigarh. She is a recipient of various fellowships such as Indian Council of Medical Research's Doctoral Fellowship (2009), University Grants Commission's Post-doctoral Fellowship for Women (2014) and Shastri Indo-Canadian Institute's Post-doctoral Fellowship at the University of British Columbia (2017). Her research interests include South Asian health, mental health, and Indian cinema. Her research interests include Punjabi cinema, Hindi/Urdu cinema and South Asian health particularly mental health and environmental health. (reetinder1986@gmail.com)

Sneha Gupta completed her doctoral research at the Department of Anthropology, University of Delhi. Her dissertation is based on fieldwork carried out on drug de-addiction centres in Delhi. Her research interest includes Psychological Anthropology, Medical Anthropology, Addiction Studies and Public Health. (snehagupta.050386@gmail.com)

Shrila Soren is a Senior Research Fellow in the Department of Anthropology, University of Delhi. Her doctoral research is based on long-term fieldwork on Santhal folklore. Her interest areas include Medical Anthropology, Gender Studies and Anthropology of Religion. (shrila30anthro@gmail.com)

Srishti Bhatnagar is working as Research Analyst at the Institute of Economic Growth, Delhi. She is currently working on a qualitative study of asthma and air pollution, an interdisciplinary project, a joint venture between University of Edinburgh and IEG. She is interested in health, gender and social perception. She earned her Master of Science degree from the University of Delhi, with a specialization in social anthropology. (srishtibhatnagar10@gmail.com)

Subhadra Mitra Channa is the senior Vice-President of the International Union of Anthropological and Ethnological Sciences (IUAES) and the Co-Chair of the Commission of Marginalization and Global Apartheid (CMGA). Until recently she was teaching Anthropology at the University of Delhi. Her areas of interest are marginalization and identity, gender, religion and cosmology, ecology and landscapes. She has received several prestigious international awards and fellowships; Charles Wallace Fellow to UK (Queen's University, 2000), Visiting Professor to MSH, Paris (2002), Fulbright Visiting Lecturer to USA (2003) and Visiting Professor in 2008-09 to USC, USA. She is the author/editor of ten books and has about fifty scholarly published papers. She was President of the Indian Anthropological Association, editor of the journal '*Indian Anthropologist*'. Her important publications include, *Gender in South Asia* (Cambridge University Press); *The Inner and Outer Selves* (Oxford University Press); *Life as a Dalit* (Sage); *Gender Livelihood and Environment* (Orient Blackswan) and *Anthropological Perspectives on Indian Tribes* (Orient Blackswan). (channa.subhadra@gmail.com)

Sukhbir Singh is working at the Population Research Centre, Panjab University, Chandigarh. He has earned his Ph.D. in Anthropology from Panjab University, Chandigarh. His academic training is in Social Anthropology and his research interests include medical anthropology. Dr. Singh research focuses on maternal and child health, HIV/AIDS, social aspect of leprosy, impact assessment studies including CSR activities, factors influencing health and illness behaviour. He has published more than 25 research articles in national and international journals. He is national consultant for National AIDS Control Programme and member of their evaluation team. (drsukhbirsingh85@gmail.com)

Sunita Reddy is an Associate Professor at the Centre of Social Medicine and Community Health, School of Social Sciences, Jawaharlal Nehru University, New Delhi, India. She taught briefly at the Indian Institute of Technology, New Delhi and Department of Sociology, Delhi School of Economics, Delhi University before joining JNU in 2004. She is an anthropologist, specializing in medical anthropology. She has researched on various issues of women's and children's health: breastfeeding practices, tribal women's health, childbirth, and child-rearing practices among the tribes. She has researched on disaster issues from social science perspectives and her current area of research is medical tourism and reproductive tourism and surrogacy issues. Dr. Reddy is also the founder chairperson of the Anthropos India Foundation which engages in anthropological research and works for solving the various social issues of communities. She has written extensively in national and international journals and has published books with reputed publication houses including Springer. (sunitareddyjnu@gmail.com)

1

Introduction: Emerging Challenges in Indian Medical Anthropology

P.C. Joshi and *Chakraverti Mahajan*

Changing Canvas of Medical Anthropology

With a very humble start in the beginning of twentieth century, Indian medical anthropology has shown remarkable dynamism and flexibility in its subject matter and research pursuits. Till India's Independence, the primary concern of anthropological studies on disease and cure was in collection of ethnographic description of illness beliefs, practices, medical lore and healing traditions, healer's practices and medicinal substances. India's independence was a turning point, as India was now looking to find pragmatic solutions to its pressing problems related to development of its vast rural areas and foreseeing population. The health related challenges facing the neophyte nation were enormous looking at the inaccessible landscape, large population, poverty, illiteracy and intense ethnic and cultural diversity.

The adoption of a vertical approach to cover a vast population for vaccination and disease eradication along with decentralization of health care services became a national strategy in effective health care delivery. These massive efforts resulted in mixed results—there was grand success in some areas and active resistance in other areas. In such a scenario, social scientists in general and anthropologists in particular directed their research in understanding the causes of resistance by adopting systems approach and the independent variable of culture. Along with this, anthropologists also started considering non-tribal rural areas as legitimate theatres for their field studies. A large number of studies focusing upon the social dynamics in health care started appearing from many nooks and corners of India. Anthropological studies on people's beliefs and practices concerning disease and health care directly contributed to India's struggle to bring fruits of new knowledge to its masses.

By the mid-seventies, the biomedicine's hegemonic sway was beginning to be challenged and India started looking for alternative means to reach its population by various measures that were adopted. Programmes strengthening primary health care approach, adopting bare foot doctor strategy and streamlining the indigenously available medical systems including the widely distributed folk and tribal systems of traditional medicines were some important steps undertaken to make health care accessible, available and affordable to the masses.

Post-liberalization, privatization and globalization in the 1990s further reoriented the perspectives and focus of medical anthropology as in this rapidly changing era, private players, insurance agencies and multinational market forces became very important actors in health care delivery. This along with information technology improvement in the form of internet and social media further decentralized the health care industry. The sudden explosion of information rapidly expanded the complementary and alternative medicines. India's health care delivery system has matured after three successive National Health Policies and a number of innovative health care programmes. At present, medical anthropology is grappling with the ever changing problems pertaining to health care of the people. We are seeing the saturation of the biomedically inspired model of health care and consequently emergence of new age therapies and at the same time the very concept of health is transforming into quality of life and well-being. Technological innovations in the field of medical sciences have offered additional challenges to medical anthropologists. Even in the traditional areas of research like the tribal and rural hinterland, the arrival of globalization and commercialization is resulting in opening new and complicated research topics.

Medical Anthropology of India and Medical Anthropology for India

From the very beginning medical anthropology has been seen as contributing to our understanding of the indigenous health care system with ostensible aim of human welfare. However, the subject matter of medical anthropology has been pursued in two distinctive directions, namely, medical anthropology of India and medical anthropology for India.

The scholars pursuing medical anthropology of India enriched our understanding of the nuances of the health care system in urban, rural and tribal regions and as such contributed immensely to the theory and methods of medical anthropology. Works by scholars such as P.O. Boddings, M. Carstairs, C. Leslie, M. Nichter, R.S. Khare, K.A. Hasan,

W.S. Sax, M. Bentley, J.M. Langford and many others would fall under this category. People involved in medical anthropology of India were deeply interested in understanding India as a place of medical anthropology knowledge production. Their valuable work enhanced our understanding of the functioning of medical systems at the local level, psycho-socio-biological perspective of shamanism, status and functioning of Ayurveda system, culture of food consumption and myriad other features of rich Indian medical culture. The resultant knowledge had good potentials for application in ameliorating the health care delivery and programme implementation deficiencies but the overt intention in medical anthropology of India was never in this direction.

For Indian medical anthropologists and few foreign medical anthropologists like Tylor, on the contrary, the use of medical anthropological knowledge in improving the health status of the people has always been the core concern. Thus, Indian scholars furthering medical anthropology for India investigated medical anthropological themes with a view to identify useful elements in the tangible and intangible aspects of medical culture so that the knowledge is put to immediate use for the community in question. Study of medicinal plants, stigmatic disorders such as leprosy, HIV/AIDS, reproductive health, vector borne diseases, tuberculosis, malnutrition and many such pressing health related problems have been the primary focus of medical anthropological investigations. Studies done by T.N. Madan, R.K. Mutatkar, P.C. Joshi, H.K. Bhat, R.K. Kar, B.V. Sharma, V. Menon, N. Khatua, B. Chaudhary, B.G. Banerjee, D.N. Kakar and many more are examples of creation of extremely useful knowledge having direct bearing on the improvement of the health of millions, especially the vulnerable and marginalized sections of the Indian society.

Role of Universities, Research Institutes and Government Bodies

Indian medical anthropological knowledge has been extensively produced in the universities, with teaching courses in medical anthropology and masters, M.Phil. and doctoral researches covering myriad themes related to medical anthropology. Universities are also places where a large number of journal articles and research project reports have been generated. Finally, universities also promoted research of theoretical nature as well. The research institutes such as Tribal Research Institutes, ICSSR-funded institutes, ICMR institutes and many other privately funded research bodies have been commissioning researches related to various themes of medical anthropology. Most of the researches undertaken by the research institutes have covered themes of relevance to application of the knowledge whether it was to do with promotion of a health activity or planning for a health facility; implementation of a programme; initiation of a health education campaign and many other initiatives. Research institutes have also been placed where the university trained researchers were absorbed to conduct research and therefore there has always been a close collaboration between universities and the research institutes even though at times it appears that both are working independent of each other. The unpublished researches in the form of dissertations and project reports are lying unutilized in universities as well as research institutions which particularly in the field of medical anthropology have immense relevance for the public policy and programme implementation.

The government institutions, like the Ministry of Health and Family Welfare, the Planning Commission/NITI Ayog and the departments directly controlled by the Government are also involved in generation of medical anthropological knowledge. Immediately after India's independence, the need to collect information on the knowledge, attitudes and practices of people, many of whom were illiterate and unaware of the new medical knowledge and technologies, was felt and at the same time it was realized that to reach such a large heterogeneous mass, health education promotion will be needed at a large scale. The establishment of the Central Bureau of Health Intelligence and Central Health Education Bureau at the centre and subsequent offices at the states produced a large amount of knowledge on the grass root situation. In recent decades, the National AIDS Control Organization, which receives more than ninety per cent of its funding from outside India, has initiated and monitored a large number of studies focusing upon the behavioural and social aspects of HIV/AIDS of both theoretical and applied nature.

While the production of medical anthropological knowledge in India has followed different routes, there is a need to freely share and collaborate between the universities, research institutes and the government bodies. The university researches and to a large extent the research institute based findings which are quite often published but rarely converted into policy briefs usable by the government. The government also accumulates continuous data for programme formulation and implementation but rarely involves universities and research institutes in project formulation and adoption of appropriate research methodology and tools so that the outcomes are based on the latest research strategies. There is a need to urgently address the issue of weak communication between the agencies producing medical anthropological knowledge. Free sharing of data and research strategy between different agencies involved in production and management of medical anthropological knowledge would go a long way in amelioration of the health care problems of the Indian masses.

Issues in Tribal Health and Indian Systems of Medicines

The traditional medicines in Indian context are multi-layered in tune with the medical system model given by Dunn (1976), there are pan-Indian regional great traditional Indian Systems of medicines like Ayurveda, Unani, Siddha, Yoga, etc. and at the same time there is galaxy of small-scale, cultural-specific little traditions spread around the length and breadth of the country in the form of tribal and folk medicines. While the Indian great traditional regional system were recognized as important, especially after India's independence, the full-fledged official support for such systems was forthcoming only in the nineteen eighties by forming a separate department within the Ministry of Health and Family Welfare with the title 'Indian Systems of Medicines and Homoeopathy' (ISM&H). Till that time, the hegemonic influence of biomedicine was quite apparent and medicalization was the norm. Though officially recognized and regulated, the reign of biomedicine over all other systems was clearly visible. In fact, the practice of non-biomedical systems was primarily tailored along the biomedicine's symbols and mannerism.

Creation of ISM&H and subsequently the separate Ministry of AYUSH provided not only the much needed autonomy to the India-based medical systems but also accelerated the research, development, teaching and extension activities. All this happened at a great cost to the tribal and folk medicines. In fact, a new trend is emerging under which the hegemonic design of the AYUSH over the tribal and folk medicines can be clearly seen and some kind of ayushaization is prevailing with respect to the so-called local medical traditions. The AYUSH bureaucracy is increasingly becoming custodians of the local medical traditions or the folk and tribal systems of medicines by identification and validation of the tangible medicinal heritage of such communities and re-introduction of the established remedies known to the AYUSH into such systems. The attempt to appropriate the local medical traditions amounts to undermining the autonomy and independence of such systems on one hand and de-contextualization of such systems from their immediate surroundings and eco-systems on the other. Eventually, the local medical traditions are being converted into second-grade appendages of Ayurveda, Unani or Siddha, losing in the process their distinctive, locally rooted and culturally supported ethnomedicines.

Are We Seriously Going to Lose Tribal Medicinal Knowledge?

The danger that the ethnomedicinal heritage of the tribal and folk communities is eventually going to be lost is imminent since the traditionally available remedies are becoming less popular in situations of new forms of therapies being adopted by the people. This phenomenon can be easily observed by medical anthropologists doing fieldwork when people report that the traditional remedies are being replaced by adoption of doctor's medicines. Sometimes, people report that the traditional medicines are losing on their effectiveness or people no longer use traditional medicines. Along with this, people as well as scholars working in the rural and tribal areas have been emphasizing that there is a real danger of losing traditional knowledge about medicines as the younger generation of the tribal youths is not keen to learn about traditional medicines.

In many places, the forces of modernization and globalization have inversely affected the use of traditional remedies. This has prompted many organizations and scholars to document the tribal medicinal heritage before it is lost for ever. A closer look at the actual situation regarding tribal medicines leads to negative as well as positive outcomes. In many places, the loss of medicinal heritage is very fast and there are very few people having good knowledge about the medicines and mostly such knowledge is with very old people who have reluctant and uninterested pupils. There is also a class of neo-educated people who consider such knowledge to be of inferior kind consisting of mumbo-jumbo superstitions. On the contrary, it is also seen that in many other places the traditional medicines are being looked as part of heritage and therefore the society is making deliberate attempts to conserve and revive this knowledge. The latter trend is particularly visible in the tribal societies which have educationally and economically progressed in the recent times.

The revivalist trend with respect to traditional medicines is a good sign that ultimately the traditional medicines will not be lost for ever. A good example in support of this argument can be the revival of Hebrew language which was almost a dead language. The tribal medicinal heritage is just like the barren arid area which suddenly springs up to become lush green as soon as the rain arrives.

Medical Anthropology and Non-Communicable Diseases

The paradigm shift in the last century with the near control over infectious diseases drastically altered the model of curative and preventive health care. The impact of globalization, privatization and liberalization leading to homogenization in the lifestyle and food habits resulted in drastically changing the morbidity pattern on a global scale. The importance of public health approach and incorporation of social science orientation to understand the nuances of human behaviour and habit formation became all the more important in tackling the newly emerging and fast expanding non-communicable diseases. The paradigm shift was also seen when the questions of mortality were replaced by the idea of disease burden and terms such as Disability-Adjusted Life Years (DALY), Quality-Adjusted Life Years (QALY), Disability-Adjusted Life Expectancy (DALE), Healthy Life Years (HeaLY) and Quality of Life (QoL). All these conceptual entities came into existence because non-communicable and lifestyle dependent disorders started showing preponderance by the turn of the last century (Murray and Lopez, 1996).

The burden of diabetes, cardiovascular diseases, cancer, HIV/AIDS and many other lifestyle related disorders need an effective strategy incorporating behaviour change and alteration in the lifestyle rather than pills. For such a strategy, the public health expert has to be a good social anthropologist having a grasp over the understanding of social relationships and foundations of human behaviour. After all, changing of habits and behaviour cannot be achieved overnight. It requires patient manoeuvring and persistent action on part of a social scientist. Medical anthropology with ostensible focus on patient-oriented experiential understanding is best suited to intervene in behaviour changing lifestyle disease intervention.

Medical Anthropology and Mental Health

Mental health issues are fast getting mainstreamed because of two important factors. Firstly, the mental illnesses are on the rise due to rapidly changing world, population movement and emergence of globalization and subsequent glocalization forcing people to adapt to new conditions and quite often new environments. These along with the stiff competitive and ever challenging surroundings have made life more stressful and exigent. Secondly, the stigma attached to mental illness is increasingly getting reduced and people are more open in psychiatric consultations resulting in better diagnosis and reporting of the mental illnesses. The net result is that mental illness is coming to the center stage and is on the agenda of the governments. Recent estimates are indicating that we were wrong in our earlier calculation of the magnitude of the mental health problems. A recent chapter in *The Lancet* (Vigo, Thornicroft and Atun, 2016) suggested that the actually Global Burden of mental illness is 32.4% of years lived with disability (YLDs) highest for any other category of diseases and 13.0% of disability-adjusted life-years (DALYs) equivalent to cardiovascular and circulatory diseases. This was far more than the earlier estimates of 21.2% and 7.1% for YLDs and DALYs, respectively.

Medical anthropology has been collaborating with psychiatry for a very long time. In fact, many of the famous medical anthropologists were psychiatrists as well. Looking at mental health problems from 'cultural' perspectives and investigating the culture-specific patterning of symptomatology and therapeutic care has been the hallmark of medical anthropology. The religion-based mental health care is another area that has fascinated medical anthropologists. Works done under the theme of shamanism, trance and possession, witchcraft and sorcery, ecstatic religion, voodoo, oracle and divination have covered the psychiatric dimensions of culture. The whole field of culture-bound syndromes and trans-cultural psychiatry is medical anthropologically inspired. In the coming days, collaboration between medical anthropologists and psychiatry is going to become closer as psychiatry is not only changing in its approach but also finding medical anthropological methods to be of use in understanding mental health issues.

Overview of the Sections

This book is devoted to the recent trends and developments in Indian medical anthropology. We have grouped the chapters under broader themes to provide logical sequence. It is divided into five parts:

Part I: Disciplinary Practices and Knowledge Production
Part II: Modes of Healing
Part III: Mental Health and Well-being
Part IV: Life Course and Gender
Part V: Medical Pluralism and Policy Issues

The part I of the book, 'Disciplinary Practices and Knowledge Production', examines evolving disciplinary practices in contemporary Indian medical anthropology. The chapters in this section critically engage with the evolving role of Indian medical anthropology with the issues of public health, health policy and colonial knowledge production. K.K. Ganguly in his chapter details the development of medical anthropology and its collective engagement with public health in the global context. By recounting how medical anthropology has so far contributed and can contribute to public health in future, Ganguly offers a brief account of how the discipline has moved its focus from ethnomedicine to the discourse of critical medical anthropology (CMA). CMA studies how health care is embedded with dominant relationships such as those of class, race, and gender and how these variables must be kept in mind when looking at the health care system. Ganguly advocates that the discipline of medical anthropology has much potential. If explored and utilised well, medical anthropology may add a critical value to the public health discourse. Ganguly suggests that there are many ways in which medical anthropology can influence public health policy and research by understanding how culture affects the research and by avoiding the one biocentrism to the public health issues. Anthropology's critical perspective to medicine and public health is crucial in policy-making. But for doing so, anthropology must be away from the hegemonic philosophies of Western biomedicine. By focusing on CMA and it is functioning at various levels: individual level of patient experience, the micro level of physician-patient relationship, relation between treated and the treatment giver, at intermediate level the local health care system such as hospitals and clinics and finally at the macro level of global political economic system, Ganguly makes a case for importance of CMA to the public health domain.

In a country like India where public health is crucial for development, the role of anthropology is of great significance not only in understanding the various aspects related to health and disease but also in policy-making. Sunita Reddy chronicles origin and growth of Indian medical anthropology and its contribution to public health. The author relates the Political Economic Medical Anthropology (PEMA) perspective closely to the states' perspective in looking at different health problems in the Indian context. By deliberating on Parker and Harper's differentiation between 'Anthropology in Public Health' and 'Anthropology of Public Health' in the Indian context, Reddy argues for use of anthropology in public health by emphasizing on the study of public health processes through anthropological perspectives. Reddy also highlights the role of practices such as CMA and international health development and concludes by discussing new frontiers in medical anthropology.

In her chapter, Subhadra Mitra Channa discusses the politics of colonial knowledge production in medical practices and its hegemonic nature which relegated other existing practices as indigenous and therefore inferior to the modern medicine. To understand the core of this issue,

Channa invokes Sandra Harding and Donna Harraway's idea of 'situated knowledge' and Bourdieu's concept 'cultural arbitrary'. Global rise and acceptance of alternative medical practices such as acupuncture (China) and Yoga (India), according to Channa can be attributed to the inefficiency of the Western medicine and the increasing disillusionment among the people towards it. In the current scenario when antibiotics are viewed suspiciously, people are trying to experiment with age old systems of remedy. With this, the hegemonic notion of Western knowledge and rationality has broken down and now these alternate forms of medicines are considered as viable options among many other forms of available medical facilities. Weaved around this framework, Channa also looks at the role of subjectivity in the perception of illness, prognosis of illness and restoration of the culturally perceived condition we call health.

The part II of the book is titled 'Modes of Healing'. The chapters in this part of the book discuss the role and relevance of indigenous/traditional healing practices. Traditional healing practices are an important way of dealing with the various health problems among the communities living around the globe. Based on a study conducted in western Himalayas, Asaf Sharabi describes the role of 'mediums' in deep healing. Mediums are consulted by the local people to seek solutions to their medical, physical and mental ailments. The chapter focuses on the local god 'Mahasu' and his mediums referred to as *mali*. Sharabi begins his chapter by detailing the process of becoming a *mali* and the social positioning of the *mali* in the regional caste hierarchy. The chapter also provides a detailed ethnography of the encounter of the locals with the Mahasu through mediums. Sharabi contextualises the ritual healing offered by Mahasu's medium as deep healing, an individual and non-generic treatment of the patient. Unlike a blessing or general *puja*, deep healing, Sharabi argues, is based on negotiations between the therapist and the patient.

Himalayan region is one of the most important biodiversity regions of the world having more than 2000 medicinal plants. Thus, most of the communities living in the mountainous region practice one or other kind of traditional medical system. Abhishek Sharma describes the Tibetan medical system known as Sowa Rigpa which is prevalent in the tribal region of Kinnaur. The traditional healers in Kinnaur are known as Amchi (superior to all) whose role is to provide therapeutic measures to the members of the community. The chapter explains the processes of diagnosis and the treatment process with a list of common herbal plants used by traditional healers to prepare medicine. Sharma attests that in spite of the government's recognition of this practice in 2010, it is being practiced by traditional healers without any organizational setup. The chapter concludes with the fact that a strong partnership between the practitioners and the authority is required to revive and sustain this practice. The author has strongly argued that medical anthropologists in India and the Anthropological Survey of India need to play an important role in saving this practice.

Biomedicine is the most sought after medical system across the globe. While anything packaged in the name of biomedicine is always considered scientific, however, indigenous healing practices are most often considered to be inferior and unscientific. Based on fieldwork among the Tharus of southern Nepal, Bamdev Subedi documents the culture of ethnomedicine including different types of healers, guruwa, *baidawa* and *surenya* who perform specialised healing practices. Subedi notes that for the Tharus use of both indigenous healers and medical practitioners is complementary. Subedi passionately urges to go beyond documenting the vanishing healing practices and argues that the mere documentation cannot prevent the indigenous knowledge from further erosion. Furthermore, he stresses that the indigenous communities haven't benefited from the current documentation projects because the documented knowledge is not accessible to them. Tharu healers not only provide health care services but also play a customary role in the community. Unlike the biomedical doctors, the Tharu healers are directed by obligations to serve in the community. Thus, they are an important resource whose contributions must be acknowledged and apprcciated by the state. A holistic approach is required to not only support and promote the indigenous practices but also make them part of the mainstream.

Srila Soren and P.C. Joshi discuss practices of healing among the Santhals by critically engaging with P. O. Bodding's detailed work, *Studies in Santhal Medicine and Connected Folklore* (1925). Through the idea of medical lore, Soren tries to understand the relationship between folk medicine, indigenous knowledge and traditional healing. Medical lore transmits and communicates traditional knowledge regarding healing and folk medicine from generation to generation. The medical lore tells us about seamless knowledge of the practitioners of folk medicine. Soren also argues that the often used oppositional dichotomy between the traditional and the modern medical systems does not hold good in the Santhal context as in everyday life their existence shows robust co-presence.

In part III of the book, we bring together theoretical, methodological and empirical issues interconnecting varied concerns about mental health and well-being. At present, there is a growing burden of mental illness in

India but we have very limited mental health care resources. Recognising the importance of indigenous healing resources, National Mental Health Policy (2014) suggests that the primary role of research is to generate knowledge understanding of mental illness in the cultural context and identification of effective indigenous systems of healing which could lead to a reduction in the burden of mental illness in India and provide therapeutic choices. Reetinder Kaur, in her chapter, sketches the psychiatric pluralism in India by emphasizing on studying a shrine as a resource for mental health care. The study is based on an in-depth account of *dargah* near Mohali city of Punjab which is a popular shrine for the treatment of mental illnesses. On the basis of the present study, Kaur concludes that the community mental health care models in India must include and understand the indigenous knowledge, cultural explanations and locally available resources for effective mental health care. *Dargahs* play an important role in providing mental health care to the individuals suffering from mental illness. Both *Dargahs* and healing performed at *dargahs* must be recognised as locally available and culturally fitting mental health care models in India.

Sneha Gupta in her chapter presents insights on a drug de-addiction centre using the concept of therapeutic communities. Addiction, although, is defined as a disease by the World Health Organization, however, popularly it is believed to be a form of madness and insanity. The notion is taken seriously in the organizational structure of the institutions and family members which deal with addicts. With the help of firsthand interviews with the patients living in therapeutic communities, she explains how the patients become a passive member in the whole treatment period and the staff acts as active members. In the name of keeping addicts busy, staff turns addicts into servants. When addicts are sent to these therapeutic communities, they are kept and treated at the cost of their individuality and freedom. The wrong treatment by the staff and negative attitude of family create more identity disorders due to harm done to an individual's self-respect and freedom which are perhaps the most important virtue of one's life. The chapter calls for active engagement of medical anthropology and its practitioners as to understand and renovate the conception of addiction, the addict and its management.

Chakraverti Mahajan focuses on the situation in Jammu & Kashmir, one of the most militarized regions of the world, where the prolonged conflict has left its mark upon the social and mental fabric of the community and its people. The militancy and militarization in Jammu & Kashmir have turned the region into a zone of mass psychological suffering. By engaging with, the Kashmir Mental Health Survey, 2015, which reported that one third of Kashmiri men and nearly half of Kashmiri women suffered from poor psychological health, the chapter raises concerns over the little understanding of the local patterns of distress which is experienced and the psychosocial impact on the people in militarized regions. There has been fast growth in medicalization of mental health care and the number of patients seeking treatment has continued to rise. The chapter questions the deliberate avoidance of analysing the impact of military presence on people's mental health.

Ravinder Singh in his chapter discusses the state of mental health India where 13.7 per cent of the general population has issues of mental illness or disorders. The chapter brings together issues of traditional medicine, indigenous healers and Intellectual Property Rights (IPRs) to give a holistic picture of the issues related to mental health challenges in India. The chapter states that due to fast lifestyle, complexities of living and breakdown of support systems and challenges of economic instability have increased the prevalence of stress, anxiety and mental disorders. The social stigma associated with the mental health problems check the family to see a psychiatrist or psychologist and most of the patients suffering from mental illness seek treatment from the traditional healers or religious shrines like *mazars* or *dargah*. By discussing the implementation of the *Dawa* and *Dua* Project (DDP), a successful experiment where traditional healers and modern doctors come together for treatment of mental illness, Singh argues for the integration of the traditional healers who hold people's faith and trust into the mainstream of the health care system. With a brief sketch of mental health policies and Acts in India, Singh emphasizes on the role and contribution of Traditional Knowledge (TK) and Traditional Medicine (TM) practices used by indigenous healers for treatments of mental health. The nexus of pharmaceutical industries and their dominance in the mental health care system in India and all-over the world including the US and other countries have made it medium to prescribe antipsychotics and anti-depressants in excessive quantities. The chapter reveals how the Diagnostic and Statistical Manual of Mental Disorders prepared by American Psychiatric Association turns common ailments into mental illness such as grief as the clinical depression. With the examples of Navajo nation and Maori system of healing in New Zealand, the chapter tries to look at the traditional mental healing practices, various questions such as the authenticity of the healer, place of healing and rising culture of traditional healing systems even in the modern clinical setup. In the third and the last section, the chapter throws light on the definition of Traditional Medicine and Traditional Knowledge by WHO. Further it discusses the Indian National Policy on Traditional Medicine (1940), the emergence of various institutes such as Department of Medicine and Homeopathy, national research institutions such as central council of Indian Medicine (1970), the Ayurvedic and the Unani pharmacopoeia. With the examples of case studies from Amazon Rainforest Plant Patent, Neem oil case and the plants of Trichopus zeylanicus collected by the Tropical Botanic Garden and Research Institute (TBGRI) with the help of Kani tribe of south-western India, the author comes to the last and most important issue of Intellectual Property Rights (IPR) where he discusses the issue of feasibility to protect the existing IPR system and the protection of traditional medicine. In short, the chapter casts light on various dimensions of mental health issues and the traditional knowledge and medicine for its cure.

Khirod Chandra Moharana, examines the role of globalisation on increasing mental health problems and the role of medical anthropology in mental health research. He emphasizes the complexities of mental health and illness and tries to find out the reasons for failing approaches to treat mental illness. Moharana further argues that a major reason behind such increase in mental illness is due to globalization and increased competitions in all walks of life. Few people control most of the resources around. The widening gap creates competition, struggle, structural violence and suffering among a large proportion of the world population today. Further, the chapter analyses various reasons such as the chemical imbalances, social factors and the ontological uncertainties as the reason for increasing mental illness. Moharana analyses the role of medical anthropology in understanding mental health issues with the help of anthropological methods. Specifically, he advocates for the method of ethnography which can be best used for diagnosis and healing of mental illness. The chapter also stresses upon the need to focus on 'lived experiences' and 'social suffering' framework in mental health research. The chapter argues that medical anthropology needs to play not only the role as a critique but as a responsible insider in mental health research, policy and interventions.

The ideas, knowledge and individual experiences of health have been the realm of anthropological studies particularly medical anthropological studies. The IV part of the book, 'Life Course and Gender', deals with the issues of menstrual health, childbirth, women's experiences of health, social care and artisan's health. Srishti

Bhatnagar, based on her fieldwork in a Punjabi village, highlights various issues related to menstrual health. Menstruation, as it is well known now, is a recurrent physiological process experienced by nearly all adolescent girls and women (of reproductive age) around the globe. As a part of the culture of silence, menstrual blood is a symbol of impurity, disease and pollution and consequently, a menstruating body is rendered pathological, silent and shameful. Bhatnagar attempts to understand the perception of menstruating bodies through a socio-cultural study of menstrual health, beliefs and practices. Based on ethnographic fieldwork conducted among women of Gurdaspur district of Punjab, Bhatnagar focuses on the lived experiences of menstruation that were explored through theories of gender and life-course perspective. Underscoring low levels of awareness, interest and many misconceptions regarding menstruation, Bhatnagar argues that education, access to sanitation, media and adherence to and/or deviation from the traditional menstrual beliefs and customary practices are the proximate determinants of menstrual health.

Priyanka Ghosh and Mathew George examine the process of decision-making regarding the mode of delivery in clinical settings. The chapter highlights three major components: the opinions of pregnant women, their obstetricians, and the institutional medicolegal factors, which decide the mode of delivery. The chapter casts light on the fact how women become passive patients in clinical settings where they have no control on the choices of giving birth. This chapter is based on researcher's interviews with the recent mothers regarding the decision-making, and the experiences shared by their obstetricians. The findings of this study are categorized in three sections that are, convenience of the obstetricians, women as passive patients and the last section is mode of delivery chosen against patients' will. In the first section, the findings of the study says that it is the obstetrician who takes all the decisions as per his own convenience and the women play no role in taking the decisions. The next part emphasizes that women who get delivery under midwives have greater control over an agency during the childbirth. The chapter concludes with the fact that for various reasons the doctor makes decisions regarding the mode of delivery and due to lack of required knowledge and available data most of the women fear to ask questions or express their feelings regarding the whole process. Ghosh and George argue that the process of decision makes a shift towards 'imposition of decision' on the pregnant women by the obstetricians, which is largely based on the convenience of obstetricians, the power of their profession and the technocentric settings in which they practice.

Focusing on the subjectivities and lived experiences of urban women working in white collared jobs in Delhi, Gunjan Arora seeks to study the various aspects of illness and disease in relation to the body. Arora has shown that illness and health care may be viewed as socio-cultural products and the knowledge that we develop around our health and illness is basically the culmination of our beliefs and our interaction with the medical system. A study on the life cycle events of a female with a focus on childbirth, menstruation and menopause and the consequent interaction of Arora's informants with the medical system, not only highlights the hegemony of the scientific medical system but also on the experiential aspects of the body. The body which is the locus of concern during any health care or illness demands a discussion. The whole discourse till now either has swayed to the biological aspect or to the body image studies. Arora has argued for a middle plane, i.e. focussing on the biological events through the cultural lens.

Ashwin Tripathi tends to bring out the relationship between ageing, system of care and health. Her chapter is based on ethnographic fieldwork of the Indian migrant community in Northern Ireland. Tripathi aims to reflect on how we understand and define care as practised within Indian migrant families and the research is conducted from the perspective of caregivers. The two questions that the researcher seeks to answer are how is care defined by middle aged care-givers as they are for the old and the young? And the other question is how this care work given by families changed over time? If it has changed then what are the new ways of caring. This study concentrates on the "sandwich generation", aged 60-80, who are "caught in the middle": caring for both elderly parents and adult children, whilst looking ahead to receiving care themselves. The research focuses upon their perspectives, and how they are adapting to the changes that they face. The study considers the changing nature of caring, evolving cultural expectations, the modern technologies that have emerged as significant tools in virtual caring, and the changing intergenerational relationships. Tripathi argues that care cycles are constantly being re-negotiated, with less expectation of reciprocal care, and more acceptance of externally provided care. With increased resources, and less stigma involved, the migrant community is more accepting of elder-care homes.

Drabita Dutta has focused on the occupational health of artisans working in the metal craft cottage industry of Assam. By using Walton's theoretical framework of occupational health and safety model, she has examined the nature of health risks and the problems faced by the artisans. Dutta observed that the metal craft clusters and the working units are characterised with long working hours, poor housekeeping, lack of public utility areas, ventilation and lighting, poor work postures and work methods, exposure to chemicals and deficiency of personal protective equipment (PPE). The study recommended: (a) developing of exclusive health care programmes targeting awareness regarding minimum safety standards, (b) develop comprehensive occupational safety and health insurance scheme for them to counter the effect of occupation related mishaps and injuries, and (c) training of local health care officials in the diagnosis and treatment of occupational hazards in the metal craft cluster of Assam.

The fifth section is related to policy-making and issues related to the health care systems from different aspects. India faces a challenge of global health burden, considering this, India ventured into a new reform of integrating traditional alternative medical systems to the existing health care infrastructure as a step towards achieving universal health coverage. But with the already existing huge disparities in the health sector, low health GDP, high out-of-pocket expenditure, high infectious disease burden and many more, it still seems to be an unachievable dream. Avani Khatri and A.K. Sinha question the politics of medical pluralism in Indian context. For them, promotion of medical pluralism in an unequal society masks several social and economic constraints to access to health care services.

Multiple systems of therapy and healing are employed by people for their or significant other's illness experience. These multiple systems of medicine, based upon their history, ideology, present day politics, their treatment/healing regime, are often considered to be contrasting and competing by both the users of these systems and the providers. However, this contrast moves in a universe of ambiguity, and complementarity emerges when actual implementation of healing strategies is chosen. The distinction between traditional and modern in terms of health and illness is not perceived as absolute but the two rather manifest as a paradoxical mix for people who live with these notions as embedded in their lives. This holds true both for village based communities and urban centres. This chapter by Gurinder Kaur and Sukhbir Singh attempts to locate the plurality of healing systems in the world of people in a single village of Bhatgarh located in hilly terrain of district Sirmaur in the northern state of Himachal Pradesh, India. It explores the continuity, hybridity and change in the perception and choices for healing systems in the village over a decade. Where the distinction between traditional and modern in terms of health and illness cannot be put in closed boxes but rather emerges as a paradoxical mix for people who live with these notions as embedded in their lives.

Ravin Srivastava presents his account of women health workers who have made it possible to improve health care at the margins and who have become the flag bearers of India's health programme. The chapter is based on the researcher's extensive interaction with women health workers across the six North Indian states— Jammu & Kashmir, Uttarakhand, Himachal Pradesh, Punjab, Haryana and Delhi and Union Territory of Chandigarh. Srivastava argues that the social capital these women enjoy in village settings make access to health care easy for other women. However, their contributions often go unrecognised. They are often paid less and the nature of their employment is uncertain. The selection procedure is not fair and transparent. They are often subject to hostilities from the powerful. There are lapses on part of the health workers too which require to be addressed along with the challenges that these women face. Srivastva argues that women are taking to the job of a community health worker for the self-reliance and respect that it brings to them in spite of various constraints.

Through a critical review of health policies in India, Prashant Khattri and P.C. Joshi in their chapter deliberate on the situation of Indian tribal population which is about 8 percent of the Indian population. They argue that tribal health gets little attention in the health policy documents which are strongly guided by the bio-medical discourses on health. Motivated by exhausting the allocated funding received for providing health care, the issue of tribal health remains an administrative and managerial matter largely. The overall approach of the ernment can be visualized in terms of having more contact with the tribes which in turn is aimed at providing medical facilities by giving incentives to both the health-seekers and health-providers for their services in the tribal areas. However, the ground reality is an antithesis to what is desired. The health policy is largely driven by the capitalist model that has its base in bio-medicine. It has been argued that most of the major institutes and authorities that are dealing with public health in India have reiterated time and again that public sector spending on health care in India needs to be enhanced.

REFERENCES

Dun, Frederick. (1976). "Traditional Asian Medicine and Cosmopolitan Medicine as Adaptive systems." In Charles Leslie (ed.), *Asian Medical Systems: A Comparative Study*. University of California Press, Berkeley, pp. 133-158.

Murray, C.J.L. and Lopez, A.D. (1996). *The Global Burden of Disease: A Comprehensive Assessment o f Mortality and Disability from Disease, Injuries and Risk Factors in 1990 and Projected to 2020.* Harvard School of Public Health, Boston.

Vigo, D., Thornicroft, G. and Atun, R. (2016). "Estimating the True Global Burden of Mental Illness." *The Lancet Psychiatry*, *3*(2): 171-178.

PART I
DISCIPLINARY PRACTICES AND KNOWLEDGE PRODUCTION

2
A Dialogue between Anthropology and Public Health: Issues and Perspective

K.K. Ganguly

The discipline of anthropology played second fiddle in the field of medicine and in public health as well. It was never felt that the discipline could play significantly in the development of public health policy. The present chapter will try and make an attempt to assess how far the discipline of anthropology can meaningfully contribute to public health policy formulation and decisions making for a greater good.

Premises of anthropology has undergone significant paradigmatic shift over the period of time (from the colonial era to this day). The classical anthropologists of late nineteenth century through middle of twentieth century have changed their classical exploratory pattern, from rite de passage of colonial era to more pragmatic and prudent issues of contemporary world both rural and urban. Today anthropologists are dealing with the domain of hard reality and vagaries of people's life and their institutions. Anthropologists are rare breeds who either glorify the existing norms and practices to a large extent under the banner of ethnographic study or deride the local medical care practices as non-scientific, therefore, public health issues never featured on the canvas of ethnography.

To understand need and benefits of medical anthropology, it is necessary to know about the nuances of the subject. The sub-disciplines of anthropology has both advantage as well as disadvantage. From disadvantage point of view, the experts attributed every small bit of activity of a community as culture bound, therefore, beyond the reach of perceptible change, while from the vantage point of view, an attempt is made by the scholar to see the actor and action holistically (on the broader canvas).

The discipline or the sub-disciplines are tangled with complexities of norms, values, system and so forth which are very much in-built in the system. But one has to deal with such complexities tactfully to gauge the issues in right perspective. In order to understand medical anthropology by the very definition, can be stated that it has established a degree of independence from its parent discipline of social/cultural anthropology. Despite this autonomy, medical anthropology's disciplinary evolution has been tardy and affected by the changes in the larger arena.

Ethnomedicine, a subfield of medical anthropology developed by scholars to satiate persistent need of better understanding of local medical practice, its need and utility. It helped to develop an understanding of local medical beliefs and practices which could be beneficial for biomedical services. McElroy states that since the 1940s anthropologists have helped health care providers understand cultural differences in health behaviours (McElroy, 1996).

Kleinman's emphasis on exploring aspects of medical anthropology led to the development of the 'Explanatory Model' framework (Kleinman, 1978) and the benchmark volume 'Clinically Applied Anthropology' by Chrisman and Maretzki (1982) are few remarkable works among many others. These works focused heavily on doctor-patient interaction and how anthropology can be used as a tool in biomedicine.

Subsequently, new waves of thinking that parallel the turns to reflexivity in social anthropology. Baer in 1983, coined the term 'critical medical anthropology'. This new domain of medical anthropology was similar to the new reflexive social anthropology which was critical, holistic and inward looking: "it is the work of anthropology turned in upon ourselves, our own society" (Scheper-Hughes, "Three Propositions"). Nancy Scheper-Hughes goes on to draw explicit parallels between colonial social anthropology and clinical medical anthropology (a group of people who would be judged for their acts and deeds by others, non-insider) by saying that medical anthropologists played a vital role in establishing the cultural hegemony of biomedicine (Scheper, 1990).

To understand the role of anthropology in general and medical anthropology in specific one has to understand different domains of public health practices and to correlate public health issues with the anthropological parameters that reflects upon understanding of public/community health.

A Different Flavour of Medical Anthropology

Hans Baer (1990), defines critical medical anthropology as a tool that aspires to merge theory and praxis in [a] desire to promote experiential health as opposed to the functional health associated with contemporary political economics around the world. Since the emergence of critically applied medical anthropology, several anthropologists have brought this brand of anthropological enquiry to the world of public health policy.

Cecil Helman (2007) in his "Culture, Health and Illness", stated, "Inadvertent as it may have been, utilizing anthropology in this role in public health often inherently used techniques of 'victim blaming' — that is, seeing the poor health of a population as the sole result of its culture, instead of looking also at their particular economic or social situation."

To my understanding, anthropology of public health can be well-delineated by perceiving critical medical anthropology. While, Parker and Harper (2005) described the anthropology of public health as, which remains passionately concerned about ill-health and deprivation and the need for public policy; but also remains committed to a rigorous and critical analytical perspective.

To understand public health and role of anthropology, I have explored the inter-phase through the prism of critical medical anthropology (CMA) [though many scholars may or may not endorse my point of view in this regard]. One need to comprehend the basic premises of critical medical anthropology clearly, which is defined as focusing attention on understanding the origins of dominant cultural construction in health, including, social class, gender or ethnic group's interests particular health concepts express and under what set of historic conditions under which they arise (Singer & Bear, 2011).

Helman's understanding is so prudent that even today faulty implementation of a public health programme is often squarely attributed to outdated cultural practices and those practices are rubricated as "unscientific". He is in pain to state that the science of anthropology and its practitioners most often acted tout for "so called rationalist" against the interest of minority and marginalised at large (Helman, C., 2007).

Furthermore, Chrisman *et al.* (1982) stated, often weaken their contributions to an understanding of infectious diseases by making "immodest claims of causality." These claims are immodest because they are wrong or misleading. They are immodest because they divert attention from the possibly doable interventions that could treat and cure people. And they are blatantly immodest because they defy plausible preventable social disorder that exacerbates biological disorder.

Epidemiological model of understanding public health is more rationalistic scientifically oriented tool for comprehending public health. Public health's first and foremost responsibility is to improve the health status of a population. This all encompassing pursuit has brought epidemiology to be the most influential discipline in health policy formulation as it does statistical sampling which can be theoretically extrapolated to draw conclusions about the state of health of entire populations/community and for various surveillance studies. According to public health scholars, the discipline stands on five scaffoldings, "i.e. epidemiology, biostatistics, management sciences, socio-behavioural sciences and environmental science".

Full potentiality of anthropology has not been utilized for informing health policy hence its contribution remained near negligible. Keeping anthropology in the bandwagon as one of the five other behavioural sciences could not make mark distinctly on policy-making in public health. One of the probable reasons of it being light weight tool in behavioural science to a large extent could be assigned to its "ethnographic" methodology. The policy-makers in any policy formulation be it public health are always on look out for a method sound enough to strength be repeated and could be validated under any circumstance. Ethnographic research involves observing and conducting interviews with a small group of people. Small numbers does not provide the strength of replicability.

Despite all odds, the methodology used in anthropological and ethnographic studies, ethnographic inquiry has the potential to generate a great deal of rich information which can influence policy formulation and execution.

Wedding Anthropology with Public Health

Anthropology can influence public health policy in ways that epidemiology or other methods cannot. (a) The ability to understand culture in its proper perspective to visualize how culture affects all research. (b) Potentiality to not to trivialize acts of an actor, however, insignificant may it look while doing scientific analysis, i.e. thematic analysis of metaphors, while analyzing interviews/FGDs. (c) Often able to maintain independence from bio-centric models of interpretation, gives distinct voice to medical anthropologist to add a critical value to the public health discourse. (d) To be able to retain objectivity in qualitative data in the all pervasive area of quantitative data and its element of reliability of data.

Parker and Harper (2005) describe the anthropology of public health as that "which remains passionately concerned about ill-health and deprivation and the need for public policy; but also remains committed to a rigorous and critical analytical perspective."

Critical outlook and reflexivity of understanding gives anthropology strength to the development of public health policy. Williams (2001) states that "a multidisciplinary approach could best address the public health needs of a population". It can be visualized that the field of public health, policy development requires research contributions from various streams of behavioural and health sciences.

A. Visualizing Culture in Right Perspective to Guide Research Meaningfully

According to Curnow and Smith (1975), to comprehend disease etiology in a given population, they frequently use a "multifactorial model of disease", is the ideal purview of public health specialists and human ecologists. This model has a number of distinct factors that are thought to contribute to disease in the population. Culture is one of these factors, amongst many others, i.e. genetics, environment and so forth. The factorial model seems consistent with earlier medical anthropological research, relating to the method of the clinically applied anthropologist. Involvement of anthropologists on a clinical level likely to reduce the impact of the 'culture factor' on disease prevalence.

Sufficient number of medical anthropologists see this model of interpretation and understanding of disease as archaic and inaccurate as well as, it reduces the investigation of social and cultural aspects of disease to discrete, static, quantifiable 'beliefs' held by the study population (Parker, M. & Harper, I., 2005). According to factorial notion of disease causation biology and environment are beyond the reach of culture. Today, culture, as accepted by most anthropologists as more complex and over-arching, it is believed that all research, even the most behavioural and scientific, is culture bound.

Contemporary medical anthropology is well-versed to see beyond the factorial model of disease. A group of anthropologists have seen the Cartesian dualism paradigm of mind-body axis. Dichotomy between the mind and the body of an individual. This conceptualization is ridden with a mechanistic view of disease etiology, very similar to that in the factorial model. Medical anthropologists accepted the Cartesian paradigm of Western medicine (diseases of somatic and psychological origin) and the view persisted for long. Of late, under the context of the 'new' critical version of medical anthropology, this concept is being scrutinized.

Scheper-Hughes and Lock argued for the need to question such a seemingly simple dualism. They reiterated that it is not so simplistic as it may seem. They defied medical anthropologists and clinicians to view humans and the experience of illness and suffering from an integrated perspective (Scheper-Hughes & Lock M., 1987).

Even today also most of the clinicians endorse "the Cartesian Legacy," while, anthropologists have been working for years at developing an integrated model. Medical anthropologists can contribute significantly to public health policy by providing an integrated model (a genuine need of the hour) to aid provide an alternative to the well recognized factorial model of disease in public health.

B. Panoptic Assessment

According to Porter (2006), the new medical anthropology's "inclusion of the whole" is another important tool that has the potential to be of great use in policy development. Anthropology is in a vantage position to deal with the entire situation in a given community. Participant observation helps capture the smallest details in the events of individuals' lives in a community. This also involves structures (institutional) and resultant function of structural interplay that are acting on individuals.

The importance of anthropology's comprehensive assessment/ holism defies the factorial model. In case of factorial model culture is an independent entity it works in isolation. Helman (2007), calls such approach as, 'victim blaming', as the victim of the situation is helpless and the very upbringing and lifestyle are reasons accountable. Public health policy is no exception, if culture is considered in isolation from political, social and economic factors, no public health policy can operate.

Insight from an anthropological point of view is essential to avoid any kind of counter-productive policy formulation. Holistic approach is comprehensive assessment to illness and is important in order to identify all pertinent factors for comprehending any endemic/pandemic event. John Porter (2006), an epidemiologist, has said regarding anthropology: "The discipline concentrates on what is actually happening and looks to 'the root' of where things come from." The 'root' at the level of social interactions is essential to be known. Anthropological methods of investigation have proven successful to know more about root.

Critical Insight

A valuable contributor to public health practice is its freedom from the theories and views of Western biomedicine. Today's health science is very rationalistic as well as atomistic in nature. Biomedicine, epidemiology and the other contributing sciences are inherently atomistic and hence have very narrow scope in which to view the phenomenon of illness or epidemic. Understanding of any bio-medical phenomena has not crossed (most often) the boundaries of hard core science.

Often the discipline of anthropology faces resentment from corners as (probably due to its past) 'handmaiden' of colonialism. One scholar delineated a vivid account of how the Public Health institution in the Philippines functions as an extension of the state in enslaving people to external/foreign practices in order to invoke control and command over the public (Warwick Anderson, 1995). This kind of situation is evinced now-a-days in most of the drug trials being conducted in most of the low to middle resource countries, while, different phases of clinical trials are being carried out.

Anthropology's critical perspective of medicine and public health makes it very important to the development of further policy. Scheper-Hughes (1990) states that it is "imperative to position ourselves squarely on the side of human suffering" (Three Propositions). Anthropologists have gone far from being the stooge of colonial power to amelioration, affliction and suffering.

Debate is necessary to stimulate improvements in structures or programmes that are promulgated without any sanity (most of the time). Critical medical anthropology probably is able to provide unique chance to deal with public health issues and policies in greater humane way.

A critical comprehension of biomedicine can be pursued if and when anthropology retains distance from the biases and philosophies of Western medicine. Many funding agencies in one or the other way draws upon the discipline of medical anthropology to fulfil their vested interest in biomedicine and such effort need to be digressed. This type of funding arrangement prohibits a fully critical interpretation and thus compromises what anthropology has to offer as a discipline (Parker and Harper, 2005).

Qualitative Data Generation and Inferences

Significant contribution of anthropology in the development of public health policy framing by applying qualitative techniques is need of the hour. Anthropological qualitative data collection technique helps inform public health policy immensely, through systematic data collection. The qualitative methodology of ethnographic data collection separates anthropology from all of the natural sciences and from many of the social sciences as well. Ian Hacking (1982) explains why qualitative data is so important in comparison to pure quantitative data: "The fetishistic collection of overt statistical data about a population has as its motto "information and control" but it would more truly be "disinformation and mismanagement". He argues that quantitative analysis requires extensive categorization.

Many of the categories that are used in essence constructs of the investigators and do not even exist in the worldview of the informant, this creates a false perception of reality in the minds of policy-makers.

A similar critique was voiced by Parker and Harper (2005), about supposed qualitative research conducted by many traditionally quantitatively oriented social scientists. It is the null hypothesis driven model of research executed by rapid assessment survey to assess field situation helps promote a tailored outcome which many of our planners love to see and work with. This type of approach often makes the policy planner quite handicap to develop and deliver a truly people-oriented public health model.

True ethnographic data helps sidestep different misconstrued skewed representation by understanding cognizable worldviews of its participants. Such an approach is in opposition to traditional public health research, which imposes an alien view upon informants, or counts them and in doing so categorizes them into culturally constructed groups that support the researchers vested viewpoint. While developing appropriate policy, it is essential to gain thorough understanding of the situation and more so, how those at the receiving end (non-pejorative) think and feel about the situation. Ethnographic inquiry only can justify acts very prudently. Quantitatively speaking "outliers" also speaks and probably that can reveal the unknown, unfortunately, often-times outliers are given "a miss".

Can Critical Medical Anthropology be a Game Changer in Public Health

Critical Medical Anthropology (CMA) upholds the idea that human health is a resultant of interplay of biosocial and political ecological product. However, CMA is critical of the tendency to naturalize the process of health and illness in the health and social sciences. CMA's ideation began in the 1980s, though it has deeper roots in critical theory concerning the social determinants of health. Critical medical anthropology adds an anthropological dimension to traditional critical approaches and helps to look into factors across the board. To put it squarely, CMA as a discipline and its proponents appreciates the interaction between the macro-level of social structure, the meso-level of social organization and meaningful interplay and the micro-level of individual experience and health.

The field of public health can only be meaningful if and only when the positivist, technocratic notion of public health practice is done away with towards a more inclusive and multidisciplinary enterprise.

Critical medical anthropology raises important questions about the impact of various social and cultural institutions, i.e. global political and economic structures and processes on health and disease. The disease, endemic or pandemic cannot be seen in void. Constant interplay of myriads of factors and culture of different involved group need to be understood for detecting public health maladies.

It broadens the canvas in the context within which medical anthropology operates and proximate to the perspective of public health practice by overtly seeking to contribute towards the creation of universal health systems that will help serve the people. Critical medical anthropology focuses on health care systems and how they function at multiple levels, viz., the individual level of patient experience, the *microlevel* of physician-patient relationships, the close interaction of treated and treatment giver, as the nuances only can help develop or modify existing policy more meaningfully. Similarly, the *intermediate* level of local health care systems, particularly hospitals and clinics the institutional setting both secondary or tertiary need to be assessed very closely to be understood in regard to public health policy framing and its execution. While at the *macro social* level of global political-economic systems, the market forces the political undercurrent towards removing or implementing a policy for larger good. And very often global decision can make a sea change in health policy as we often see the vertical programmes of the government changes its priority in terms of its execution. And it is very glaring to note that mother and child health policy, HIV/AIDS care and cure Malaria, TB eradication keeps changing its goal post as per national/international priority.

At each of these levels, the goal is to understand how existing social relations structure the relationships among the participants in the systems at all levels. Preçisely speaking, critical medical anthropologists study the way health care is embedded within dominant relations such as those of class, race, and gender and public health policy cannot be framed without taking into account the above factors.

One has to be attentive and vigilant regarding public health programmes, those have been executed or even for that matter those which are in the pipeline and the state is the executor. The system (state mechanism) does not envisage public awareness programme before most of the public health programmes getting launched. The key question, the policy planners need to respond is how best, how long (to eradicate any disease) and how economically the programme will serve the interest of the people, be it, TB (all kinds) eradication, vector-borne disease control, water-borne disease eradication, besides, vaccine preventable diseases, which are still incapacitating our children in many ways in large number.

The Polio eradication is the recent flagship public health programme of success, but there is still little apprehension in many minds, are the children of the country safe from the disease for times to come. This is a situation, probably where CMA and its proponents along with public health experts can come close for purposeful dialogue to check any reversal of success. As we are really vulnerable due to our endemic neighbourhood and the cessation of any communicable disease is not "once for all phenomena", it is always in the state of dynamic equilibrium so is the resurgence of the disease.

Critical medical anthropology should be able to make status chapter on most of the public health issues. The (sub)discipline should not be mere onlooker from the sidelines and neither it should be matter of credit points for those who opt for the CMA in course work. The CMA has the strength of ethnography, ways to understand the political economy both at the national and international level, so any programme getting implemented in the area of public health need to enrich itself with the wherewithal of CMA.

Public health cannot remain in the exclusive domains of epidemiologist. Public health engineers and last but not the least in the hands of few physicians (both at national and international level) who assess the disease pathways and progression in a factorial fashion. Preparation and dispensation of drugs are really mechanistic way of dealing with public health issues. Anthropologists with the tool of critical medical anthropology should purposefully intervene and work with paternalistic state (where public health is one of the deterministic instruments of control of state power) and also see to it that the cardinal ethical principles are truly adhered with for larger good of the people. As many state-run "health freebies" becoming replete without actually serving the cause of public health in the country, anthropologist need to do their bit now.

REFERENCES

Chrisman, N. & Maretzki, T. (1982). *Clinicially Applied Anthropology*. New York: Springer.

Curnow, R.N. & Smith, C. (1975). "Multifactorial models for familial diseases in man." *Journal of the Royal Statistical Society*, *138* (2), 131-169.

Hacking, I. (1982). "Biopower and the Avalanche of Printed Numbers." *Humanities in Society*, *5*, 279-295.

Hans, B. (1990). "The Possibilities and Dilemmas of Building Bridges between Critical Medical Anthropology and Clinical Anthropology: A Discussion." *Social Science of Medicine*, *30* (9), 1011-1013.

Helman, C. (2007). *Culture, Health and Illness* (5th ed.). London: CRC Press.

Kleinman, A. (1978). "Concepts and a Model for the Comparison of Medical Systems as Cultural Systems." *Social Science and Medicine*, *12*, 85-93.

McElroy, A. (1996). "Medical Anthropology." In: D. Levinson & M. Ember (Ed.) *Encyclopedia of Cultural Anthropology* (pp. 759-763). New York: Henry Holt.

Parker, M. & Harper, I. (2005). "The Anthropology of Public Health." *Journal of Biosocial Sciences, 38*, 1-5.

Porter, J.D.H. (2006). "Epidemiological Reflections of the Contribution of Anthropology to Public Health Policy and Practice." *Journal of Biosocial Sciences*, *38*, 133-144.

Scheper, H.N. & Lock, M. (1987). "The Mindful Body: A Prolegomenon to Future Work in Medical Anthropology." *Medical Anthropology Quarterly*, *1*, 6-41.

Scheper, H.N. (1990). "Three Propositions for a Critically Applied Medical Anthropology." *Social Science in Medicine*, *30*(2), 189-197.

Singer, M. & Hans, B. (2011). *Introducing Medical Anthropology: A Discipline in Action*, (2nd ed.). Lanham: Alta Mira Press.

Warwick, A. (1995). "Excremental Colonialism: Public Health and the Poetics of Pollution." *Critical Inquiry*, *21*(3), 640-649.

Williams, H.A. (2001). "Caring for Those in Crisis: Integrating Anthropology and Public Health in Complex Humanitarian Emergencies." *National Association for the Practice of Anthropology Bulletin*, *14*(4), 1-16.

3
Medical Anthropology and Public Health

Sunita Reddy

Introduction

The present chapter looks at the field of medical anthropology, concepts, theoretical understanding, and methodological strengths. Further, it looks at the application of medical anthropology to public health, the dominance of Western influence and the need to look at the health inequalities, felt needs and health culture, calling for an interdisciplinary approach to understand public health issues.

Origins of Medical Anthropology

Anthropology is the only contemporary discipline that approaches human questions from historical, biological, linguistic, and cultural perspectives. Cross-cutting the subfields of anthropology are a number of sub-disciplinary foci that have much to contribute to the achievement of public health objectives. The most important for public health is medical anthropology, has rapidly grown to become one of the largest areas of research and practice within anthropology. Medical anthropology as a distinct sub-discipline did not emerge until the 1950s, nevertheless, Otto von Mering (1970: 272) contends that the formal relationship between anthropology and medicine began when Rudolf Virchow, a renowned pathologist interested in social medicine, founded the German Anthropological Society in 1869, and in the same year, the Berlin Society of Anthropology, Ethnology, and Prehistory. He also edited the journal of the Society. W.H.R. Rivers, a physician-anthropologist was one of the first anthropologists to discuss health-related issues cross-culturally, argued in "*Medicine, Magic, and Religion*" (1924: 51) that "medical practices are not a medley of disconnected and meaningless customs" but rather an integral part of the larger social-cultural systems within which they are embedded. Erwin Ackerknecht (1971) and others wrote chapters and chapters on topics that would today be considered medical anthropology during the 1940s (quoted in Baer, H.A. *et al.*, 2016).

After Second World War, an increasing number of anthropologists turned their attention to health-related issues, especially applied ones. Norman Scotch (1963) is often credited with popularizing the term "medical anthropology". Medical anthropology received its initial impetus from two main sources: one was the involvement of various anthropologists in international health work; Cora Dubois became the first anthropologist to hold the formal position with an international health organization and secondly, the involvement of anthropologists in the clinical settings as teachers, researchers, administrators, and clinicians. 'Anthropology of Public Health' draws upon a long tradition of research within medical anthropology, dating back to Paul's key text *Health, Culture and Community* (Paul, 1955) and the classic work of social anthropologists such as Evans Pritchard's *Witchcraft, Oracles and Magic Among the Azande* (1937).

Rooted in applied research, medical anthropology was expected to facilitate the introduction of Western biomedical health care into impoverished communities of the allegedly developing world. Chapters by Marriott (1955) and Carstairs (1955) are examples of the same. Post-World War II medical anthropology tended to emphasize the cognitive dissonance between the indigenous and biomedical constructs (Sargent, C.F. *et al.,* 1996). Gradually medical anthropology took strides in 1970s, Landy (1983: 193) asserted that medical anthropology "has begun to come of age, or at least to have left its childhood and entered its adolescence." While this dynamic sub-discipline has certainly not yet reached full maturity, one might argue that it has reached late adolescence or even early adulthood (Baer, 2003).

Medical Anthropology Today

Today, medical anthropology constitutes an extremely broad area of work that no single textbook can possibly summarize. At the theoretical level medical anthropologists are interested in topics such as evolution in ecology of disease, paleopathology, and social epidemiology; the political economy of health and disease; ethnomedicine and ethnopharmacology; medical pluralism; cultural psychiatry; the social organization of health professions, clinics, hospitals, national health care systems and international health bureaucracies; human reproduction; nutrition and many more topics.

At the applied level, medical anthropologists work in areas such as community medicine; public health; international health; medical and nursing education; health care delivery; mental health services; health programme evaluation; health policy; health care reform; health activism; advocacy; biomedical ethics etc. In applied medical anthropology, the efforts are to control and eradicate a wide area of health-related problems, including malaria, cancer, alcoholism, drug addiction, AIDS, malnutrition, and environmental pollution. Most disciplines have evolved from mono-disciplines to interdisciplinary to resolve complex issues. In many ways, the work of medical anthropologists overlaps with that of medical sociologists, medical geographers, medical psychologists, medical social workers, epidemiologists, and public health professionals. In the past, medical anthropologists tended to focus on health problems at the local level and, less often, at the national level (Baer *et al.*, 2003: 28). Physician-anthropologist Cecil Helman (1994: 338) maintains that future research in medical anthropology "*will involve adopting a much more global perspective—a holistic view of the complex interactions between cultures, economic systems, political organizations and the ecology of the planet itself.*" He identifies overpopulation, organizations, AIDS, primary health care, pollution and global warming, deforestation and species extinction as some of the areas with which medical anthropologists will need to concern themselves.

The richness of this sub-discipline is apparent in the range of theoretical perspectives encompassed by it. Anthropology has also made important methodological contributions to public health, especially with regard to the use of ethnography for the systematic collection of field data; qualitative methods for the collection and analysis of descriptive, interpretative, and formative data; and the integration of qualitative and quantitative approaches. The ability to translate scientific knowledge into effective practice at the community level is a third area where anthropological approaches have much to offer to public health. Public health is often described as having the population or community as its patient, in contrast to the individual-level focus of clinical medicine. This focus on community creates a natural foundation for the partnership between public health and anthropology, which takes as its primary focus the study of people in groups and especially in local communities.

Anthropological theory and methods have much to offer to public health in the area of translating public health knowledge into effective action (Hahn, 1995). Contributions range from basic issues of cultural sensitivity to enhance the acceptability and effectiveness of proven practices in clinic settings to the development of policy for the provision complex treatment regimens for intersecting emerging epidemics under conditions of inequity in access to health care. As such, anthropologists are asking questions about the root causes of public health's toughest problems. These problems are not often amenable to study using controlled clinical trials or cross-sectional survey designs. Rather, they are dynamic, systems-level problems that require field-based observation and the use of multiple methods that are both qualitative and quantitative.

Anthropology in Public Health and Anthropology of Public Health

Lambert & McKevitt (2002) note that most of the chapters in *Journal of Biosocial Science* attempt to understand the prevalence and distribution of disease and sickness within and between populations as well as local responses to biomedical interventions and public health policy more generally. They fall broadly within the remit of human ecology, and they embrace a 'factorial' model of disease in which social and cultural factors are deemed to be just one of a number of factors to be considered alongside a range of other factors. These include biological features of the infecting organism; nutritional factors; environmental factors; psychological factors; and genetic factors influencing susceptibility to disease at an individual and population level. The authors share a sense of disquiet at the continuing predominance of this approach. They recognize that it is vital to document and understand the changing distribution of disease(s) within and between populations as, apart from anything else, effective public health policy cannot be formulated without such information. They also recognize that no single discipline has a monopoly of insight; and that effective public policy cannot be formulated without harnessing insights from the biological and social sciences. However, working with a 'factorial' model of disease is problematic as it embraces conceptual splits that may be more misleading than they are helpful. For example, a separation is implicitly made between 'science' and 'culture'. Leaving aside the question of what these two complex terms might mean, the suggestion is made that scientific knowledge and endeavour is quite separate from the context in which it is used or the social circumstances to which it might be applied. There is little, if any, recognition of the fact that what appears, in any specific context, to be 'scientific knowledge' has emerged and been shaped by multiple and overlapping ways of thinking and seeing embedded in complex social processes. These processes include power relations and economic hierarchies as well as conceptions generated by previous public health interventions. The mainstream public health literature also makes a conceptual split between 'science' and 'culture'. The analysis is dominated by the combination of the 'factorial' model with biomedical epistemology and conventions of clinical practice. This type of approach typically reduces the investigation of social and cultural aspects of the disease to discrete, static, quantifiable 'beliefs' held by (or sometimes even about) the study population. The separation of these beliefs from the ideas of medical science and its intended humanistic outcomes has led researchers to investigate 'barriers' to the effective provision of health care services. Surveys documenting the 'knowledge, attitudes and practices' of the study population and, more recently, 'focused ethnographic studies' have sought to understand the gaps between the provision and uptake of services in the health sector; and the emphasis is frequently given to 'cultural factors' inhibiting their effective delivery. It is often looked at our 'knowledge' and their 'beliefs'.

Medical sociologists Freidson notes the existence of "very large body of sociological and anthropological information 'about popular knowledge' and attitudes towards health and disease, but finds most of it to be 'grossly descriptive'." "Aside from cultural designations like Mexican, Subanun, and Mashona", he writes, "there is no method by which the material is ordered save for focusing on knowledge about a particular illness. Such studies are essentially catalogues, often without a classified index" (Freidson, 1970: 10 in Foster, G.M., 1976). Most popular and often used is the deductions from KAP survey data about explaining health-seeking behaviour. Questions related to Practices in KAP surveys usually inquire about the use of preventive measures or different health care options. Normally, hypothetical questions are asked (what do you do if your child is ill?). They, therefore, hardly permit statements about actual practices. Rather, they yield information on people's normative behaviours or on what they know should be done (or they expect the interviewer wants to hear). In this sense, they check well on people's knowledge about practices, as heard in educational campaigns for example. Above all, KAP surveys yield highly descriptive data, without providing an explanation for why people do what they do. Unfortunately, many investigators who use KAP studies do use them, implicitly or explicitly, to explain health-seeking behaviour. Their studies are based on the underlying assumption that there is a direct relationship between knowledge and action. They assume that by changing knowledge, behaviour is automatically changed as well. Neglected are other factors like treatment expectations, satisfaction with health care services, decision-making for health care, and external barriers (e.g. financial constraints, accessibility of health services). All this makes clear that knowledge is just one element in a broad array of factors, which determine health-seeking behaviour (for a critique of KAP studies, see also Nichter, 1993).

Public health discourses and biomedical ways of seeing (which are generally linked to the entrenched hierarchies of clinical practice) *construct* rather than discover 'knowledge', and are embedded in the social circumstances they observe. As Farmer (1999) has shown, the adoption of culture as a kind of variable in public health discussion has actually detracted from the development of broader understandings of the ways in which political, economic and social processes influence the prevalence, distribution, and response to disease(s) within and between populations. Indeed, Farmer and many others (including Ogden, 1999; Baer *et al.*, 2003) have shown that critical medical anthropology can offer much more than an understanding of social and cultural factors. It can, and should, 're-configure the boundaries of the problem', offering (new) conceptual frameworks, substantive knowledge and methodological insights (Lambert & McKevitt, 2002).

Differentiating between Anthropology in *Public Health and Anthropology of Public Health*, Parker and Harper (2006) observe that a great deal of funding allocated for research in medical anthropology comes from organizations committed to the 'factorial' model; and many colleagues have been drawn into work that fits this scheme (see, for example, Gove & Pelto, 1994; and many of the chapters in the book edited by Hahn, 1996). Their research is described as 'anthropology in public health'. That is anthropological research that sets out to generate data that fits within pre-existing categories embraced by the 'factorial' model frequently compromises, what anthropology has to offer as a discipline. However, they feel that there is a need for an 'anthropology of public health' which remains passionately concerned about ill-health and deprivation and the need for public policy; but also remains committed to a rigorous and critical analytical perspective. In other words, 'anthropology of public health' should not be divorced from the world of practitioners. It should engage and comment upon public policy in such a way that it helps to alleviate the distress and suffering caused by infection and disease.

Theoretical Contributions

Scholars have proposed a wide range of explanations for the forms of human sickness and healing found in different cultural and historical settings. Three basic theories underlying a variety of explanations are *an environmental/evolutionary theory, cultural theory, and political economic theory*. Environmental/evolutionary theory argues that the physical environment and human adaptations to it are the principal determinants of sickness and healing. In cultural theory, cultural systems of beliefs, values, and customs are basic determinants and in political economic theory, the economic organization and contending relationships of power are the principal forces controlling human sickness and healing (Hahn, 1996).

The medical ecological approach links biomedicine with biological and cultural anthropology, resulting in important contributions to understanding health and disease as dynamic, adaptive population-based processes. The ecological model builds on three key assumptions (after McElroy & Townsend, 1989: 20 in Singer, 1989):

1. There is no single cause of disease; rather, the disease is ultimately due to a chain of factors related to ecosystem imbalances.
2. Health and disease are part of a set of physical, biological, and cultural sub-systems that continually affect one another.
3. The ecological model provides a framework for the study of health in the environmental context but does not specify what factors maintain health within any given local system.

Critical medical anthropology seeks to understand health and illness from a holistic biological, socio-cultural, political and economic perspective. This approach attempts to identify and understand the determinant interconnections between one or more health conditions, sufferers and the community understandings of illness in question and the social, political, and economic conditions that may have contributed to the development of ill-health. To frame this kind of big picture of dialectical thinking in health, critical medical anthropologists introduced the concept of "syndemic" (Singer, 2013) as a new term in epidemiological and public health thinking.

The past decade has witnessed a significant increase of studies in political economic medical anthropology (PEMA). Some publications specify political economy in their very titles; others are not similarly explicit. Still, other works carry the label critical medical anthropology (CMA) (Baer, H.A., Merrill Singer and John H. Johnsen, 1986). Critical medical anthropology (CMA) raises important questions about the *impact of global political and economic structures and processes on health and disease*. It expands the context within which medical anthropology operates and brings it closer to the perspective of public health practice by explicitly seeking to contribute to the creation of global health systems that "serve the people" (Baer, Singer & Susser, 1997: 33).

CMA focuses on health care systems and how they function at *multiple levels*, including:

1. The *individual* level of patient experience.
2. The *micro-level* of physician-patient relationships.
3. The *intermediate* level of local health care systems, particular hospitals, and clinics.
4. The *macro-social* level of global political-economic systems.

At each of these levels, the goal is to understand how existing social relations structure the relationships among the participants in the systems. In particular, critical medical anthropologists study the way health care is embedded within dominant relations such as those of class, race, and gender. For CMA, the future has already arrived, making micro-macro connections—that is, likely patients suffering to the global political economy.

From the perspective of CMA, health can be defined as access to and control over the basic material and non-material resources that sustained and promote life at a high level of satisfaction. Health is not some absolute state of being but an elastic concept that must be evaluated in a larger social-cultural context (Baer, 2003). The relevance of culture is not restricted to ethnomedical conceptions but extends to issues of power, control, resistance, and defiance surrounding health, sickness, and healing.

Anthropological Methods to Public Health Problems

The application of anthropological methods to public health problems has been another important area of contribution. The use of systematic descriptive qualitative methods has proven effective in identifying context-specific factors that contribute to health and disease outcomes. Another important methodological contribution is the use of triangulation or the systematic application of multiple methods in order to reduce bias in situations where controlled comparison is not feasible. For example, anthropologists typically use natural observation of behaviour along with self-report data and descriptions or normative expectations to obtain highly accurate descriptions of events and social relationships.

The development of rapid assessment techniques, variously called rapid appraisal, rapid assessment, and rapid rural appraisal is a prime example of anthropological contributions to the public health methodological toolkit (Scrimshaw *et al.*, 1991; Beebe, 1995). As described by Beebe (1995: 42) this is a multidisciplinary team-based approach designed to generate reasonably valid, reliable qualitative results within a short time frame. Rapid assessments can provide the contextual information needed to design in-depth community-level and community-based public health research and to guide decisions about implementing programmes in local settings.

A key anthropological contribution to health research lies in its empirically based grasp of the context-specific nature of social processes. This focus on the particular, which anthropology insists on through documenting the complex details of everyday life, provides an important corrective to misleading generalizations and abstractions that can, according to Singer, "grotesquely flatten" the diversity of different settings (Singer M. in Lambert, 2002). However, analysis of specific situations or cases can also provide more general insights into the type of phenomenon under study, through anthropology's comparative approach. Comparing primary data with secondary evidence about similar issues (such as a particular health problem) in different settings can produce stronger analytical insights with greater potential generalizability. This is achieved through logical (rather than statistical) inferences that make use of relevant empirical knowledge and theoretical principles (Clyde Mitchell J. in Lambert & McKevitt, 2002).

Emphasis on methods in health-related qualitative research obscures the value of substantive knowledge and theoretical concepts based on some social sciences. Anthropology views the familiar afresh by focusing on classification and on understanding rationality in social and cultural context. It highlights the value of data gathered informally and the differences between what people say, thinks, and do. Its emphasis on empirical particularity helps to avoid inaccurate generalizations and their potentially problematic applications. Truly multidisciplinary research needs to incorporate the conceptual frameworks and knowledge bases of participating disciplines (Lambert & Mckevitt, 2002).

International Health

International health development work is among the most personally challenging, intellectually engaging, and potentially frustrating areas of medical anthropological practice. International health is the term that is most frequently used when health policy planners speak about health in the developing world. Although the United States and other industrialized nations are normally included in the concept international, in the case of health development work they are most commonly the planners, and less developed nations such as Egypt, Liberia, India, Bangladesh are the recipients. Thus, in practice, international health refers to the flow of advice, health professionals, and health technology from the wealthier nations to the poorer. There have been historic trends in international health work, and anthropologists have mainly played roles in two opposing camps: those who work on the projects and those who became the critics (Banerji, 1986).

The assumptions of international health work have, according to George Foster (1987) historically included the assumptions that: (1) Wealthier countries have the capital, the talent, and know-how to solve the health problems of the poorer countries; (2) The million countries should, therefore, plan and direct such efforts; and (3) Western health care institutions and approaches will work in solving health problems in the LDCs. Nonetheless, the major themes of health development work involve the exporting by the West to the developing world its concepts of medicine and health care. These general assumptions are elements of a professional worldwide that persists despite repeated demonstrations that it is inadequate. Benjamin Paul (1955) then a professor at the Harvard School of Public Health, an anthropologist published a book *Health, Culture and Community* in having 16 case studies is a trendsetter in developing curricula for education and training of social scientists in health fields in developing countries. Pelto & Pelto (1992) used applied medical anthropology in Third World countries to solve the problems. Medical anthropological research by Indian anthropologists has started appearing.

McKeown describes how the social movements of the 19th century in England led to the provision of clean water and improvements in nutrition and housing, which were responsible for the reduction in infectious diseases. The resulting decrease in mortality rates, especially among infants and children, happened before the advent of antibiotics. Thus, health care alone may not be the best method of improving the health of people internationally, particularly when their health problems stemmed directly from poverty. Many health problems of the developing world, results from inequality. It follows that the greatest improvement in health can be achieved by improving economic status, nutrition, water supply, and other environmental conditions, education, social and political relations.

Health services—promotive, preventive, curative and rehabilitative—form but one of the means of improving the health status of a society. In fact, there is a synergistic relationship between these factors and health services. The progress of these fields creates conditions for more effective use of health services; reciprocally, effective health services often make significant contributions to advancement in socio-economic status.

The approach has to be an integrated interdisciplinary one. Research on community involvement in health service development will require studies of cultural aspects of health, health services, health institutions and health practices, the modes of production and social structures. Health service development is thus a socio-cultural process, a political process and a technological and a managerial process, involving epidemiological and sociological approaches. These should also include analysis of the distribution of power, political organization, mobilization of resources and the pattern of their use within the community as well as their effectiveness in the context of the cultural perception and cultural meaning of health problems (Banerji D., 1986).

There are many factors, which determine the use of social sciences in health service development in a country like India. For health administrators, there is a need for commitment, increase the effectiveness of services and most important of all, a sensitivity to the interdisciplinary nature of health administration. For social scientists, it is necessary to have scholars who have strong foundations in the methods and concepts in social science, which are relevant to public health. They should have the capability to visualize health services as a complex system with interdisciplinary dimensional, make social science contributions for health service development and have interpersonal competence and participate effectively as members of interdisciplinary teams (Banerji, 1985, 1986). Mere grafting or even adaptation of the knowledge of the discipline of health administration as it has developed in the affluent industrialized countries will not be enough. The intellectual challenge to scholars in health administration in India is to build, wherever needed, an alternative body of knowledge (new public health) that is rooted in the cultural, social, political, epidemiological, administrative and economic conditions of the country (Banerji, 1985, 1986).

To develop a meaningful approach to social scientists have to get away from what has been termed as "Western reference frame" by Yogendra Singh and build an alternative body of social science knowledge which is rooted in the conditions obtaining in the country but they are also often required to distance themselves from the Western reference frame in the disciplines such as medical sociology, medical anthropology, and health economics and formulate alternatives. Thus, above all, the involvement of social scientists in an interdisciplinary team to build an alternative body of knowledge for the discipline of health administration in India calls for high degree of ethical commitment and competence (Banerjee, 1986).

Social scientists have produced a large volume of literature in the course of their work in health fields in India. They have also covered an extensive field—health education, health behaviour in relation to rural and urban health services, family planning, maternal and child health, health systems development, communicable disease control programmes, environmental sanitation, health professions and medical education, socialization of health professionals, hospital administration, organizational behaviour, health economics, and political economy of health and so on. According to the imminent Indian sociologists and psychologists like I.P. Desai, Ramakrishna Mukherjee, Roy K. Berman, S.C. Dube, Surajit Sinha, and B.N. Mukherjee, most of the studies did not live up to the requirement due to their heavy dependence on the Western reference frame. The review of ICSSR had observed, "much of the current research effort has no relevance to contemporary social and national problems and suffers besides from lack of rigour in its analysis of phenomena and the synthesis of facts. It is largely oriented to micro-level research to the neglect of macro-level problems. It has not yet emancipated from its tutelage to Western theories and has failed to develop research tools, models of its own, appropriate to the Indian situation."

Foster (1982) has made a very insightful observation: "almost all assume that effective health care can be achieved only when members of traditional communities change their health behaviour. Rarely, if ever, the question is asked, 'how can anthropologist's help to change bureaucratic behaviour that inhibits the design and operation of the best possible health care system?'" Foster belongs to the minority group of 'Western' scholars who have contributed to the formulation of an alternative paradigm.

Health is a part of overall development. Its analysis will acquire meaning and significance, only when the medical anthropologists, relate in the present social, cultural, economic, political and ecological and biological milieu and carry out with broader imagination and holistic framework in the developing world.

Several studies in India by Hasan (1967), Takulia *et al.*, (1967), Dhillon and Philip (1994), Marriot (1995), Carstairs (1955), Opler (1963), Gould (1965), Djurfelt and Lindberg (1975), Van Veen (1981) have obtained reliable and valid data on certain anthropological aspects of health, besides inadequate understanding of the overall institutional framework for making medical care services accessible to the people. Sahu (1991) feels that these studies were far removed from the reality. Works of Minocha (1980), Karna (1976), Kakar *et al.*, (1972), provide further evidence to demonstrate the inadequacy of anthropologists in developing an overall framework of the relevance of their discipline to the field of health (Sahu, 1991).

Very few studies have taken a comprehensive, holistic approach which is embedded in the concept of health culture (Banerjee, 1993, Sahu, 1991). It is necessary for anthropological studies on health in India to take a holistic view of all the cultural, socio-economic and political dimensions that are related to the health and health services of a community and to relate such a holistic perspective to the overall culture of the community. It may be observed that all these aspects related to health problems and health practices can be studied only in the context of the overall culture of the community.

The concept of health culture flows from the concept of felt need. It is apparent that cultural and social perception and meaning of health problem, the health institutions that are available and accessible to members of a community and health behaviour, all interact with one another to form a sub-cultural complex; one factor cannot be described or studied without having reference points for the other interacting factors. This sub-cultural complex has been termed as health culture of a community. In this cultural context, community health programmes that are introduced from outside can be considered as purposive interventions to bring about a change in the pre-existing health culture. This holistic and interdisciplinary concept of health culture provides a valuable framework for analysis, in the domain of medical anthropology (Banerji, 1993 and Sahu, 1991).

New Frontiers in Medical Anthropology

One major area of inquiry in medical anthropology is 'medical systems'. Till recently anthropologists have been studying 'ethnomedicine' that deals with the study of traditional medicines; not only those that have relevant written sources (e.g. traditional Chinese medicine, Ayurveda), but especially those, whose knowledge and practices have been orally transmitted over the centuries. Recent studies are debating and questioning the legitimacy of asking biomedicine as so-called 'dominant' and others as 'alternative'. Scholars have argued that biomedicine too is an 'ethnomedicine' and 'medicine as a culture' (Deborah, 2003). Often 'biomedicine' is seen in opposition to all other 'alternative medicines'. *Biomedicine* is referred to the predominant medical theory and practice of Euro-American societies, a medicine widely disseminated throughout the world (Bosk, 1980 in Hahn and Kleinman, 1983). Each of its many denominations, "Western," "Cosmopolitan", "Modern", "Scientific," "Allopathic" and "Biomedicine" as well, captures one of its characteristics, while misleading in other ways. While Biomedicine may have its principal origins in Western civilization and has even been a leading edge of modernism (MacIntyre, 1981, in Hahn and Kleinman, 1983), it has incorporated and now penetrates other traditions as well. Even though it is widespread, the exclusive erudition and Catholicism connoted by "Cosmopolitan" is inaccurate. Biomedicine may have appeared more recently and changed more rapidly than many other traditions, but nonetheless, these other traditions also manifest contemporary, "modem" versions (Leslie, 1976 in Hahn and Kleinman, 1983). Moreover, non-Western ethno-medicines evidence "scientific" approaches, while Biomedicine discloses certain magical non-rational elements. We use "Biomedicine" as a name for this medicine, referring to its primary focus on human biology, or more accurately, on physiology, even pathophysiology. Other medicines, e.g. contemporary Chinese (Hahn & Kleinman, 1983) demonstrate a similar focus, though cast in a different orientation. Thus, Biomedicine is the version of bio-medicine founded and dominant in Euro-American societies and spread widely elsewhere.

Western biomedicine is a cultural construct and should, therefore, be seen as only one of many complementary alternatives within the field of healthcare. To reach this conclusion, Hopwood (1997) examines the construction of the body, and the ways in which culture affects the types, causes and incidences of illness.

Biomedicine, then, is an *ethnomedicine*, albeit a unique one. In making this claim they do not deny a natural connection. Biomedicine and other socio-cultural systems continually remake nature, including human nature; but nature reciprocally constrains what can be made of it. Biomedicine is thus the product of a dialectic between culture and nature. By making this dialectic a central focus, medical anthropology, we aver, will confront general anthropological theory with a vital problematic and offer a subject matter for its exploration. A focus on the nature-culture dialectic as a primary theoretical problematic for medical anthropology, they *recommend the strategic integration of medical and anthropological epistemologies as a primary methodological problematic of this field.* Socio-cultural phenomena such as the social production of disease and the placebo effect may then be included within medical theory and practice rather than excluded either as "non-medical" or as "controls" for purportedly more real effects. Methodologies combining ethnography and cultural analysis with epidemiology and clinical research techniques are being applied in non-Western settings (Hahn and Kleinman, 1983). Other significant works of medical anthropologists are on pain, suffering, structural violence (Farmer, 2005) and Inhorn's (2007) work on ethnographies of reproductive disruptions.

More recent work of Indian medical anthropologists, Bhasin (2007) on reviewing medical anthropology, Prasad (2005) on narratives of sickness and illness taking a case of malaria, Naraindas (2003, 2006, 2011) on Pox, on Ayurveda, on healings across borders. Joshi *et al.* (2011) work on disasters. My own work on HIV, medical tourism, surrogacy, (Reddy *et al.*, 2013, 2015, 2016) and disasters (Reddy, 2005, 2011, 2013, 2015) have been looked at from anthropological lens. In methodology, Savyasachi and Thapan's work (1998) on looking into the reflections into the fieldwork and Srivastavas' (2004) work on 'Methodology and Fieldwork' is the new addition into the Anthropological perspectives and methods.

Medical anthropology studies have thus built upon historical and cultural analysis over a long period of time that indicate an array of difference with respect to the metaphors and meanings that signify health. These studies emphasize cultural fabrics that give coherence and depth to these meanings such that cosmology and ethical traditions come to define the body in states of sickness and well-being. Anthropological studies of health focus on local contexts where health and illness are recognized and responded to culture, affects health as much through the culture of biomedicine.

Thus, there is a huge scope for application of anthropological concepts, theories, and methods for better understanding public health issues in India. What is required is a good grounding in anthropological theories, methods, conceptual clarity, epidemiology to address public health issues.

REFERENCES

Baer, H.A., Merrill Singer and John H. Johnsen (1986). "Towards a Critical Medical Anthropology", *Social Science and Medicine*, *23*(2), pp. 95-98.

Baer, H.A., Singer, M. & Susser, I. (1997). "Medical anthropology: central concepts and development." *Medical Anthropology and the World System: A Critical Perspective.* Westport, CT: Bergin & Garvey, 3-19.

Baer, H.A., Singer, M. & Susser, I. (2013). *Medical Anthropology and the World System: Critical Perspectives:* Praeger.

Baer, H.A., Singer, M., Long, D., Erickson, P., Cheyney, M., Finkler, K., & van der Geest, S. (2016). "Imagining the Whole: Toward an Articulation of Health Anthropology." *Current Anthropology*, *57*(4), 000-000.

Banerjee, D. (1986). *Social sciences and health service development in India*, New Delhi, Lok Prakshan.

Banerjee, D. (1993). "A Social Science Approach to Strenghtening India's National Tuberculosis Programme." *Ind. J. Tub*, *40*, 61-82.

Beebe, J. (1995). "Basic concepts and techniques of rapid appraisal." *Human Organization 54*: 42-51.

Bhasin, V. (2007). "Medical anthropology: A review." *Studies on Ethno-medicine*, *1*(1), 1-20.

Carstairs, G.M. (1955). "Medicine and faith in rural Rajasthan." *Health, Culture and Community*, 107-134.

Dhillon, H.S., & Philip, L. (1994). *Health promotion and community action for health in developing countries*. World Health Organization.

Djurfeldt, G. & Lindberg, S. (1975). *Pills against poverty: a study of the introduction of Western medicine in a Tamil village*. Student litterature.

Evans-Pritchard, E.E. (1937). *Witchcraft, oracles and magic among the Azande* (Vol. 12). London: Oxford.

Farmer, P. (1999). "Pathologies of power: rethinking health and human rights." *American Journal of Public Health*, *89* (10), 1486-1496.

Farmer, Paul (2005). "On Suffering and Structural Violence" in *Pathologies of Power*. Univ. of California Press.

Foster, George M. (1987). "World Health Organization behavioural science research: problems and prospects." *Social Science and Medicine 24*: 709-15.

Foster, G.M. (1982). "Community development and primary health care: their conceptual similarities." *Medical Anthropology*, *6*(3), 183-195.

Gould, H.A. (1965). "Modern medicine and folk cognition in rural India." *Human Organization*, *24*(3), 201-208.

Hahn, R.A. & Kleinman, A. (1983). "Biomedical practice and anthropological theory: frameworks and directions." *Annual Review of Anthropology*, *12*(1), 305-333.

Hahn, Robert A. (1996). *Sickness and healing: an anthropological perspective*. New Haven: Yale University Press.

Haimendorf (1945). *The Reddis of the Bison Hills*. Macmillan, London.

Hasan, K.A. (1967). *The Cultural Frontier of Health in Village India: Case Study of a North Indian Village*. Manaktalas.

Helman, Cecil. (1990). *Culture, Health and Illness*. London etc. Wright.

Hopwood, A.L. (1997). "The social construction of illness and its implications for complementary and alternative medicine.' *Complementary Therapies in Medicine* (1997) *5*, 152-155.

Joshi, P., Kaushal, S., Aribam, B.S., Khattri, P., D'aoust, O., Singh, M.M., & Guha-Sapir, D. (2011). "Recurrent floods and prevalence of diarrhea among under five children: observations from Bahraich district, Uttar Pradesh, India." *Global Health Action*, *4*(1), 6355.

Kakar, D.N., Murthy, S.S., & Parker, R.L. (1972). "People's perception of illness and their use of medical care services in Punjab." *Indian Journal of Medical Education*, *11*(4), 26-94.

Karna, M.N. (1976). "Etiology of Disease: A Sociological Study in the Rural Context." *Man in India*, *56*(1), 50-64.

Lambert, Helen Christopher McKevitt (2002). "Anthropology in health research: from qualitative methods to multidisciplinarity", *BMJ volume*, 325, 27 July.

Landy (1983) Landy, D.(ed.). (1977). *Culture, disease and healing: Studies in medical anthropology.* London: Collier Macmillan.

Marcia Inhorn (2007). "Introduction: Defining Women's Health: A Dozen Messages from More than 150 Ethnographies" in *Reproductive Disruptions*. Berghahn Books.

Marriott, M. (1955). "Western Medicine in a Village of Northern India", *Health, Culture, and Community*, 239.

McKeown, T. (1978). "Determinants of health." *Understanding and Applying Medical Anthropology.*

Meenakshi Thapan. (1998). "Unlearning Fieldwork: The Flight of an Arctic Tern" by Savyasachi, in the Book *Anthropological Journeys: Reflections on Fieldwork*' (Ed.) Orient Longman.

Mering, Otto von. (1970). "Medicine and psychiatry", In Otto von Mering and Leonard Kasdan (Eds.) *Anthropology and the Behavioural and Health Sciences*, 272-307. Pittsburgh: University of Pittsburgh Press.

Minocha, A.A. (1980). "Medical pluralism and health services in India." *Social Science & Medicine. Part B: Medical Anthropology*, *14*(4), 217-223.

Naraindas, H. (2003). "Crisis, charisma and triage: extirpating the pox." *The Indian Economic & Social History Review*, *40*(4), 425-457.

Naraindas, H. (2006). "Of spineless babies and folic acid: Evidence and efficacy in biomedicine and Ayurvedic medicine." *Social Science & Medicine*, *62*(11), 2658-2669.

Naraindas, H., & Bastos, C. (2011). "Healing holidays? Itinerant patients, therapeutic locales and the quest for health: Special Issue for Anthropology & Medicine." *Anthropology and Medicine*, *18*(1), 1-6.

Nichter, M. (1993). "Social science lessons from diarrhea research and their application to ARI." *Human Organization*, 53-67.

Opler, M.E. (1963). "The cultural definition of illness in village India." *Human Organization*, *22*(1), 32-35.

Parker, Melissa and Ian Harper (2006). "The Anthropology of Public Health" *J. Biosoc. Sci.* (2006) 38, 1-5.

Paul, B.D. (1955). *Health, Culture, and Community*. Russell Sage Foundation.

Pelto, P.J., & Pelto, G.H. (1992). "Developing applied medical anthropology in Third World countries: Problems and actions." *Social Science & Medicine*, *35*(11), 1389-1395.

Prasad, P. (2005). "Narratives of sickness and suffering: A study of malaria in South Gujarat." *Sociological Bulletin*, *54*(2), 218-237.

Reddy, Sunita (2013). *Clash of Waves: Post Tsunami rehabilitation in Andaman and Nicobar Islands*, Indus, New Delhi.

Reddy, Sunita (2005). "Understanding Cultural Resources from HIV/AIDs Control: An Interdisciplinary Approach". *Indian Anthropologist*. Vol. 35. No. 1 & 2, March and September 2005.

Reddy, Sunita (2011): "Understanding Disasters from Anthropological Perspectives", *Indian Emergency Journal*. Vol. VI, Issue I.

Reddy, Sunita & Tulsi Patel (2015): "There are many eggs in my body: Medical markets and commodified bodies in India", *Global Bioethics*.

Reddy, Sunita, Tulsi Patel, Malene Tanderup, Birgitte Bruun Nielsen. (2015) "Breast Feeding and Bonding: Issues and Dilemmas in Surrogacy", In Tanya Cassidy and Abdullahi El-Tom (Ed.) *Ethnographies of Breast Feeding: Cultural Contexts and Confrontations*, Bloomsbury Publishing PLC.

Rivers, W.H.R. (1924). *Medicine, Magic, and Religion*. London: Kegan Paul, Trench, Trubner and Co.

Sahu, S.K. (1991). *Health culture in transition: a case study of Oraon tribe in rural and industrial nexus*. Khama Publishers.

Sargent, C.F. and Thomas M. Johnson (eds.) (1996). "Political economy in medical anthropology" In *Medical Anthropology—Contemporary Theory and Method*. Praeger, London, pp. 21-40.

Scotch, N.A. (1963). "Medical Anthropology. *Biennial Review of Anthropology*, *3*, 30-68.

Scrimshaw, S.C., Carballo, M., Ramos, L., & Blair, B.A. (1991). "The AIDS rapid anthropological assessment procedures: a tool for health education planning and evaluation." *Health Education Quarterly*, *18*(1), 111-123.

Singer, M. (1989). "The limitations of medical ecology: the concept of adaptation in the context of social stratification and social transformation." *Medical Anthropology*, *10*(4), 223-234.

Singer, Merrill. (1994). "AIDS and the health crisis of the urban poor: the perspective of critical medical anthropology". *Social Science and Medicine*, *39*: 931-48.

Takulia, H.S., Taylor, C.E., Sangal, S.P., & Alter, J.D. (1967). *The health centre doctor in India*. Baltimore: Hopkins

van der Veen, K.W. (1981). "Socio-cultural aspects of medical care in Valsad District, Gujarat state." *The Social and Cultural Context of Medicine in India*, 168-194.

van Hollen, C. (2003). *Birth on the threshold: childbirth and modernity in South India*. University of California Press.

4

The Relevance of Indigenous Medical Perspectives

Subhadra Mitra Channa

The Genesis of the Concept Indigenous

I wish to focus on not just indigenous systems of medicine but on the legitimizing processes of certain forms of knowledge and the close association between knowledge and power as pointed out by Michel Foucault (1980). During the process of colonization, a particular form of knowledge that seemingly emanated from the West was established as the *only* form of knowledge. That it was purely a knowledge originated from the West is a misleading information as large and fundamental aspects of this knowledge was built up on what was borrowed from the thriving Islamic Civilization of the Middle East and also from other sources. One may refer to the highly influential medical treatise created by Iranian scholar and philosopher Ibn Sina, known throughout the European World as Avicenna. Written originally in Arabic in 1025, this remained the most referred medical text for centuries and was the most important text in Europe through the entire 18th century. In India, it still forms base of the Unani system of medicine. Today, very few people overtly acknowledge the debt to Islamic civilization, and take Western system of medicine as indigenously developed by European scholars. Worse still, by virtue of colonization and the establishment of Western civilization as the civilization, this form of medicine is now established as the form of medicine; all other systems being relegated to a marginal position by being labelled as 'indigenous' medicine. The possibility of having one objective 'truth' was also manipulated by the Western political domination to be that which originated from the West. Thus, the philosophy was given an ontological status by the power equation. Today the term indigenous has come to represent politically the former colonized and marginalized peoples of the world. In this context, this term has acquired political significance and has become a negotiating platform. But, when applied to a body of knowledge, it implies the same marginalization to a core system that is taken as the valid system.

Thus, the term indigenous form of medicine or indigenous knowledge can be understood as an example of what Bordieu (1980) refers to as 'symbolic violence'. By taking them away from the centre and giving them exotic status, delegitimizes them as knowledge systems that are primary and central. In other words no mainstream medical system gives validity to these systems of knowledge that seem attractive only to anthropologists and persons likely to be adventurous. Further by lumping large numbers of diverse systems under one label is an essentializing process that homogenizes the 'other', takes away from multiple forms of knowledge their claims to uniqueness and identity. Thus, is South Asia itself, there co-exist diverse forms of medical philosophies, such as Ayurveda, Unani, tribal medicines and shamanistic practices; which all get grouped under one label, denying them their specific paradigms and techniques.

A very significant aspect of this 'othering' is that few if any ethnographies, record the actual efficacy of these systems of medicine, even if these are described in detail. What actually happens, how many persons get cured and how many do not? There are questions that are rarely addressed in anthropological writings! Anthropologists tend to be swayed by the philosophical and cosmological, rather than by the practical aspects of these systems.

It is important for us to understand that what gains prominence in the eyes of the lay public or even of practitioners of medicine is very much derivable from the changing power equations both global and local. As decolonization took place across the globe, and different regions gained in the global power arena, various systems that were earlier only identified as superstition and ignorance, began to find their place in the sun. One has to recognize the popularity of Chinese medicine in the West, after China has become a global economic power; but African medicine is still categorized as Voodoo.

Indigenous as Identity

Knowledge and systems of medicine are often revived as an aspect of resurgent nationalism. With the emergence of India as a predominantly

Hindu nation; there has been a complete change in status for Ayurveda. This can be compared with the era when Ayurveda and all indigenous forms of medicine were being relegated to the category of ignorance under British rule and by the emergent generation of young men educated in the English system. The Gyan Peeth award winning Bengali author, Tarashankar Bandopadhyay narrated in his classic novel, *Arogya Niketan*, the rejection by a young man trained as a medical doctor in the British system, of his father's vast knowledge as an eminent Ayurvedic practitioner. Against the background of the colonial period, the author has described how a knowledge backed by centuries of experience and practice is outright ridiculed as civilization and rationality come to be defined only in terms of those who established political supremacy. This is one of the most moving and authentic narrations about the colonization of the mind that Chatterjee (1993) has mentioned. Yet the novel ends by not granting supremacy to the new and the acceptance of the efficacy of age old knowledge systems.

In the post-colonial nationalist resurgence, that took more than a generation to properly establish itself, India's nationalism is turned towards establishing its ancient knowledge like that of Yoga, globally and it is succeeding (Channa, 2004). Even hospitals, especially the state-run ones have begun to have departments devoted to Ayurveda. Although there is no doubt about the efficacy of these ancient form of wisdom, yet one remembers that for many years, even after the Independence of India, all such traditional forms were kept aside as 'non-scientific' and 'non-rational'. The educated people looked down upon them as unreliable, unproven forms of knowledge that could not compare with the Western form of medicine, that symbolized modernity, education and in the cosmology of colonization, civilization itself.

About fifty years after Independence, a new generation of post-colonial Indians began not only to take pride in the emerging global power status of the Indian nation, there was in addition a right wing resurgence of Hindu upper caste identity and Ayurveda, based on ancient Sanskritic texts was the right kind of symbol of pride in a 'glorious' Hindu past. The more popular Unani system of medicine was relegated to a back seat along with Homoeopathy and the indigenous forms of medicine that are part of the Little Tradition of India, in the words of Redfield, were kept in their marginal position.

What is more interesting is the change in the class component of the clientele that catered to these forms of medicine. Till recent times mostly people belonging to rural areas and poorer economic sections relied on the indigenous medicine systems. In the rural areas, the people are faced with the practical aspects of non-availability of so-called modern medicine and medical practitioners, the prohibitive cost of such medicines and the callous attitude of medical practitioners towards the uneducated and poor masses of people.

While a large section of the Indian people had always relied on the traditional or local forms of healing, the upper crust has also now begun its exploration of what has now come to be known as 'alternative' forms of medicine. For one thing, the identity and nationalist aspects are gaining prominence. Secondly, there is disillusionment with respect to Western system of medicine whose efficacy is increasingly coming under the scanner. More and more drugs, including the popular broad spectrum anti-biotics, are now viewed with suspicion. Educated people are more willing to experiment with what is regarded as 'age-old' systems of cure. The media too is playing a key role in popularizing household remedies and non-conventional modes of healing. The internet plays a key role in propagation and introduction of ideas. At the same time at the lower end of the scale, the rural people and the working classes are turning to what they describe as 'modern medicine'. For those striving to achieve a higher status and respectability, using what they identify as a 'modern' (read superior) system of medicine is like moving up the ladder. It is an information passed down by many medical practitioners that private medical practice thrives most in small towns and semi-rural areas. Doing fieldwork in a semi-urban small town/village in Himachal (in 2014) had also given the same finding that most people were relying on local hospitals and doctors in order to use their enhanced incomes from farm produce and also salaried jobs. The result was an inordinate number of women with hysterectomies, done by unscrupulous practitioners who also find it easier to misguide people with less outside awareness.

The Disenfranchisement of Western Medicine

Globally too there is now a disillusionment with the purely Western form of medicine that also reflects the processes, not only of globalization, in the form of migration and sharing of knowledge and values but also a decentralization of the power centres of the world, especially away from its Eurocentric base. With the shifting of economic power towards the East, an ancient culture like China is also getting a global base. Chinese acupuncture is finding its global recognition and market along with Indian Yoga. There are proliferation of Chinese medicine clinics and of Yoga training centres all-over the USA, for example. This corresponds to the considerable economic and social presence of South Asians and Chinese in the USA. They form an elite section of the migrant population who have considerable political and economic clout leading to popularization of Chinese and with it Tibetan medicine.

This global trend looking beyond the efficacy of the Western forms of medicine can also be traced to the transformations in the philosophy of science from pure positivist objectivism to a more tempered and holistic concept where the earlier strict mind/body duality of the Renaissance period is increasingly being discarded. With the transformations in Physics from Particle Physics to Quantum Physics, with the realization that there is a Dark universe way beyond the reach of current human knowledge, the increasing disillusionment about the efficacy of industrial technology in the wake of the climatic and environmental disasters facing the world, This is backed up by the political disillusionment with Western civilization, that comes not only in the form of a post-colonial critique based in theory but also in the present day political turmoil that is putting a question mark on the historically received concept of 'civilization'.

Increasingly the euro-centric notion of 'rationality' is being realized as a just another mode of thinking among many others; what Feminists like Harding (1991) and Harraway (1988) have referred to as 'situated knowledge' and Bordieu has called a 'cultural arbitrary'. In the post-colonial world, knowledge is no longer seen to be confined to a particular regime or region and neither is that of reason and rationality. Earlier, in another place I had referred to P.O. Bodding's ethnography of Santal medicine to show how the Santal shaman's rationality in terms of protecting his interests is in no way different from the manner in which modern hospitals protect their legal interests. The Santal shaman, when asked to treat a patient shows great reluctance in the initial stage and makes sure that the family proactively make a request in a way that demonstrates their eagerness to have him treat their patient. Even when he begins his treatment, he makes it very clear that he is not responsible for the final outcome and everything is actually in the hands of God. This is very similar to the modern hospital making a patient and her relatives sign a bond to say that the hospital is not responsible for the final outcome of an operation or procedure.

In terms of the medical narratives of any patient, irrespective of the cultures or regions they come from, we find that the desire to be cured is the fundamental logic that underlies recourse to treatment. The concept of medical pluralism is also universal in that in almost every culture, people will go looking for alternative cures. The process again almost always involves moving from low cost, easily available cures to high cost and difficult to achieve ones. People move from home and above the counter, non-prescriptive medicines to the local doctor, easily available clinic to a speciality hospital in the urban areas. Those who can afford it can move region and country as well.

The real difference between indigenous forms of cure and what we may refer to as Western or modern form of medicine lies in the basic premises of philosophy and cosmology on which beliefs and practices regarding health and healing are based. While Western medicine treats each individual body as an independent entity and seeks to find the condition of illness to the body itself, non-Western forms of medicine do not make a distinction between mind and body but also makes the body analogous to the person, the social person embedded in his or her relationships. Thus, illness is not caused simply by conditions that affect the individual but by any kind of disturbances in the total social universe of which the individual is only one part. Thus, illness is the result of the moral lapse on part of the person, his or her failure to honour the traditional morality. Earlier, it was thought by Western scholars that only their premises were correct and that of the 'others', the politically marginalized people of the world, were superstitious, non-rational and hocus-pocus.

In contemporary times, the evolution of global knowledge is itself proving a critique of these earlier essentialist and Eurocentric viewpoints.

The Efficacy of the Indigenous

Anthropologists and medical anthropologists in particular have seized upon the holistic perspective characteristic of most non-Western medical system.

I will focus only upon one aspect of the earlier divergent approaches in Western and indigenous forms of healing, namely how the entity to be healed or cured was perceived. In the Western system of medicine, this entity was a human body, bounded and separated from the rest of humans. The understanding of disease was focused upon this unique body as separate from all other, except in terms of its biological and environmental aspects like genetics and infections. The modern medicine is not concerned with the nature of sociability or social interactions except in a limited way for mental illnesses. But in indigenous systems of healing sociability or nature of one's social interactions may play a primary role in both the causative and curative aspects of illness. People fall ill because they fail in the discharge of their social duties, or have breached a cultural or moral rule that makes the spirits or deities angry. Cure consist of restoring the social balance, of expiation of the misdeed and so on. A very good example of such a form of healing is found in Victor Turner's *The Ritual Process*, in the ritual of Isoma, practiced by the Ndembu. This ritual, that seeks to cure women suffering from reproductive disorders, seeks to restore the balance between a woman's loyalty to her maternal kin and her relationship to her husband. Among the matrilineal Ndembu, the women must keep their responsibility towards their maternal ancestors and not deviate too much towards their husband and the ritual recreates harmonious relationships and cures the woman of anxiety that she may feel. The relationship between anxiety, tension and miscarriages is well known to all medical doctors. Thus, what the Ndembu achieve by rituals may well be a state of mental well-being that a modern gynecologist would like to advise to their own patients. But they lack the expertise of the Ndembu shaman in this respect.

Among the Bhotiyas of the Upper Himalayan region (Channa, 2013), the first cause of all illness is in some deity becoming angry. So the first step in the process of cure is, rationally enough, the determination of the cause of the illness. The first stage of divination, comprises determining which supernatural being has been displeased and for the patient to confirm the cause of this displeasure. Once determined and self-confirmed, the second stage comprises asking the offended being, what can be done as compensation for the misconduct, most often unwittingly done. The first stage of divination is usually done through consulting the house deity or lineage deity, through their medium. If no result is forthcoming then a larger possession ritual may be held that invites a larger pantheon of deities.

If no satisfactory result is obtained from the local supernatural beings, then a Buddhist lama is consulted. Failing the intervention of the lama, a Hindu Tantrik (holy man) or priest may be consulted. Only when all available supernatural sources are exhausted will a person venture out to consult a medical doctor. Usually, the first level is of the local village doctor, whose qualifications are equivalent to a compounder or a Registered Medical Practitioner (RMP). At the second level is the medical centre of the local army cantonment. Very few, if any go beyond this level. The last resort will be the hospital in the nearest town of Uttarkashi.

Some of the common causes of offending local deities are already spelled out and deeply ingrained through the acculturative process. While in the upper altitude village, young and beautiful persons, men or women, should only go to the forest with their faces smeared with dust. No one should wear bright coloured clothes; especially yellow, orange and red, as these are the colours of the forest deities. These deities are easily jealous of humans, if they feel they are good looking. Once jealous they will make the person ill. The landscape is a sacred space that contains places of many spirit beings. One needs to be very careful and sensitive to these beings in the environment, and the different parts of the landscape are also alive and need to be treated with caution.

The village deities are sovereign deities that are treated like local rulers. They must be obeyed and their commands adhered to. No important work can be done without permission from these deities. When offended, the deities can bring *own disaster* on the individual as well as the collective. The lineage deities or *kuldevta* are also potent. They are like the family elders, when pleased they take care of a person and also protect and fight on behalf of them. But they too are easily displeased and when angry are the most potent cause of ill health.

People also clearly distinguish between the kinds of illness that are most likely to be caused by supernatural causes and those that are more directly related to specific triggering events. If you fall and break a leg, then one needs to go to a bone setter. If it is clear that it was caused because of anger of a supernatural being, then additional offerings need to be made to ensure that the leg heals properly. Most supernaturally caused diseases are those that appear as mystical illnesses; loss of appetite, paleness of colour, listlessness, weakness, unexplained aches and pains, loss of fertility, gynaecological disorders and bad dreams are usually traced to supernatural wrath.

The important aspect of the medical trajectory is cure. It is almost with certainty that most people reported that they were cured once the cause of the illness was removed. This most often consists of doing some kind of atonement. Basing one's self on the premise that all persons everywhere have common sense and rationality, it would be hard to believe that practices and beliefs would continue to be accepted if they were inefficacious. I will quote the words of a young girl in the Bhotiya village to support this. She was about fourteen years old at that time and a serious student of science. She told me that she wanted to become a medical doctor. I asked her if she wished to go to the city to work as a doctor. But she replied that she wished to come back to her own village because the "outside doctors do not understand us. They believe that all our customs and beliefs are nonsense. That is not true. I want to come back here and treat my people according to their beliefs. What *we believe to be true*."

In contemporary times neuro-sciences are oriented towards

deconstructing the false dichotomy between mind and matter or between the body and its social/cultural environment. The entity that needs to be cured is not simply to be viewed as a bounded physical body, but as a social/biological entity enmeshed in relationships that affect the state of the mind and of the body as well. Recent researches on the plasticity of the brain—neurocognitive and psychological sciences indicate the link between social practices and the mind. The brain and the body are linked and the brain is linked to our sociability, the nature of our relationships, our cultural practices and environment. Thus, what was always understood by the traditional healer, the indigenous *shaman* and practitioners, is now being understood by modern scientists. The human being is not just a body, she or he is a complete entity comprising mind and body in an amalgamation where treatment must always be holistic.

This truth was realized by the indigenous healers, discarded by the positivist Western science and is now making a comeback globally. The indigenous medical systems are still to be given their due and their underlying rationality accepted as logical and efficacious. It should be our endeavour as anthropologists to bring about this awareness and to foreground it to the medical community and others.

REFERENCES

Bodding, P.O. (1986). S*tudies in Santal Medicine and Connected Folklore*, Calcutta: The Asiatic Society.

Bordieu, Pierre. (1980). *The Logic of Practice, T*r. Richard Nice, Stanford: University of Stanford Press.

Channa, Subhadra Mitra. (2004). "The Re-emergence of traditional Medicine and health care in Post-Colonial I*ndia and National Identity." In Paul Sillitoe, Alan Bic*ker and Johan Pottier (Eds.), Investigating Local Knowledge: New Directions, New Approaches, UK: Ashgate: pp. 189-207.

Channa, Subhadra Mitra. (2013). The Inner and the Outer Selves, New Delhi: Oxford University Press.

Chatterjee, Partha. (1993). *The Nation and its Fragments, Princeton: Princeton Uni*versity Press.

Foucault, Michel. (1980). Power/Knowledge: S*elected Interviews and other w*ritings (ed) Colin Gordon, New York: Pantheon Books.

Harding, Sandra G. (1991). Whose Science? Whose Knowledge? Thinking from Women's Lives. Ithaca: Cornell Univ*ersity Press.*

Harraway, Donna. (1988). "Situated Knowledges: *The Science question in Feminism and the Privilege of Parti*al Perspectives", Feminist Studies. *14*(3): 575-99.

Turner, Vict*or* (1969). *The Ritual Proces*s: Structure and Anti-Structure, Aldine.

PART II
MODES OF HEALING

5

Mediums and Deep Healing: Ritual Healing in the Western Himalayas

Asaf Sharabi

Mediumship is one of the most important religious roles in the Western Himalayas, because through mediums it is possible to communicate with the local god (*devtā*). One reason to appeal to the god is to obtain solutions to medical, physical or mental problems. Thus, turning to a medium is one option available to those who seek healing, along with appeals to other specialists such as astrologers, herbalists, and doctors (Joshi, 2000, 2004). In this chapter, I will focus on the mediums of a local god named *Mahāsū*, who has temples dedicated to him in parts of the Shimla district of Himachal Pradesh, and Uttarkashi and Dehradun districts in Uttarakhand (see also: Bhatt, 2010; Sutherland, 2003). First, I will describe the process whereby people become mediums of *Mahāsū* and I will portray the social situation of mediums. I will then describe the encounter of the locals with the *Mahāsū* through mediums, and their inherent skepticism about how the mediums function.

I refer to the ritual healing offered by *Mahāsū*'s mediums as deep healing (Sharabi, 2014; Guzmen-Carmeli and Sharabi, Forthcoming). In deep healing, as opposed to standard therapy, there is individual and non-generic treatment of the patient. In other words, the treatment is not a blessing or a general *puja*, it is tailor-made for the individual supplicant, since deep healing relies on negotiations between the therapist and the patient and/or other social elements.

How to become a *mālī*

The mediums of *Mahāsū* are called *mālīs*. According to Claus Peter Zoller, the word *mālī* (which is a homonym of *mālī*—'gardener') derives from the Sanskrit *mahallaka*—'venerable, old'. Theoretically, anyone from the two high status castes (Brahmins and Rajputs) can be a *mālī*, but in practice most *mālīs* belong to the Rajput caste, which is also the majority group in the region. Most *mālīs* become mediums independently, seeing it as an expression of the will of God. They often say they felt bothered by intense physical sensitivity, a feeling that something was wrong, that they were not functioning properly. This liminal stage, which is related to the psychological and psychiatric aspects of the individual, can last for several years (Joshi, 2010). The *mālīs* say that it was these feelings and medical problems led them to appeal to *Mahāsū* (in other words, they met with a *mālī* in order to communicate through him with the deity), and in this way they could ascertain whether these feelings indicated that they too could be mediums. In the event that *Mahāsū*, by means of the *mālī*, affirms that this is indeed the case, they can function as a *mālī*. To be on the safe side, some will ask for confirmation from a number of *devtās*/*mālīs* until they receive an answer that satisfies them. Some may also ask for permission from the *mālīs* in the central temple of Mahāsū in the village of Hanol.

Another way to become a *mālī* is if residents of a village without a medium want a *mālī* to live in their midst. In this case, several villagers can approach *Mahāsū*, usually at the temple in Hanol, to ask which of them he chooses to be the *mālī*. Either the same day or a few days later one of the villagers will fulfil the role by suddenly becoming possessed. Here too, the institute of the *mālī* is an expression of the god's choice rather than a hereditary position that passes from father to son (Berreman, 1964; Bhatt, 2010).

Either way, recognition of the *mālī* is not based on any formal confirmation other than consultation with the deity. Moreover, no great importance attaches to his good name in adulthood before he discovered that he could function as a *mālī*, for there are cases of young people who began functioning as *mālīs* before the age of 18. The locals' acceptance of the *mālī* depends to a great extent on his performance and his good (or bad) reputation as a *mālī*.

There is at least one *mālī* in most of the villages in Mahāsū's territory. In the event that there are none, the villagers turn to the *mālī* in the temple of a nearby village. In Hanol, where *Mahāsū*'s main temple is located, there are a number of *mālīs*, some permanent, others transient. The locals say that for minor problems they can appeal to the *mālīs* in the villages, but for more weighty matters they turn to the *mālīs* in Hanol (see also: Handa, 2004). This encounter usually takes place in the area of the temple, but if necessary it can be held in the home of the patient or the home of the *mālī*.

The *Mālī* as a Medium

There is a clear disjuncture between the times when the *mālīs* are possessed and other times. This disjuncture is evident at both the operational and the societal level. At the operational level there is a clear distinction between the times when the deity is presumed to speak through them and other times. This phenomenon does not occur everywhere in the Himalayas. Berti (Forthcoming), for example, finds that in the Kullu Valley 'the deity's presence is not marked by continuity but comes and goes' during the medium session. In cases described in other parts of the world, a relationship develops between the medium and the spirits, outside of the possession itself (Boddy, 1988; Lambek, 1981; Masquelier, 2002; Pierini, 2016).

At the societal level, the villagers assume that at moments of possession *mālīs* are the conduit through which the deity communicates with his devotees, nothing more than that. They themselves have no special holiness or social role, neither before nor after possession. As with other instances of mediums (e.g. DeBernard, 2006: 301; Clart, 2003: 155), the status of mediums is only relevant when they are possessed. Furthermore, this phenomenon does not occur everywhere in the Himalayas. Lecomte-Tilouine (2009: 52), for example, notes that in Nepal there are mediums who wear special clothing on a daily basis and "any harm done to them, even when they are not possessed, is seen as an attack on the god they incarnate". Gaborieau (1976: 226), also writes about a medium in Western Nepal who "is authorized to marry but does not work; he is careful about his food and never wears pants; he never leaves the village."

However, in the case of *Mahāsū,* when the *mālīs* are not possessed they function normally and are not revered (unlike *pujārīs*, for example). Although in theory they are supposed to observe certain practices in their daily routine (Joshi, 2010), it seems that at least in recent years many do not strictly adhere to this (Sharabi and Shalev, 2018). The *mālīs* do ordinary work, they do not strictly adhere to a vegetarian diet, nor do they fast extensively. *Mālīs* in *Mahāsū*'s territory have 'normal jobs': a taxi driver, an art student, small photography shop owner, a janitor in a hospital, and so on. Some *mālīs* do not work in the public or the private sector but have their own apple orchards. This occupation is prevalent among the people of the region, and many of those with jobs also own orchards.

The *mālī* must pass tests of charisma and performance as well as reliability and integrity. Unlike *pujārīs,* who operate in an established market where the position is fixed for several days a year (and in some cases, for the whole year), *mālīs* operate in a free market where anyone can become a *mālī*. Therefore, the *mālī* must provide a convincing cultural performance so that the locals will trust him and continue to use his services. In other words, it depends on is his ability to convince those who come to him that the deity is speaking through him. This does not mean that a *mālī* can do whatever he pleases, in fact quite the opposite. If the locals suspect the *mālī* is a fraud, they will no longer trust him and he will be left without clients. The *mālī*, therefore, relies on charismatic authority (Weber, 1948), and is constantly under examination. Like any charismatic authority, his authority is not guaranteed and can disappear at any time. Since *Mahāsū* has many *mālīs* and because there are many mediums of other gods working alongside them, most *mālīs* function as mediums in a part-time capacity, and need to maintain their charisma when possessed in order to retain their popularity as mediums in the local market (Sharabi and Shalev, 2018).

The Encounter between the *Mālī* and the Supplicants

The meeting with the *mālī* is structured as a ritual event. It begins with a brief meditation during which the *mālī* performs some kinds of physical gesture indicating that an alien entity has possessed him. This may take the form of loud breathing, placing one hand over the other, passing both hands behind his ears, loud exhalations, and more. The voice that emerges from the *mālī* is then perceived to be that of *Mahāsū*. The ensuing dialogue is between the supplicants and the deity. Sometimes, the supplicant explains the reason that brought him to *Mahāsū*, but at other times the problem is arrived at through a series of questions posed by the *mālī*.

Once the problem has been clarified, the *mālī* will determine whether it is due to *greh/graha* (fate, influence of the planets), whether it is caused by *doṣ* (curse by gods), *burī nazar* (evil eye cast by people), or *Chhua* (the prohibition on touching the food of some people, as a result of a conflict that occurred in previous generations) (see also Headley, 2007, 44-45). If the *mālī* concludes that the problem is due to the person's *graha*, not much can be done by *Mahāsū*, and the person should embark on bio-medical treatment. If the *mālī* diagnoses the problem as not relating to the person's *graha*, he usually gives the devotee rice to eat or to place on his body. He is instructed to return after a specified time (e.g., a week, a month, or several months) in order to see if he has experienced any relief. Once the person has experienced relief he may want to know the cause of his problem in order to ensure that it will not recur. In that case, he may appeal once again to *Mahāsū*, who will ascertain whether the problem relates to an ancestor, a land dispute, *burī nazar*, the *doṣ* of another *devtā*, and so on. Finally, *Mahāsū* will provide a solution that usually involves the client offering *chapatti*, coconut, or *bali* (animal sacrifice) to *Mahāsū* or another deity. The treatment of *Mahāsū*, then, is ongoing therapy. It usually does not end with one meeting.

Elsewhere, in the context of Judaism in Israel, I made a distinction between regular healing and deep healing (Sharabi, 2014; Guzmen-Carmeli and Sharabi, Forthcoming). Regular healing is generic, applied uniformly to everyone, like a rabbi's blessing in Judaism or *puja* in Hinduism. Deep healing, however, is linked with more complex performances of ceremonial healing, in which the healing relies on negotiations between the healer and the patient and/or additional social elements. So ultimately the healing will be tailored according to the nature of the patient. Treatment by *Mahāsū* through the *mālī* is also related to the interaction between the *mālī* and the patient, and can be described as deep healing. This is due to the fact that this role relies on charismatic authority which depends, to a large extent, on the market (Sharabi and Shalev, 2018). As a result, the *mālī* must know who he is facing, and on this basis he will offer a suitable diagnosis and a solution. For example, he will tell him to bring *puja*, sacrifice a goat (*bali*), carry some rice wherever he goes, go to a doctor, and so on.

Deep healing is most evident when in the interaction between the *mālī* and the patient, the *mālī* is uncomfortable with the solutions he has offered. In this case he may respond in such a way that the patient will be satisfied with the meeting, as can be seen from the following case: Two men, a woman and a girl came to consult with *Mahāsū* in Hanol. One of the problems that troubled them was the girl's mental distress. While the four of them were sitting on the floor in front of the *mālī*, the girl began to breathe heavily, shake her head so her hair became dishevelled, and moved her body repetitively up and down. At one point one of the men said:

> **Man:** She remains sick all the time. We have taken her to many places for curing her, we have taken her to big-big hospitals but we don't know what her disease is and she is not getting well.
>
> **Mālī:** Do one thing! You have problems of your heart-beat and also physical problems. You must be having headache problems also. And you also must be getting bad dreams. Today I'll make you to feel better.
>
> **Girl:** Yes, I want to feel better.
>
> **Mālī:** Yes, I'll make you to feel better. Today you'll feel better. For that you need to trust yourself. (The girl said "ok". The *mālī* turned to the man:) I am saying you that sometimes she is totally fresh.

Man: Yes, that's true.

Mālī: And sometimes she is totally down.

Man: So what's the reason for that? We did treatment for it once. But she was not cured.

Mālī: You'll always have my blessings. But today it's not possible. And you'll definitely get benefit from tomorrow. Okay! You should take an appointment of the doctor, who will cure you.

Girl: You are only our doctor.

Man: Yes, we don't want any doctor.

Mālī: Okay, I'll tell you. Listen! Doctor is also a kind of god. He provides solution for all problems. He'll check all the veins for a disease.

As can be seen, *Mahāsū*'s diagnosis satisfied the group that came to him. But the solution he suggested—going to see a doctor—displeased them. *Mahāsū*, through the *mālī*, tried to persuade them to seek biomedicine ("Doctor is also a kind of god"), but to no avail. Since the three adults and the girl insisted that *Mahāsū* provide some treatment for the girl, he asked the girl to carry a handful of rice with her at all times. Thus negotiations between the four supplicants and *Mahāsū* about the correct treatment for the girl ended to the satisfaction of the whole group. Appealing to a medical doctor through *Mahāsū* is not unheard of. Sometimes, the problem is related to the fate (*grah*) of the person requiring treatment. As elsewhere in India (Ranganathan, 2007), biomedical therapy and temple healing can coexist.

Skepticism regarding the Mālī's Possession

Skepticism regarding the institution of mediumship is inherent in any encounter with the *mālīs*. Skepticism also exists elsewhere in the Western Himalayas (Berti and Tarabout, 2010) and there are practices that seek to reassure the locals that they are indeed speaking with the gods when they do so through the agency of the mediums (Berti, 2016). In the case of *Mahāsū*, the locals have a practice called *goti* which is meant to "confirm" that they are speaking with *Mahāsū* when they interact with the *mālī*. The word *goti* means small pile, and as part of this practice the locals present *Mahāsū* with several options, usually in the form of small piles of rice. Each pile represents a problem: a physical ailment, a land dispute, problems of livelihood, mental problems in the family, and so on. Sometimes, the rice pile does not represent anything, but the supplicants do not reveal to the *mālī* what each pile represents (or doesn't represent). Sometimes, the *goti* is repeated several times. For example, in the first round, the *mālī* may indicate that the problem is medical, and the second round of the *goti* may present him with several possible medical problems. It is then up to him to indicate the specific ailment which is troubling the supplicants. The following example is a good illustration: A father and his two adult sons came to the main temple of *Mahāsū* in Hanol. They approached a *mālī*, seeking to speak to *Mahāsū* through him. They were particularly concerned about financial problems in the extended family. The conversation between the three men and *Mahāsū* went as follows:

> **Father:** Oh Mahāsū devtā! Please keep unity in my family.
>
> **Mālī:** I have kept. I, Mahāsū devtā has not kept deficit for anything.
>
> **Father:** (while putting *goti*) Okay. Take this.
>
> (The *Mālī* is selecting a *goti*)
>
> **Younger Brother:** Botha Mahāsū, this is [the] right [*goti*]. But now you must do something. I want your shelter also.
>
> **Older brother:** To be very honest with you. He (the younger brother) is not having good *kismet*.
>
> **Mālī:** Yes, he has bad luck (*buri kismat*).
>
> **Older brother:** In that case, I'll require your blessings.

As can be seen from this example, the father opened the conversation with the intention of practicing *goṭī*. From the three heaps before him the *mālī* chose the correct one. After his conversation with the *mālī*, the father told me that the correct heap represented problems in the family's destiny. What concerned the three was not whether the *mālī* knew the precise problem for which they had come to speak with *Mahāsū*, but whether he would identify the correct heap. This is indeed what happened, and so the oldest brother could immediately appeal to *Mahāsū* for advice and a blessing regarding the specific problems of the younger brother.

The villagers are not always satisfied when the *mālī* chooses the correct heap. Sometimes, they want to see if he knows the specific problem that the heap of rice represents. In many cases *mālīs* are successful. If the locals appeal to the *mālī* of their village or a neighbouring village, there is a good chance that the *mālī* can identify the problem for which they have come, since he is familiar with the characters involved. In these cases, the harder part is choosing the correct heap. If the locals turn to a *mālī* in a distant village (for example, appealing to the *mālīs* in Hanol), choosing the correct heap may be easier than knowing precisely what it represents. One way or another, the conversation with *Mahāsū* through the *mālī* is a delicate dance of negotiations about the details the *mālī* is required to know with regard to *goti*, as we can see from the next example: a village *pujārī*, his son and another man went to *Mahāsū* in Hanol to inquire whether the *pujārī* had acted correctly by leaving his position. Towards the end of the conversation, after agreeing with *Mahāsū*'s answers regarding his resignation from the post of *pujārī*, he asked to conduct the *goti*. Seeing that the *pujārī*'s son and another villager had accompanied him, the *mālī* turned his back while the three arranged the *goti*, preparing three small heaps of rice and deciding between them which heap was the correct one. After turning around, the *mālī* was asked the following by the *pujārī*:

> **Pujārī:** Oh *devtā*, I have put up *goti*, kindly select only one *goti*.
>
> **Mālī:** (Selecting one *goti*) What do you want?
>
> **Pujārī:** You tell me—You have selected the *goti*. You can say it loudly too. There is nothing difficult for you. I'll worship you next month. Kindly grant me peace.
>
> **Mālī:** I gave you, whatever you asked for I gave you. Now you don't delay in my worship.
>
> **Devotees together:** We will not do.

In this instance, the *mālī* chose the correct heap but did not say what it signified. The *pujārī* tried to press him gently, asking what it meant, but swiftly backed down, asking instead for peace and tranquility in his life. For example, in the following case, where a local named Bittu wanted to know whether the curse *(doṣ)* and the evil eye *(burī nazar)* that had afflicted him and the house that he built had been lifted. He went to see a *mālī* from a nearby village. After *Mahāsū* reassured Bittu that the curse and the evil eye had been lifted from him and his household, Bittu suggested applying the *goṭī*:

> **Bittu:** Oh lord! Now I want to put *goṭī*.
>
> **Mālī:** Yes, yes, why not!
> (Bittu arranges three heaps of rice, representing three different *goṭīs*. The *mālī* chooses one and turns to Bittu).

> **Mālī:** I have selected this *goṭī* in which you have desired to sell this house or property. But it all depends upon your wish.
>
> **Bittu:** But *devtā*, the *goṭī* chosen by you was empty! It means I have not kept any desire in it.
>
> **Mālī:** It means you don't have any kind of *doṣ* (curse). So you should not worry now.

In this case Bittu did not think the *goṭī* chosen by the *mālī* was the correct one—the *goṭī* relating to his home. The *mālī* had actually chosen an empty *goṭī*. When Bittu drew the *mālī*'s attention to this, the *mālī* responded that it was the correct *goṭī*, because the empty *goṭī* signified the fact that there is no curse or evil eye upon him and his household. Bittu accepted this explanation for the failure to choose the correct *goṭī*, but nevertheless he went on to ask whether he and his family should remain living in their house or whether they should leave. *Mahāsū*, through the *mālī*, reassured him again that everything is fine now and he can stay in his house.

The *goṭī*, then, enables the devotee to obtain a response for his epistemological questions—Am I talking to *Mahāsū*?–either through the correct choice of the rice heap, or through a correct determination of the specific request made symbolically through the rice heap. When one or both of the *mālī*'s statements are not realized, the locals have the option of challenging his decision, his diagnosis of their problems, or his method of solving them. "He doesn't speak the truth" is the common statement made by locals who have had an experience with a *mālī* that didn't have a positive outcome in their eyes. Vinod, a young teacher, met three times with a famous *mālī* to consult him about a medical problem. Each time the *mālī* maintained that the problem lay in the fact that Vinod did not have sufficient belief in the *devtās*. Vinod repeatedly rejected this diagnosis until he met another *mālī* who told him something that seemed acceptable to him—he was suffering from a curse. On the other hand, as we saw in the previous instance where the *mālī* did not choose the correct heap of rice, not every failure results in epistemological confusion. Thus, to a great extent, the *goṭī* not only makes it possible to determine whether the deity is present in a state of possession, it also challenges the agency of the deity and enables supplicants to negotiate about his existence and his message.

Conclusion

In recent years, the institution of mediumship is being challenged in parts of the Western Himalayas (Sharabi and Shalev, 2016) and in other parts of India (Mallebrein, 2014). Alongside the inherent skepticism regarding the phenomenon of mediums, more and more people, and especially the younger generation, believe less and less in mediumship, and certainly fewer people are availing themselves of it. This is due in part to the ongoing process of Sanskritization that is taking place in the Western Himalayas (Berreman, 1964, Shalev and Sharabi, 2018). This reality requires the *mālīs* to retain their charisma even in the face of competing knowledge systems, such as Western medicine (See also Bindi, 2012). One way to do this is to deepen cooperation with them. Indeed, in other places in South Asia, psychological, medical, and scientific rational discourse plays a role in traditional healing (Dein, Alexander and Napier, 2008; Ranganathan, 2017). In the case of the *mālīs* of *Mahāsū,* cooperation with Western medicine mainly takes the form of the *mālī* referring the patient for biomedical treatment. It seems that this practice does not weaken the institution of mediumship but on the contrary, it reinforces its diagnostic dimension (see also Joshi, 2010). One way or another, the strength of the *mālīs* therapy is related to the deep healing it offers, healing related to the interaction between the *mālī* and the patient, and the ability of the *mālī* to assess and respond to each specific situation.

REFERENCES

Berreman, Gerald D. (1964). "Brahmins and Shamans in Pahari Religion." *The Journal of Asian Studies*, *23* (S1): 53-69.

Berti, Daniela (2016). "Technicalities of Doubting: Temple Consultations and Criminal Trials in India." In Daniela Berti, Anthony Good and Gilles Tarabout (Eds.), *Of Doubt and Proof: Ritual and Legal Practices of Judgment*, 19-38. London and New York: Routledge.

Berti, Daniela, (Forthcoming). "Possession, Communication and Power in India." In Pocs Eva and Zempleni Andras (Eds.), *Spirit Possession: European Contributions to Comparative Studies*, New York Budapest: Central European University Press.

Berti, Daniela and Gilles Tarabout (2010). "Possession." In *Dictionnaire Des Faits Religieux*, edited by Hervieu-Léger Danièle and Azria Régine, 941-947. Paris: Presses Universitaires de France.

Bindi, Serena (2012). "When there were Only Gods, then there was no Disease, no Need for Doctors: Forsaken Deities and Weakened Bodies in the Indian Himalayas." *Anthropology & Medicine 19* (1): 85-94.

Boddy, Janice (1988). "Spirits and Selves in Northern Sudan: The Cultural Therapeutics of Possession and Trance." *American Ethnologist, 15* (1): 4-27.

Clart, Philip. (2003). "Moral Mediums: Spirit-Writing and the Cultural Construction of Chinese Spirit-Mediumship." *Ethnologies*, *25*(1): 153-189.

DeBernardi, Jean Elizabeth. (2006). *The Way that Lives in the Heart: Chinese Popular Religion and Spirit Mediums in Penang, Malaysia*. Stanford, CA: Stanford University Press.

Dein, Simon, Malcolm Alexander, and A. David Napier. (2008). "Jinn, psychiatry and contested notions of misfortune among east London Bangladeshis." *Transcultural Psychiatry, 45*(1): 31-55.

Gaborieau, Marc. (1976). "Preliminary Note on Masta God." In John T. Hitchock and Rex L. Jones (Eds.), *Spirit Possession in the Nepal Himalayas*, 217-243. Warmintser: Aris and Phillips Ltd.

Guzmen-Carmeli, Shlomo and Asaf Sharabi. (Forthcoming). "Textual Healing: Tailor-Made Kabbalistic Therapeutics in Jerusalem." *Anthropology and Medicine*.

Handa, Omacanda. (2004). *Naga Cults and Traditions in the Western Himalaya*. New Delhi: Indus Publishing.

Headley, Zoé E. (2007). "Genealogies of Affliction: Aetiological Regimes and Causal Thinking Assessment in a South Indian Sub-caste." *Indian Anthropologist, 39*(1): 29-48.

Joshi, P.C. (2000). "Relevance and utility of traditional medical systems (TMS) in the context of a Himalayan tribe." *Psychology and Developing Societies, 12*(1): 5-29.

Joshi, P.C. (2004). "The world of tribal healers." In Aloke Kumar Kalla and P.C. Joshi (Eds.), *Tribal Health and Medicines*, 202-241. Delhi: Concept Publishing Company.

Joshi, P.C. (2010). "Psychotherapeutic Elements in Shamanistic Healing in the Context of Himalayan Traditions." *Delhi Psychiatry Journal, 13*(2): 254-257.

Lambek, Michael. (1981). *Human Spirits: A Cultural Account of Trance in Mayotte*. Cambridge/New York: Cambridge University Press.

Lecomte-Tilouine, Marie. (2009). "The Social Dimension of Himalayan Mediumism." In Marie Lecomte-Tilouine (Ed.) *Bards and Mediums: History, Culture and Politics in the Central Himalayan Kingdoms*, 29-54. Almora: Almora Book Depot.

Mallebrein, Cornelia. (2014). "The Divine Play on Earth: Forms of Possession in Odisha." In Tina Otten and Uwe Skoda (Eds.), *Dialogues with Gods: Possession in Middle Indian Rituals*, 31-76. Berlin: Weissensee Verlag.

Masquelier, Adeline. (2002). "From Hostage to Host: Confessions of a Spirit Medium in Niger." *Ethnos, 30*(1): 49-76.

Pierini, Emily. (2016). "Becoming a Spirit Medium: Initiatory Learning and the Self in the Vale do Amanhecer." *Ethnos, 81* (2): 290-314.

Ranganathan, Shubha. (2017). "'God's hospitals' with 'No Superstition!' On the place of healing shrines in contemporary India." In B.V. Sharma (Ed.). *Medical Anthropology: Tradition and Change*. New Delhi: Concept Publishing Company.

Shalev, Hagar and Asaf Sharabi. (2018). "Sanskritization of the Upper Castes: The Case of Mahāsū Followers". *Anthropos*, *113*(1), 258-267.

Sharabi, Asaf. (2014). "Deep Healing: Ritual Healing in the Teshuvah Movement." *Anthropology and Medicine,* 21 (3): 277-289.

Sharabi, Asaf and Hagar Shalev. (2016). "From Ruler to Healer: Changes in Religious Experience in the Western Himalayas." *Himalaya, 36*(2): 22-35.

Sharabi, Asaf and Hagar Shalev. (2018). "Charismatic Mediumship and Traditional Priesthood: Power Relations in a Religious Field." *Religion, 48*(2): 198-214.

Sutherland, Peter. (2003). "Very Little Kingdoms: The Calendrical Order of West Himalayan Hindu Polity." In Georg Berkemer and Margret Frenz (Eds.), *Sharing Sovereignty: The Little Kingdom in South Asia*, 31-61. Berlin: Klaus Schwartz Verlag.

Weber, Max. (1948). *From Max Weber: Essays in Sociology*. Great Britain: TJI Digital, Padstow, Cornwall.

6
Tibetan Medicine in Kinnaur, Himachal Pradesh

Abhishek Sharma

Introduction

Based on the natural herbal resources, Tibetan medicine or *Sowa Rigpa* (science of healing) is an age-old traditional medicine system which was officially recognized by the Government of India in 2010. In the wake of this recognition, a notification was published by the Himachal Pradesh Government in January 2011 for laying down rules of recruitment and promotions of four *Sowa Rigpa* practitioners to be delegated in District Kinnaur and District Lahaul & Spiti.[1] However, later visits to District Ayurvedic Hospital in Kinnaur, unveiled that *Sowa Rigpa* clinic is still non-functional and no recruitment has been made by the state government. Tibetan medicine system functional in Kinnaur still works in the traditional way without any organizational setup. One cannot deny the fact that prior to infrastructure development of the region traditional medicine was the only accessible health care services for the people for years.

In all rural societies curing measures are taken against ailment by utilizing indigenous therapeutic knowledge practiced for generations. Health problems are fundamental difficulties faced by every society and to cope up, different societies have developed various methods in the form of health care systems.[2] Majority of tribal communities all-over the globe are dependant on traditional medicine for primary health care.[3] The World Health Organization defines traditional medicine as "The health practices, approaches, knowledge, and beliefs incorporating plant, animal and mineral-based medicines, spiritual therapies, manual techniques and exercises, applied singularly or in combination to treat, diagnose and prevent illnesses or maintain well-being".[4] Traditional medicine is the system of knowledge that has developed through generations and much before the advent of modern medicine.[5] Ethno-botanical knowledge, socio-cultural and spiritual beliefs have largely contributed to the formation of traditional systems of medicines.

Some traditional medicine systems are highly developed and well-documented; these are based on systematized knowledge. India is a land where many traditional medicine systems originated and existed for centuries. Ayurveda is one of the oldest documented traditional medical literature (Leslie, 1968) legally sanctioned by the Government. It is an integral part of the public health care sector.[6] In some African and Asian nations, up to 80 per cent of the population relies on traditional medicine for their primary health care needs.[7] In India, a large number of people depend upon the traditional medicine and there are a number of traditional systems in different parts of the country.[8] Himalayan region of India is one of the mega biodiversity regions of the world having more than 2000 medicinal plants. The Western Himalaya consist of unique habitats to sustain several endemic and rare herbs which number more than 800 and is home to many traditional practices.

Sharma *et al.* (2006) observed the traditional medicinal use of herbal plants by the inhabitants of the cold desert of Spiti in Himachal Pradesh.[9] The rich repository of herbal plants is utilized for treating diseases like gastrointestinal, malaria, and cancer. The research concluded that the development of proper plantation and harnessing plan may result in developing a unique biosphere. Namsa *et al.* (2011) conducted research in parts of Arunachal Pradesh and documented medicinal plants used by Monpa ethnic group in the traditional health care. The locals still possess a great knowledge of the medicinal plants and their role in health care.[10]

Tag *et al.* (2012) documented the use of herbal medicine to treat diabetes mellitus by the Khampti tribe residing in remote areas of Lohit District of Arunachal Pradesh.[11] Traditional healers known as *Chau Ya* were interviewed to record treatment methods and production of medicine. The healers reported that by observing the symptoms like excessive urination, swelling of legs and healing of wounds they are able to diagnose diabetes in a patient. Borah *et al.* (2006) interviewed traditional healers to collect information about herbal plants used to treat various gastrointestinal diseases by the population of Dibrugarh District in Assam. It was concluded that there is an urgent need of conserving herbal plants and validating its use by conducting clinical studies.[12]

Kala (2006) studied the health tradition of Trans-Himalayan regions of Tibet, Lahaul & Spiti and Ladakh. Documenting the historical perspectives of the health care system and the role of Traditional healer from Ladakh and Lahaul & Spiti it was concluded that this system is fading away with the time and it is the need of the hour to recognize the importance of this system and also work for its integration with the modern medicine system.[13] Similar study by Ballabh and Chaurasia (2007) on the traditional medicine utilized by the Boto tribe of Ladakh region was conducted which revealed that Tibetan medicine is popular among the inhabitants.[14] Studies by Nautiyal *et al.* (2001), Negi and Subramani (2002), Khan *et al.* (2004), Singh *et al.* (2005), and Natarajan *et al.* (2000) documented the utilization of herbal medicine in the Himalayan region.[15, 16, 17, 18, 19]

The present research gives an insight into the basic principles, treatment process and diagnostic techniques of Tibetan medicine system prevalent in Kinnaur. Although many studies have been conducted in this field, however, there is a persistent gap in the knowledge regarding functioning of Tibetan medicine in Kinnaur.

Area and Methods

The present research was conducted in the District Kinnaur in the state of Himachal Pradesh. The state is also known as 'abode of god' *Devbhoomi*, as it is cuddled in the western Himalayas surrounded by Jammu & Kashmir in the north, Punjab in the west and to the east is India's border with Tibet (China). Kinnaur district is situated in the eastern part of Himachal Pradesh with an area of 6401 square kilometres and population of 84,121 persons. Inhabited by the *Kinnuara* tribe it is one of the remotest areas of the state with the entire rural setup. Administratively, the District is divided into three Development Blocks (Nichar, Kalpa and Pooh), which are further subdivided into five Tehsils. The present research was undertaken in villages (Chango, Nako, Ribba, Lippa, Pooh) located in Pooh Block/ Block 3 (Upper Kinnaur). Pooh block is located near Indo-China border and a major part of the region is cold desert comprising dry temperate and dry alpine scrub forests with altitude varying from 3000 to 5000 metre.[20] Large part of Pooh block falls mainly in the rain-shadow resulting in arid climatic condition, similar to the climate of Tibet. During long winter season district remains cut-off from rest of country due to heavy snow deposits seizing the transportation. Western Tibetan dialect is most popular in the region. Majority of people follow Buddhism although in some villages a beautiful synchronization of Buddhism and Hinduism is observed in religious ceremony and customs.

Anthropological researches are characterized by their holistic nature of study based on data gathered through the first-hand contact. Keeping in mind the desired objectives and resources qualitative research method had been used to collect data. The primary empirical data were collected by employing data collection techniques of in-depth interviews, narratives and quasi-participant observation. A total of six traditional healers were interviewed to collect data. Secondary data was gathered from different books, journals, and government official websites.

Results

Sowa Rigpa based on the Tibetan medicine principles has its origin in the region of Tibet (China). During the reign of King Trisong Deutsen of Tibet, literature pertaining to different medical systems from countries like India, Nepal, and China were translated into the Tibetan language. This led to the writing of Tibetan medicine literature known as '*Rgyudbzhi*' also known as four *tantras* and it was compiled by a most popular physician of the time Yuthog Yongtan Gonpo in the 8th century also regarded as the founder of *Sowa Rigpa*. It follows the basic principle of balance of biological elements of the body. This medicine system is based on the principle of *Nespa Gsum* (three humours; *Vata, Pitta, Kapha* or Air, Bile, Phlegm) and *Jung-wa-ina* (five elements; earth, water, fire, air, and space). A healthy body is described to be in balance of these humours and elements.

Three humours, i.e. *vata* (air), *pitta* (bile) and *kapha* (phlegm) are locally known as *vayu, thema,* and *pakhad,* respectively. Humours are basics for categorizing human physique into three divisions similar to the concept of body composition in anthropometry, i.e. ectomorph, mesomorph, and endomorph. Balance among the three humours helps individual in maintaining good health. Along with these humours, the balance of five body elements, i.e. Earth/*Prithvi* (Bones and Muscles), Water/*Jal* (Blood), Air/*Vayu* (Breath), Fire/*Agni* (Heat), and Space/*Akash* (vacuum) is also paramount for a healthy individual. Traditional healers believe that key to longevity is maintaining balance of elements. Illness is characterized by the imbalance of these humours and elements in the body.

In Kinnaur, traditional healer is known by the term '*Amchi*' (derived from Mongolian language meaning 'Superior to all'). *Amchi* is an individual whose role is to provide therapeutic measures to the members of the community. Common culture and belief system of the patient and healer benefits the curing process as the healer takes into account the physical, mental and social aspects of the individual before starting treatment. Most healers rely on the oral knowledge obtained during the learning process, although some healers have kept few handwritten texts for their own convenience. All healers interviewed practice medicine from their homes, however, visits are made when required.

Transmission of knowledge generally happens through community, family and elderly of the village (healers). The predominant form of transmission of medical knowledge is through family lineage, however, Tibetan medical colleges across India also impart government recognized degrees of Tibetan Medicine. In the present research, two healers have attained bachelor degree from 'Mein Si Khang' in Dharamshala, while the others obtained knowledge from the family. The duration of learning varies from 6-10 years. Apart from medical education, students have to learn the Tibetan language as all the old medical literature followed is written in Tibetan.

Diagnosis

Diagnosis is the process of identification of illness and determining the health condition of a person by observing symptoms. Prior to treatment, it is necessary to accurately diagnose the condition of the ill person and then select the required treatment. Unlike modern medicine (Allopathic), the diagnosis is performed manually without the use of equipment. Diagnostic techniques used by the traditional healer start with questioning and is followed by pulse examination and visual examination. During questioning, the healer inquires about the perception of the patient regarding his/her health condition. It begins as a casual conversation between the two about the symptoms, case history, dietary pattern, and habits of the patient. Along with the personal aspects of the individual seeking treatment, his/her social and cultural environment is also enquired upon.

> *"kya hua, kaise hua, kab hua, kahan hua, ye sabse zaruri hai puchna"*
> (What happened, how, when, where it happened is asked from the patient and it is very important for the diagnoses of the diseases.)
> (*Aged 56, Healer, Block 3*)

This conversation is generally in the local dialect which helps in the appropriate understanding of the health problem. The patient is accompanied by family members or friends who provide useful information about the environment of the locality, patient's behaviour, food intake, habits and the past medical history. Pulse (*nabz*) examination is followed after questioning which is most important diagnostic technique is as it gives an insight into the physiological condition of the patient and an account of the individual's three humours, i.e. *Vata, Pitta,* and *Kapha*. The technique of pulse examination incorporates critical subtle elements, for example, the best time of day to take a pulse, the correct method on how and where to place fingers when pursuing the beat. Pulse examination is carried out with the index, middle, and ring finger. By placing fingers on the radial artery of patient's left hand number of pulse beat per respiratory cycle is counted. The efficacy of treatment depends upon the pulse examination: "a good healer is one who can accurately examine the pulse". At last visual and urine examination is conducted in required cases which include examination of the shape of the body, the colour of the skin, and colour and texture of tongue. Urine analysis is done by examining major aspects of urine like colour, odour, and formation.

After completion of the diagnosis and overall assessment of the body, illness is specified and treatment is started.

Treatment Process: Treatment begins with dietary and behavioural changes administered by the healer, followed by oral medicines, ointments, and other external therapies if required. Dietary changes suggested are in accordance with the patient's social, psychological and physiological condition. Apart from dietary regulations, the timing of meals is also specified as it plays a vital role in maintaining good health.

> "*Timing sahi hona chahiye khane ka, baar baar khanaa or betime khane se bimari hoti hai*"
> (Timing of the meals should be fixed; taking meals at irregular intervals increases the risk of illness) (Aged 50)

Food taken at proper intervals provides good nutrition and boosts immunity of the body. Home grown and locally produced food is strongly recommended for better health. The types of food recommended include *Sattu* (Barley), milk, curd, millet, and local cereals. The treatment prohibits intake of certain kinds of food and beverages such as fried food, high-fat diet, and alcohol. Efficacy of the treatment purely depends on these prohibitions and instructions given by the healer.

The most common modes of treatment involve prescription oral medicine, oil or ointment which is indigenously prepared by the healer. Herbal powder or pills prepared using different combinations of herbs are administered to be taken orally with water, milk or herbal tea. Few healers strongly believe that the efficacy of the medicine depends on the technique used for preparation of medicine. For injuries related to muscles, tendons, ligaments, broken bone, migraine and arthritis, oil massage is prescribed which promotes blood circulation and helps in timely healing. Indigenous techniques such as hydro-distillation, oil mills, and decoction are used to extract oil from herbal plants. Ointment or '*lep*' is prescribed in case of external injuries, bacterial infection, burns, skin infections, and bone or muscle injuries. Two healers of the region procure herbal medicine from Tibetan Medicine College '*Mein TsiKhang*' in Dharamshala, Himachal Pradesh, and the other prepare medicine indigenously.

Cupping and Bloodletting is external surgical method which involves the creation of vacuum around the painful part of the body using metal cups. These cups are heated from inside before placing on the affected part which results in the suction of blood on the spot. The healer then removes the cup and uses a blade to make a cut at the point where stagnant or impure blood has accumulated (bloodletting). This method has its roots in Chinese traditional method which was later incorporated in the Tibetan medicine. Cupping is known as '*Zang Boom*' in local language and bloodletting goes by the name of '*Tar*'.

It is observed that the number of people availing traditional medicine has been decreasing in the region and it has dropped by almost 50 per cent in the last decade. Levels of acculturation are held accountable for this behavioural variation which is alarming for the existence of *Sowa Rigpa*.

Table 6.1: Common herbal plants used by the traditional healers to prepare medicine

Scientific name	*Local name*	*Active Components*	*Used for*
Saussurea lappa	Kuth	Costunolide and Dehydrocostus Lactone	Skin diseases, digestive problems
Bunium persicum	Kala zeera	Limonene, γ-Terpinene, ρ-Cymene, β-Pinene, α-Pinene, Cuminaldehyde, and Myrcene	Blood purification, common cold, and digestive problems
Piccorhizaa kurroa	Karu	Iridoid Glycosides and Cucurbitacins (Triterpenoids).	Pain relief, common cold and cough, fever
Morchella esculenta	Guchi	Tocopherols, Carotenoids, Organic acids and Phenolic Compounds.	Common cold and cough, fever and immunity booster

(*Contd.*)

Scientific name	Local name	Active Components	Used for
Dactylorhiza hatagirea	Shalampanja	Mucilage, Starch, Glucoside, Dactylorhins A-E	Used for energy
Prunus armeniaca	Chulli oil	Benzaldehyde, Mandelonitrile, Benzoic acid	Rheumatic pain and burn marks, toothache, skin infection.
Ephedra gerardiana	Somlata	Calcium oxalate, Tannin	Pain relief, asthma, and fever
Saussurea gossypiphora	Khaspal	3-Stigmastanol, Beta-sitosterol, and Ergostan-3	Stops bleeding from injuries
Cannabis sativus	Bhang	C21 Terpenophenolic Cannabinoids	Headache and insect bites
Achillea millefolium	Saigun	Eucalyptol, Camphor, α-Terpineol, β-Pinene, and Borneol	Digestive and liver diseases

Table 6.1 enumerates different herbal plants along with their active compounds used by the healers of Kinnaur to treat various illnesses.

Discussion

Use of herbal plants for therapeutic purposes dates back to the ancient times as evident from manuscripts such as the *Rigveda* regarded as the oldest written account, and *Charaka Samhita* which documents use of 341 medicinal plants (Pullaiah, 2002)[21], similarly use of plants in their everyday life has been a well established routine with regards to the population of Kinnaur. Traditional healers of Kinnaur acquire vast ethnomedicinal knowledge during training and it forms the basis of medical practice. In India, *Sowa Rigpa* is also practiced in other parts of Himachal Pradesh and in the states of West Bengal, Jammu & Kashmir, and Sikkim (Gurmet, 2004).[22] Kala (2006) documented the history and evolution of *Sowa Rigpa* and its use by the inhabitants of Tibet, Ladakh and Lahual-Spiti. Upper Kinnaur has socio-cultural similarities with Tibet and primarily Buddhist population, which accounts for the belief in *Sowa Rigpa*.

Traditional healers of Kinnaur equate health with the balance of humours and elements, similar concept is also popular among Siddha and Ayurveda system of medicine (Scharfe, 2009) stating that each humour has a different function (Wangchuk, 2007).[23, 24] It is observed that the diagnostic technique applied by the traditional healers of Kinnaur is holistic in approach as it includes all aspects of an individual (physiological, socio-cultural and psychological). It starts with questioning which provides the healer an idea of the lifestyle of the patient, his/her dietary habits and socio-cultural environment. Technical similarities were observed in the diagnosis methods applied by healers of Kinnaur and Ethiopia as the use of questioning is common among the healers of both the regions (Kassaye, 2006).[25] The conversation between the healer and patient regulates the two-way flow of knowledge and the patient never feels isolated from the diagnostic and treatment process. In Kinnaur, this conversation is an integral part of diagnostic and treatment process. The accomplishment of compliance between the two helps in providing appropriate treatment which signifies the role of patient-provider relationship in health care as reported by Gupta and Sinha (2008), Mahmud (2009), Roter (1977), Bartlett *et al.* (1984) and Smith (1983).[26, 27, 28, 29, 30] Pulse examination conducted by the healers in Kinnaur is also prevalent among the Siddha and Unani medicine systems. A similar practice is common among the folk healers of Jaunpur (Uttarakhand) who believe that shape, size, and motion of the pulse helps in diagnosis (Langford, 2003).[31]*Jariyara* (traditional healer) belonging to Jaunsari Tribe of Central Himalayan region also believe that pulse reveals everything about the illness (Joshi, 2000).[32] Traditional healers of Lohit District of Arunachal Pradesh known as *Chau ya* have also been reported to diagnose urine sample for treatment of diabetes mellitus (Tag *et al.*, 2012).[33]

Healers of Kinnaur believe that indigenous preparation methods maintain the efficacy of medicine and any change in these could decrease the effect of medicine. The significance of indigenous methods of medicine making was illustrated by Tu Youyou that led to the extraction of artemisinin (anti-malaria) from Chinese herb Qinghaosu, for which she was conferred Nobel Prize in 2015 in the field of Medicine (Venkateswaran, 2015).[34]

Common modes of transmission of indigenous medical knowledge reported by the healers of Kinnaur (informal) included oral instruction, demonstration, and participation although few healers obtained a formal degree in Tibetan medicine. Learning process incorporates various aspects of medicine such as diagnostic techniques, treatment methods, collection of herbs, and preparation of medicine using indigenous techniques. Lozada (2006) also documented a similar source of transmission of traditional medicine knowledge among the rural community of north-western Patagonia, Argentina.[35] Socio-cultural changes and decreasing number of healers in Kinnaur is prompting a decline in number of people availing traditional medicine.

As described earlier *Sowa Rigpa* was officially recognized in 2010 by the Government of India and a notification regarding the appointment of healers (with a formal degree) was published by Himachal Pradesh Government in 2011, but no appointment in Kinnaur was made. Even after seven years the policy meant for appointing *Amchis* is still on chapter rather than in practice. This clearly depicts the negligent approach towards traditional medicine and gap in the implementation of health policy.

Conclusion

Partnership and active role of traditional medicine practitioners and authority can ensure that modalities of these indigenous systems can be saved. This chapter generates comprehensive data on traditional health care system of Kinnaur and elucidates the basic gap in the health policy of the State. Anthropological research has to play a key role in health-related policy and planning but yet the majority of published data is ignored and is not included in these policies. Participatory research by the anthropologists will help in understanding traditional medicine within the cultural context of a group and aid in designing health policies.

REFERENCES

1. Notification regarding appointment of Tibetan medicine practitioners. Available at: http://hpayurveda.nic.in/. Accessed on 21 January, 2016.
2. Oyeneye, O.Y. (1985). "Mobilizing indigenous resource for primary health care in Nigeria: a note on the place of traditional medicine." *Social Science & Medicine*, *20*(1), 67-69.
3. Singh, K.N. (2012). "Traditional knowledge on ethnobotanical uses of plant biodiversity: a detailed study from the Indian western Himalaya." *Biodiversity: Research and Conservation*, *28*, 63-77.
4. World Health Organization (2002). *WHO traditional medicine strategy 2002-2005*.
5. Bannerman, R.H. (1983). *The role of traditional medicine in primary health care*, 318-27.
6. Leslie, C. (1968). "Division of Anthropology: The Professionalization of Ayurvedic and Unani Medicine." *Transactions of the New York Academy of Sciences*, *30*(2), 559-572.
7. WHO, *Traditional Medicine*. 2008 World Health Organization. Accessed

on 11 September, 2015. Available online: http://www.who.int/mediacentre/factsheets/2003/fs134/en/.

8. Mukherjee, P.K. (2001). "Evaluation of Indian traditional medicine." *Drug Information Journal*, 35(2), 623-632.
9. Sharma, P.K., Sethi, G.S., Sharma, S.K., and Sharma, T.K. (2006). "Ethnomedicinal observations among the inhabitants of cold desert area of Himachal Pradesh." *Indian Journal of Traditional Knowledge*, 5(3), 358-361.
10. Namsa, N.D., Mandal, M., Tangjang, S., and Mandal, S.C. (2011). "Ethnobotany of the Monpa ethnic group at Arunachal Pradesh, India." *Journal of Ethnobiology and Ethnomedicine*, *7*(1), 31-45.
11. Tag, H., Kalita, P., Dwivedi, P., Das, A.K., and Namsa, N.D. (2012). "Herbal medicines used in the treatment of diabetes mellitus in Arunachal Himalaya, North-east, India." *Journal of Ethnopharmacology*, *141*(3), 786-795.
12. Borah, P.K., Gogoi, P., Phukan, A.C., and Mahanta, J. (2006). "Traditional medicine in the treatment of gastrointestinal diseases in upper Assam." *Indian Journal of Traditional Knowledge, 5*(4), 510–512.
13. Kala, C.P. (2006). "Indigenous uses, population density, and conservation of threatened medicinal plants in protected areas of the Indian Himalayas." *Conservation Biology*, *19*(2), 368-378.
14. Ballabh, B., and Chaurasia, O.P. (2007). "Traditional medicinal plants of cold desert Ladakh—used in treatment of cold, cough and fever." *Journal of Ethnopharmacology*, *112*(2), 341-349.
15. Nautiyal, S., Rao, K.S., Maikhuri, R.K., Semwal, R.L. and Saxena, K.G. (2001). "Traditional knowledge relative to medicinal and aromatic plants in tribal societies in part of Himalaya." *Journal of Medicinal and Aromatic Plant Science, 22-23*(4A-1A), 528-541.
16. Negi, P.S. and Subramani, S.P. (2002). "An ethnobotanical study in the village Chitkul of Sangla Valley, District Kinnaur, Himachal Pradesh." *Journal of Non-Timber Forest Products, 9*(3-4), 113-120.
17. Khan, Z.S., Khuroo, A.A., and Dar, G.H. (2004). "Ethno-botanical survey of Uri, Kashmir Himalaya." *Indian Journal of Traditional Knowledge, 3*(4), 351-357.
18. Singh, V. and Chauhan, N.S. (2005). "Traditional practices of herbal medicines in the Lahaul Valley, Himachal Himalayas." *Indian Journal of Traditional Knowledge, 4*(2), 208-220.
19. Natarajan, B., Paulsen, B.S., and Korneliussen, V. (2000). "An ethnopharmacological study from Kullu District, Himachal Pradesh, India: Traditional knowledge compared with modern biological science." *Pharmaceutical biology*, *38*(2), 129-138.
20. Geographical features of Himachal Pradesh. Available at: http://hpplanning.nic.in/GEOGRAPHICAL%20FEATURES%20OF%20HIMACHAL%20PRADESH. Accessed on 10th September, 2016.
21. Pullaiah, T. (2002). *Indian Medicinal Plants.* Regency Publications, New Delhi, 1-4.

22. Gurmet, P. (2004). "Sowa-Rigpa: Himalayan art of healing." *Indian Journal of Traditional Medicine, 3*(2), 212-218.
23. Scharfe, H. (1999). "The doctrine of the three humors in traditional Indian medicine and the alleged antiquity of Tamil Siddha medicine." *Journal of the American Oriental Society*, 609-629.
24. Wangchuk, P., Wangchuk, D., & Aagaard-Hansen, J. (2007). "Traditional Bhutanese medicine (gSo-BA Rig-PA): An integrated part of the formal health care services." *South East Asian Journal of Tropical Medicine and Public Health*. *38*(1), 161-167.
25. Kassaye, K.D., Amberbir, A., Getachew, B., & Mussema, Y. (2006). "A historical overview of traditional medicine practices and policy in Ethiopia." *Ethiopian Journal of Health Development*, *20*(2), 127-134.
26. Gupta, A. & Sinha, A.K. (2008). "Doctor-Patient Relationship: Aspects of Social Structure of a Rural Referral Hospital in Himachal Pradesh." *Bio-social Issues in Health*, 56.
27. Mahmud, A. (2009). "Doctor-patient relationship." *Pulse*, *3*(1), 12-14.
28. Roter, D.L. (1977). "Patient participation in the patient-provider interaction: The effects of patient question asking on the quality of interaction, satisfaction and compliance." *Health education monographs*, *5*(4), 281-315.
29. Bartlett, E.E., Grayson, M., Barker, R., Levine, D.M., Golden, A., & Libber, S. (1984). "The effects of physician communications skills on patient satisfaction; recall, and adherence." *Journal of chronic diseases*, *37*(9-10), 755-764.
30. Smith, C.K. (1983). "Achieving patient compliance: The psychology of the medical practitioner's role." *JAMA*, *250*(17), 2376-2376.
31. Langford, J.M. (2003). "Traces of folk medicine in Jaunpur." *Cultural Anthropology*, *18*(3), 271-303.
32. Joshi, P.C. (2000). "Relevance and utility of traditional medical systems (TMS) in the context of a Himalayan tribe." *Psychology and Developing Societies*, *12*(1), 5-29.
33. Tag, H., Kalita, P., Dwivedi, P., Das, A.K., and Namsa, N.D. (2012). "Herbal medicines used in the treatment of diabetes mellitus in Arunachal Himalaya, North-east, India." *Journal of Ethnopharmacology*, *141*(3), 786-795.
34. Venkateswaran, T.V. (2015). "Nobel Prizes 2015: Physiology or Medicine—Mao, Malaria and the Discovery of Artemisinin." *Science Reporter*. NISCAIR-CSIR. *52*(12) 43-47.
35. Lozada, M., Ladio, A., & Weigandt, M. (2006). "Cultural transmission of ethnobotanical knowledge in a rural community of North-western Patagonia, Argentina." *Economic Botany*, *60*(4), 374-385.

7

Unavoidable Ethnomedicine: Indigenous Healers and Healing Practices among the Tharus

Bamdev Subedi

Introduction

Ethnomedicine refers to the medicinal knowledge, skills, perceptions and practices of ethnic communities. Ethnomedicine occupies an important place among the indigenous ethnic communities[1] across the developing world (Joseph & Phillips, 1984; Kleinman & Sung, 1979; Leslie, 1976; Nichter, 1980). It is well-known that the indigenous ethnic communities continue to rely on indigenous healers for health care services (Joshi, 2004; Lambert, 1996). The indigenous ethnic communities are more close to the nature and possess knowledge and skills about the medicinal plants available around their ecological habitation. The use of locally available medicinal plants (including vegetables, spices and animal products) constitutes an important source for treating various ailments. The knowledge and skills of using these medicinal plants vary among the indigenous healers. By and large, the aged and experienced ones know more than the younger and educated ones. The indigenous healing practices are deeply rooted in the culture and religious tradition of indigenous populations and hold a long history of development.

Tharus are one of the indigenous ethnic communities of southern Nepal and are also found in adjoining areas across the Indo-Nepal border. There are various types of healers with different capacities and specialities among the Tharus. These healers recite healing mantras, conduct healing rituals, use various plants, animals and mineral resources to treat wide range of illnesses (Acharya & Acharya, 2009; Ghimire & Bastakoti, 2009; Paudyal & Ghimire, 2006). These practices correspond to the community perceptions and are culturally important. A common perception is that for some of the culturally understood illnesses such as evil spirit, soul loss, nightmare can only be treated by the indigenous healers. These practices also serve as complementary and alternative medicine to the expensive official medicines. However, the indigenous healing practices are not codified and lack textual tradition, even though some traditional healers possess hand written material and manuscripts about medicinal plants and healing mantras. The healing knowledge is passed informally from aged and experienced healers to the younger ones through an oral tradition. The interaction between indigenous healers and patients takes place in an informal setting, unlike the official medicine, in which interaction takes place in an institutional setting. The indigenous healers are the important health care resource for the majority of the rural and indigenous population in Nepal.

The indigenous healing practices continue to exist even after the total neglect, attack and threat of extinction. The wide existence and use of indigenous healers *per se* shows its importance. Even today, in most rural areas, people depend on the indigenous healers for their primary health care needs. However, there is concern over the withered state of indigenous healing practices. With the rise of official medicine, the concerns of declining state of ethnomedicine were expressed with an assumption that 'when modern development appears, folk system disappears', 'biomedicine would replace indigenous medicine', 'traditional medical practices would soon die out', 'folk medicine will wither away as biomedicine advances' (Attewell, Hardiman, Lambert, & Mukharji, 2012: 2; Lock & Nguyen, 2010: 61; Najunda, Annapurna, Midatala, & Laxmi, 2009: 706). Though even after the introduction and expansion of official medicines (including scholarly traditional medicines such as Ayurveda), people have not stopped to resort to the indigenous healing practices. They remained pluralistic, in that they always sought to use multiple systems of medicine according to situation and need (Sujatha, 2014: 237). They continued to resort to the local healers at times of illness. Noticeably, not only the rural, illiterate, poor ethnic communities but also urban, educated and well-off sections from non-ethnic communities have been making use of the services of these healers. A study conducted in India also shows that people have recourse to the folk healers not only because of official medicine is unavailable, inaccessible and unaffordable but because of the 'felt need' for services other than that of the modern system (Priya & Shweta, 2010: xxiii). They turn to the indigenous healers when they are not cured by official medicine (Regmi, 2003; Singh & Agrawal, 2009).

There can be difference among the various sections of people in the level and extent of reliance on indigenous healing practices. But there is no denying that people take recourse to both academically qualified practitioners and academically not qualified but experienced healers such as herbalists, midwives, and spiritual and shamanic healers (Brodwin, 1996). The services of these healers are accessible, affordable and acceptable and the healers and patients enjoy a better relationship. The treatment procedures are non-invasive, safe, efficacious and free from iatrogenic effect. The continued recourse to such healers also points to the fact that the indigenous healing practices have something creditable to offer in many aspects of health and healing. Even so, the decline of indigenous healing practices and erosion of indigenous knowledge system has placed ethnomedicine in question. In this context, this chapter looks into the indigenous practices among the Tharus and their importance to the community. The chapter seeks to understand the changes as well as continued use of indigenous healing practices.

Methods

The Tharus

The ethnic communities constitute more than one-third of the total population of Nepal. Tharus are one of the ethnic communities of Nepal which constitute 6.6 per cent of the total population of Nepal (i.e. 2,64,94,504, according to 2011 Census) (CBS, 2012). They live in southern region of Nepal Tarai. They are also found in some of the districts of Uttarakhand, Uttar Pradesh, and Bihar in India and are also recognized as scheduled tribe in those states (Guneratne, 2010; Krauskopff, 1995; Maiti, 2004). The original place of the Tharu is believed to be 'Thar' of Rajasthan (in India) from where they had fled to the Tarai region of Nepal in the ancient times. They were called Tharu because of their migration from "Thar" (Bista, 1969; Gurung, 1992; Rajaure, 1981a). They speak Tharu language and follow animistic tradition and Hindu religion with some modification. The main occupation is agriculture supplemented by animal husbandry and seasonal labour. They grow rice, wheat, maize, potato, pulses and vegetables in their lands. They also collect wild vegetables, fruits and medicinal plants from the forest. Though the collection of forest products including medicinal herbs, according to the community people, is declining over the last few years. With an intervention in agriculture, education, transport, communication and expansion of markets and interaction with broader communities, they have experienced a change in their lives and livelihoods. Now, a number of youth are working in Malaysia and Gulf countries as unskilled or semi-skilled labourers.

The study was conducted in Dang district of mid-western Nepal. The qualitative field data were collected from Saudiyar village development committee (VDC), where a dozen of caste and ethnic groups live together but the Tharus constitute 53.24 per cent of the total population (i.e. 12101) of the VDC (CBS, 2014). According to 2011 Census, the literacy rate of the VDC was 73.8 per cent (of the population aged five years and above), which was higher than the national average (i.e. 65.9 %) (CBS, 2012). The Saudiyar VDC is located about eight kilometres south from the district headquarters (Ghorahi) and is well connected by road transport. In the recent restructure of local government, Saudiyar VDC comes under the Ghorahi sub-metropolitan area.

Study Participants

The study participants were healers, patients and key members of the community. A total of 65 healers identified from Tharu community and of them 18 were selected purposively for interview. They were approached by making home visits. They were explained about the study objectives and requested for participation. All of them agreed to participate in the study. Among the patients, who had consulted these healers, 27 were also approached and interviewed. Some of the healing episodes were observed seeking permissions with both the healers and the patients. They were assured of anonymity and later interviewed at their preferred time and venue. Besides, nine key community members such as local leaders, social workers, school teachers, health post staffs were also interviewed. The fieldwork was conducted from October 2012 to February 2013.

Results

Tharu Healers and Healing Practices

There were various types of indigenous healers among the Tharus known mainly as *guruwa*, *baidawa* and *surenya* (Adhikari, 2006; Dahit, 2008; Rajaure, 1981a, 1981b; Shafey, 1997), whose healing practices differ considerably. There are various types of *guruwas* who mainly follow shamanic or faith healing practices and use *mantras* and ritualistic healing to treat illnesses of social, psychological, supernatural or spiritual nature.

The *mantras* are considered powerful to appease angry deities and to drive out the evil spirits. The *mantras* are recited to perform various healing rituals such as swinging the saucer with burning cotton wick, sweeping down and blowing out the evil spirits with hand broom, reading rice grain to diagnose the illness, offering blood of rooster to appease ancestral deities, making an amulet to wear to protect from evil spirits. They also involve in cultural, religious and ritualistic activities to prevent illness and misfortunes and worship deities as village priests. Some of the *guruwas* also know and use various types of medicinal herbs.

The healers who use medicinal herbs, animal and mineral substances, fix sprains or set broken bones, treat snake or dog bites, toothache and stomach problem are known as *baidawas*. The *baidawas* largely follow herbal practices, bone setting or body manipulation massage practices. Some of them are consulted for tooth extraction, thorn extraction, snakebite healing, navel dislocation, nasal problems and problems of the women and children. They read pulse rates and do physical examination of the patients. They collect crude herbs from the village or nearby forests and use animal products and mineral substances as medicines. In most cases they suggest patients about the medicinal herbs of common knowledge and give instruction on how to use. They also deal with the veterinary problems. Some of them reported the unavailability of certain herbs (such as asparagus) in the jungle because of overcollection of these herbs for commercial purpose. Some of them had started to buy certain herbs from vendors and local manufacturers to sell to the patients who need them.

A *baidawa* can never become a *guruwa* unless he fulfils the ritualistic procedures called *baan-chirna*. Every year, in Dashain festival, the *guruwas* have to make small cuts on their body parts (forehead, shoulder, chest, knee and feet) and offer blood which is known as *baan-chirna* to be and to continue as *guruwa*. The distinction between *guruwa* and *baidawa* is that the inclination of *guruwa* is more on the use of *mantras* and ritualistic healing, whereas the inclination of *baidawa* is more on herbal healing. The position of *guruwa* (particularly of *ghar-guruwas* or *desh-bandhya guruwas*) is hereditary whereas *baidawa* is not hereditary. Some *guruwas* also possess the knowledge of treating the kind of illnesses which a *biadawa* can treat and they are also called *baidawa*. Because of this, the distinction between *guruwa* and *baidawa* becomes blurred and tentative. All the *guruwas* and *baidawas* were male whereas all the *surenya* were female. No women *guruwas* and *baidawas* were found in the area, though they might be found among other groups of the Tharus.

The *surenyas* are traditional midwives and follow massage and midwifery practices. They assist in childbirth and provide midwifery and massage services to the mother and newborn baby and also to other people, particularly women and children, who need such services. Some of them are also familiar with medicinal properties of some of the plants, vegetables and spices, and know how to prepare and apply as medicines in conditions of reproductive problems, abdominal pain, minor injuries, wounds and sprain. They also provide post-partum care and massage, and massage for sore back, stomach pain, joints pain, and fatigue. They use mustard oil, cow ghee, homemade alcohol, turmeric and herbal preparation to massage. Some of them have also started to use manufactured balm, Vicks and ointments bought from the local pharmacies. There are no other healers or medical practitioners who provide the kind of services which the *surenyas* provide. The midwifery services are highly demanded from both Tharu and non-Tharu communities.

These healers are compensated by providing them with tea and snacks and/or petty cash as *bheti* (offering) and kind (as gift items, which includes fruits, green vegetables and foodstuff). Some of the *guruwas* (*ghar guruwas* and *deshbandhya guruwas*) are compensated by providing one or two day's free labour at the time of plantation or harvesting of crops). It is said that some of them used to have *Laal mohar* (*Royal edicts*), an authority to perform preventive rituals to protect the village from evil-spirits, disease and epidemics, wild animals, and to collect local revenues and to trap wild elephants for royal need (Rajaure, 1982: 74). The *baidawas* are paid with an amount which is considered reasonable for their services and products (for example, the cost of medicine needed to prepare medicine by themselves or the price of the drugs supplied by the local manufacturers). *Surenyas* are also provided with food items, petty cash or kind for their episodic services. For birthing and post-delivery services, which may continue for a couple of weeks, they are provided with footwear and cloths and an amount that covers their daily wages.

Most of the healers are aged and experienced members of the community and provide services to wide range of illnesses. The patients who had come to visit *guruwas* had problems of nightmare, evil spirit, headache, heart palpitation, sudden vomiting, dizziness (nausea), and soul lose and those who have visited *baidawas* had problems of swelled leg, thorn prick, stomach ache, wasting and physical weakness, nasal problem, stomach problem, joints pain, snake bite and sleeplessness. Mostly it is the patients who go to visit the healers but sometimes when there is a call from the patient's family, the healers also go to the patients' home to provide services. The *surenyas* generally provide their services in the patients' home. In some of the illnesses, the patients prefer these healers over the medical practitioners. The reason which they gave were that the healers deal with different kind of illnesses which a medical practitioner cannot deal with. The healers' services costs very less in comparison to medical practitioners and it does not take a long time to visit a village healer. Some of them have strong faith in the indigenous healing practices. The socio-economic and cultural factors also contribute to the use of indigenous healers.

They make a choice among the healers based on the kind and condition of their illness. They feel that only indigenous healers can provide better care (than the medical practitioners) for some of the illnesses. For instance, the illness caused by supernatural forces are considered untreatable by medical practitioners. The *guruwas* or shamanic/faith healing is the best option for *lagu-bhagu,* evil spirits, soul loss (supernatural illnesses) while *baidawas* or herbal healing is the best option for the naturalistic illnesses and for physical injuries. *Surenyas'* services are considered to be the best for midwifery, post-delivery care and massage. The services of these healers are sought by both Tharus and non-Tharus, villagers and people from outside the village, rich and poor, educated and uneducated.

In the village, similar types of healers are also found among non-Tharu communities. There are other vendor herbalists who come from mountain region to sell various medicinal herbs such as *padamchal* (Himalayan rhubarb), *chiplekira* (dried limax), *dalchini* (cinnamomum leaves and bark), *bhakimlo* (*Rhus javanica*), *timur* (*Zanthoxulum armatum*), *yarsagumba* (*Cordyceps sinensis*), and *silajit* (black bitumen). These herbs are most commonly used for various ailments. Some of the healers also come from UP and Bihar of India to sell various herbs and provide treatment services for chronic problems such as body pain, arthritis, rheumatism etc. Thus, a wide variety of healers and informal practitioners have been serving many of the health care needs of the villagers.

Most of the family members know some plants which are of medicinal values. They are familiar with the local plants such as *tulsi* (*Ocimum sanctum*), *bojho* (*acorus calamus*), *ghodtaapre* (*Centella asiatic*), *kurilo* (*Asparagus filicinus*), *pudina* (*Menthe piperita*), *titepati* (*Artemisia dubia wall*), *neem* (*Azadirachta indica*), *bel* (*Aegle marmelos*), *harro* (*Chebulic myrobalan* or *Terminalia chebula*), *barro* (*Terminalia bellirica*), *amala* (*Emblica officinalis*), *bar* (banyan tree or *ficus benghalensis*) and *pipal* (*Ficus religiosa*) etc. and their medicinal values. The healers specially the *baidawas* or traditional herbal healers know wide range of plants which are available in the local forests (Manandhar, 1985; Paudyal & Ghimire, 2006).

Continuity of Indigenous Healing Practices

The volume of official medicine, especially of biomedicine, has increased significantly in the recent years as biomedicine has been expanded remarkably, provided by both public and private sectors. Biomedicine dominates in terms of official provision, markets and medical education. Ayurveda has greater presence among the scholarly traditional medicines. The Tharus also take recourse to the co-existing systems which include biomedicine, Ayurveda, homeopathy, acupuncture etc. General tendency is that one should not solely rely on indigenous healers but also seek treatment from the practitioners of official medicine. This types of perceptions are widely held and simultaneous use of both indigenous healers and medical practitioners were also reported. According to them, both indigenous healers and medical practitioners are complementing each other. The *guruwas* also hold similar perceptions, as (Guneratne, 2001: 14) quotes, "The *gurau* (*guruwa*) by himself is useless, the doctor by himself is useless."

The participants responded differently when they were asked whether the indigenous practices are declining. However, more than half were of the view that the indigenous healing practices are in a declining trend. They gave various reasons for the low use of the indigenous healing practices. The main reasons, according to them, were the lack of highly experienced healers, lack of teaching-learning activities among the healers, non-availability of medicinal herbs, adulteration in the herbal preparation, irrational and unscientific practices (undefined drug dose), and the availability of modern medicines in their localities. They pointed to the establishment of hospitals, health posts, training schools and medical colleges, private pharmacies and medical clinics and increasing use of modern medicine.

However, some of them were of the view that the indigenous healing practices are not vanishing because people have not stopped using them. These practices are, according to a participant "are not avoidable". He continued, "When an illness befalls you, such practices automatically come into your imagination. At times of illness, you cannot keep local healers out of your mind." Most of them viewed that the illnesses caused by supernatural forces needs to be dealt by indigenous way and all of them had strong faith in *jadi-buti* (literally barks and roots of herbs). Showing the importance of *jadi-buti* one of the participants compared herbal medicine with compost manure and biomedicine with chemical fertilizers. According to them, the compost manure keeps the quality of soil intact whereas chemical fertilizer gives quick result but damages the soil quality. By saying this, the participants meant that the biomedical injection and drugs work as chemical fertilizer in a human body, shows quick results but can damage with side-effects.

The indigenous healing practices are of great importance for both ethnic and non-ethnic communities. The indigenous healing practices comprise vast knowledge of healing *mantras*, knowledge of medicinal herbs, specialist techniques such as bone setting, and the knowledge of traditional massage and midwifery. There has been a change in the healing practices with the current change and development. There is no encouragement and incentives to the indigenous healers to continue such practices. The healers are facing economic pressure, getting low compensation for their services, facing difficulty in accessing medicinal plants from the jungle and in many instances, accused of superstitious, unscientific and harmful cultural practices. The younger generation has been demotivated to practice the traditional practices because of disincentives.

Even so, the indigenous healers have an obligation to play an institutional role. The community expects a customary role from them. For example, a *guruwa,* after his father's death had to take the responsibility to serve his clienteles, even though he was aspiring for a foreign job. There are some rituals which can only be performed with the help of one's *guruwas*. So, even if someone in the family does not believe in faith healing, he or she cannot make an overt objection. Some of the practices such as *lausari* (a ritual performed twice a year for the children's health at the family level), *gurrai* (a ritual performed for community health at the village level) are associated with the cultural tradition and disrespect to these traditions is not acceptable. Moreover, the *guruwas* are the respected elder members of the community with rich knowledge of healing and skill of dealing with the many family and community problems. They help in performing rites and rituals which are inseparable part of Tharu life. Hence, the *guruwas* and their healing roles may change but some of their healing practices may continue. The popularity of the herbal medicines for its safer and efficacious quality (free from iatrogenic effect) has not declined and hence, the role of *baidawa* may continue. As Kunwar *et al.* (2006: 1) state, "the importance of plants as medicine has not diminished in anyway in recent times" and popularity of some of the herbal healers who are reputed for specific illnesses such as jaundice, gastritis, joints pain and the like will help continue such practices. But as has been seen, with the market influence, the *baidawa* may also change in their use of herbal preparations. The importance of assisting in birth and post-delivery care and massage cannot be undermined. The role of the *surenyas* may change as the government is encouraging institutional deliveries but there is no substitute for their role to provide post-delivery care and massage services. Besides, still a large majority of the poor families depend on the traditional birth attendant for the delivery.

Many of the studies associate ethnomedicine with supernatural causation and professional traditional medicine and biomedicine with natural causation. However, as has been seen, ethnomedicine also deals with natural causation. Because of the association of faith healing, some of the indigenous healing practices are often tagged unscientific and irrational, and even harmful. The faith healing is a part but not the whole of indigenous healing practices. Besides, from the villagers' eyes faith healing can be equally scientific. Many studies have shown the importance of shamanic/faith healing in emotional, spiritual and social health and the important role in psycho-social counselling.

The role of local healers, however, has not been the same. The increased use of over the counter drugs than a homemade herbal preparation also signals to the minimized (or changed) practices. The practices of self-medication has been increased with the mushrooming of privately run pharmacies/clinics in the small towns and villages. These pharmacies, which are known as "medical hall" supply biomedical drugs (and some popular ayurvedic drugs and products) on demand, without the prescription of medical doctors. Even the indigenous practices are not free from the influence of commercialization of medicine. Some of the participants are of the view that there has been changes in the indigenous healing practices over the years. They said that the indigenous healers are less consulted than the previous times, and those who are consulted have started to charge for their services and products, and a visible trend is that people have started visiting urban hospitals and "medical hall" more than ever before. The healers also have started to buy and sell manufactured herbal medicines instead of collecting and preparing themselves. The specialist healers such as bone setters, snake-bite healers, herbal specialists and even the traditional midwife (*surenya*) and massagers have started to see their services in terms of market value. This indicates to an influence of market and consumerism.

Discussion

Viewing the declined enthusiasm among the younger generation and disappearance of some of the practices, studies have drawn attention to safeguard indigenous healing practices. Indeed, there is variations in the extent of utilization of indigenous healing practices among the different sections of the people. However, people have not stopped utilizing the services of indigenous healers even after the development of official health care services. Rather, there is a renewed interest in natural medicines and herbal practices. The recent resurgence of ethnobotanical and ethno-pharmaceutical studies are contributing to bioprospecting and drug discoveries. The importance of indigenous herbal practices and the need of revitalization of local health tradition in India also shows the importance of local herbal medicines. Though there is a commercial interest in herbal practices and research studies have contributed exploitation of, rather than the advancement of, indigenous knowledge and empowerment of indigenous people.

The protection of locally available medicinal herbs and promotion of the indigenous healing practices and indigenous healers is crucial for strengthening of the indigenous knowledge systems. The indigenous healing practices will worsen further if these were not given importance and incentives. The state indifference and inaction would further the erosion of the indigenous knowledge. The modern dominant perception is that anything traditional is superstitious, irrational and unscientific. The challenge is to seek science and rationality in the indigenous healing practices. Some studies have pointed to the declining state of indigenous healing practices and have shown an urgent need to document before they vanish. Mere documentation cannot prevent the indigenous knowledge from further erosion. Moreover, the indigenous communities have not been benefited from the current documentation project because documented knowledge is not accessible to them. One of the issues is that on the one hand, a large majority of the rural population relies on indigenous healers for various health problems and these healers have been making a great contribution in providing primary health care services to the rural masses. On the other hand, they do not have an official support, because they lack official legitimacy and are often ignored, neglected, stigmatized and discriminated.

With the growing illness and chronic disease conditions, the world is recognizing the importance of herbal medicine. In this context, the indigenous healers, with the indigenous knowledge base, can play an important role. The promotion of indigenous health practices contributes in providing affordable and sustainable primary health care to the indigenous populations. The irony is that the importance of indigenous herbal knowledge has been recognized but there has been a hesitation to recognize the knowledge holders, the healers. The national health policies and programmes emphasize on the production, utilization and management of medicinal plant resources and herbal products as an opportunity of trade and commerce (MoHP, 2014; MoHP, GoN, 2015). However, the indigenous healers and healing practices often get no mention in the recent policy documents. The indigenous healers are appreciated and acknowledged for their *significant* role in the past when people were without options and had to rely on them but they get *insignificant* support, except involving some healers in occasional training and interaction programmes, and "peripheral and lukewarm" efforts to link them with the public health systems (NESAC, 1998: 60). Policy and programmatic intervention is needed for the recognition, legitimacy and revitalization of the indigenous healing practices. The accreditation of the indigenous healers is necessary if state wants to link them with the public systems and facilitate them to play a meaningful role in the national health care system.

The indigenous healers have been contributing to help meet some of the primary health care needs and more importantly provide diagnostic, treatment and referral services, saving time and resources of the people. The state is trying to increase accessibility of official health care services as well as provide quality (safe and effective) services. A system of ensuring quality health care services including from indigenous healers is necessary for the common benefit of the people. The herbal medicines are considered safe and efficacious as they are non-toxic and have no or fewer side effects. Enhanced knowledge and capacity of indigenous healers is what is needed to ensure quality services from them and to contribute to the revitalization of indigenous healing practices.

Everyone has some knowledge of medicinal plants and can handle many of the illnesses with the domestic knowledge base and expertise. However, the use of over the counter drug (manufactured pills, tablets, syrups etc.) is preferred over the home-made herbal remedies. Thus, the domestic front has also been affected by the recent development intervention which welcomes something packaged in 'science' and discourages indigenous and traditional practices as 'irrational and unscientific'. With this change and development, on the one hand people are losing their indigenous healers and their knowledge base and expertise of health care, and on the other hand, with the maximized role of private sectors, markets and mounting out-of-pocket spending they have found official medical service unaffordable (Subedi & Joshi, 2018). They have got themselves in a situation what a key informant describes, "*Na ubhine hango chha, Na samatne hango chha* (neither they have base to stand on nor something to catch)". The imposition of Western ideas and technologies in the name of science and rationality, development and modernity can be counter-productive and likely to increase dependency and health care cost.

The indigenous healing practices are the community resources. The decline and damages of these resources can have an adverse impact on the community. This can disempower and deprive them of their rights and resources. With the help of indigenous healers many of the ailments are treated at the community level without wasting much time and resources. For those who are poor or who have no access to official medicine, these healers are the only source. The indigenous healers come handy for minor ailments as well as for backup source before, during and after getting services of medical practitioners. Sometimes, they are the only hope for biomedically untreatable conditions. However, there is a threat of losing such an important indigenous knowledge base. The protection of locally available medicinal herbs and promotion of the indigenous healers is crucial to strengthen indigenous knowledge.

Conclusion

The Tharu healers not only provide health care services but also play a customary role in their community. The existence and continuity of the indigenous healing practices are also associated with the culture and tradition of ethnic communities. The indigenous practices are important culturally, economically and also environmentally for the sustainable use of plant resources. The promotion of indigenous knowledge and indigenous practices empowers indigenous ethnic communities, and this also contributes to the development of scholarly traditions giving a lifeline to the most important source of knowledge. Because "the ethnomedicinal practices are the mother of all other traditional systems such as Ayurveda, Siddha, Unani and even today's most popular modern therapeutic system or allopathic system" (Katewa, 2009: 34). The indigenous healing practices are the untapped resources with enormous possibility. The indigenous healers, on whom the indigenous ethnic communities have strong faith, should be provided with encouragement and incentives to contribute to the official health care system.

NOTE

1. Nepalese scholars prefer 'ethnic groups' over the 'tribal people' (Dahal, 2012: 139). They are also recognized as indigenous nationality (*Aadivasi Janajati*) defined as "a tribe or community having its own language and traditional rites and customs, distinct cultural identity, distinct social structure and written or unwritten history" (NFDIN, 2003: 32). Tharus are one of the 59 indigenous nationalities notified by the Government of Nepal. In this chapter 'ethnic communities' refers to the 'indigenous nationalities'.

REFERENCES

Acharya, R., & Acharya, K.P. (2009). Ethnobotanical Study of Medicinal Plants Used by Tharu Community of Parroha VDC, Rupandehi District, Nepal. *Scientific World*, *7*(7), 80-84.

Adhikari, K. (2006). Indigenous Healing Practices among Tharus of Amrai Village in Dang. *Education and Development*, *22*, 106-116.

Attewell, G., Hardiman, D., Lambert, H., & Mukharji, P.B. (2012). Agendas. In David Hardiman and Projit Bihari Mukharji (eds.), *Medical Marginality in South Asia: Situating Subaltern Therapeutics.* London: Routledge.

Bista, D.B. (1969). *People of Nepal*. Kathmandu: Ratna Pustak Bhandar.

Brodwin, P. (1996). *Medicine and Morality in Haiti: The Contest for Healing Power* (*Cambridge Studies in Medical Anthropology*). Cambridge: Cambridge University Press.

CBS (2012). *Volume 1, NPHC 2011: National Population and Housing Census 2011* (*National Report*). Kathmandu: Central Bureau of Statistics, Government of Nepal.

CBS (2014). *National Population and Housing Census 2011* (*Village Development Committee/Municipality*) *DANG*. Retrieved from Central Bureau of Statistics website: http://cbs.gov.np/image/data/Population/District%20Level%20 Detail%20Report/Volume05Part02.pdf

Dahal, D.R. (2012). Adibasi/Janajati/Indigenous/Nationalities of Nepal: Socio-economic Situations and Some Questions on Change and Development. In B.C. Upreti and Uddhab P. Pyakurel (eds.), *Contemporary Nepal*. (pp. 139-150). New Delhi: Kalinga Publications.

Dahit, G. (2008). *Research Brief: Inclusion/exclusion of Tharu indigenous knowledge and practices*. Kathmandu: Social Inclusion Research Fund (SIRF)/SNV, Nepal.

Ghimire, K., & Bastakoti, R.R. (2009). Ethnomedicinal Knowledge and Health care Practices among the Tharus of Nawalparasi District in Central Nepal. *Forest Ecology and Management*, *257*, 2066-2072.

Guneratne, A. (2001). The Shaman and the Priest: Ghosts, Death and Ritual Specialists in Tharu Society. *Himalaya, The Journal of the Association for Nepal and Himalayan Studies*, *19*(2), 9-20.

Guneratne, A. (2010). Tharu-State Relations in Nepal and India. *Himalaya, The Journal of the Association for Nepal and Himalayan Studies*, *29*(1), 19-28.

Gurung, G.M. (1992). Socio-economic Network of the Terai Village: An Account of the Rana Tharus of the Urma Urmi. *Contributions to Nepalese Studies*, *19*(1), 19-25.

Joseph, A.E., & Phillips, D. (1984). *Accessibility and Utilization: Geographical Perspectives on Health Care Delivery 1984*. Harper & Row Ltd.

Joshi, P. (2004). The World of Tribal Healers. In A.K. Kalla and P.C. Joshi (eds.), *Tribal Health and Medicines,* pp. 202-241. New Delhi: Concept Publishing Company.

Katewa, S.S. (2009). Indigenous People and Forests: Perspectives of an Ethnobotanical Study from Rajasthan (India). In K.G. Ramawat (ed.) *Herbal Drugs: Ethnomedicine to Modern Medicine.* (pp. 33-56). Udaipur, India: Springer.

Kleinman, A. & Sung, L.H. (1979). Why do indigenous practitioners successfully heal? *Special Issue: Parallel Medical Systems: Chapters from a Workshop on "The Healing Process"*, *13*(1), 7-26. https://doi.org/10.1016/0160-7987(79) 90014-0

Krauskopff, G. (1995). The Anthropology of The Tharus: An Annotated Bibliography. *Kailash Journal of Himalayan Studies*, *XVII* (3 & 4), 185-213.

Lambert, H. (1996). Popular Therapeutics and Medical Preferences in Rural North India. *The Lancet*, *348*, 1706-1709.

Leslie, C. (1976). The Ambiguities of Medical Revivalism in Modern India. In Charles Leslie (ed.), *Asian Medical Systems: A Comparative Study,* pp. 356-367. Berkeley: University of California Press.

Lock, M., & Nguyen, V.-K. (2010). *An Anthropology of Biomedicine*. West Sussex: Wiley-Blackwell.

Maiti, S. (2004). *The Tharu: Their Arts and Crafts*. New Delhi: Northern Book Centre.

Manandhar, N.P. (1985). Ethnobotanical Notes on Certain Medicinal Plants Used by Tharus of Dang Deokhuri District, Nepal. *International Journal Crude Drug*, *23*(4), 153-159.

MoHP. (2014). *Rastriya Swasthya Niti 2071 [The National Health Policy 2014]*. Ministry of Health and Population, Government of Nepal.

MoHP, GoN. (2015). *Nepal Health Sector Strategy 2015-2020*. Kathmandu, Nepal: Ministry of Health and Population, Government of Nepal (GoN).

Najunda, D., Annapurna, M., Midatala, R., & Laxmi, J. (2009). Medical Pluralism and Health Seeking Behaviour of Primitive Society: A Medico-Anthropological Study. In Najunda D.C. (ed.), *Social Anthropology in India: An Ethnography of Policy and Practice,* Vol. 3, pp. 696-711. New Delhi: Sarup Book Publishers Pvt. Ltd.

NESAC. (1998). *Nepal Human Development Report, 1998*. Kathmandu: Nepal South Asia Centre (NESAC).

NFDIN. (2003). *National Foundation for Development of Indigenous Nationalities:*

An Introduction. Kathmandu: National Foundation for Development of Indigenous Nationalities (NFDIN).

Nichter, M. (1980). The Layperson's Perception of Medicine as Perspective into the Utilization of Multiple Therapy Systems in the Indian Context. *Social Science & Medicine. Part B: Medical Anthropology*, *14*(4), 225-233.

Paudyal, S., & Ghimire, G. (2006). Indigenous Medicinal Knowledge among Tharus of Central Dang: A Note on Gastro-Intestinal Diseases. *Education and Development*, *22*, 98-105.

Priya, R. & Shweta, A.S. (2010). *Status and Role of AYUSH and Local Health Traditions under the NRHM*. New Delhi: National Health Systems Resource Centre.

Rajaure, D. (1981a). Tharus of Dang: The people and the social context. *Kailash Journal of Himalayan Studies*, *17*(3 & 4), 155-188.

Rajaure, D. (1981b). *The Tharu Women of Sukrawar*. Tribhuvan University, Kathmandu: Centre for Economic Development and Administration.

Rajaure, D. (1982). Tharus of Dang: Tharu Religion. *Kailash Journal of Himalayan Studies*, *9*(1), 61-96.

Regmi, R.R. (2003). Ethnicity and Identity. *Occasional Chapters in Sociology and Anthropology, Central Department of Sociology and Anthropology, Tribhuvan University.*, *VII*, 1-11.

Shafey, O. (1997). Medical Pluralism among the Tharu People of Far West Nepal: The Logic of Shamanism at the Jungle Frontier (Ph.D. Dissertation). University of California, San Fransisco.

Singh, N. & Agrawal, B. (2009). Health Communication among Scheduled Tribes of Chhattisgarh: An Anthropological Analysis. *The Eastern Anthropologist*, *62*(4), 491-498.

Subedi, B. & Joshi, L.R. (2018). (Un)popular traditional medicine: Community perceptions, changing practices, and state policy in Nepal. *e-Social Science and Humanities*, *1*(2), 157-167.

Sujatha, V. (2014). *Sociology of Health and Medicine: A New Perspective*. New Delhi: Oxford University Press.

8

Connecting Folk Medicine with Medical Lore: Examining Bodding's Perspective of Santhal Medicine

Shrila Soren and *P.C. Joshi*

Introduction

For as long as one can remember folk medicine has depended on the traditional knowledge. The ideas, beliefs and habits held by the members of any community are shaped by their lived experiences. More often these are communicated among each other orally and over generation to generation and could be clubbed under oral traditions.

These lived experiences of the people constitute the medical lore which again acts as a system dealing with the interactions between health and disease, habitat, environment or space, and one's body (Sujatha, 2007).

The focus of this chapter is on the Santhals, their medical lore and how it is related to the medical system observed by them and *vice-versa*. P.O. Bodding has done an extensive work on Santhals and his work *The Studies in Santal Medicine and Connected Folklore* (1925) throws some light on their traditional knowledge as well as their medicine. This, however, has to be noted that these works were published almost a century ago and that too during the colonial period. Therefore, all the observations presented cannot be expected to be holding true even today.

Santhals have a rich cultural background and take their traditions very seriously. The way they are geographically situated is really fascinating as majority of areas inhabited are surrounded by dense forests and mountains. They have access to the medicinal plants/herbs, and roots which are in abundance in those regions. They have profound knowledge about the type of plants and trees which could be of medicinal value and can distinguish between the variants. Not just plants or trees, their knowledge encompasses the details about different parts like flower, fruit, roots, bark, stem etc. This botanical knowledge puts them at an advantage. Likewise, the belief in supernatural is very strong and prevalent in Santhals like many other tribal communities. When the disease does not heal even after medical attention they seek refuge in the supernatural (Bodding, 1925). Aptly said by Rivers, medicine, magic and religion are: "*three sets of social processes…so closely interrelated that the disentanglement of each from the rest is difficult or impossible*" (Rivers, 1924). Hence, the thoughts that are shared by the members of the community become part of their experiences. These shared ideas find its place in their folklore too which shows a plethora of examples or situations wherein the 'medical aspect' comes up; be it the disease or illness caused by the evil eye or just due to natural reasons, *ojha* or medicine man curing or treating the disease or illness etc. This chapter does not propose to provide a complete list of types of diseases or unusual physical states as encountered in the folklore or any cure or measure, but, instead it simply tries to show how these people deal with the medical problems when they occur. It could be implied that folk medical belief and practices are adopted by the people according to the needs of the folklore, for instance, consuming a particular food item will promote long life.

General Perception of Health, Disease and Illness, and Body

In the Western world people generally do not make a distinction between illness and disease. These two terms often seem to mean the same thing and are, therefore, usually used interchangeably. However, it is important to define illness and disease differently when considering some non-Western cultures, particularly the tribal communities in India. A disease is more or less a pathological condition of the body which is measured objectively. Tooth decay, measles, or broken bones are few examples. In contrast, illness is a feeling of not being normal and healthy. Illness may occur due to a disease or could be because of a feeling of psychological or spiritual imbalance. Like any other society, Santhals do have their own explanations for health and ill-health (Bhasin, 2007).

Santhals are aware of the natural causes of illness. These beliefs emerge from their daily experiences and this knowledge shared by them arises out of the interconnection between mind, body and environment. They believe in the concept of 'cause and effect' when it comes to diseases (regardless of this they always have their own suspicions that the natural cause might not the real or original one). They have a view that human body is similar to a *'machine carriage'* or as they say *'kol gadi'*. This *'gadi'* or vehicle moves through a machine and this is precisely how their body functions. As long as the engine is working, their body functions normally. Bodding was told by them that this *'machine'* is comprised *'sirs'* or *'seers'* (singular: *sir* or *seer*). By *sir* it is to represent the muscles, sinews, the nerves, arteries and veins. This *sir* is generally where the blood is found to be present or flowing. In case the *sir* is not functioning properly people complain of ill-health. So, if these *sirs* are twisted or dislocated or sprained, it results in irregular blood flow. Headache, cold or cough, body ache all are the result of disrupted blood flow throughout the *sirs* which again could be due to incorrect posture or injuries. Also, Santhals compare almost all organs of their body to a machine, for instance, the comparison of their stomach to that of a railway engine. Just like the engine of a train needs coal to function, a human body also needs food to sustain. If one does not consume sufficient food or nutrient their body would lose energy or stamina to regulate properly. The human body according to them *'breaks the air'* or passes gas exactly like the smoke that gets out of the engine. The food first passes into the stomach where it is broken down. The food and water consumed is ultimately converted into blood. Most of the water is excreted out of the body as urine and whatever is leftover is then expelled out of the system as excreta. Hence, what one eats or drinks in a way balances or maintains the whole system. Whenever one disturbs this balance by eating or drinking too much or too little it manifests in some kind of disorder. Seasonal change has direct impact on one's body and if not taken proper measures one succumbs to the disease.

Although they attribute medical reasons for disease, according to Bodding, Santhals think illness and disease occur due to something 'unnatural'. They believe that the spirits, whom they refer to as *'bongas'*, if and when angry, envious, hurt or not pleased with them, harbour evil intentions and as Bodding quotes "they supposedly '*eat*' them (the people)" or in Santhali: "*jom kedeya ko*" and this 'eating' or '*jom*' is a common Santhal expression which means the consuming of the soul or health of the person on whom the wrath is projected. Apart from these *bongas*, they also believe that ill-health or disease could be attributed to the wrongdoings of a witch or *'dain' (dan)* or a sorcerer. In case these two are the ones behind the falling health of an individual they consult an *ojha*. The witch is almost always a woman, although, a case of evil eye could be traced back to the doings of any of the sexes (Bodding, 1925).

Existing Medical Practices and Modes of Diagnosis: Generalised and Specialised

Santhals do not consult a 'doctor' immediately when someone falls ill rather they wait to confirm the intensity of the illness. They have an expression: 'one should let the disease become tired' (Bodding, 1925). They do have generalised knowledge about first aid or minor ailments. These household remedies are very effective considering their knowledge regarding different herbs. Most common is the existence of something called '*rehet ran*'which literally means 'root medicine'. Sometimes, some ailments require simple massage which they call '*ota*' or '*iskir*' depending upon the intensity and nature of '*hasu*' or pain.

Bodding (1925), in his writings, has mentioned the existence of '*tiju*' which could be understood close to larvae, worms etc. These *tijus* could be of varying size; from as small as to be invisible to the naked eye to being fairly large. Large number of diseases, like rabies, epilepsy, cancer of the jaw, leprosy, ringworm, eczema occurs due to specific type of *tijus*. The concept of *tiju* shows that there is an understanding among Santhals with respect to their body and the environment and how it affects their health.

If the disease does not heal or get cured even after the administration of household remedies and persists they seek the attention of a 'doctor', a medicine man or an *ojha,* either from the village or the neighbouring villages.

A doctor, medicine man, and an *ojha* are basically all physicians but the difference is that while the doctor only gives medicine to a patient, an *ojha,* in contrast, in addition to giving just medicines tries to drive away the disease using supernatural ways (magic, incantation, divination etc.). A medicine man on the other hand is sometimes a person with a natural talent or gift for 'medical' related works. The knowledge these individuals have regarding medicinal plants and herbs are exceptional and they expertise in particular diseases or illness. One can specialise in only one disease. They are often called '*raranic*' by the person, which means 'the one who cures or administers medicine' (Bodding, 1925). The medicine men and the *ojha* could be labelled as traditional healers; of which the former is more of an herbal specialist, whereas the latter specialises as ritual and magico-religious healer (Bhasin, 2007). These folk practitioners have codified knowledge and irrespective of the fact that it might not be their full term profession they could classify diseases and come up with diagnosis and treatment borrowing their traditional knowledge.

Even though the people seek for the *ojha* or the medicine man to treat the disease or cure the illness initially, but when the situation does not get better they ultimately see a doctor who specialises in Western or 'modern' medicine. These doctors often reside in nearby small towns and cities or may be in the same village. They earn their livelihood through the practice of medicine and are somewhat more refined with the modern 'medical' terminologies.

Amalgamation of Folk and Modern: Medical Pluralism in Santhal Setting

It is not uncommon to find that in Santhal community the belief in the traditional folk medicine and the modern medicine co-exist. People let the disease take its course and when considered to be an inconvenience, visit a traditional healer at first. When the results are not desirable and the root of the problem cannot be found they turn to the 'modern' doctors and avail the medical facilities. What is important to understand here is that these people do not view these medical systems as superior or inferior to one another but a mere alternative to each other. They decide to choose the one which suits the intensity or nature of their situation. There is a "synchronic existence" of at least two medical systems in a society which could be based entirely on different worldviews, that is medical pluralism. Nevertheless, it is not uncommon to find competition among the local traditional healers and the physicians or the medical doctors. Sometimes, the rivalry becomes very intense and it affects the medical choices of people when they seek medical help. However, this competition is merely a choice for Santhals. People do not hesitate to go to a professional medical doctor in the nearby town or cities and ask for their counselling instead of traditional healers. With the onset of the millennia and with the technological innovations in the field of Western and bio-medicine people are accessing the facilities more than ever. One such facility would be the availability of Primary Health Centres in the villages and different government schemes and policies regarding health care.

Irrespective of all this one cannot ignore the fact that the traditional medicine still finds its way among the locals. It is a part of their culture and at times they find it easier to tell their problems to a fellow villager who specialises in some kind of medical knowledge than to a total stranger.

Conclusion: Medical Lore *vis-à-vis* Folk Medicine

The chapter presents the Santhals mostly based on the descriptions provided in the works of Bodding (1925) hence the data is secondary in nature. Bodding was a missionary and even though he lived among Santhals for three decades and learnt their language the Anglo-Saxon tone in his writing could not be missed. Although he has provided an 'in-depth' description of Santhal medicine but the way he has described the notions and beliefs gives readers an exotic impression. He does propose that Santhals believed in 'modern medicine' but somehow maintains the 'dichotomous' distinction between the Western and non-Western counterparts. From his perspective, the folk understanding of health and disease would always be 'invalid' when compared with 'modern' medicine. Traditional beliefs, mainly those with respect to supernatural, would remain as 'superstition' to him. What he failed to understand is that what is labelled as 'superstition' to one might be a lived experience for someone else. These experiences would be classified as 'subjective' and never given a valid ground. This leads to the need to understand that 'others' experiences' are parallel truths, therefore, not invalid (Sujatha, 2007). Bodding mentions that many of (their) medical practices are 'undoubtedly worthless' and many of the remedies may likely have 'little or no value'. There is also mention about Santhals (at that time) being in a 'stage of development'. He justifies his remarks by borrowing concepts of evolutionism and in the process gives away his ethnocentric mind-set. He added that 'proper pharmacological investigation' would help show the 'real worth' of the medical practices of Santhals (of that time).

It is not just Bodding but anyone who has worked among the so-called 'savages' in the colonial periods have had the notion that they were entitled to a higher position and that those under their study were in a stage where their practices and beliefs were exotic and nothing but rudimentary.

When working among people who come from a different cultural background than the researcher, it is necessary to understand that while the one studied becomes an 'other' to the researcher, the researcher also, on the other hand is an 'other' to that particular community. Hence, there is a need to focus on the 'multiple voices' (Good, 1994) rather than being blinded by the biases. Of course, it is important to be objective to an extent so that one does not get swayed by the biases favouring the community under research.

There is plenty evidence from the work of Bodding that the medical lore existing among the Santhals are to be accounted as valid when talking about the folk medicine as well as the modern medicine. The people have a general idea about their body, their environment, as well the causations of the diseases but that does not negate the fact that they deny modern medicine also works. Instead, more and more people these days are availing biomedicine or modern medicine as much as they are relying on their own folk medicine. There is a clear existence of both of these medical systems in the community and it all comes down to a simple inference—the patient's choice.

Bodding does point out the relationship between the patient and the healer, or the patient or the doctor. This relationship is as important as the relationship between the patients and its surroundings, which again applies to both personalistic and naturalistic causes of a disease. Understanding of one's body and having the generalised ideas about health and disease, having a clear acceptance of the existence of *tiju*, attributing supernatural reasons for certain diseases are all projected from their own experiences which represent their reality. These experiences and knowledge govern the underlying principles of their society which manifest in their lifestyle, mainly the dietary pattern and health care. Their folklore provides reference about their botanical and zoological knowledge, how they perceive it and how it is associated with their day to day lives. Common expressions and proverbs stating the do's and don'ts are shaped according to their worldview and in no way suggests that their truth cannot exist as a parallel truth. Even though Bodding stresses that the folk healers or practitioners share the common worldview with the patients, one cannot ignore the fact that after so many decades people have come to terms with the Western medicine as well. The co-existence of multiple genres of medical knowledge is the reality of the society at present, without one undermining the other.

REFERENCES

Acharya, D. and Shrivastava, A. (2008). *Indigenous Herbal Medicines: Tribal Formulations and Traditional Herbal Practices.* Jaipur: Aavishkar Publishers Distributor.

Bascom, W.R. (1977). *Fontiers of Folklore*. Boulder: Westview Press.

Bhasin, V. (2007). Medical Anthropology: A Review. *Ethno-Medicine,* Vol. 1 (1), pp. 1-20.

Bodding, P.O. (1925). *Studies in Santal Medicine and Connected Folklore.* Calcutta: Asiatic Society of Bengal.

Chaudhuri, B. (eds.). (1986). *Tribal Health: Socio-cultural Dimensions.* New Delhi: Inter-India Publications.

Cohen, David William. (1989). The Undefining of Oral Tradition. *Ethnohistory*. Vol. *36* (1), pp. 9-18.

Doshi, S.L. and Vyas, N. (1992). *Tribal Rajasthan: Sunshine on the Arawali.* Udaipur: Himachal Publications.

Foster, G.M. and Anderson, B.(1978). *Medical Anthropology.* New York: Wiley.

Geertz, C. (1973). *The Interpretation of Cultures.* New York: Basic Books.

Good, Byron J.(1994). *Medicine, Rationality and Experience: An Anthropological Perspective.* Cambridge: Cambridge University Press.

Grobman, Neil R. (1973). Eighteenth-Century Scottish Philosophers on Oral Tradition. *Journal of the Folklore Institute.* Vol. *10* (3), pp. 187-195.

Harms, Robert. (1979). Oral Tradition and Ethnicity. *The Journal of Interdisciplinary History.* Vol. *10* (1), pp. 61-85.

Harrah-Conforth, J. (1987). Review of *Oral Tradition as History* by Jan Vansina. *The Oral History Review.* Vol. *15* (2), pp. 212-213.

Landy, David. (1977). *Culture, Disease, and Healing: Studies in Medical Anthropology.* New York: Macmillan.

Rivers, W.H.R. (1924). *Medicine, Magic and Religion.* London: Kegan, Paul, Trench, Turner and Co.

Singh, C.S.K. (1995). *The Sound of Drums: Tribal Movement in Rajasthan (1881-1947).* New Delhi: Manak Publications.

Sujatha, V. (2007). Pluralism in Indian medicine: Medical lore as a genre of medical knowledge. *Contributions to Indian Sociology.* Vol. *41* (2), pp. 169-202.

Tonkin, Elizabeth. (1986). Investigating Oral Tradition. *The Journal of African History.* Vol. *27* (2), 203-213.

Vansina, Jan (1965). *Oral Tradition. A Study in Historical Methodology* London: Routledge & Kegan Paul.

Vansina, Jan.(1985). *Oral Tradition as History.* Madison, Wisconsin: University of Wisconsin Press.

Vidyarthi, L.P. & Rai, B.N. (1976). *The Tribal Culture of India.* New Delhi: Concept Publishing Company.

West, F. (1966). Review of *Oral Tradition: A Study in Historical Methodology* by Jan Vansina and H.M. Wright. *History and Theory*, Vol. *5* (3), pp. 348-352.

PART III
MENTAL HEALTH AND WELL-BEING

9

Recovering from Mental Illness in a North Indian Muslim Shrine

Reetinder Kaur

There is a growing burden of mental illness in India and limited mental health care resources are available to cater mental health services to the needy. Recognising the importance of indigenous healing resources, National Mental Health Policy (2014) suggests that the primary role of research is to generate knowledge (understanding of mental illness in the cultural context and identification of effective indigenous systems of healing) which could lead to a reduction in the burden of mental illness in India and provide therapeutic choices. With this background, the present chapter deals with the understanding of mental illness in a cultural context with special focus on explanatory models of mental illness and exploration of healing at *dargah* as a resource for mental health care in India. An attempt has been made to understand the patients' idioms of distress, their explanatory models, healer's explanations of the mental illness and the healing process.

Introduction

Within the specific context of mental health, there exist multiple systems of healing such as psychiatry, Ayurveda, naturopathy, homeopathy and faith healing in India. Due to huge burden of mental illness, limited mental health care resources, associated stigma and culturally rooted explanations, people resort to these traditional systems of medicine and healing apart from what is called 'mainstream medicine'. Bhattacharyya (1983) identifies three varieties of psychiatric pluralism in India: (a) social institutional pluralism of the diverse specialists; (b) cultural cognitive pluralism of the client's conceptual framework; and (c) pluralism resulting from the divergent perspectives of clients and specialists. The places of faith healing such as temples and *dargahs* are an especially important part of this pluralistic system. The healing practices differ at different places of faith healing, but uniformity lies in recognition of the role of the divine, understanding individual's relation to the divine and situating role of healer as a mediator in healing. The beneficial aspects of faith healing include understanding illness in the religious-spiritual spectrum, the inclusion of patients in the healing process and cultural continuity with the local community (Davar and Lohokare, 2009; Davar, 2014). Pluralism not only exists in the availability of treatment options to the clients, but in terms of explanation of symptoms, causes and cures of mental illness, which Campaner (2014) calls as 'explanatory pluralism'. In India, mental illnesses are largely attributed to non-medical factors, such as social causes, spirit possession, supernatural forces and *karma* (Kaur and Pathak, 2017). As a consequence, traditional healing resources play a vital role in addressing mental health needs due to easy availability and reported benefits (Raguram *et al.*, 2002).

Dargahs **and their Role in Indian Mental Health care**

A Dargah is a Sufi Islamic shrine built over the grave of a revered religious figure, often a Sufi saint or *pir*. The *pir* is a Persian word meaning an elder. Within the Sufi tradition, a *pir* is a religious guide (*murshid*) who shows his disciples (*murid*) the straight path (*rashid*) to spiritual fulfilment (Pinto, 2004). *Dargahs* have a distant relationship with formal Islam and closer relationship with healing (Davar and Lohokare, 2009). According to the Sufi thought, illness as well as their ways of healing comes from *Allah* and curer is just a person who mediates between *Allah* and the sufferer. In India, the *dargahs* known to heal various mental health include Nizzamudin and Patteshah *dargahs* in Delhi, Mira Datar *dargah* in Gujarat, Erwadi *dargah* in Tamil Nadu, Peeran Kaliyar Sharif *dargah* near Haridwar and Mempuram *dargah* in Kerala.

Dargah is a site where social control of bodies takes place (Basu, 2009; Davar and Lohokare, 2009). It is a liminal space, passage between profane (outside world) and the sacred spheres of life (worship of *pir*) as described by Basu (2009). Similarly, at a psychiatric hospital[1], the practices such as institutional care, admission of patients for treatment, wearing uniforms and closed structures of the hospital differentiates it from the outside world. The works by Kakar (1982) and Basu (2009) suggest that difference between *dargah* and the psychiatric hospital lies in the healing/treatment process. At a *dargah,* greater communication between the patient, family, the larger community and the healer is facilitated as a part of the healing process, and ill are not merely passive recipients rather they are actively involved in the healing process. At a psychiatric hospital, a formal distance is maintained between the medical professionals (who know) and the ill (who do not know). The involvement of the sufferer and the family in healing process makes *dargahs* a popular choice for the patients and their families. Moreover, the healer at *dargah* is more specialised than the Western psychiatrist or a psychotherapist. The healer explicitly covers a part of 'disorders' in the religious-spiritual spectrum, which are generally hidden and unavowed by psychiatry or psychotherapy (Kakar, 1982). In a shrine, the mentally ill are included in, not excluded from, the community of believers (Basu, 2009). The healing at *dargah* has positive aspects and holistic healing offers social and safe spaces to those experiencing vulnerabilities and crisis in their lives (Davar and Lohokare, 2009). The traditional healers draw upon extensive knowledge of healing methods and materials accumulated, and passed down from one generation to the next. It is based on a complex socio-cultural and religious belief system. The traditional healing systems address the question of identity and belonging, may reaffirm or alter prevailing social norms and structures, and serve as quasi-judicial moral courts resolving community conflicts and power relations (Kakar, 1982). The cultural continuity with the local communities, adaptation of their processes to the local needs, and the complex web of relationships that the healers and the centres share with communities makes the traditional healing practices a popular choice (Davar, 2014). These healing centres are often seen as spaces of refuge for those in distress (Ranganathan, 2014). The central part of religious healing is the process of being at the place, familiarising oneself with the shrine culture and "becoming a pilgrim" (Ranganathan, 2015).

Research Setting and Methods

This chapter deals with the understanding of mental illness in a cultural context, explanatory models of mental illness and exploration of healing at *dargah* as a resource for mental health care. The study is an in-depth account of a *dargah* near Mohali city (Punjab) that caters health services to the people suffering from various illness such as mental illness, skin ailments, infertility, somatic complaints such as bodyache, backache and sleeplessness, *nazar lagna* (evil eye), *jadu* (witchcraft), and *tona*[2] (sorcery) etc. *Dargah* chosen for the study is the oldest *dargah* in the city and has a historical value attached to its healing tradition. It belongs to a Sufi saint popularly known as Lalan wale *pir*.[3] The term '*lal*' refers to the son, the *pir* was known to bless his followers with sons. The *pir* is also referred to as '*Nigahe wale pir*' and '*Sakhi Sarvar*'.[4] A number of legends associated with him suggest that he was a great healer. The *pir* himself travelled from Shahkot (Pakistan) to various places such as Baghdad (Iraq), Gujranwala (Pakistan), Multan (Pakistan) and Sakhi Sarvar (a town in Pakistan named after the *pir* and a tomb has been built there) during the thirteenth century. Prior to advent of Sikhism, worship of Lalan wale *pir* was a part of popular culture in Punjab.[5] *Dargahs* were built at places visited by the *pir* himself and at other places, his followers built shrines in his memory (Bhatti, 2000), one such shrine is a *dargah* chosen for the study.

I conducted fieldwork at *dargah* from May 2015 to December 2016 during Thursdays (the healing day) and weekends (when the healer meets patients who are in emergency need of care). My fieldwork began with the rapport establishment with the healer[6] and his family, observing the interactions between healer and visitors, the healing process and the rituals performed by the healer. The healer was the first person to be interviewed and the interview guide for healer focused on the healing process, his understanding of the patient's and family's explanatory models of mental illness, his 'theory of mental illness', his knowledge about mental illness and its typology etc. After few months of observation, the visitors began to recognise us as one amongst them and we were able to talk to them freely. Therefore, I began interviews with the people suffering from mental illness and their families about their experiences of mental illness. Through this chapter, we aim to seek answers to the following questions: how do *dargah* fit into their help-seeking model? Whether they benefit from healing at *dargah*? The interviews and interactions with all the identified respondents were carried out repeatedly during their *chaunkis* (visit to the *dargah* as a part of the healing process). As it was mandatory for the people undergoing healing to visit the *dargah* for five Thursdays, we were able to interview them repeatedly. The participants were chosen using purposive sampling technique. The data were collected in the form of case studies, narratives and conversations. The socio-demographic characteristics of the respondents and the information regarding their health-seeking behaviour were taken into account. The data are analysed thematically and presented in the form of three themes: healer and his visitors; Patients' idioms of distress and the healer's explanations; and the healing process. Quantitative data are expressed as percentages.

The study has a number of limitations. First, the data is generated from single *dargah* but the fieldwork is conducted for a considerable amount of time. Second, the sample size of seventy participants is chosen from a specific field site.

Healer and his Visitors

The characteristics of the healer are given in the Table 9.1 in the form of a Curer Stylistic Inventory adapted from Press (1971).

Table 9.1: Curer Stylistic Inventory

Reputation of healer	Mediator between patients and the *pir*, specialist in curing a variety of illnesses including mental illness.
Personal and environmental impressionistic phenomena	Aged 64 years, male practicing at a Sufi Islamic shrine located at heart of the city.
Origin of curer's vocation as claimed	Healer's own desire.
Origin of curer's ability or knowledge	Apprenticeship with father (who was specialised in healing cases of possession) followed by learning through practice.
Power source of the curer	Supernatural combined with patient's faith in his abilities.
Personnel involved in the cure	Healer, patient, family and the larger community as healing takes place in the public arena and rarely in a private space.
Diagnostic technique	Questioning, patient confession and divination.
Socio-cultural classification of the cure	Locally, culturally and historically rooted healing practices that cater to all socio-economic groups, especially those who are socially disadvantaged—women, poor and the homeless.
Healing techniques	Ritual performance, herbal medicine and minor exorcism, including *jhara*.
Degree of specialisation of the curer	Specialist in cases related to mental illness, reproductive health, childlessness, evil eye.
Manner of establishing payment	Voluntary donation in the form of money or *prasad* (food offered to God) in the form of fruits or cooked sweet rice (*nayaz*).

Two categories of individuals/families visit the healer: one, those who come for healing of bodily or mental ailments and second, those who visit the healer for receiving divine help for a favourable outcome of uncertain situations such as court cases, employment, family conflicts etc. A well-known psychoanalyst, Kakar (1982) calls the first category as 'patients' and second category as 'supplicants' in his work on traditional healers.

The patients include those suffering from 'tension', alcohol dependence, reproductive health problems, childlessness, skin problems etc. The socio-demographic characteristics of the healer's patients are given in Table 9.2.

Table 9.2: Socio-demographic characteristics of the healer's patients

Socio-demographic variables	*Respondents N=70 (in per cent)*
Gender	
Male	37.1
Female	62.9
Age-wise distribution (in years)	
1-2*	2.9
11-20	14.3
21 and above	82.9
Marital status	
Married	65.7
Unmarried	31.4
Widow/Widower	2.9
Religion	
Hindu	91.4
Sikh	5.7
Muslim	2.9
Educational status	
Illiterate	4.3
Primary	12.9
Middle	11.4
Matric	31.4
Senior Secondary	21.4
Graduation and above	15.7
Not applicable*	2.9
Occupation	
Homemaker	22.9
Labourer	40.0
Student	20.0
Business	8.6
Job (Private and government)	5.7
Not applicable*	2.9
Category	
Patients	87.1
Supplicants	12.9

* Includes two children (below 2 years of age) brought by their mothers for healing evil eye. All other respondents are above the age of 11.

Many people come to *dargah* to be cured of *kita kraya, khavis, dabav paina, opri kasar, hawa*, other existential, psychological or spiritual questions manifested as mental disturbances. These illnesses are explained in detail in the following section. The patients included 87.1 per cent of the total sample. The percentage distribution of all patients is given in Table 9.3. Those suffering from mental illness formed the largest part of the healer's patients and majority self-reported to be suffering from depression. Majority patients choose traditional healing as their first resort to cure and at the time of their interview, 74.3 per cent received only traditional healing. Another 25.7 per cent received both traditional healing and psychiatric treatment for curing their illness.

Table 9.3: Percentage distribution of patients

Illness	*Male (N=22)*	*Female (N=39)*	*Total (N=61)*
Mental illness	26.3	47.5	73.8
Reproductive health problems	–	4.9	4.9
Skin ailments	3.3	1.6	4.9
Bone related	0	4.9	4.9
Evil eye	3.3	0	3.3
Others	3.3	4.9	8.2
Total	**36.2**	**63.8**	**100**

Patients' Idioms of Distress and the Healer's Explanations

The idioms of distress are experiences and expressions of distress by the sufferers (Nichter, 2010). The respondents in the present study expressed their psycho-social distress in terms of *dabav paina* (heaviness of the body while sleeping), *kita kraya* (suspicion of *jadu* or *tona*), possession (the three terms *khedna/hawa/opri kasar* are used) and *khavis* (man overpowering a woman for sexual intercourse in her dreams). The explanatory models of these mental illnesses are given in Table 9.4.

Dabav paina: *Dabav paina* (heaviness of the body) takes place while sleeping. It means overpowering by an outside force which does not allow a person to get up and as a result the person feels scared, full of sweat and tired.

> A girl (25 years, unmarried) complained that she sees a spirit in the form of 'flying dark clouds' around her. These spirits exert pressure on her body and suddenly her body becomes heavy and she finds it difficult to lift herself and get up. On her

Table 9.4: Explanatory models of mental illness

Patients' and family's explanation of symptoms	*Medical diagnosis of the patients (self-reported)*	*Patients' and family's self-diagnosis*	*Healer's explanatory model*
Social withdrawal, sadness, incapability to do routine work, loss of desire to live	Depression	*Opri kasar/kita kraya/ Dabav paina*	Tensions, familial problems, interpersonal conflicts within the family and outside
Anger, excessive cleaning, bathing, social withdrawal	Obsessive Compulsive Disorder	*Kita kraya*	Tensions, familial problems, lack of care at home, interpersonal conflicts
Excessive consumption of liquor or drugs	Dependence syndrome	*Kita kraya*	Influence of peer group, familial problems, weakness of one's own personality
Hearing voices	Schizophrenia	*Opri kasar*	Tensions, non-fulfilment of desires
Violent behaviour, rotation of head, change in voice etc.	Not clearly known	*Khedna/hawa/opri kasar*	Way of social expression, attention seeking behaviour
Bad dreams, appearance of *khavis* in dreams	Not clearly known	*Opri kasar/hawa*	Unfulfilled sexual desires, marital conflicts

complaint, the family first took her to a general physician in a government hospital who referred her to a psychiatrist. The psychiatrist diagnosed her with schizophrenia and for first few months she underwent treatment. The girl and the family felt that the psychiatrist was not able to explain her 'flying dark clouds' theory, and decided to visit a healer who stays in a village at the outskirts of Chandigarh. The healer performed *jhara* (a minor ritual of exorcism) and gave *vibhuti* (ash to apply on the whole body to save the patient from spirit attack). She did not feel much relief. The family moved on to another healer, i.e. healer at the *dargah* under study. The healer asked about the illness in detail, listened to both father and the girl about their explanations of the illness, and counselled the girl. The healer also performed *jhara* and gave her *dhaga* (sacred thread) for protection. By the end of five *chaunkis* (visits to *dargah*), the girl felt relief in her symptoms and she continued with her psychiatric treatment on advice of the healer.

The healer explained the symptoms such as social withdrawal, anger, incapability to do routine work and loss of desire to live in terms of tensions, familial problems, interpersonal conflicts within the family, and lack of care. Depression was the only mental illness that the healer knew of but he preferred to use the term 'tension'. He described depression as a 'brain disease' and 'illness of thought'. He himself used the term 'tension' to cover a wide range of symptoms. He attributed tension to a variety of socio-cultural (role conflict, gender roles, belief system) and economic factors (financial status).

Kita kraya: The expression *kita kraya* includes the suspicion of *jadu* (witchcraft) or *tona* (sorcery). The findings of the study suggest that a large number of patients attribute their illness to *kita kraya.* The symptoms such as social withdrawal, obsessive and compulsive behaviour and dependence syndrome are considered to be an outcome of *kita kraya.* The healer attributes the majority of these symptoms to 'tensions', familial problems, lack of care at home, interpersonal conflicts and weakness of one's own personality. He categorises drug addiction and alcohol dependence as a lifestyle and habitual problem, and avoids healing these patients as they are mostly abusive and non-cooperative.

Hearing voices: Another idiom of distress explained by participants is 'hearing voices' which Western psychiatry refers to as auditory hallucinations (a symptom of schizophrenia). Two respondents (both young girls) reported hearing voices repeatedly. One of the participants (aged 22 years, postgraduate student) reported listening to 'voice of a man' repeatedly while she is under stress (when she thinks too much). Her parents do not allow her to discuss these symptoms with anybody outside the family (her gender, age and stigma being the major reasons). On advice of their tenants, family brought the girl to *dargah* and consulted the healer. The healer attributed the illness to her young age (he suggested that she might want to get married to someone of her choice) and her lifestyle (use of mobile phone).

Possession: Some patients behave violently and strangely when they come to healer and some of them start 'playing'. This playing involves physical activities (rotating head, moving body at a fast pace) performed not by the individual but by the spirit that possess the individual and usually is characterised by glazed eyes, a change in voice and the whirling around on the head, with hair flying loose. The healer refers to it as '*khedna*' (the term means 'to play' and is used to designate possession).

In present study, the participants used the terms such as *hawa ka ana*, *opri kasar* and *khedna* for possession.

> A girl (aged 11 years) came to *dargah* with her mother on pretext of *khed* (possession) that happened three days back. The mother came to *dargah* in emergency on Wednesday (one day prior to the healing day) and narrated the incidence to the healer. She explained that while her family was coming back from their native place in Uttar Pradesh, her daughter complained of a head-ache and started shivering. Soon she started uttering things which were not there, such as: there is blood on roof of the train; there is a dead rat lying on the floor; the train has caught fire; somebody would die etc. The girl started behaving violently, shouting at her mother and wandering around. Her mother, who had seen similar cases before, immediately understood her behaviour as *khed.* She held her tightly from hair and slapped her daughter and tried to ask the spirit about its identity: Who she was? Who send the spirit? Why her daughter? The girl replied to none of her queries and collapsed.
>
> On understanding the whole situation, healer performed *jhara* and gave sacred thread to the girl. The next day, i.e. Thursday the girl again visited the healer along with her mother. The healer asked the mother, "*how did she address you while she was possessed?*". To which she replied, "*mummy*". The healer immediately refuted it as a case of *khed.* He suggested that girl must have seen somebody else doing it and has imitated the behaviour to seek attention. The mother argued with the healer that her daughter has never seen a '*khed*' and she cannot imitate something which she has not seen. The healer assured that he has prayed to *pir*, everything would be fine and told the mother to take the girl home.

The healer considers *khed* as a way of social expression of a socially disadvantaged person or an attention seeking behaviour and not a mental illness or possession. He tries to counsel these individuals, and claims that in most cases, counselling works. He believes that possession is a rare phenomenon and cannot take place that often. According to the healer, the majority of individuals pretends to be possessed and small fraction of them are actually possessed. The healer explains that the socially disadvantaged individuals such as women pretend to be possessed as they are allowed to express, abuse or violate the social norms of society in the state of possession which otherwise is not possible. The 'possessed' are not held responsible for their behaviour and the families try to regain their health by seeking divine help.

The respondent's belief in spirits suggests that they believe in the presence of the soul and liberation of the soul after death. The respondents believed in 'body-soul duality'. They explained that the soul gets liberated after death and in case of untimely death, such as accident, sudden death or death of a person with no children, the soul may wander. These wandering souls may themselves harm others or may be controlled by *seane* for benefit of others. The healer refers to professional, self-proclaimed healers whom he calls as *seane* and suggests that these healers diagnose such cases as possession in order to make money from the family of the sufferer. For him, such behaviours are rooted in conflicts within the family or strained interpersonal relationships or non-fulfilment of the desires (such as marriage to a person of choice), and lack of care and attention.

Khavis: The expression of distress in terms of *khavis* is common among married women, especially those who stay alone, away from their husband or whose husband work in night shifts/till late night. These women generally complain of bodyache, tiredness, inability to work etc. In such cases, the healer counsels the husband more than the suffering woman. He relates these kinds of dreams to their disturbed family life and views it in socio-economic context.

> A woman (aged 35 years, married, having two children, visited *dargah* with her husband) complained of 'bad dreams' where she sees a man in disguise of her husband and this man forces her into an intimate relationship. As a result, she feels tired next morning. While talking to the couple, healer mentioned about *khavis* (a spirit that belongs to low caste and is a Muslim). He explained that *khavis* appears in the dreams of a woman either in disguise of husband, father or brother. In the disguise of a husband, he develops an intimate relationship with the woman and when the woman gets up next morning, she feels tired. Although the healer mentioned that he has not seen *khavis* himself, but as elders believe, he too believes in its presence. The healer told that elders call it '*hawa*'. The woman too agreed with the healer's interpretation of her dream.
>
> After the discussion of *khavis*, the healer asked about the financial condition of the family and the occupation of the husband. The woman complained that her husband earns very less and works in a night shift. The healer told the man to find some other job and suggested him to spend time with his family especially his wife.

This case study can be analysed in light of the works of psychoanalyst Freud (1899) who consider dreams as disguised hallucinatory fulfilment of repressed desires. His theory affirms that the main cause of dreams is unsatisfied sexual appetite, and especially those sexual or quasi-sexual impulses which are repressed violently in infancy. Kakar (1982) presents similar case studies in his work '*Shamans, Mystics and Doctors*' and explains that narration of a dream acts as a therapeutic lever, enabling the patient to communicate a symbolised account of his/her inner conflicts. Similarly, in the above mentioned case, the healer tries to address the woman's problem by interpreting her dream in her own cultural understanding. The healer, too, counsels her husband regarding their financial worries and his inability to spend quality time with his wife.

The participants in the study provided a detailed account of various culture-specific illnesses difficult to comprehend in terms of Western psychiatric categories that follow the International Classification of Diseases (ICD-10). The existence of such categories demands for their careful analysis and utilisation of such knowledge for development of culturally relevant and appropriate mental health care models.

The Healing Process

On seeing a patient, the healer first asks family for medical diagnosis. For him, doctor is like a God and he places a doctor next to *pir.* A number of patients visit the healer as their first resort to cure. In some of the cases where healer feels that medical diagnosis is important, he suggests the family to take the patient to a doctor and then revisit him with a medical diagnosis. In the meanwhile, he starts his healing based on his own diagnosis. The healer makes diagnosis by: listening to the patient and the family, observing and understanding the socio-cultural context of the illness, and taking into account age, gender and socio-economic status of the patient. He counsels both patient and the family, and reassures both that everything would be fine. The healer tells the family to visit the *dargah* for five consecutive Thursdays for *chaunki* except women who are allowed to break this continuity (during their menstruation). It is noteworthy that women are considered as 'ritually impure' during their menstruation and they cannot take part in religious ceremonies especially within the context of Hinduism. By doing so, the healer heals the patient by providing them satisfaction and at the same time maintains the number of visitors to *dargah*. The healer keeps on repeating this cycle for his patients. On Thursdays (day of *pir*), the healer witnesses a great rush and providing privacy to his patients is not possible. In case, a patient requires special attention or needs privacy, he attends his patients on Saturdays or Sundays and in case of an emergency, on any other day as well. Table 9.5 describes the patient's, family's and healer's perceptions about the healing process.

Table 9.5: Patient's/family's and healer's perceptions about the healing process

Healing process	*Patient's/family's perception*	*Healer's perception*
Performing *jhara*	Heal all kinds of *kita kraya*, evil eye, illness	Provides satisfaction to the patient
Preparing *dhaga* (sacred thread) for the patient	Protection from supernatural forces, illness, evil eye	Provides satisfaction to the patient
Preparing *laung* (cloves) for the patient	Treats the disease, tensions, help in manipulating others for own benefit	Hot properties, provide relief to the body
Suggesting patients to light *dhup* (incense sticks) at home	Protection from supernatural forces, *kita kraya*, marks the territory of *pir*, smoke generated has mystic healing powers	Positive energy at home
Suggesting patients to keep a bottle of mustard oil with its lid open overnight	Helps to find out if some *bhut pret* or *jinn* reside at one's place	Procedure to find out if some *bhut, pret* or *jinn* reside at one's place, but in all cases refute the same
Tying a black thread at *dargah* for fulfilment of a wish	Helps to fulfil one's wishes and desires	Provides satisfaction to the patient
Putting mustard oil in *chirag* (sacred lights) at the dargah	The way to worship the *pir*	Provides satisfaction to the patient

The healer follows a set pattern to heal his patients and this pattern involves understanding biological origins of illness, psychological impacts of the illness and social reaction to the illness.

1. Asks the patient for the medical diagnosis and on the basis of severity or complexity of the disease/problem, he initiates the healing process. If medical diagnosis is not available, he makes use of his wisdom and previous experience to cure the illness.
2. Gives *laung* (cloves), *dhaga* (black sacred thread) and *dhup* (incense stick) after enchanting *mantras* (sacred hymns) and praying to *pir*. He also performs *jhara* with peacock feathers, a minor ritual of exorcism. He touches the head repeatedly for four times and each of the shoulder once.

3. Tries to understand the social, cultural and economic context of the illness or problem. He tries to address these problems through counselling and discussions with patients and their family.

Initially, the healer mentioned that *pir* listens to and fulfil all his prayers. The *pir* has chosen him for the welfare of the society and he feels blessed. In later interviews, he confided that he merely addresses the social, cultural and economic context of the illness/problem and listens to the patients and their family members who visit him. He narrated: *For people, I am God, they trust me, they feel satisfied by visiting me*. Kakar (1982) and Frank and Frank (1991) suggest that the healing power resides primarily within the patient's mind rather than the healer or healing process. In the present study, it can be observed that the healer has been performing rituals for over five weeks. This time period helps healer to establish rapport with the visitors, offer them a suitable 'theory of illness' and to cure the illness of the patients or to fulfil the desires of the supplicants (Pfleiderer, 1981).

Discussion

In addressing the issues related to mental health care in India, one must realise the importance of understanding the needs in a local context. As the explanations of mental illness are rooted in culture-specific context, the narrow biomedical approach that focuses solely on physical symptoms may not be adopted. Jadhav (2004) suggests that development of psychiatric models is largely confined to Euro-American countries. The application of these models, Jadhav (1995) suggests, often leads to marginalisation of locally available resources and replacement of culturally relevant concepts with scientifically explained universal categories. Jadhav (1995), further, suggests that development of 'indigenous taxonomies' and recognition of local healing systems is crucial to develop knowledge base for clinicians. This would further help to develop what Jadhav (2004) calls as 'locally generated models' based on local illness experiences and explanatory models. In this direction, National Mental Health Policy of India (2014) suggests that researchers must focus on understanding of mental illness in culture-specific contexts and identification of effective indigenous systems of healing to increase the therapeutic choices for people.

The present study takes into account explanatory models of mental illness and explores healing at *dargah* as a resource of mental health care. The participants described their mental illness in terms of various culture-specific categories such as *dabav paina, khedna, hawa, khavis* and relied on healing at *dargah* for their cure. These categories are specific to culture and have not been mentioned in 'International Classification of Diseases'.[7] Therefore, the Western psychiatry does not recognise these explanations or behaviours and outrightly reject the patient's explanatory models of mental illness. On the other hand, a traditional healer who has knowledge of culture, local understanding of symptoms, causes and explanatory models of mental illness is able to understand and communicate with the patient and the family as well. In the present study, the respondents reported benefits of healing at *dargah* and expressed that healer attempts to bring significant changes in their social environment and understands their explanatory models. Moreover, the healers, according to them are easy to approach and available whenever required. Previous research also suggests that the people suffering from mental illness benefit from traditional healing (Davar and Lohokare, 2009) and report pleasant experience of healing (Raguram *et al.*, 2002). Some of the psychiatrists and researchers have rejected the idea of traditional healing being beneficial citing the beating, chaining and other inhumane practices. It is noteworthy here that violations of human rights have also been reported at psychiatric hospitals in India. National Human Rights Commission (2008) suggests that the psychiatric hospitals still retain certain old practices (shaving the heads of inmates and wearing uniforms) and infrastructure (closed structures, non-maintenance, unclean toilets and sleeping areas etc.) that violates the basic human right of life with dignity.

The findings of the present study suggest that:

1. *Dargah* provides an opportunity to talk about desires, conflicts and disagreements, and the healer acts as a mediator between the two conflicting parties. The healer is considered spiritually powerful, respectable and wise, and the followers share their personal problems with the healer. For them, he acts as a counsellor.
2. The healer heals a wide range of illness, including mental illness and provides culturally relevant and fitting explanatory models. The cost of healing in terms of *nayaz* (sweet rice), *chadar* (green cloth offered at *dargah*) and *charahwa* (monetary offering) is minimal as compared to a biomedical doctor (cost of diagnostic tests, consultation and medication). Moreover, the patients receive attention and are free to meet the healer whenever they require.
3. The healer does not outrightly reject the patient's views and try

to explain everything in their own cultural context. On the other hand, most of the patients report rejection of their explanatory models by their psychiatrists and this creates a barrier between the two.

4. The secular and syncretic features of *dargah* attract the people from different religions and across communities. *Dargah* provides an opportunity for the visitors to discuss their personal problems with the healers. As the healer heals in the public arena, all the illness and problems are discussed in open and without any hesitation.
5. The public expression of sexuality is uncommon, especially among women. *Dargahs* provide a place for this outlet (e.g. narration of one's dream) and in a way which is acceptable to the family as well as the healer.

On the basis of the present study, it can be concluded that the community mental health care models in India must include and understand the indigenous knowledge, cultural explanations and locally available resources for effective mental health care. *Dargahs* play an important role in providing mental health care to the individuals suffering from mental illness. Both *Dargahs* and healing performed at *dargahs* must be recognised as locally available and culturally fitting mental health care model in India.

Religious healing practices have, however, been criticised for violation of human rights, especially after Erwadi tragedy that led to death of 28 chained inmates at a *dargah* located in Indian State of Tamil Nadu. Despite criticism, the efforts to integrate religious healing into psychiatric care have begun in various states. One such attempt, *Dawa Dua* (medicine prayer) clinic at Erwadi *dargah* initiated by the National Human Rights Commission in 2012 has proved to be successful and could be extended to other places of religious healing (Scott, 2015). Recently launched Ministry of AYUSH (2014) and National Mental Health Policy of India (2014), too, lay emphasis on indigenous systems of healing that provide therapeutic choices to the patients and develop a deeper understanding of the bio-psycho-social determinants of mental health in India.

[**Acknowledgment:** This chapter is dedicated to my mentor Late Professor R.K. Pathak who edited its first draft. The cooperation of all the participants and postdoctoral funding received from the University Grants Commission, New Delhi by Reetinder Kaur for successful completion of this study is highly acknowledged.]

NOTES

1. The term mental hospital was replaced by psychiatric hospital in Mental Health Act, 1987.
2. The term '*tona*' means sorcery (Turner, 2008).
3. The term '*Lalan wale pir*' is commonly used in Indian State of Punjab.
4. The name 'Sakhi Sarvar' is more popular in Pakistan.
5. The *dargahs* are places of spiritual power to which one can appeal for protecting and favour. *Pirs* have the power to grant boons, fulfil wishes and cure illness in addition to their basic protective functions. They have been a part of popular culture in undivided Punjab prior to the advent of Sikhism (Bhatti and Michon, 2004).
6. There was only one healer at the *dargah* and he healed his visitors of various physical and mental illness, and other concerns such as evil eye.
7. However, ICD-10 recognises some culture-specific syndromes such as amok, latah, koro etc.

REFERENCES

Banerjee, G. and S. Roy (1998). Determinants of help-seeking behaviour of families of schizophrenic patients attending a teaching hospital in India: An indigenous explanatory model, *International Journal of Social Psychiatry,* 44:199-214.

Basu, Helene (2009). Contested practices of control: Psychiatric and religious mental health care in India, *Curare* (32): 28-32.

Basu, Helene (2010). Healing madness through ritual trials. In K.I. Leonard, G. Reddy and A.G. Gold, *Histories of intimacy and situated ethnography*, pp. 215-238. Manohar Publications, Delhi.

Bhattacharyya, D.P. (1983). Psychiatric pluralism in Bengal, India, *Social Science and Medicine, 17*(14): 947-956.

Bhatti, H.S. (2000). *Folk Religion: Change and Continuity*. Rawat Publications, Jaipur.

Bhatti, H.S. and Daniel M. Michon (2004). Folk Practices in Punjab, *Journal of Punjab Studies, 11*(2): 139-154.

Campaner, R. (2014). Explanatory pluralism in psychiatry: What are we pluralists about, and why?, *New directions in the philosophy of science*, Volume 5 of the series *The Philosophy of Science in a European Perspective*, pp. 87-103.

Campbell-Hall, V., I. Petersen, A. Bhana, S. Mjadu, V. Hosegood and A.J. Flisher (2010). Collaboration between traditional practitioners and primary health care staff in South Africa: Developing a workable partnership for community mental health services, *Transcultural Psychiatry, 47*(4): 610-628.

Chakraborty, K., G. Das, A. Dan, G. Bandyopadhyay and M. Chatterjee (2013). Perceptions about the cause of psychiatric disorders and subsequent help seeking patterns among psychiatric outpatients in a tertiary care centre in Eastern India, *German Journal of Psychiatry*, http://www.gjpsy.uni-goettingen.de/gjp-chapter-chakraborty6.pdf.

Champion, J., and D. Bhugra (1996). Experience of religious healing in psychiatric patients in south India. *Social Psychiatry and Psychiatric Epidemiology, 32*(4): 215-221.

Crawford, T.A. and M. Lipsedge (2004). Seeking help for psychological distress: The interface of Zulu traditional healing and Western biomedicine, *Mental Health Religion and Culture, 7*(2): 131-148.

Davar, Bhargavi V. (2014). Globalizing psychiatry and the case of 'vanishing' alternatives in a neo-colonial state, *Disability and the Global South, 1*(2): 266-284.

Davar, Bhargavi V. and M. Lohokare (2009). Recovering from psychosocial traumas: The place of dargahs in Maharashtra, *Economic and Political Weekly, 44*(16): 60-67.

De Souza, A., and D.A. De Souza (1984). *Psychiatry in India*. Bombay: Bhalani Book Depot.

Frank, J.D. and J.B. Frank (1991). *Persuasion and Healing*. The John Hopkins University Press, London.

Freud, Sigmund (1899). *The Interpretation of Dreams*. Basic Books, United States of America.

Ganguli, H.C. (2000). Epidemiological findings on prevalence of mental disorders in India, *Indian Journal of Psychiatry, 42*: 14-20.

Jadhav, Sushrut. (1995). The ghostbusters of psychiatry. *The Lancet, 345*: 808-810.

Jadhav, Sushrut. (2004). How 'culture bound' is 'cultural psychiatry'? *Bulletin of the Board of International Affairs of the Royal College of Psychiatrists 4*: 6-7.

Jugal, K., R. Mukherjee, M. Parashar, R.C. Jiloha and G.K. Ingle (2007). Beliefs and attitudes towards mental health among medical professionals in Delhi, *Indian Journal of Community Medicine, 32*:198-200.

Kakar, S. (1982). *Shamans, mystics and doctors: Psychological inquiry into India and its healing traditions*. Oxford University Press, New Delhi.

Kapur, R.L. (1979). The role of traditional healers in mental health care in rural India, *Social Science and Medicine, 13B*: 27-31.

Kate, N., S. Grover, P. Kulhara and R. Nehra (2012). Supernatural beliefs, aetiological models and help seeking behaviour in patients with schizophrenia, *Industrial Psychiatry Journal, 21*(1): 49-54.

Kaur, Reetinder, and R.K. Pathak. (2017). Treatment gap in mental health care. *Economic and Political Weekly, 52*(31): 34-40.

Khare, R.S. (1996). Dava, daktar, and dua: Anthropology of practiced medicine in India, *Social Science and Medicine, 43*(5): 837-848.

Kleinman, A. (1988). *Rethinking psychiatry: From cultural category to personal experience*. Free Press, New York.

Kumar, A., U. Goyal, K.S. Ganesh, M.K. Srivastava, B.D. Gautam and R. Kumar, (2001). Attitude of postgraduate residents towards psychiatry, *Indian Journal of Psychiatry, 43*:2.

Lal, Sunder and B.M. Vashisht (2002). Moving away from mental institutions: Towards community mental health care, *Indian Journal of Community Medicine, XXVII* (4): 147-150.

Manohari, S.M., Pradeep R. Johnson, and R.B. Galgali (2013). How to teach psychiatry to medical undergraduate in India? A model, *Indian Journal of Psychological Medicine, 35*(1): 23-28.

National Human Rights Commission (2008). *Mental health care and human rights*. National Human Rights Commission, New Delhi.

Nichter, Mark (2010). Idioms of distress revisited, *Culture, Medicine and Psychiatry, 34*: 401-416.

Padmavati, R. (2005). Community mental health care in India, *International Review of Psychiatry, 17*:103-107.

Pfleiderer, B. (1981). Mira Datar Dargah: The psychiatry of a Muslim shrine. In: *Ritual and religion among Muslims in India*, ed. by Imtiaz Ahmad, pp. 195-233. Manohar Publications, New Delhi.

Pinto, D. (2004). Muslim spiritual masters. In T.N. Madan (Ed.), *India's religions: Perspectives from sociology and history*, pp. 185-195. Oxford University Press, New York.

Raguram, R., A. Venkateswaran, J. Ramakrishna and M.G. Weiss (2002). Traditional community resources for mental health: A report of temple healing from India, *British Medical Journal, 325*: 38-40.

Reddy, V.M. and C.R. Chandrasekhar (1998). Prevalence of mental and behavioural disorders in India: A meta-analysis, *Indian Journal of Psychiatry, 40*(2): 149-157.

Scott, DJ Walter (2015). NHRC prescribes 'Dawa Dua' clinics for mentally ill, *The Hindu*, November 24.

Seby, K., S. Chaudhury, and R. Chakraborty (2011). Prevalence of psychiatric and physical morbidity in an urban geriatric population, *Indian Journal of Psychiatry, 53*(2): 121-127.

Sheehan, H.E. (2009). Medical pluralism in India: Patient choice or no other option?, *Indian Journal of Medical Ethics, 6*(3): 138-141.

Srinivasan, T.N. and R. Thara (2001). Beliefs about causation of schizophrenia: Do Indian families believe in supernatural causes?, *Social Psychiatry and Psychiatric Epidemiology, 36*: 134-40.

Subba, S.H., V.S. Binu, M.S. Kotian, N. Joseph, A.B. Mahamood, N. Dixit, A. George, P. Kumar, S. Acharya and P. Reddy (2012). Future specialization interests among medical students in Southern India, *The National Medical Journal of India, 25*(4): 226-229.

Thacore, V.R., and S.C. Gupta. (1978). Faith healing in a north Indian city. *International Journal of Social Psychiatry, 24*(4): 235-240.

Thirunavukarasu, M. and P. Thirunavukarasu (2010). Training and national deficit of psychiatrists in India: A critical analysis, *Indian Journal of Psychiatry, 52*(7): 83-88.

Turner, R.L. (2008). *A comparative dictionary of the Indo-Aryan languages* (Volume 1). Motilal Banarsidass, New Delhi.

Venkatashiva Reddy, B., A. Gupta, A. Lohiya and Pardip Kharya (2013). Mental health issues and challenges in India: A review, *International Journal of Scientific and Research Publications, 3*(2): 1-3.

World Health Organisation (2011). *Mental Health Atlas*. World Health Organisation, Geneva.

World Health Organisation (2015). *The ICD-10 classification of mental and behavioural disorders*. World Health Organisation, Geneva.

10

The Disease, Diseased and Solution: Exploring Addiction as Madness

Sneha Gupta

Introduction

Freedom is just a word now which can grab everybody's attention. Travelling from the age of early man to modern man has cost us our freedom. A virtue that was functional in practice got embedded into theory. The evolution of identity has evolved into identity crises and the worst entangling of identity can be seen in people suffering from psychiatric illness and addiction disease. Although when referred in a lay-man language these people are called as mad and insane, respectively. The two major works done on madness and addiction by two pioneer thinkers Foucault and De Leon respectively will help to renovate the concept of contemporary freedom. Therapeutic Community (TC) at functional level has lots of caveats which can be eliminated with the understanding of Foucault concept of madness and freedom.

Part I: Understanding Madness and Addiction

The comparison of two different times and two different works which shows certain similarities between organizations formed to tame madness as described by Foucault and addiction TC conceptualized by De Leon in practice.

"Seventeenth century created enormous houses of confinement which seemed to assign the same homeland to the poor, to the unemployed, to prisoners and to the insane. These places were referred to as houses of correction which established order and work for welfare measures. Further investigations into these houses reveals that the same walls could contain those condemned by common law, young men who disturbed their families' peace or who squandered their goals, people without profession and the insane" (Foucault, 1989: 35, 36, 40, 41). These words used by Foucault described to a great extent about the functionality of contemporary TCs as the same kind of heterogeneity could be seen where the staff got uncontrolled natural power in the garb of welfare, correction, morality to change the person. The origin of this uncontrolled yet justifiable power could be traced in the written philosophy of TC which permits giving consequence to addicts to develop consequence thinking and many other such measures. It is important to mention here that theoretically TCs are well framed measures to curb addiction but unfortunately its implication depends upon the person who demands respect for addicts but forget themselves to give one. Coming to Foucault second description which is about idleness that "from the beginning, the institution set itself the task of preventing mendicancy and idleness as the source of all disorders" (Foucault, 1989: 43). Similar thinking can be seen in TCs where addicts are kept busy all day in work as the concept of TCs says that everything should be done by the members only and nobody from outside whether cooking, cleaning, keeping records etc. It appears to be a very efficient way of keeping addicts busy but when seen in practice it is more like turning addicts into servants where staff have all the rights to make them do any work in the name of treatment. Both houses of confinement and TCs have served a new solution where negative measures of exclusion were replaced by a measure of confinement. As said by Foucault, "the unemployed person was no longer driven away or punished, he was taken in charge, at the expense of the nation but at the cost of his individual liberty. Between him and society, an implicit system of obligation was established. He had the right to be fed but he must accept the physical and moral constraint of confinement" (Foucault, 1989: 44, 45). Addicts are no more excluded instead they are send to TCs for treatment where outsiders think that they are bearing the expense of keeping him included but it is his "addicts" freedom which is the biggest cost. He has to change himself morally as per the terms laid by staff and family to retain freedom and space in society. This conversion is a very responsible process where staff and family have to make lots of effort keeping individual in mind. But unfortunately what happens is exactly reverse of it with a series of blaming and favours done to him. With irresponsible implication of TCs measures, this new solution has turned into new problem in addict's life. This wrong treatment by staff and negative attitude of family create more identity disorder due to harm done to an individual self-respect and freedom which are perhaps the most important virtue of one's life. To sum up this whole series of comparison with some more lines by Foucault which ironically also characterize contemporary TCs:

- "Houses of confinement plays double role to reabsorb employment or at least eliminate its most visible social effects" (Foucault, 1989: 50).
- "Measured by their functional value alone, the creation of the houses of confinement can be regarded as a failure" (Foucault, 1989: 51).
- "An important phenomenon, this invention of a site of constraint, where morality castigates by means of administrative enforcement" (Foucault, 1989: 56).
- "It must not be despaired of correcting the man who has strayed" (Foucault, 1989: 59).
- "Confinement represents in the form of an authoritarian model" (Foucault, 1989: 59).

TCs absorb addicts who are of no use to family and society while eliminating problems of social stigma with other social effects. They are made correct or to say made to do anything and everything through TCs functional authoritarian model. Therefore, it is not wrong to say that TCs are functional failure which could also be the reason behind its low recovery rate. The question that arises is: If TC is failure then why these intuitions are flourishing more than ever now? The answer is hidden into two things, first more number of people falling into the trap of substance abuse and addiction. Second, the whole reason of not being able to recover is seen in the individual rather than in any other thing. But, it is important to take into account that TCs do not have neutral effect on addict where if it is neither doing any good to him nor any harm. It contains the potential of doing great amount of welfare but the practice in reality is showing the great amount of injury done to the individuality and identity of a person which largely goes unnoticed.

As explained by Foucault that "the mad man had become a social individual, it was the first time that anyone had entered into conversation with him and that once again, he was questioned (Foucault, 1989: 190). The birth and spread of TC has turned the addiction madness into a social disease thereby giving opportunity to an addict once again to become a social individual rather than left isolated in his own world of addicted substances. This social virtue at the cost of his individual liberty is for good or worse is a big question. But one thing that cannot be denied is the shift from absolute ignored freedom to absolute ignored constraint.

As discussed above, the two—Madness and Addiction has travelled a long journey from in-house exclusion to outhouse inclusion and achieving the tag of disease. With all the illusionary achievements that can boost about the unfortunate truth is the worst affected part of both the diseases is THOUGHTS. As cited by Foucault, "I can easily conceive of a man without hands, feet, and head. But I cannot conceive of man without thought; that would be a stone or a brute" (Foucault, 1989: 66). It is their thoughts which get disoriented to such an extent that they started living in illusionary world where consequence thinking exists in its most diminished form. These disoriented thoughts determine their behaviour which seems to be the symptoms of madness and addiction. Foucault talked about the fundamental role of passion, citing it "as a more constant, more persistent and somehow more deserved cause of madness" (Foucault, 1989: 80). Passion is an undeniable reason for onset of substance abuse and addiction. There is a very thin line between passion and addiction where former is a very thoughtful positive process of surrendering yourself but latter is "the result of our blind surrender to our desires, our incapacity to control or to moderate our passions" (Foucault, 1989: 80). Crossing of that thin line results into diminished consequence analysis where "external objects do not produce the same impression on the sufferer's mind as on that of a healthy man; his impressions are weak and he rarely pays attention to them, his mind is almost totally absorbed by the vivacity of certain ideas which are his illusionary imaginations" (Foucault, 1989: 86). "Madness is no more than the derangement of the imagination" (Foucault, 1989: 87), and similar can be said about addiction. Therefore, the terms often associated with substance use disorder are delirium, illusions, hallucinations etc.

Imagination is the ground where madness and addiction found absolute freedom. "Still imagination is not madness, madness begins only beyond this point, when the mind binds itself to this arbitrariness and becomes a prisoner of this apparent liberty" (Foucault, 1989: 88). Whether healthy, mad, addict, all can imagine that they are dead but affirmation to this imagination makes all the difference. Therefore, both madness and addiction begins only in the act which gives the value of truth to the image (Foucault, 1989). An addict has a passion towards his substance of choice and even getting harmed by it, he kept on imagining that it is not causing any harm rather people around him are the reason behind everything. When the person succumbs to his imagination and takes his substance of choice in spite of damage, that act symbolizes him as addict. Passion, imagination and act, when all used in a combination without consequence thinking leads to destruction of one's own self and to a terrible state of addiction and madness. Both these diseases toil in one's thoughts which create an image that mind is incapable of escaping, therefore, very aptly put by Foucault that "madness is nonetheless more than imagination forming an act of undetermined content" (Foucault, 1989: 89).

Part II: Space or No Space

"At once, so great was the confusion of those years; so difficult was it, at the moment when "humanity" was being re-evaluated to determine the place madness was to occupy with in it; so difficult was it to situate madness in a social sphere that was being restructured" (Foucault, 1989: 228). Today, humans are living in a fast growing world of substance abuse and addiction. The time is quite appropriate to talk about the place occupied by *Homo addictus* in contemporary social structure. Addicts were there in society but not a part of social structure. This invisibility of addicts in social structure has brought with itself a need for philanthropic approach. With this comes the introduction of second pioneer named De Leon who is largely responsible for bringing a new wave of philanthropic treatment termed as Therapeutic community. The words used by Foucault will best describe physicality of today's TCs, "the houses of confinement are no longer with bars, grills on the windows but large farms surrounded by a great, walled garden" (Foucault, 1989: 230). This is the picture of contemporary TCs.

Therapeutic Community as Visualized by De Leon

"Therapeutic community is a self-help group with systematic methodology for transforming lives and understanding the disorder which lies with the person and not with the drugs" (De Leon, 2000: 20, 57, 58). Drug intake is only the act (Foucault term) or to say symptom (De Leon term) of disorder. The real problem lies in thoughts not behaviour which has to be changed for wholesome and long term recovery. TC has a very unusual way of bringing change in thoughts by emphasizing on behaviours. It is a very well justified way because it is not possible to know about what going on inside person in a short span of 3 to 6 months. On the contrary, behaviour is a visible part which is worked upon believing that if thoughts affect behaviour so *vice versa* also occur. This is a very delicate process which should be done with utmost care.

Guilt and Responsibility: There is a very slight apparent difference between making a person guilty and making him responsible but the inner effect it does is very big. Both Foucault and De Leon emphasize on responsibility in place of guilt as reflected in following words:

- "The obscure guilt that once linked transgression and unreason is thus shifted; the madman, as a human being originally endowed with reason, is no longer guilty of being mad; but the mad man, as a madman and in the interior of that disease of which he is no longer guilty, must feel morally responsible for everything within him that may disturb morality and society, and must hold no one but himself responsible" (Foucault, 1989: 234).
- "In their many and varied reasons for using drugs, substance abusers deny or do not accept their own contributions to their problems, nor do they fully recognize their own potential for the solutions. Essential element of the disorder is the failure of individuals to take responsibility for their decisions and actions" (De Leon, 2000: 59, 60).

TC understands the reality behind addict's behaviour which can never be realized by family members and the person himself while living in outside world. It is a disease where the person view got severely affected due to impaired skills. They do not recognize or fail to consider how their actions affect others or how the behaviour of others affects them along with impaired judgement skills in problem-solving, decision-making, assessment of consequences, poor impulse control and an inability to delay gratification. They do not see themselves, others, or circumstances as they actually are with the unwillingness to confront the everyday issue of their lives and tend to avoid or escape these in their thinking and behaviour. They do not understand the relationship between their drug thoughts or actions and the various emotions and circumstances that serve as cues or triggers for these (De Leon, 2000). It is very important to make them feel responsible for all these things but not to be held guilty because "addicts are already plagued by various feelings of guilt and shame which is most destructive for them" (De Leon, 2000: 71). In TC, recovery begins with behaviour change as expressed in common TC axioms "Act as if" or "Do it right, then you'll understand why you've been doing it wrong." Addicts are made to understand the reason behind their thoughts and behaviour while making them enabled to recognize the triggers to their drug use (De Leon, 2000: 89, 90). As addiction is a disease of thoughts reflecting in behaviour so TC is a treatment of behaviour with change reflecting in thoughts. The only reason behind repeating some of the lines from De Leon's book is to represent the goodness and human nature of TC treatment and no other treatment can provide a person plagued with dismantle identity, an altogether new identity.

Part III: Therapeutic Community: A Boon or a Bane?

Addiction is something that an addict thinks is in his control but at the same time it is something not in his control unconsciously. The gap between this unconscious and conscious is bridged by de-addiction-*cum*-rehabilitation centre where addicts are brought forcibly (most of the time) to change their habitus of behaviour associated with substance abuse or better called as substance use disorder as the latter term reduces the stigma attached to it to certain extent in theory. It was a choice of a person to induce substance into their life but eventually it becomes a tacit activity where an addict induces substance of their choice (SOC) due to habitus but they are brought to rehab to change that habitus.

Patients[1] in Therapeutic Community: Active or Passive Members

Yash, age: 75 years, SOC: alcohol, Period of stay in the centres: 9+ years

> I took alcohol in the form of beer for the first time at the age of sixteen when I was a student in an institute teaching brewing technology. The whole class was taken to the alcohol factory for educational visit where I tasted my substance of choice for first time. I like the after effects of having it and then I started taking occasionally. I was always surrounded by alcohol because of my working environment. Gradually, I became addicted to alcohol and from past nine years my son has admitted me into one centre after another.

One drink as a part of study has brought him to this condition where he has not seen outside world for almost a decade. In the name of treatment, his son has left him in centres because nobody believes him. The whole TC philanthropic approach has been turned into money business where in exchange of money one can keep other person captive and addict has no say in it.

Rohan, age: 40 years, SOC: cannabis, Period of stay in the centre: 3+ years

> I took tobacco at the age of twelve from my father's pocket. Within one year of this I started taking cannabis product with friends. I belong to a small village where cannabis is easily available at tea shops. I also started drinking alcohol occasionally in parties and functions. I took cannabis and alcohol simultaneously for twenty four years.

It has been more than three years and his family members have not come even once to meet him. It seems like treatment is a good way of getting rid of these people.

Abdul, age: 26, SOC: cannabis product, Period of stay in the centre: 2+ years

> I am a refugee from Afghanistan and came to India because of threat to my life. I felt very lonely here away from my family. I made some friends here who asked me to take drugs in order to forget all kinds of problems. I want to study further and go out of India to USA or Canada but was not getting help from UNHCR. Therefore, I tried to commit suicide. Due to this attempt I was brought to the centre.

He is not an addict but a problematic user who has this escaping tendency in the form of drugs and suicide. He is in the centre for more than a year and it seems to having done more harm to him rather than any good. Therefore, time period is very important, one should not be kept inside for more than six months.

Devansh, age: 45 years, SOC: heroin, Period of stay in the centres: 10+ years

> I started smoking at the age of fourteen and then after four years I started consuming cannabis out of curiosity which was told to me by seniors in college. I kept taking alcohol side by side and gradually shifted to higher forms of drugs. Lastly, I ended up being an addict of heroin.

He is there in the centres from last ten years and finally got absorbed in the centre as a cook. His family has left him in the centre and come only to collect his salary once a month. The need was to rehabilitate him into the society and not in the centre.

Rehaan, age: 23, SOC: cannabis products, Period of stay in the centre: 3+ years

> I have taken various cannabis products for a period of three years. I started with cigarette at the age of seventeen because my friends told me to try it once and then became regular with it. I was twenty when my family told me about this centre and I agreed to come here as they told me it is for four-five months. But, I am here for more than three years and want to go home.

He has spent more time in a de-addiction centre as compared to the time spend in addiction. His brother comes every month to meet him and also wants him to get well. But the staff always says "his condition is worse than before or he is not showing any improvement." The point here is one cannot keep a person locked in the centre for so long because others think his improvement is zero. It is the responsibility of treatment staff and here they act as passive part with patient as active part and it is his mistake. But when views are taken, it is staff which is active part and patient being passive. There has to be a right amount of balance in it of shared responsibility and shared opinions. TCs were made with the aim to serve addicts but under the garb of it, motive of family members and centre owners are getting fulfilled. This raises a very alarming yet unfortunate question—what is doing more harm ADDICTION or ADDICTION TCs? Having said that, the intention is not to point towards universality of the above mentioned pattern on the part of TC owners, staff and family members but to put light on suffering of people due to misuse of TC model, if the recovery of one day and one person matters so as the suffering of one person. As rightly said by Strang (1992) "perhaps the bad results of treatment may be no more than the results of bad treatment" (p. 972).

This is where critical medical anthropology can contribute significantly by shaping treatment or so-called solution not only from the eyes of health care providers but also from the experiences of those who are receiving it.

Recent Evolution in Medical Anthropology

"Anthropologists have been interested in medical practices for many decades; however medical anthropology as a distinct subfield is a relative newcomer in the world of academia" (Campbell, 2010: 76). Therapeutic community treatment turned from boon to bane because of inadequate treatment. There is need to focus on treatment givers' and treatment receivers' interaction and anthropology can be used as a tool for this. Critical medical anthropology calls for merging of theory and practice to promote experiential health as opposed to functional health (Baer, 1990). It is extremely important to put focus on the experiences of patients to bring out critical perspective. As stated by Scheper-Hughes (1990: 196) that it is "imperative to position ourselves squarely on the side of human suffering". Anthropology's distinct character as integrated, critical, holistic and qualitative makes it a very potent force in encouraging public health by bridging the gap between treatment and its practice (Campbell, 2010). The humane nature of anthropology as a discipline contains the great potential for understanding and renovating the disease, the diseased person and the solution.

Conclusion

To sum up the whole discussion with Foucault lines aptly suitable to addiction illness. "It is a modern tragedy with irreversible interiority of passion and unfulfilled desire, a disease of sensibility which is no longer controlled by the movement of nature, but by all the habits, all the demands of social life" (Foucault, 1989: 203, 207). To an addict, "everything seems without sentiment and without life, because they are trying to find out what does not exist in nature" (Foucault, 1989: 208). With all these characteristics of an addict, "it is neither reasonable enough not to be confined, nor wise enough not to be treated as wicked, it is all too true that those who have lost the use of reason must be hidden from society" (Foucault, 1989: 216), sometimes as forbidden figures in home and other time as forbidden figures in centres. The only question left is—These addiction stuck people have lost the sensibility of thoughts but what made non-addicted one so insensible and thoughtless to behave like this? Lastly as Foucault said "Confinement is open to criticism because of the repercussions it can have..." (Foucault, 1989: 221). Therefore, limit the confinement to the right amount, to the right degree and to the right treatment.

Beginning with freedom and ending with confinement seems unjust to the whole argument of revamping disease, sufferers and treatment but unfortunately there is no other way of bringing real freedom in their life as said one has to see for opportunity in adversity. Addiction is an unconscious part of addict's life where unknowingly it gives a new imagination to the person. Unfortunately, it is a disease of being unaware and unconscious of that new imagination which is causing damage. He became conscious of this only when he came to a rehab where he accepted the identity of an addict which he shared with many others like him and become part of that group. This change from unconscious to conscious is the first step towards rehabilitation where he knows with whom he has to fight to win....

NOTE

1. Pseudonyms are used to maintain anonymity.

Abbreviations

SOC:	Substitute of Choice
TC:	Therapeutic Community
UNHCR:	United Nations High Commissioner for Refugees

REFERENCES

Baer, Hans. (1990). "The possibilities and dilemmas of building bridges between critical medical anthropology and clinical anthropology: A discussion." *Social Science of Medicine, 30*(9), 1011-1013. Retrieved from: https://doi.org/10.1016/0277-9536(90)90147-K

Campbell, Dave. (2010). "Anthropology's contribution to public health policy development." *McGill Journal of Medicine, 13*(1), 76-81. Retrieved from: https://www.ncbi.nlm.nih.gov/pmc/articles/PMC3277334/

De Leon, G. (2000). *The therapeutic community, theory, model and method* [kindle Version]. Retrieved from: https://play.google.com/books/purchases

Foucaut, M. (1989). *Madness and civilization: A history of insanity in the age of reason*. New York: Vintage Books.

Scheper-Hughes, Nancy. (1990). "Three propositions for a critically applied medical anthropology." *Social Science in Medicine, 30*(2), 189-197. Retrieved from: http://digitalassets.lib.berkeley.edu/anthpubs/ucb/text/kas069_070-006.pdf

Strang, J. (1992). "The fifth Thomas James Okey memorial lecture: Research and practice: The necessary symbiosis." *British Journal of Addiction*, 87, 967-986. Retrieved from: https://www.ncbi.nlm.nih.gov/pubmed/1643405

11

Militarization and Mental Distress in Jammu & Kashmir

Chakraverti Mahajan

Medical Anthropology of Conflict and Militarization

For decades, medical anthropology has carried the responsibility of understanding the linkages between human health and its social, cultural and biological determinants. The discipline has documented the experience and distribution of illness, the prevention, and treatment of sickness, healing processes, the social relations of therapy management, and the cultural importance and utilization of pluralistic medical systems (Society for Medical Anthropology, 2017). However, for some reason, medical anthropology has not generated enough scholarship on the linkage between human health and wartime realities. The impact of continuous and prolonged conflict on the physical, social and mental fabric of societies is an area which has not received enough attention by medical anthropologists. Similar observation was made by Marcia Inhorn in 2008 during her presidential address at Society for Medical Anthropology, where she heralded that medical anthropology and medical anthropologists had "turned away from the brutal realities, the embodied suffering, the psychological devastation, the sexual violence, and the refugee aftermath of wars" (Inhorn, 2008: 421). She challenged the 'new millennium' generation of medical anthropologists to take a stand against war by revealing its harmful effects. A year before that, Gusterson (2007) tried to ascertain the relationship between anthropology, colonialism, and militarism. Explaining the complex relationship, he pointed out that war and militarism has a similar relationship as anthropology has with colonialism (*ibid.*). He remarked that the choice of research topics and access to the field for the earlier generation of anthropologists was shaped by colonialism but colonialism itself was 'rarely brought into focus as a topic of ethnographic research or reflexive self-questioning' (2008:156). In a similar way, he stated, anthropology has been "more or less subtly moulded by the priorities of the national security state and the exigencies of other peoples' wars, but until recently, anthropologists have written little about militarism or international conflict" (*ibid.*).

What is more noteworthy is that the nature of armed conflict and wars has changed substantially over time, both in terms of causality and casualty. "Wars today take a different form than in the past and most strategic analysts agree that in the second half of the 20th century, contemporary wars are less of a problem of relations between states than a problem within states" (Pederson, 2002: 176). The contemporary wars, or the "wars of the third kind" (Rice, 1988) are local in nature and often termed as 'low-intensity warfare'. It is the warfare where the "local population and not the territory is the target for psychological warfare, terrorisation, and other traumatic experiences" (Pederson, 2002: 176). Such a type of warfare is taking place across nations and the number is alarmingly high. These conflicts, irrespective of where they are taking place, bring "suffering and illness, revealed both in very direct ways like visible wounds, severed limbs, or dead bodies, but also in innumerable indirect ways: somatic expressions of fear, exposure, and vulnerability" (Henry, 2006: 391). Even a fleeting look at the existing literature suggests that not enough attention has been paid to the "local patterns of distress being experienced and the long-term health impact and psychosocial consequences of the various forms of political violence against individuals, communities, or specific ethnic groups" (*ibid.*:182).

While work on war and mental health of those ravaged by it is beginning to catch the attention of anthropologists around the world, the awakening has been painstakingly slow in the Indian context. The only significantly visible work contributed in the field is of Saiba Verma (2012; 2018) who has focused upon the conflict-ridden region of Jammu & Kashmir. Her work is grounded in medical and cultural anthropology where she draws together the psychological and political to understand how mental health is understood, explained and treated in the region of Jammu & Kashmir. Using relevant literature, surveys and analyzing them together the present chapter also takes the case of Jammu & Kashmir to establish how prolonged conflict has left its mark upon the social and mental fabric of a community and its people. After establishing the deteriorating status of mental health in the region, the chapter attempts to explain the causative factors using the concept of 'ecology of suffering'

(Jadhav *et al.*, 2015). The concept of "ecology of suffering" facilitates the understanding that militarization of the region by Indian state has aggravated the existing 'social stressors' and created a 'mental health emergency' in the region. In order to understand how this "ecology" is created in Jammu & Kashmir, a brief understanding of militarism and militarization is presented.

Militarization is a "larger phenomenon than war...which can be practiced during times of peace and (it can) be part of institutions and structures not directly concerned with war" (Chenoy, 1998: 101). Today, militarization is an integral part of the global society. It can be seen around the world in the form of "standing armies, paramilitaries, military contractors, the stockpiling of weaponry, burgeoning state surveillance programmes and the circulation of militarized imagery in popular culture" (Gusterson, 2007). In other words, it is the "domination of the military over the civilian, an undue preponderance of military demand, and emphasis on military considerations, spirits, ideals, and scales of value, in the life of states" (Vagts, 1959: 14). Chenoy has (1998) differentiated between militarization and militarism. In her words, "militarization is the process that emphasizes the use of coercive structures and practices and militarism is the ideology that valorizes and glorifies such reliance and practice" (1998:101). She explained militarization as a social process and militarism as a worldview. In case of Jammu & Kashmir, which is the northern-most region of Indian state, militarization was achieved through military presence and heavy surveillance. The armed conflict in Jammu & Kashmir began in the year 1989. However, the reasons for such an insurgency were drawn from long-term political and ideological differences between Kashmiri aspirations and the Indian state.

Jammu & Kashmir Timeline of Major Events[1]

1845-1946	Kashmir as a Princely State
1946	Political Unrest in Kashmir
1947	Partition of India Kashmir's invasion Kashmir's accession to India
1948	India raises Kashmir issue in the UN Security Council, Resolution 47
1951	Elections held in J & K
1957	Constitution of J & K framed as a part of India
1962	Indo-China war over Aksai Chin region
1965	Indo-Pakistan war

(Contd.)

1971-72	Indo-Pakistan War in East Pakistan (Bangladesh), Simla Agreement
1987	Disputed State elections and pro-independence insurgency
1990	Armed Forces Special Powers Act (AFSPA) imposed in J & K
1999	Indo-Pak War
2001	Attack on the assembly of Indian-administered Jammu & Kashmir in Srinagar
2010	Protests erupt in the Kashmir Valley after a demonstrator is killed by the Indian Army.
2013	Kashmiri Jaish-e-Mohammed member Mohammad Afzal Guru hanged over the role in 2001 Indian Parliament terror attack, prompting protests in which two young men were killed.
2015	Muslim separatist leaders in Kashmir close shops, businesses, and government departments in protest at the enforcement of a colonial-era ban on eating beef.
2016	The killing of Burhan Wani, a popular militant and top commander of the Hizbul Mujahideen group sparks violent protests.

The insurgency movement against the Indian State first gained strength in the Kashmir Valley and eventually spread to the Jammu region as well. Acts of violence such as killings, attacks on state-owned buildings, bombings were carried out by militants in an attempt to establish their rule in the region. This led to mobilisation of huge army troops in the region by the Indian government. The Indian state attempted to snuff out the movement using brutal force to gain control and administer the region. Killings, encounters, and conflicts multiplied, bringing the locals in direct contact with it. The conflict has raged on for more than three decades now and shows no signs of ending anytime soon. The militarization of the region has also steadily increased and the number of security personnel deployed in the region has been on the mount. As early as in 1997, it was reported in the report titled 'Wounded Valley Shattered Souls' that Kashmir has one military person per seven Kashmiris, making it "one of the most heavily militarized places in the world" (Duschinski, 2009: 703).

Militarism is often found in amalgamation with nationalist ideologies in variable and complex ways. In the state of Jammu & Kashmir, it is well documented. Indian Government uses the rhetoric "Kashmir is an integral part of India" to justify its actions in the region. Chenoy (1998) has provided that "non-state actors are also sites and agencies for militarization" (1998:102). Movements which are secessionist, communal or sectarian can advocate or pursue militarist methods and practices. Another important feature of militarization is that it "can exist in select and isolated regions within states at specific times, coinciding with normalcy elsewhere" (*ibid.*). The observation sits perfectly in the case of Jammu & Kashmir where the degree of militarization varies both at an intra-state level and inter-state level. For example, militarization in Kashmir is heavier as compared to the Jammu or Ladakh region. It is on account of comparative normalcy observed in the regions.

This chapter discusses mental health in conflict zones and points to the lack of medical anthropologists in conflict zone studies. Using the concept of "ecology of suffering" (Jadhav *et al.,* 2015), it is argued that individual mental suffering is tied to a wide range of local factors. The concept of "ecology of suffering" in Jammu & Kashmir is given substance by analyzing the existing literature on the subject matter. Jadhav *et al.* (2015) stated that "each person's suffering occurs within a specific ecology", a network of interrelated forces with variable directionality." It is argued in this chapter that the "ecology" in Jammu & Kashmir is created by the combined factors of living in tough terrain, poor employment opportunities, chronic conflict and militarization of the region. These factors together create a condition of perpetual suffering for the people which translates into a highly poor mental health situation in the region.

The chapter is divided into three sections. The first section deals with mental health and highlights how conflict and militarization have a negative impact on mental health. The second section presents the mental health scenario in Jammu & Kashmir. The third section argues about the need for medical anthropologists to explore more conflict-ridden regions in the country.

I
MENTAL HEALTH IN CONFLICT ZONES

Mental health, as defined by World Health Organization (WHO), represents "a state of well-being in which every individual realizes his or her own potential, can cope with the normal stresses of life, can work productively and fruitfully, and is able to make a contribution to her or his community." It further lists the determinants of mental health stating that multiple social, psychological, and biological factors determine the level of mental health of a person at any point in time. For example, violence and persistent socio-economic pressures are recognized risks to mental health. Poor mental health is also associated with rapid social change, stressful work conditions, gender discrimination, social exclusion, unhealthy lifestyle, physical ill-health, and human rights violations. WHO states that war and disasters have a large impact on mental health and psychological well-being and rates of mental disorders tend to double after emergencies.[2]

Inhorn (2008) observed that definitions of war, conflict, armed struggle, and revolution are imprecise and depend heavily on the vantage point of those doing the fighting. In her essay on 'Medical Anthropology Against War', while focusing on the war in Iraq and Afghanistan, she brought to light the mental health crisis in conflict-ridden countries. As reported by Chambers (2018), almost half of children surveyed in their research said they felt grief, and more than 80 per cent of young people aged 13 to 17 said that they did not feel safe walking alone. Since the U.S. invasion, cases of post-traumatic stress disorder (PTSD) increased by 35 per cent, particularly following some of the major battles and explosions that devastated urban neighbourhoods in Iraq (Tarabay, 2006). Martín-Baró (1989) iterated that social disturbances correspond to personal and somatic disturbances, and this can develop into the complex forms of psychotic alienation which is observed in some youth in the populations of conflictive areas. Arcel and Kastrup (2004) observed that a single factor creating long-lasting physical and mental health problems in women was sexualized violence and rape of women before, during and after an armed conflict. They reported that if diagnosed by psychiatrists and psychologists, sexually traumatized women in armed conflicts will often get the diagnosis of post-traumatic stress disorder. Panter-Brick *et al.* (2009) conducted a survey in Kabul and found that "consistent with other published research on war zones, exposure to traumatic events was strongly associated with mental health outcomes." They observed that experience of five or more traumatic events trebled the risk of probable psychiatric disorders and post-traumatic stress, also increasing depression symptoms in the children. Roberts *et al.* (2009) in his study of post-conflict Sudan had also established how experiences of violence result in increased rates of mental disorders.

Rozanov *et al.* (2019) have presented a detailed analysis of the consequences of war conflicts on the mental health of individuals. It has been noted by them that, traditionally, the impact of war conflicts on humans has been measured in terms of mortality. But, in contemporary times, where the nature of war and conflict has transformed into "local, low-intensity, surrogate, terroristic and information wars" mortality alone is not enough measure of the harmful effects of war. "The present wars are associated with less direct mortality but with growing and long-lasting mental health consequences" (2019 : 282). As Rozanav *et al.* (2019) further describe the consequences of war on mental health, they note that these consequences are found in both the sides, i.e. the military personnel involved in the conflict and the civilian populations. It also presents a detailed account of conflict-related psychological suffering in military personnel and methods used to overcome such negative consequences. However, it has also been noted that the mental health consequences are higher and graver in civilian populations as they are untrained for dealing with situations that arise in conflict-ridden areas. Civilians always suffer immensely during wartime, and it has been observed that unlike the wars of the past, civilians are the main target of violence in present-time wars. In previous wars, 90 per cent of casualties were military, while casualties in recent wars are 90 per cent civilians (Ugaide, 1999). This is especially true for mental health casualties and long-term mental health consequences.

Women and children are found to be at a greater risk of mental disorders, the severity of experienced stress correlating with psychological and psychiatric outcomes (Rozanov *et al.,* 2019). It was also reported that negative mental health effects can sometimes be transgenerational[3] as well.

Thus, it is not a matter of speculation that in times of conflict and war, the mental health of individuals suffer greatly. The repeated encounter with violence and terror begins to corrode the psyche of the people which is seen in terms of elevated levels of mental health distress. The impact of the conflict on mental health is always severe for those at the receiving end than those perpetrating it. In cases where militarization is a part of the cycle of violence and conflict, such as in Jammu & Kashmir, the impact on mental health can be unprecedented. Thus, in such types of low-intensity and persistent conflict zones, the role of medical anthropologists becomes indispensable to analyse the bearing on individual's and community's mental health.

II
MENTAL HEALTH IN JAMMU & KASHMIR

A long history of political instability in the state of Jammu & Kashmir has had a negative bearing on the social, economic and mental fabric of its people. This has led to an increase in the number of stressors affecting the everyday life and livelihood of the people of the region. For the last three decades, the valley has been a scene of heightened conflict between the military forces and the militants. Bomb attacks, shoot-outs, pressure from both sides have affected the daily lives of ordinary citizens. Violent incidents happen every now and then and the risk of getting caught in the crossfire is always present. Security concerns are a dominant theme in the minds of people living in the region. This owes to the fact that death, injury, and destruction of property is a notable feature of everyday life here, thus leading to the creation of "ecology of suffering" (Jadhav *et al.* 2015).

This "ecology" is created and persists through a vicious cycle of events comprising torture, disappearances, displacement, killings, ballistic trauma etc. parallelled by a state of mind wherein grieving, insecurity, oppression, poverty, uncertainties of career and relationships etc. are the major themes.

Kashmir Mental Health Survey Report, 2015

In the year 2015, Médecins Sans Frontières (MSF) in collaboration with the Institute of Mental Health and Neurosciences, Kashmir and Kashmir University conducted a mental health survey in Jammu & Kashmir. The survey (KMHS) was conducted in all ten districts of the Kashmir Valley and it serves to provide valuable information on the prevalence of mental distress in Kashmiri adults, as well as a record of community perceptions and knowledge of mental health and access to services in the Kashmir Valley. The survey revealed that people in the valley grapple with a number of problems in their everyday life. These problems vary from financial issues to poor physical health and unemployment. It was reported that one-third of Kashmiri men and nearly half of Kashmiri women suffered from poor physical health. This was common to all age groups, with the highest proportion in the 35-54 age groups. Both men and women stated unemployment as a significant problem in their daily life.

In order to cope with the stress of their daily life problems, people used to pray, talk to family members or friends and try to keep busy. Men and women utilized similar coping strategies in this case with the exception of using tobacco (21% men, 4% women) and visiting a mosque or shrine (12% men, 2% women). Apart from this, as already reported by some previous studies, substance abuse is present in the valley. The survey found that nearly 30 per cent of Kashmiri adults used tobacco in its various forms, and nearly half of all Kashmiri households stated that at least one person in their family used it. Using tobacco was one of the main coping strategies for men. Very few Kashmiris reported consuming alcohol, taking cannabis or opioids.

The survey found that the language of distress, in the region, is largely somatic, i.e. suffering is understood only in terms of physical symptoms. This is indicated by the fact that the survey found that nearly two-thirds of respondents reported having experienced headaches in the past four weeks, and a high proportion also indicated feelings of nervousness, tension and experiencing heart palpitations. The high reporting of physical symptoms in the survey was reflective of the more common somatic manifestation of mental distress in the Kashmiri population. People did not consider cognitive symptoms worthy of attention but somatic symptoms were viewed as legitimate (Varma, 2012).

The focus group discussions (FGDs) carried out during the survey showed that Kashmiris did not recognize cognitive, behavioural and social symptoms in terms of mental distress and their knowledge of services available for the treatment and management of mental illness was largely limited to a biomedical understanding of doctors and medicine. This biomedical understanding is combined with traditional approaches, such as seeking the guidance of a *pir* (spiritual healer). The *pir* is frequently the first point of care, as mentioned by the people in the survey. Participants in the survey had reported taking the affected individual to a *pir* (spiritual healer), or less commonly a *Hakeem* (traditional healer). The *pir* uses amulets, verses from the *Quran* and instructs the individual to perform *niyaaz* or *taweez* (ritual acts that will cure them). If treatment is unsuccessful with the *pir*, the family may seek out another *pir* or go to a hospital to see a doctor. Respondents reported that doctors give medicine and that they adhere to the treatment of both the doctor and the *pir*. While many reported visiting the *pir* first and then the doctor, the reverse was also true; when their symptoms were not relieved after visiting the doctor they would go to the *pir*. While the majority of participants in the survey referred to the *pir* and the doctor when asked about the services that were available for people with mental illness, in all focus groups carried out during the study someone would always refer to the 'mental hospital' or '*pagal khana*'. Little was known about other mental health services on offer. Some individuals mentioned 'tensionee' doctors, the English word tension being commonly used in Kashmir to describe all forms of stress and mental distress. Even though the 'mental hospital' was mentioned in all focus groups, it was largely a place people had just heard about rather than considered as an accessible service. It was often referred to as a last resort: when all other treatments and efforts had been exhausted the person would need to go to the 'mental hospital'.

Few participants had knowledge of specialist mental health service providers, beyond the 'mental hospital'. The survey presented a wide and detailed analysis of the mental health situation in Kashmir. However, it did not encompass the region of Jammu and refrained from analyzing the reasons behind such high rates of mental disorders in the valley. The survey report mentioned militant attacks and military crackdowns as reasons of trauma but it was done only in passing. The report abstained from closely analyzing and commenting on the impact of military presence on people's mental health.

Mental Health Crisis in Making

The KMHS report on the prevalence of mental health disorders in the region was a first of its kind, and a comprehensive survey study in terms of the number of individuals and number of parameters covered. However, there have been several more studies on mental health distress in the region, that have time and again tried to shed light on the existing and ever-growing mental health crisis in Jammu & Kashmir. Kumar (1999) had reported that overwhelming fear, uncertainty, and stress caused by the conflicts had led to a ten-fold increase in psychiatric disorders and the number of cases had risen from 1762 in 1990 to 17,584 in 1994. It was reported by Hassan and Shafi, 2013) that a lot of people suffer from stress (normal or related to a traumatic event) in the region and high amounts of psychosocial problems (substance abuse, distrust) are registered and disorders like anxiety, mood, and post-traumatic disorders are mounting (2013 : 105).

According to a nationwide survey conducted by the Ministry of Labour and Employment in 2012-2013, it was found that Jammu & Kashmir had the highest youth unemployment rate across India, with a high percentage of university graduates unemployed. The uncertain atmosphere in the state over the past 30 years has prevented outside investment. At the state level, the number of registered job seekers had increased by 190 per cent between 2008 and 2013. On the downside, the employment-generating sectors such as commercial agriculture, forestry, fisheries, and floriculture have been curtailed due to the prevailing political circumstances in the region. Where tourism was once the source of employment and economic growth, in the past 27 years it has become fractured and unreliable. In 2011, a Kashmir-based report by Mercy Corps reported risks associated with high youth unemployment, which included feelings of failure, isolation, lack of social status, delayed marriages and an increase in tensions among disenfranchised young people, all of which have been compounded by the impact of future uncertainty related to ongoing political conflict. Expressions of disappointment, anger, and hopelessness in addition to conflict-related stress, mental illness, suicide, and drug addiction have been reported as prevalent in Kashmir's youth (Kashmir Mental Health Survey, 2015). Media reports highlight the fact that Kashmir has one of the highest rates of post-traumatic stress disorder (PTSD) in the world, with approximately one-third of the population exhibiting traumatic symptoms (Matloff and Nickelsberg, 2008). Similarly, a 2006 report by Human Rights Watch entitled, "Everyone Lives in Fear", described an "epidemic of trauma" underway because of sustained human rights abuses. Kashmiri psychiatrists have also reported exponential increases in the number of patients visiting the only state-run psychiatric hospital in Kashmir, from 1,000 per year in 1989 to 1,00,000 per year in 2009.

Amin and Khan (2009) carried out a cross-sectional study of general population to determine characteristics of depression in Kashmir. The subjects were selected from both urban and rural areas of Kashmir from all the districts (except Ladakh). The results revealed that the prevalence of depression in respondent population was 55.72 per cent and it was highest in the 15-25 years age group. Hassan and Shafi (2013) reported that before the onset of militancy certain mental disorders, which were unknown to Kashmir, showed a phenomenal presence after the conflict. They reported that there was no case of Post Traumatic Stress Disorder (PTSD) before 1990 and this kind of disorder was completely unrecognized in Kashmiri society. But after the conflict situation, 15 to 20 per cent patients in the outpatient department (OPD) were suffering from this mental disorder, followed by Major Depressive Disorder. Mir and Joshi (2010) reported in their study that "adolescents who were affected by the militancy related traumatic events showed more psychological distress than their counterparts who had not been affected by the militancy directly" (2010:70).

The picture of mental distress in Jammu & Kashmir became clearer and a part of popular discourse by the end of twentieth century. A key feature of all the above-cited studies is that majority of them were carried out beginning from early 2000s. Researchers began to focus on the negative impacts of prolonged conflict on everyday life of the people and on physical and mental health. However, as mentioned beforehand, anthropologists arrived late on the scene and studies focusing on conflict zones have been sparse, more so in the South Asian part of the world. An exception to the rule is the work of Saiba Varma who has deeply studied the conflict zone of Jammu & Kashmir with respect to mental health status and provided anthropological insight to the overall situation in the region. Varma (2012) conducted extensive ethnographic research on the perceptions of psychosocial programmes in the Kashmir Valley. She identified the Kashmir valley as a zone of mass psychological suffering. In her chapter 'Where There are only Doctors: Counsellors as Psychiatrists in Indian-Administered Kashmir' she talked about the ongoing psychosocial intervention programmes being run by various non-governmental organizations. Varma used ethnographic material to showcase how the local staff negotiated with the cultural limitations of explaining and understanding technical mental health terminologies to the local patients, i.e. 'vernacularization of biomedicine'. In the chapter, Varma stated that biomedicine, having been already vernacularized—acts as a culturally familiar buffer to psychosocial knowledge, which is newer and less recognized among the Kashmiris. Talking about the training given to psychosocial workers by psychiatrists, Varma explained how the psychosocial counsellors were able to successfully diagnose the illness which later led them to the next two steps which were—"(mis)reading" the medical record, and then choosing technical, biomedical treatments, rather than psychosocial ones. Explaining the step two, i.e. "(mis)reading" the medical records, Varma observed that although the counsellors were unable to read or comment on patients' medical cards, they mimicked the reading practices of doctors because they recognized that it was an important step in the biomedical care for patients. They read the medical cards without any ability of comprehension. Varma explained this practice as an attempt by the counsellors to make non-biological, psychosocial interventions more legible to their patients who understood the biomedical model of treatment where reading the medical cards was a significant step. Talking about the illegibility of the concept of counselling in the Kashmiri context, Varma explained how the psychosocial counsellors themselves felt at times that their job was made more difficult by the fact that their patients did not understand the meaning of 'counselling' and how hard it was for them to explain to other Kashmiri people what they did for a living. Another challenging aspect for the counsellors was to translate technical, English-language concepts like "cognition" or "emotion" into Kashmiri or Urdu language for their patients, and ultimately they had given up on it. They continued to use the English terms. Explaining the third and the final step taken by the psychosocial counsellors where they acted as doctors, was the part where the counsellors considered biomedicine as the best and the most efficacious kind of treatment not just for their patients but in their personal lives as well. Saiba commented that such an approach to biomedicine situated the counsellors as a part of, rather than apart from, the individuals and communities who sought their help. She concluded in the chapter that, in Kashmir, the blending of the medical and psychosocial models of care is neither entirely accidental nor entirely designed; it is borne of individual practices and acts that attempt to respond to a powerful local ontology of medical care and illness. As a result, the medical model of care is sometimes gifted, other times smuggled in, and at still other times, downright demanded by the people.

In her another published work, Varma (2016) explored substance abuse in Kashmir and how patients at a Drug De-addiction Centre (DDC) learn to overcome their *nasha* with the help of biomedical and penitentiary techniques. DDC, where the research work was carried out, was located in the headquarters of Jammu & Kashmir Police Department. DDC majorly relied on group therapy sessions where the patients discussed and performed narratives of how they got their addiction and how the DDC helped them overcome their addiction. Saiba observed that the narratives often involved reveries of love and heartbreak which the patients used to negotiate and justify their addiction. However, the narratives provided by the patients at DDC differed in public and private space. In the group sessions, the patients offered a narrative where they seemed to have understood their past 'mistakes' of drug use and expressed gratitude to the DDC for their help. But, in more private moments, the patients, particularly those who identified as Sufis, narrated reveries of romantic love in which they understood their drug use and pasts in radically different ways from the DDC's clinicians. They viewed the intoxication (*nasha*) as a valuable experience that allowed them to maintain temporal and phenomenological links with their past selves and behaviours, and, in contrast to public recovery narratives, absolved themselves of responsibility for their addictions. Varma explained how the *nasha* offered the patients a discursive and experiential capsule through which they could express and recast illicit experiences of drug use, love, madness, and jealousy that are thick with emotion, deeply painful, and otherwise intangible. Its presence—along with the durability of love reveries—showed how patients have alternative therapeutic and narrative resources than those that the clinic authorized.

In Varley and Varma (2018), the authors used a jinneaological approach to study the chronically ill mental patients in the state hospital in Gilgit Town of Pakistan-controlled Kashmir and in a psychiatric hospital in Srinagar, Indian-administered Kashmir. A jinneaological approach provided them an alternative to the theories of abandonment that have become hegemonic in medical anthropology. Within the study, the authors equated the severely mentally ill patients with *jinns* and argued that like *jinn*, they are a separate species of being, different from other humans. They tried to explain how ill patients and human others are intimately related to each other. The study brought forth a narrative of state neglect, institutionally forgotten experiences and sectarian violence. This was achieved through the ethnographic study of the mental institutions and how the severely ill mental patients were viewed and treated by the doctors, the staff at the institutions and by the public at large.

In her more recent publication, Varma (2018) looked into the recognition of mental health consequences in Kashmir valley and through her work she observed how trauma and PTSD are being used beyond clinical diagnosis. She cited that "the term 'trauma' has rhetorical power in Kashmir, but its analytical power is diluted due to its multiple, varying usages" (2018 : 131). In the recent decade, mental health is being identified as a key component in the medical humanitarianism efforts in Kashmir. This involves efforts by both international and national organizations and the state and the union government. Varma observed that "the recognition of trauma and PTSD in Kashmir can be partly attributed to the global trends in medical humanitarianism, but the shift from the language of terror to that of trauma is also shaped by local and national politics" (2018:130). Through her chapter, she raised critical anthropological questions about "the implications of using trauma and PTSD to make political claims, including when trauma therapies are imagined by the state as alternatives to political solutions." After narrating the proliferation of mental health cases in the region, the chapter discussed how the Indian state institutions were working with international and national organizations on mental health projects and this resulted into "depoliticizing the efforts carried out by these organizations and transforming political agitators into medical victims" (2018: 137). This is followed by a critical reflection of trauma as a marker of human rights violations where trauma is "a rhetorical tool used by the political establishment to assert empathy with victims of violence and to underscore the long-term and insidious effects of occupation" (2018:135). The chapter shows how human rights activists have used trauma and PTSD as evidence of the ongoing brutality of Indian occupation and how the Indian state has used medical humanitarian techniques to justify and soften its ongoing military rule. The Indian government has initiated a number of "healing touch" policies to humanize its presence in the region. The 'winning hearts and minds' and other psychological initiatives are being run by the government which Varma highlights are "directly shaped by the interests of the Indian state and military" (2018:142). In the last segment, she showed how the doctors and psychiatrists are using trauma and PTSD to find global recognition and legitimize the status of Kashmiris as sufferers under Indian occupation. The research work has shown that various involved parties in Kashmir's conflict zone have tried to capitalize on trauma and PTSD and that despite the global proliferation of trauma and PTSD, the factors are highly contingent on local interests. Varma has raised points where she highlighted how a political and interest-driven popularization of trauma and PTSD can result in complications of hierarchizing the victims. She offers a way out by suggesting that we have new languages and tools that can go beyond trauma and PTSD and even beyond medicine, which tend to pathologize suffering.

III
"ECOLOGY OF SUFFERING" IN A MILITARIZED JAMMU & KASHMIR

Militancy and militarization in Jammu & Kashmir have turned the region into "a zone of mass psychological suffering" (Varma, 2012: 520). Years of ongoing conflict and military presence has disrupted people's lives in insidious ways. Violence, death, and trauma are part of people's everyday lives. The locals often find themselves facing the barrel of a gun or in the midst of a bomb attack or in interrogation camps. This has led to an alarming status of mental health deterioration in the region which has been confirmed by a range of mental health studies conducted in the region. As the studies report, the environment of fear and hostility has resulted in a rapid increase in the incidence of mental disorders such as anxiety, depression and post-traumatic disorder. This radical decline in people's mental health, however, can be better understood using the concept of "ecology of suffering" which proposes that "suffering is profoundly affected by ecological relations that are contingent on local particularities" (Jadhav *et al.* 2015: 12). This "ecology" refers to "the network of forces acting on and by the people suffering and those around him and her" (*ibid.*:12). These forces are a mix of social and natural elements.

In the case of Jammu & Kashmir, the "ecology" is created through a mix of natural factors such as hard terrain, geographical isolation, and poor connectivity. Socio-economic factors that work to the disadvantage of the people are poverty, unemployment, lack of infrastructure, family and personal issues. This "ecology of suffering" was exacerbated by the arrival of militancy in the region followed by heavy militarization. A far-reaching shift was brought in the economic, social and religious life of the people that gave rise to more vectors and forces to act upon the people.

Thus, the conventional psychiatric notion which emphasizes upon the narrow focus of social stressors having an impact on the psyche as the primary site of morbidity is only partly true. The fact of the matter is that individual mental suffering is related to a wide range of local factors that contribute to mental health. Thus, the mental health crisis in Jammu & Kashmir is the result of local ecology which involves poor socio-economic condition, conflict, and militarization. As the number of mental health cases has risen in the region traditional systems of healing, mainly magico-religious methods formed the first line of defence. Mushtaq and Margoob (2006) had explained the role of religious leaders in the psychosocial intervention of trauma in Jammu & Kashmir. Talking about Sufism in Kashmir, they stated that Sufi mystic and psychotherapist shared the experience of balance between inner and outer life in the community. Mushtaq and Margoob had observed that the turmoil of the conflict had reinforced the faith in God and religion as a coping method to deal with trauma and loss resulted in a massive rush to faith healers, shrines and other religious places (along with the rise in demand for psychotherapeutic and medical treatment). The authors had suggested that encouraging a working alliance between traditional healers and allopathic practitioners could help to overcome barriers to treatment acceptance and delivery.

In this context, the expertise of medical anthropologists can work to the advantage of medical health professionals. By closely studying and analysing conflict-affected societies, medical anthropologists can facilitate the state in understanding the needs of afflicted people and setting up intervention policies and measures. Traditional and religious healers can sustain the burden of the ever-growing mental health problems to a certain limit, that too in an untrained and non-professional capacity only. A cooperative linkage between professionally trained mental health professionals and religious professionals can serve to provide a better treatment module. A similar working relationship has already been applied in the case of the '*Dava* and *Dua*' project which is based on the unique concept of providing modern scientific mental health services along with traditional faith healing. The project was conceived in the aftermath of the unfortunate Erwadi fire incident in Tamil Nadu where 25 mental patients were charred to death in a local makeshift religious healing shelter. The official website of the project observes that traditional healers in developing countries have a significant role to play in mental health treatment and they can be trained to help psychiatrists. They can advise patients to continue their psychiatric treatment and follow-up while concomitantly carrying on their magico-religious treatments for patients. The '*Dava* and *Dua*' project envisages cooperation between traditional healers and psychiatrists which in turn may encourage patients to complete psychiatric treatment, prevent premature relapses, and decrease expenses in health system. As per a World Bank Blog, the '*Dava* and *Dua*' initiative has brought about the diagnosis and treatment of over 3,000 people suffering from mental illness have been diagnosed and treated (Vemuru, 2016). Similar initiatives can be started in conflict zones with the aid of medical anthropologists.

Moreover, medical anthropologists can examine how mental health challenges are expressed in conflict zones and how these are different from mental health challenges in non-conflict zones and whether or not the mental health problems arising due to war-like situations are more far-reaching and irreversible? How do the mental health consequences manifest in different conflict zones based on their cultural and religious systems? How do the traditional methods of healing evolve in the light of increasing mental health crisis and whether or not they are sufficient to meet the demands of suffering and complications arising out of conflict situations? Medical anthropologists can attempt to find whether there can be methods and ways to empower the traditional healers and knowledge systems in a conflict-ridden society so that the people can be psychologically resilient to the changes taking place around them. The questions on how the forces of globalization and technological advancements have brought a shift in social, cultural, economic and political lives of the people in conflict zones and affected the 'ecology of suffering' can be interesting to answer. Rozanov *et al.* (2019) have reported that "the massive media portrayal of terrorism and war becomes a potent source of stress for the wide public" (2019: 295). Such prolonged exposure to conflict and terror broadcasts can manifest into mental health problems in already susceptible people who are living in conflict zones.

It can also be interesting to see how the catching interest in mental health consequences has resulted in the medicalization of mental health care where psychosocial care methods are less understood and preferred. Saiba Varma (2018) observed that the number of patients seeking psychiatric and psychological treatment in Kashmir continues to rise. She suggested that it can be "read as a process of growing recognition of mental health care, and an example of the medicalization of everyday life in Kashmir, evidence for the breakdown in cultural life and coping mechanisms, or all of the above" (2018 : 147).

Thus, the participation of medical anthropologists in conflict and mental health studies can also help to find ways of strengthening traditional stress coping mechanisms and help the conflict-ridden people to carry on with their lives in a mentally-robust and dignified manner. Thus, this chapter urges the medical anthropology community to venture into conflict zones and find ways to push the limits of the discipline into newer horizons, or in the words of Marcia Inhorn, "to participate in multiple forms of antiwar activism."

NOTES

1. Kashmir profile – Timeline, BBC News. https://www.bbc.com/news/world-south-asia-16069078
2. WHO. Ten Facts about Mental Health. https://www.who.int/features/factfiles/mental_health/mental_health_facts/en/index3.html
3. Possibilities of transgenerational effects are associated with severe early life stress (including in utero effects) on developing brain with subsequent mental health problems in children and young adults.

REFERENCES

Amin, Syed and Khan, A.W. (2009). "Life in Conflict: Characteristics of Depression in Kashmir", *International Journal of Health Science, 3* (2): 203-213.

Arcel, Libby Tata, and Kastrup, Marianne C. (2004). "War, women and health", *Nora-Nordic Journal of Feminist and Gender Research, 12* (1): 40-47.

Chambers, Bill. (2018). "Mental health after war: how children in Iraq are severely underserved", *The Star.* (https://www.thestar.com/opinion/contributors/2018/07/11/mental-health-after-war-how-children-in-iraq-are-severely-underserved.html) (accessed 15 February, 2019).

Chenoy, Anuradha M. (1998). "Militarization, Conflict, and Women in South Asia", in Lois Ann Lorentzen (ed.): *The women and war reader*. New York: New York Univ. Press, pp. 101-110.

Duschinski, Halcy. (2009). "Destiny Effects: Militarization, State Power, and Punitive Containment in Kashmir Valley", *Anthropological Quarterly, 82* (3): 691-717.

Gusterson, Hugh. (2007). "Anthropology and Militarism", *Annual Review of Anthropology, 36*: 155-75.

Hassan, Asima and Shafi, Aneesa. (2013). "Impact of Conflict Situation on Mental Health in Srinagar, Kashmir", *Bangladesh e-Journal of Sociology, 10*(1): 101-125.

Henry, Doug. (2006). "Violence and the Body: Somatic Expressions of Trauma and Vulnerability during War", *Medical Anthropology Quarterly, 20*(3): 379-398.

Inhorn, Marcia. (2008). "Medical Anthropology against War", *Medical Anthropology Quarterly, 22*(4): 416-424.

Jadhav, Sushrut; Sumeet, Jain; Nanda, Kannuri; Clement, *et al.* (2015). "Ecologies of Suffering: Mental Health in India", *Economic and Political Weekly, 50*(20): 12-14.

Kashmir Mental Health Survey. (2015). Médecins Sans Frontières (MSF), India. (https://www.msfindia.in/sites/default/files/2016-10/kashmir_mental_health_survey_report_2015_for_web.pdf) (accessed on 27 July, 2019).

Kumar, Sanjay. (1999). "Mental-health problems increase as health care in Kashmir collapses", *The Lancet, 353*(9156): 908.

Martín-Baró, Ignacio. (1989). "Political Violence and War as Causes of Psychosocial Trauma in El Salvador", *International Journal of Mental Health, 18* (1): 3-20.

Matloff, Judith and Nickelsberg, Robert. (2008). "The Psychic Scars of Kashmir", *Time Magazine*. (http://www.time.com/time/audioslide/0,32187,1735822,00.html) (accessed 3 February, 2019).

Mercy Corps. (2011). "Youth entrepreneurship in Kashmir: challenges and opportunities", (https://www.mercycorps.org/sites/default/files/youth_entrepreneurship_in_kashmir.pdf.) (accessed on 20 August, 2019).

Mir, Urfat Anjam and Joshi, P.C. (2010). "Trauma Suffering and Medical Anthropology: Some Reflections in the Context of Findings from Jammu & Kashmir", in *Microdis Working Chapter Series: Symposium on Medical Anthropology and Disaster Management*, Kannada University, Hampi, India. pp. 51-88.

Mushtaq, Huda and Margoob, Mushtaq A. (2006). "Pir, Faqir and Psychotherapist: Their Role in Psychological Intervention of Trauma", *JK-Practitioner, 13*(1): 89-93.

Panter-Brick, Catherine, Mark Eggerman, Viani Gonzalez, *et al.* (2009). "Violence, suffering, and mental health in Afghanistan: A school-based survey", *The Lancet, 374* (9692): 807-816.

Pedersen, Duncan. (2002). "Political violence, ethnic conflict, and contemporary wars: broad implications for health and social well-being", *Social Science & Medicine, 55*(2): 175-90.

Pike, Ivy L. (2019). "Intersections of Insecurity, Nurturing, and Resilience: A Case Study of Turkana Women of Kenya", *American Anthropologist, 121*(1): 126-137.

Rice, Edward. (1988). *Wars of the third kind: Conflict in underdeveloped countries*. Berkeley: University of California Press.

Roberts, Bayard *et al.* (2009). "Post-conflict mental health needs: A cross-sectional survey of trauma, depression and associated factors in Juba, Southern Sudan", *BMC Psychiatry, 9*:7.

Rozanov, Vsevolod, Tanja Frančišković, Igor Marinić, *et al.* (2019). "Mental Health Consequences of War Conflicts", in Javed Afzal, Fountoulakis Kostas (ed.): *Advances in Psychiatry.* Cham: Springer International Publishing, pp. 280-304.

Society for Medical Anthropology. (2017). (http://www.medanthro.net/about/about-medical-anthropology/) (accessed on 12 June, 2019).

Tarabay, Jamie. (2006). "Iraq Mental Health Deteriorates with Violence", National Public Radio, (https://www.npr.org/templates/story/story.php?storyId=5378517) (accessed on 01 September, 2019).

Ugaide, Antonio; Richards, Patricia L and Zwi, Anthony. (1999). "Health consequences of war and political violence", *Encyclopedia of Violence, Peace and Conflict, 2*:103-21.

Vagts, Alfred. (1959). *A history of militarism civilian and military*. London: Hollis & Carter.

Varley, Emma, and Saiba Varma. (2018). "Spectral Ties: Hospital Hauntings Across the Line of Control", *Medical Anthropology, 37*(8): 630-644.

Varma, Saiba. (2012). "Where There are only Doctors: Counselors as Psychiatrists in Indian-Administered Kashmir", *Ethos, 40* (4): 517-535.

Varma, Saiba. (2016). "Love in the time of occupation: reveries, longing, and intoxication in Kashmir", *American Ethnologist, 43* (1): 50-62.

Varma, Saiba. (2018). "From 'Terrorist' to 'Terrorized': How Trauma Became the Language of Suffering in Kashmir", in Haley Duschinski, Mona Bhan, Ather Zia, and Cynthia Keppley Mahmood (ed.): *Resisting occupation in Kashmir*. Philadelphia: University of Pennsylvania Press, pp. 129-152.

Vemuru, Varalakshmi. (2019). "Dawa-Dua: How medical treatment complements prayer for people with mental illness in India", World Bank Blogs. (https://blogs.worldbank.org/endpovertyinsouthasia/dawa-dua-how-medical-treatment-complements-prayer-people-mental-illness-india) (accessed on 26 August, 2019).

IPT. (1997). Wounded Valley...Shattered Souls: Women's Fact Finding Commission Probing Army Atrocities on Women and Children in Kashmir. (http://www.iptindia.org/wp-content/pdf/report/Wounded-Valley-Shattered-Souls.pdf) (accessed on 12 August, 2019).

12

Healing Mind: Mental Health, Indigenous Healers and Traditional Medicine

Ravinder Singh

Introduction

Traditional Indian medicines—*Ayurveda*, Chinese medicine, and Arabic *Unani* medicine, as well as to various forms of Indigenous medicine around the world are grouped together as Traditional Medicine (WHO, 2002). Indigenous healings are *treatment procedures* used in the folk healing or rather traditional healing in traditional medicine. Traditional medicine accounts for approximately 40 per cent of health care in China, and 80 per cent in Africa, with methods including herbal medicines, the use of animal parts and/or minerals, manual therapies and spiritual therapies to maintain well-being, to diagnose and treat illness. In this chapter author raises the issue of mental illnesses as prevalent in our country and question if traditional healing matters in healing the mind for better mental health in our country in first part of the chapter besides analysing recent survey, NMHS-2014. Then illuminate various mind healing ways and put it in question whether we can protect these healers and medicines in existing IPR in Part-II followed by traditional knowledge, medicines, National policy and cases of Indian patents and Intellectual Property Rights (IPRs) are described in the last part.

Mental Health: Towards Healing Mind

Do we really look for solution in the mental health surveys? Or do we just enumerate the gravity of the mental health problems, i.e. how many people are suffering with which mental illness? Survey only shows gravity of the problem, *not* the solution and plan to control for these illnesses. Nobody tells how best can mental illnesses be prevented. Most of the professionals tell intensity of these diseases, but do not chalk out the effective planning resulting into appropriate solutions. Let us see the recent mental health survey, NMHS-2014 and its findings, followed by some case studies and relevance of participation of people in mental health awareness programme.

Mental Illnesses—Situational Analysis, DHMP, Mental Health Bill, Where is the Cure or Remedy?

About 13.7 per cent of general population of India has issues of mental illness or disorders and 10.6 per cent of these people need *immediate intervention* for the treatment followed by 10 per cent of the population having common mental disorders with 1.9 per cent people suffering with *severe* mental disorders (Table 11.1). The mental morbidity is very high in urban areas. There is higher prevalence of neurotic or stress-related disorders, schizophrenia and mood disorders. This situation is alarming, may be due to fast-lifestyles, experiencing stress, complexities of living, a breakdown of support systems and challenges of economic instability mentions the recent survey. A pilot study was conducted in Kolar district, Karnataka where 3,190 individuals were screened for the mental illnesses. Further NMHS-2014 was extended to 13 States viz. Punjab, Jharkhand, West Bengal, Rajasthan, Gujarat, Uttar Pradesh, Tamil Nadu, Kerala, Madhya Pradesh, Chhattisgarh, Assam and Manipur. Assam, Uttar Pradesh and Gujarat reported prevalence rates of mental illnesses less than 10 per cent and in eight of the 12 States, the prevalence varied between 10.7 to 14.1 per cent (*see* Yasmeen, 2016, NMHS-2014).

Table 11.1: Prevalence of Mental Disorders in Different Sates

Sl. No.	*States of India*	*Percentage*
1	Manipur	14.1
2.	Madhya Pradesh	13.9
3.	Punjab	13.4
4.	West Bengal	13.0
5.	Tamil Naidu	11.8
6.	Chhattisgarh	11.7
7.	Kerala	11.4
8.	Jharkhand	11.1
9.	Rajasthan	10.7
10.	Gujarat	7.4
11.	Uttar Pradesh	6.1
12.	Assam	5.8

National Mental Health Survey-2014: A Brief

An important finding in this survey is that there is huge gap in treatment of these illnesses. Further *three* out of *four* persons *(3/4)* people are experiencing severe mental disorders in our country. Apart from epilepsy, the treatment gap for all mental health disorders is more than 60 per cent. The economic burden of mental disorders is very high affecting families as they have to spend nearly Rs. 1000–Rs. 1500 a month mainly for treatment and to access care. Nearly 80 per cent of those with mental disorders had not received any treatment despite being ill for over 12 months due to the stigma of mental disorders, mentions the survey. Poor implementation of schemes under the National Mental Health Programme is the main reason for this treatment gap. There is also a paucity of mental health specialists, indicating that mental disorders are a low priority in the public health agenda in our country. The health information system itself does not prioritise mental health. Recommending that mental health financing needs to be streamlined, there is a need to constitute a national commission on mental health comprising professionals from mental health, public health, social sciences and the judiciary to oversee, facilitate support and monitor and review mental health policies *(ibid.)*.

3.1. Main Findings

Most common illnesses were: depression, anxiety and substance abuse in the NMHS-2014. These were 10 per cent to the total population studied. Most of the females in the age-group 40-49 years suffer from depression and it is almost 1 in 20 persons. 22.4 per cent of the population above 18 years suffers from *substance use disorder*. The highest was contributed by *tobacco and alcohol use disorder*. Nearly 1.9 per cent of the population is affected by *severe mental disorders*. These are detected more among males in urban areas. While prevalence of mental illness is higher among males (13.9%) as compared to females (7.5%), certain specific mental illnesses like *mood disorders* (depression, neurotic disorders, phobic anxiety disorders etc.) are more in females. Neurosis and stress related illness is also seen to be more in women. Prevalence in teenagers aged between 13 and 17 years is 7.3 per cent (Table 11.2) (*Ibid.*).

Table 11.2: Major Mental Illnesses in India

Mental Disorders	*No. of people suffer*	*Symptoms of Mental Illness*
Schizophrenia	37,37,481	Person suffers from delusion, hallucination
Mood disorders	1,99,33,232	Include depression and bipolar disorder, marked by alternating episodes of mania and depression
Cannabis users	99,66,616	Addicted to intoxicating hallucinogenic drugs
Mental retardation	12,45,827	A condition due to incomplete growth of brain, characterised by impaired cognitive, language, motor and social abilities
Child, adolescent disorders	3,08,96,510	
Geriatric disorders	30,89,651	Mental illness that onsets with aging
Dementia	18,93,657	Deterioration of an invidividual's intellectual, emotional and judgemental abilities; can occur with aging or injury to brain
Common mental disorders	2,49,16,540	Describe a state of deeper psychological distress; includes anxiety disorders, dissociative disorders, phobia and somatoform pain or acute false pain
Epilepsy	1,12,12,443	Neurological disorder with convulsive seizure
Alcohol dependency	1,24,58,270	Compulsive use of Alcohol

Source: NMHS-2014.

Healing Mind

Cases shown in Table 11.2 highlight the real picture of the common people (Mrinal, 2018). These reveals how they meet frontline healers in the local areas. Ideally NMHP was launched in 1982 with the hope of providing treatment at primary or district health centres. But real situation of DMHP-Sheohar, MP exposes their functioning at grassroots level in Sheohar.

Case-1: Jagat Ram's Sister

He had been travelling from Hapur, UP to Institute for medicines for his younger sister. She suffers from *depression*, a common mental illness in the country. He tells about his sister illness: "It all began at her in-laws' place where she uses to complain of torture", recalls the 35-year-old. In 2007, she lost her newborn and it pushed her into shock. It was another addition, as blow, to her already existing problems in her marriage. She turned quiet, lost interest in doing household chores, personal care for her appearance and even stopped bathing. Her in-laws used to accuse her of *acting* to gain attention and did not think of her treatment. Her condition continued to deteriorate and then Jagat Ram forcibly brought her back their home. Jagat Ram spent money on costly private treatment in his native place for one year. But she showed no improvement. It was by chance that the family brought her to Institute. Here she is under treatment now and being recovering. He adds further that "We now have to keep her away from negative thoughts". Though I still spend money on travel and take frequent leaves from office whenever it is required (Mrinal, 2018 *c.f.* Varsheny, 2013).

Case-2: Sanju

Sanju is a tribal boy from a village in Jhabua district of Madhya Pradesh. He shows symptoms of depression. Ratan Singh, his father, believes that he is under the spell of evil spirits, because he was fine till two years ago. But his behaviour suddenly changed. He stopped responding to calls and did not even care for himself. He would cry for no reason. In past two years, Ratan Singh and his wife have travelled several times to the *Baba Dongar* temple atop a hill, hoping that *God* would cure Sanju. They also promised to sacrifice *cocks* at the temple, if Sanju showed improvement. Though the boy did not show any sign of improvement. *Baba Dongar* is their only hope. When asked why he does not take Sanju to a doctor, a bewildered Ratan Singh says Sanju does not have any health problem (Mrinal, 2018 *c.f.* Varsheny, 2013).

National Mental Health Programme (NMHP)

The Government launched National Mental Health Programme (NMHP) in 1982. One of its objectives was to integrate mental health care in general health care by introducing mental health centres through Primary and Community Health Centres in each district. These centres are headed by psychiatrists who travel to interior parts of the district and provide treatment to patients. It is very interesting to observe the real field situation at the district level where how do the mental health professional work and encounter the everyday problems? The DMHP functioning in MP district reveals the issues at their level.

DMHP in Madhya Pradesh

The Sehore is a district in MP. There is one DMHP centre which is not able to handle the load of patients in the area. It is the only hospital, other than the Mental Hospital, Indore and Gwalior Mental Hospital, to cater to the mentally ill people of Madhya Pradesh. Between 1996 and 2007, the Central Government had sanctioned four DMHP centres in Shivpuri, Dewas, Mandla and Satna districts in the MP. But, none is functional. The Sehore DHMP centre is under-staffed as people do not wish join. There is also shortage of psychiatrists and psychologists in the entire MP because there are no PG courses on these subjects in any of the six medical colleges of the state. Secretary to the Madhya Pradesh State Mental Health Authority says DMHP failed in the state because it is not a priority for the authority. The money sanctioned for Satna and Jabalpur centres was returned to the Centre because the district authorities were not interested in the programme. Further adds "proposals have been sent to revive the defunct centres and begin DMHP in five new districts more than a year ago. But the proposals were never forwarded to the Centre", he says. The situation is no better in other states. The programme has made little headway in the past three decades (Varshney, 2013). One of the leading head of district mental hospital observes "Very few patients visit the doctor", and adds further:

> "While some fear social stigma, the rest are superstitious. We are planning to take the help of *tantriks* to bring mentally ill patients to the centre. Traditional or Indigenous healers, *Tantriks,* deal with many such patients and could be helpful to bring them here. They would perform their rituals and after that ask patients to visit the centre."

In Madhya Pradesh, the DMHP should be active in 123 districts (of 652 districts), it is barely functional in most districts, mentions *States Mental Health Policy Group*, established in May 2011 to create a mental health policy for the country and provide recommendations to improve DMHP in the 12th Five-Year Plan. The group submitted its report in June 2012. It says "...barring islands of good performance, the DMHP is yet to achieve its objectives," says the group. Inconsistent fund flow, lack of trained staff, lack of coordination between departments and non-availability of psychotropic drugs and psychological treatment are plaguing the programme. The group's report indicates that States are reluctant to take overfunding of DMHP. As per the guidelines, the Centre will fund DMHPs for five years, after which the respective state governments shall take over the programme. A clinical psychologist working with advocacy group Public Health Foundation of India highlights another flaw in the programme design. "NMHP is the only public health programme in the country where finances are routed through the Directorate of Medical Education", he says. "The deans of medical colleges are busy training psychiatrists and are not concerned about public health care whose foundation rests on awareness and reduction of stigma."

In the 12th Five Year Plan, the government plans to redesign the programme and expand it to all the districts in the country. But, will it be effectively given that India has never undertaken an official mental health survey? Several analysts are skeptical. A similar effort in 2002 to revamp NMHP and expand it to 22 districts had significantly changed the scope of the programme (Varshney, 2013).

"The new policy reduced emphasis on access to services and community participation (which were the prime aim of the 1982 policy) and moved towards provision and distribution of psychotropic medication,"(Jain and Jadhav, 2009). The authorities revamped the programme without analysing the problems that were ailing NMHP. "... there is no indication of who was involved in this (consultation) process and what resulted from it", it notes. The study holds lessons for Union Ministry of Health and Family Welfare, which plans to revamp its mental health care system. It has drafted a Mental Health Care Bill to replace the Mental Health Act of 1987.

Mental Illness: Is it a Biological Reality?

Recent advancements in technology have established it well. With the advancement of technology we could attribute emergence of mental illnesses to several factors: genetic inheritance, exposure to brain-damaging chemicals, conditions that beset people, such as work pressure, death of loved ones or even romantic rejection, which can trigger dysfunction of the brain and lead to mental disorders. The brain dysfunction may occur due to problems with neurotransmitters, where the level of the neurotransmitter serotonin is lowered in individuals who suffer from depression. Similarly, schizophrenia is linked to the disruption in neurotransmitters, dopamine, glutamate and norepinephrine.

Biological psychiatry is now an established branch of psychiatry and uses *imaging techniques* like psycho-pharmacology and neuro-immuno-chemistry to pinpoint the problem. Such understanding helps in the development of drugs to treat the problem. Using these techniques, researchers, in the past five years, have identified genes that influence susceptibility to five common psychiatric disorders, including bipolar disorder. Their finding was published in a medical journal: *The Lancet*. Using the technology, researchers at the National Institute of Mental Health in the USA are developing a classification system that would help differentiate the structure and function of a mentally ill brain from that of a healthy one. This will help researchers understand why a traumatic event leads to post-traumatic stress disorder, neurology of hallucinations and how drug addiction rewires the brain. There is still a long way to go. Scientists are not close to understand the brain the way they understand heart, kidneys and other parts of the body (Varshney, 2013).

National Commission on Macro-economics and Health (NCMH)

The National Commission on Macro-economics and Health (NCMH) published its report in 2005. It is most reliable and often quoted figure that provides some sense of prevalence of the illness. According to NCMH, at least 6.5 per cent of the Indian population—more than 80 million people—suffer from serious mental disorders, such as schizophrenia, bipolar disorder and obsessive compulsive disorder, with no discernible rural-urban difference. The share of mental illnesses is 8.5 per cent of the total burden of diseases in the country. These figures will grow substantially with increase in population. Poverty, gender discrimination, alcohol use, stress of modern life, conflicts and natural disasters—most of the identified risk factors for mental illness are common in India. But in the absence of an official mental health survey, there is little data on the number of people who suffer from the illness. Suicide cases have increased more than 22 per cent in the last one decade.

Stigma: Incurable beyond Medicine!

Tamanna, 30-year-old lives a life of rejection (Case-3), is not the only one who has been ostracized because of mental illness. A warden at the hospital, who did not wish to be named, says she has witnessed at least

12 such cases in the past two years where family members refused to take back their wards even after doctors certified complete recovery. More often than not women face institutionalization and desertion. Indore Mental Hospital alone has more than 40 women inmates compared to 20-odd men. More than 50 per cent of patients admitted to a mental hospital often end up staying there for five years or more. The most unfortunate aspect of this problem is that these patients have been in the hospital for years not because of treatment-related reasons but because their families have abandoned them. Prolonged hospitalisation has further impaired their socio-vocational skill, points out the National Human Rights Commission (NHRC) in its report submitted to the Supreme Court. NHRC has been reviewing mental health institutions in the country since 1997. That year the Apex Court had asked it to monitor mental health hospitals at Agra, Ranchi and Gwalior following complaints of human rights violation.

Table 11.3: Depressing Growth—Suicide cases in the Country

Year	*Number of People*	*Rate of Suicide*
2003	1,10,851	10.4
2004	1,13,697	10.5
2005	1,13,914	10.3
2006	1,18,112	10.5
2007	1,22,638	10.8
2008	1,27,017	10.8
2009	1,27,151	10.9
2010	1,34,599	11.4
2011	1,35,585	11.2
2012	1,35,445	11.2

Source: National Crime Records Bureau.

Case-3: Tamanna

Thirty-year-old Tamanna lives a life of rejection. Last year, her husband and his family brought her to Indore Mental Hospital. Doctors diagnosed her with *bipolar disorder* and admitted her to hospital. Within a couple of months, they declared her healthy and asked her family to take her back home. But no one wanted to take her back. Tamanna kept writing to her family for six months, but there was no response. Even her mother did not respond. Finally, the hospital administration had no choice but to shift Tamanna to a nearby shelter home with due permission of the Chief Judicial Magistrate (Mrinal, 2018, *c.f.* Varshney, 2013).

Dava **and** ***Dua*** **Project (DDP): Successful Mental Health Community Based Project**

The shrine of *Hazrat Sayed Ali Mira Datar*, a general of Ahmedabad Sultan Mahmud Begada, has attracted devotees for over 500 years. It is one of the many places of worship in India where thousands of mentally ill patients seek divine remedy. The fabled power to cure mental illness, which has a huge stigma attached to it, also draws Hindus who consist of 50 per cent of the visitors. But today, the shrine is now known for *dua* and for *dava*. The *Dava* and *Dua Project (DDP)* was initiated in 2008, which has ensured that almost half of the visitors to the shrine also consult a psychiatrist and accept an amalgamation of faith and science to treat their mental illnesses. This is one of the pioneering initiatives in which traditional faith healers work in close association with psychiatrists and psychologists, creating a model of social psychiatry that has attracted the attention of organizations such as the World Health Organization and the National Human Rights Commission. The organizations have even recommended the project's replication in other places. The model has already been implemented at shrines in Erwadi in Tamil Nadu and Hyderabad in Telangana. Another shrine in Nagpur, Maharashtra, will be part of the DDP later this year. In Erwadi, 25 persons in shackles had died in a 2001 fire accident. The tragedy had stoked outrage and spurred a nationwide drive to prevent practices such as chaining patients and beating them up to cure mental illness. The *Unava* is a shrine sharing a number of such practices.

The going was tough as *mujawar*, faith healers, vehemently protested when a team of doctors and others tried to inspect the premises in 2002, and police had to intervene. The medical practitioners did not lose hope and succeeded in starting the DDP formally in 2008. Managing trustee of Ahmedabad-based *Altruist*, a voluntary organization that manages the DDP informs in last eight years they have treated 38,500 patients who would not have gone to doctors anyway. Further adds that mental illness is stigmatized in India. So studies estimate that 82 per cent patients of common and 47 per cent of severe mental disorders never come into contact with medical practitioners. In such a situation, places like *Mira Datar* provide an opportunity to us to reach out. According to the figures released by Altruist—the NGO running the *Dava* and *Dua* Project—most patients were diagnosed for depression followed by schizophrenia, epilepsy, somatoform disorders, mental retardation, and general medical conditions. In eight years, the DDP has reached out to an average of 400 patients per month. In 2015-16, patients from Rajasthan, Maharashtra, Madhya Pradesh, Karnataka and West Bengal formed a major part of the visitor population, apart from those from Gujarat. In all, patients from 17 States had benefited from the DDP.

Case-4

Neeti, 26-year-old from Dhuliya, Maharashtra suffering with mental illness that had come for treatment with her brother to *Mira Datar Dargah* shrine, which is located in Mehsana district. It is 100 km away from Ahmedabad. The shrine is famed for its capacity to cure illnesses and '*possessions*'. Thousands people across the country visit it for the treatment. Neeti's brother tells that she was chained as she would smash things and beat up people. Neeti's family spends four months every year at Unava for her treatment. We consulted doctors but nothing worked. Now, she has become much calmer. The bouts still erupt but they last, at the most, for ten minutes (Mrinal, 2018 *c.f.* Varshney, 2013).

It is clearly visible that DDP success is because of the integration of the traditional healers who holds people's faith and trust. Similarly, government should think to induct them in their main stream of health care system.

Do We still need Effective the Mental Health Policy? Missing Participation of People and Community

An officer of PHFI expressed that public sector is small and the private sector provides most of the services. Therefore, the policy should focus on strengthening the public health care system. Simultaneously, it should regulate the role of private mental health care providers. Dependence on psychiatrists should be reduced as in the case of TB programme where not all diagnosis and treatment are done by specialists. Like HIV/AIDS programmes, mental health care system needs counsellors. The evaluation mechanism has also to be built in the policy. Similarly *Snehi*, a Delhi based NGO, suggests instead of devising a separate mental health policy, the government should make it part of the pending national health policies. Further a former director of NIMHANS expressed that we need to make mental health care accessible, affordable and acceptable to the patient. For this he suggests a three-pronged approach: involve community, integrate mental health care with general health care system so that mental illness is dealt along with other illnesses, and bring about a change in the attitude of specialist doctors who are not willing to accept that non-specialists could provide care. Adding more, the existing system is controlled by the pharmaceutical industry and the private sector lobby. Instead the government should focus on spreading awareness about mental illness. People should know what to do when they are mentally sick. Unfortunately, India does not have a diagnostic manual of mental disorders. For creating awareness, the government should use standard methods such as posters, radio and TV shows, street plays and social media. Mental illness-related information can be made available in the form of questionnaires, narratives or life stories of survivors. Networks of survivors can help patients combat the illness. The awareness would go a long way in reducing social stigma and ensuring early diagnosis. An early diagnosis is the key to fight mental illness.

Treatment is beyond Pills: Are Pills solution for Mental Illness?

Jain and Jadhav (2009) reported a clinical ethnography of a community psychiatry programme in north India, wherein they traces the biosocial journey of psychotropic pills from the Centre to the Periphery. They add that pill journeys from the Ministry of Health to the clinic, its symbolic meaning transforms from an emphasis on accessibility and participation to administration of '*treatment*'. The pill becomes central to professional monologues on compliance that mute the voices of patients and families.

The pharmaceuticals have already changed the character of National Mental Health Programme (NMHP). They studied the role of psychotropic medication in NMHP and found that instead of being a symbol of accessibility to health care, the pill ends up being a method of administering a discrete treatment. Thus, instead of empowering the community, the pill silences community voices and re-enforces the existing barriers to care (Jain and Jadhav, 2009). Pharmaceutical industries have dominated the mental health care system in India. In 2007, the psychiatrists and pharmaceutical company nexus in the US reportedly resulted in growing use of new antipsychotics in children. Between 2000 and 2005, the industry's payments to Minnesota psychiatrists rose more than six-fold. During the period, prescriptions of antipsychotics for children under the state's insurance programme rose more than nine-fold (Varshney, 2013).

The US psychiatrists are prescribing six times more antipsychotics to children and adolescents than in the UK. More than 30 million Americans take antidepressants. Another example of this unholy nexus is the recently released Diagnostic and Statistical Manual of Mental Disorders prepared by American Psychiatric Association. The manual turns even common ailments into mental illnesses. For example, it terms common experiences like grief as clinical depression, and binge eating a new category of illness. It is alleged that the manual aims at pleasing the pharma industry (*Ibid.*).

Here it is clear that these Pharmaceutical industries controlled the political economy to make their ways of profits. As already said the everyday problems are being medicalised and there is standard book where they have added as mental diseases with appropriate symptoms and their treatment strategy. Now I resume the mind, its healing ways and mental health in the indigenous healers and their healing section.

II

Indigenous Healers and their Healing

There are many definitions of indigenous or aboriginal healing, but I am giving a brief analysis of various definitions of indigenous healing or aboriginal healing practices. These healing ways have a more holistic approach to health than the approach taken in most Western medical models (Hewson, 1998; Horn, 2008; Smith, 2009) and aboriginal contexts (Adelson and Lipinski, 2008; Fiske, 2008; Fletcher and Denham, 2008; Waldram, 2008) most have common elements, found on different continents where Aboriginal populations have been colonised, e.g. in North and South America to Africa and Australasia. They also mention spiritual and emotional issues in addition to mental and physical health (Moran and Fitzpatrick, 2008). They focus on the frequent reference to 'balance' and/or 'harmony' (Chansonneuve, 2005; Ross, 2008); place emphasis on families and communities as well as on individuals (Lane *et al.,* 2002) and include references to nature or aspects of the environment. In many cases these explicitly refer to healing from the trauma caused by aspects of colonisation, such as forced removals from family and incarceration in residential schools (Castellano, 2006). There may be a deviation from Western models, there are many examples which mention the healing required by those who have hurt others, as well as those who have been injured (Archibald, 2006; Correctional Service of Canada, 2008). In Australia, the Aboriginal and Torres Strait Islander Healing Foundation Team (2009), state that healing is "a spiritual process that includes addictions recovery, therapeutic change and cultural renewal." The Team goes further to explain that:

> ....therapeutic change means dealing with trauma in a safe and culturally-appropriate environment. Cultural renewal means strengthening and reconnecting with identity, which may include language, dance and song (*see* William, Guenther and Arnott, 2011).

Most of the tribal or indigenous people undergo through trauma by forcible removal from their lands, the break-up of societies and families and the removal of children away from their cultural heritage and often into situations of cultural, physical and sexual abuse in Australia as well as in other countries of the world. Such trauma needs the healing at different level—at individual, family and community as means of alternative care (William, Guenther and Arnott, 2011).

Healing Traditions

Healing traditions are the methods which are learned and passed down from generation to generation. It also includes the *"experientially informed"* healers when a healer gains through self-motivated skills in dealing with their own trauma or problems which can be helpful to other people. They may be called as indigenous or aboriginal healers. Let us see an example of traditional healing among the Navajo. The Navajo *hataali* spend years studying and working with a master healer to learn their craft of singing healing ceremonies. These chants are long and any mistake in words is considered dangerous and the potential healers are selected for their work ethic and seriousness, and must be prepared to spend years working on their craft and paying for what they are learning (Iris, 1998; Sandner, 1979). There are other forms of healing in Navajo communities, which may be practiced by men or women with diagnostic skills or knowledge of herbal remedies (Iris, 1998), but they do not enjoy the level of status given to *hataali*. Similarly, there are long-established healing methods in east Arnhem which are still practised by *Yolngu* healers, and which require specialized training and experience to use (Wearne and Muller, 2009).

There are communities whose experiences have devastated transmission of cultural knowledge during the post-colonial period and unlikely to retain the degree of healing knowledge required for such extensive and rigorous ceremonies (Phillips, 2003). The use of traditional healing practices may be more common than is realized, at least in both South America and North America:

> In some areas of the country [Canada, in this case] and within some Aboriginal communities, traditional healing practices remain very strong. There are traditional *"treatment centres"* which are being run with no external funding, no staffing or administrative structures and which are undocumented, often at the homes of healers. Many people, both within the literature and anecdotally ascribe their healing to participation in traditional cultural practices (Lane *et al.,* 2002: 30).

Healing Methods

There are many methods in traditional indigenous healing which are normally employed. A healer tries almost every modality for healing someone. Often almost everything works for someone, and nothing works for everyone. It is clear that specific modalities are less important than the context in which they take place (Lane *et al.,* 2002). Medicinal plants are often an important component (Dobson, 2007; Swan and Raphael, 1995), but ceremonies and other healing modalities are typically even more important, and most often there is a mix of healing methods, even in the most traditional healing modalities.

A list of healing methods may include: chants, cleansing and smoke rituals, counselling, healing circles, bush trips to special sites, painting and other forms of art therapy, vision quests, massage, residential treatment and many more, often used in various combinations (Fiske, 2008; Smith, 2009; Swan and Raphael, 1995). Some approaches appear to be particularly effective, like the common emphasis on group healing involvement rather individual sessions, and the emphasis on cultural recovery. Healing circles were often cited as effective, compared to more standard Western healing models:

> … I probably could have gotten help [from a professional therapist], but what scared me was, I got in touch with my rage and for the first time, I became aware of how terrifying it was. I couldn't make myself go back to a therapist, because I'm going to be there alone, and I am going to be touching this terrible thing inside me, and I'm going to be walking away alone. I can't do any work through the Western methods. It's just too much. I have to do my work through the traditional way. I have to use the circle. I have to have people that care about me and know they care about me. I want them there to help me through whatever it

> is I have to deal with. I can't do it any other way (Bushie, 2008 *cf.* William, Guenther and Arnott, 2011).

Perhaps the single strongest claim in the literature is the importance of re-connecting to one's own cultural traditions; indeed, in many cases it appears that 'recovery' is equivalent to recovery of one's lost cultural identity and that this is vital to healing.

> The answer to improving the health of indigenous people may lay less in increasing their access to modern health services and more in their rediscovering cultural values and ways (Smith, 2003).

Probably for such reasons, Canadian Aboriginal communities are increasingly adopting the *'Culture as Treatment'* healing model across that country, sometimes in favour of more traditional local approaches, due to their perception of its special effectiveness (Lane *et al.,* 2002: 30).

Healing Places—Where to Heal?

Indigenous healers generally do heal in their home. But there are examples in other countries where there are '*Aboriginal healing centres*' where it takes place. This healing is used in many different senses ranging from frankly entrepreneurial centres that combine New Age techniques with Aboriginal healing practices. A Healing place may or may not be headed by an aboriginal person, to centres specializing in Western style medicine but in a facility designed for use by Aboriginal clients, to places offering solely traditional healing practices. In many cases, traditional healing may be offered in private homes or in community buildings not necessarily called '*healing centres*' (Lane *et al.,* 2002).

Hospital and clinics owned and operated by Aboriginal people may offer Western medical equipment and procedures, but the facility is often designed to look and operate different from a mainstream hospital or clinic, perhaps with family spaces (for extended family of well of over a dozen people), '*talking rooms*', incorporating local motifs, open spaces that do not separate healers from patients, and other culturally friendly features (Belfrage, 2007; Finke, 2009; Towne, 2009). Iris (1998) noted that:

> Today… it is not unusual for a Navajo healer to perform some piece of a healing ceremony in the clinical setting, and many Navajo people are engaged as community health representatives,

nurses, and interpreters, among others, in the health delivery system on the Navajo Nation.

Although there are facilities specifically designed to offer traditional healing, these are probably a minority; few of the Canadian Aboriginal Healing Foundations grants, for example, went to such facilities, with most going to programmes that would be operated out of other facilities and perhaps incorporated into other programmes (Aboriginal Healing Foundation, 2008). Lists of different types of Aboriginal healing places can be found in Canada (Aboriginal Healing and Wellness Strategy Management, 2003; Aboriginal Healing Foundation, 2008) but no comprehensive national lists exists, likely due in large part to the difficulty of determining what exactly should qualify as an '*Aboriginal healing centre'*.

New Zealand provides relatively comprehensive national lists of services that "deliver health and disability services to predominantly... although certainly not exclusively... *Māori* clients [within a].... delivery framework which is distinctively *Māori'* and seeks to keep the lists comprehensive and updated" (Cripps and McGlade, 2008). "In America, it is easy to find lists of services offered through the Indian Health Service for people living on recognised tribal lands, but it is difficult to find lists of services outside this system, and urban Aboriginal Americans in particular have great difficulty in accessing suitable health care" (Young, 2007).

It has proven difficult to find good sources listing Australian Aboriginal healing centres. Even discussion chapters and reports on the potential for Aboriginal healing provide little in the way of such information (Aboriginal and Torres Strait Islander Healing Foundation Development Team, 2009; Phillips and Bamblett, 2009). This may again in part reflect the difficulty of defining an '*Aboriginal healing place'* but may also reflect the lack of strategic attention to date paid to such facilities at a national level.

Healers

The literature offers far more on the healing experience from patients' perspectives than can be found on healing from the traditional healers' perspective. However, a number of important themes emerge, including contrasts between the approaches taken by traditional healers and most modern doctors, the need to sustain Aboriginal healing knowledge by passing on information, the need to care for healers, and to importance of distinguishing between genuine healers and self-proclaimed '*healer*' charlatans. The relationship between patients and their Indigenous and traditional healers differs from the patient/doctor relationship in most modern Western practices. As Hewson (1998) notes, traditional healers may not distinguish between *'curing* and *caring'*, or between *subjective* and *objective* symptoms.

> "Traditional healers probe deeply into the patient's social and psychological well-being in addition to the history of the present illness. They already know or are prepared to learn about the context of the patient's life, such as his or her social and economic status, attitudes, beliefs, hopes, and fears" (Hewson (1998), *c.f.* William, Guenther and Arnott, 2011).

It is also important to explore, where these healers heal? There is a significant relationship of these two. Here Dobson (2007) elaborates it among Arrente women that power of healing comes from the country of whoever chosen to be healer. Further Trudgen (2000) also illuminates the relationship between healing and traditional laws among *Yolngu* and context of Arnhem Land. He says further that *'health matters'* he concludes that:

> All this knowledge and the correct procedures pertaining to health and healing are encapsulated in the Yolngu law, the Madayin. (*c.f.* William, Guenther and Arnott, 2011, p. 13)

Ganesharajah (2009) explains complex relationships on the healing, country and sharing intergenerational cultural knowledge in Canada. He pointed to need for "recognition of the central importance of land to Indigenous peoples' identity, spirituality, community and culture." In Canada, the sharing healing knowledge is also an important issue for lateral knowledge transfer as well as for intergenerational transfer. The following quote from a Canadian context confirms:

> Talk of "knowledge transfer" and the "exchange of best practices" has become, of late, very much the talk of the town [but] the prospect that useful knowledge might flow "up-hill", or even laterally from community to community is ordinarily excluded from the realm of conceivable or legitimate possibilities...(see Chandler and Lalonde, 2006 c.f. William, Guenther and Arnott, 2011).

Healers are trying to improve opportunities for 'side-by-side learning' to ensure transfer of information by those who possess healing knowledge before the healers pass on. The intergenerational transmission of healing knowledge is also an important issue because such knowledge is guarded in many traditional societies. It is not shared with others. Similarly, such situations have emerged in well-established healing traditions. The *Navajo Nation* where healers are finding it difficult to get young healers interested to learn and put in their years for acquiring skills to become a qualified traditional healer. In this endeavour, a school for traditional healers was set up with the support of Cornell University but it could not produce the desired results (Iris, 1998).

Similarly, the Maori system of healing in New Zealand has been incorporated into mainstream health delivery system, interactive workshops with traditional healers revealed their difficulties with overwork and their ageing. Maori traditional healers are, therefore, currently looking at practice-based training with suitable candidates selected by older Maori practitioners and posing a problem in caring the older *Maori healers*. Here the caring of Maori older healers has become an important issue.

In Canada, the situation of aboriginal healers is similar to Maori healers. Aboriginal healing foundation and other similar organizations have helped to support these healers having serious issues of self-care and traumatic experiences in Canada. Further, the problem of distinction between qualified and non-qualified healers remains. But, such situation is being controlled by the membership of the formal organizations, recently developed, which automatically declare them as qualified healers in South Africa and New Zealand. Today healers in these countries are facing their own problems of self-injuries, ageing and unresolved legal issues (William *et al.*, 2011: 14).

Integration of Traditional Healers and their Medicines: Experiences of their Integration to Western Medicine—Some Countries

Most of the countries of the world are using traditional medicines and about 80 per cent people in rural areas in developing countries rely on these medicines for primary care. In contrast developed countries mostly use Western medicines for their day-to-day sicknesses. These developed countries are using similar medicines in their colonies and traditional healers or aboriginals people also use same medicines seldom. However, traditional medicines men do have their own medicines for such illnesses. In such countries—New Zealand, South Africa, Australia, Canada, and

USA, the policies for the best care practices are still evolving. Government, in these countries are using two strategies to increase the number of aboriginal healers/indigenous healers working in the mainstream of health care. These people increase Aboriginal workforce without enabling the incorporation of traditional practices can lead to high turnover in Aboriginal staff. One registered Nurse Emmy Mitchell (1998) expressed her concern as follows:

> Emmy Mitchell... looks at every elder as if they were her grandparents and strongly believes in the natural way of healing. To her that means hands-on healing; massage therapy, traditional medicines, soaking the elders' feet, talking to them in their own language and other comfort measures. Working first as a Licensed Practical Nurse, then as a Registered Nurse, Emmy clashed over and over again with doctors and nursing directors who believed in giving the elders muscle relaxants, sleeping pills and antidepressant pills... As I passed and graduated the RN course, it was supposed to be big celebration, but it was not because the more I learned about medication and its side-effects that our people are suffering from, it turned me away from being a nurse (Emmy Mitchell, 1998).

Now let's see how these countries look at such issues of traditional medicine and its healers? Can their integration to mainstream be a best way for them? In South Africa, some countries are colonized which are less in numbers, so they are in minority, as compared to aboriginal people living in these areas prior to colonial rules. Here colonial government has evolved an attitude of curbing them as their medicine too.

They made legislation, *Witchcraft Suppression Act, 1957* forbidding traditional healing practices. But *Witchcraft Suppression Amendment Act, 1970* replaced an attempt to partnership:

> In rural South Africa, over 60 per cent of the population seeks health advice and treatment from traditional healers before visiting a medical doctor. Those that do seek formal health care also continue to visit a traditional healer... partnering with traditional healers and bringing them into the formal health system is vital to improving health in South Africa. Their potential as a resource and point-of-contact for both rural and urban communities cannot be ignored (African Medical and Research Foundation, 2010).

WHO has also encouraged Western medical practitioners for partnership with these healers to control the problem of HIV/AIDS. Now, these healers are making associations so that their services can be recognized by the South African department of Health. But there are issues related to medical ethics, on such partnership, between Traditional Healers and Medicines and Mainstream Health Care System.

Maori constitutes 15 per cent of the population in New Zealand and have high rate of incarceration, ill health, early mortality or suicides than other people. Government has changed her attitude towards the *Tohunga* (the traditional healer in Maori) between 1907 and 1962. The *Tohunga* (*Maori traditional healer*) *Suppression Act* had the provision of penalties for using any type of sorcery or enchantment or to claim to leave super-natural power for the treatment of diseases. Such provisions have led many *Tohunga* to go underground. But their methods of healing continue (Archibalds, 2006, *c.f.* William, Guenther and Arnott, 2011). Now New Zeeland government is formally including traditional healers in the formal health care system. This way the government is also increasing Maori workforce in the mainstream of health care. Though there are challenges remains, i.e. to distinguish between legitimate and non-qualified healers, to meet patient care needs, are evaluating practices, training new healers, and protecting cultural and intellectual property right of these healers (see *Ibid.*, p. 16).

In USA, 1.5 per cent people are American Indian, or Alaska nation, or often called "Native Americans", then two groups may be attributed on "aboriginal" as I feel indigenous equally connotes same meaning for these two groups. The *Dawes Act* suppressed traditional healing practice for a long time these native Americans. This Act prevented dances and ceremonies in 1921 or it continued till 1978. But *Freedom of Religion Act* of 1978 gives same freedom for these dance and religious ceremonies. By 1960, tribal people and native Americans become politically empowered or gave a birth to American Indian movement (see Witllstock and Salivas, 2006, *c.f.* William, 2011). There are 564 recognized tribes living on the reservation in 38 States of USA and all of them are entitled Indian health services funded by the Federal government. Hospitals, health cares, community clinic or often services are operating under the supervision of federal or the tribal system. These services are dedicated to tribal peoples or aboriginal people. Though only one per cent of these resources are dedicated to other tribal or aboriginal people living off their land in the urban cities (*see* Young, 2007).

The Indian health services are being provided for more culturally appropriate spaces healing through significant process of *de-medicalise* space in their culture. A number of partnerships have also emerged between traditional healers or mainstream primary care system (Finke, 2009, Town, 2009). Through this arrangement people or patient can approach a number of healing traditions (Lamphere, 2000). They may either go to a Western clinic for any ailment, i.e. for a broken leg and may have traditional healing ceremony for it to after returning from such clinic, or they may approach to traditional healer for an effective healing directly. In USA, the government is developing a strategy for a healing model which has culture and spirituality at the base due to the increasing partnership with traditional healers and incorporation of traditional healing practice (*see* Smith, 2009).

In Canada, there are three groups of aboriginal people, viz., first Nation, Inuit and Metis, which together make 3.3 per cent of Canada's populations. These aboriginal people have been suffering from ill health, high risk of suicide, colonial trauma of forced relocation to the long "*residential school*" era—where aboriginal children removed from their families and kept in these schools for further education (see Williams, *et al.*, 2011: 17). In 1980, Aboriginal health movement began after the darkest phase between 1950 and 1980 in Canada. A re-emergence of aboriginal spirituality or culture, due to greater political empowerment developed some new initiatives for this Aboriginal people. Government started "Addiction services" in 1982 for these people based their cultural principles particularly target the Aboriginal communities (Beadman, 2009). As Beadman (2009) further writes about them:

> Many communities have experienced the revival of old ceremonies, practices and teachings such as smudging, the sweat lodge, the use of the sacred pipe, fasting, vision quests, ceremonies for naming, healing, reconciliation, and personal or collective commitment. Some communities seemed to have forgotten their own ceremonies, and so whole generations of younger men and women travelled to other communities and tribes across the continent to find spiritual teachers who would help them recover something of their own aboriginal spiritual teachings and practices. Sometimes, as the teachings and songs of another tribe were introduced in a community, the elders would begin to share their own heritage which had been hidden away in their hearts for so many years (Beadman, 2009).

In Canada, there is federal system where provinces are entirely responsible for health care. Though Central Government of Canada is especially responsible for health of aboriginal people in all the provinces. They are living on reserve provisions made for them. The Ontario Province has very well developed health care policy for the traditional aboriginal healing and has developed the agreement with a number of Aboriginal nations in Ontario for incorporation of their practices and also ensured access to other health options. One of such centre in Ontario is providing the health services to aboriginal people on—

> … holistic health services, combining traditional and Western practices. The Traditional Healing Programme uses various traditional Aboriginal healing methods and a holistic approach to individual, family and community health and wellness. Services include confidential sessions with traditional healers, access to traditional activities, learning about natural medicines, stress management workshops using traditional methods, and cross-cultural awareness training (Aboriginal Healing and Wellness Strategy Management, 2003).

There are other initiatives taken by the other provinces in Canada. These are healing for offenders about to re-enter communities, training or enabling the aboriginal to work in other parts of health care system (Lane *et al.*, 2002, Lavalles, 2007).

The development of "Aboriginal Healing Foundation" has greatly influenced the aboriginal health care system or streamlined with other system. Initially, it was set up for limited time period, but it continues to support the programme in healing legacy of Canadian residential school for emotional damage, violence or abuse by survivors, or their children (Adelson and Lipinski, 2008; Archibald, 2006; Castellano, 2006; Chansonneuve, 2005; Kishk Anaquot Health Research, 2006; Mussell, 2005; Waldram, 2008).

In Australia, 2.4 per cent of its people are aboriginal or Torres Strait Islanders based in northern territory. They are in predominantly aboriginal. They are younger, less migratory, have higher fertility and mortality rate, high population growth and wide dispersed people as compared to aboriginal people. Main problem of these people are high suicide, violence, abuse, family breakdown, health problem, life expectancy. These are more in Torres Strait Islanders and other aboriginal in Canada, New Zealand and USA (Archibald, 2008).

As already mentioned in other case that Australian government has adopted traditional healing practice into mainstream health care. Though it does not support them. About Australian government, Devanesen (2000) writes:

> "Traditional healers were employed by the Northern Territory Department of Health at various rural health centres in Central Australia in the early 1970s.... A training course to teach traditional healers about Western medical practices was attempted in 1974. It was soon realised that it would be better to train a separate group as Aboriginal health workers and to leave the traditional healers to their vitally important roles.... However, rural health centres continue to recognise and cooperate with traditional healers in the management of sick people.... The Northern Territory Department of Health's first policy on Aboriginal Health stated that 'traditional medicine' is a complementary and vital part of Aboriginal health care, and its value is recognised and supported."

But recent documents, *"Aboriginal Health and Families: a five year framework for action*"; it notes, understands and acknowledges the potential value of traditional healers:

> "...Increasingly the medical profession has recognised that 'health care belief systems are critical to the patient's healing process' and overseas studies have shown that the practice and advice of traditional healers is often valued more highly than the advice from western medical practitioners. These themes are repeated in recent decisions of the Australian Health Ministers' Advisory Council" (Northern Territory Department of Health and Community Services, 2005).

Although, this document does not propose any effective programme for the healers as remains continue to improve the Western medicine with involvement of community and the cultural activity. In contrast, Dunlop (1988) mentions the importance of "Aboriginal traditional method and their community imitations given equal status to non-aboriginal medical practice." "Bringing them home" report expressed need for holistic approach to their healing, including the partnership with traditional healers. Though Australian government respect the traditional healing practices or cultural protocols; and also recognize potential role of community leaders, traditional healers, those working to resolve the community problem (*see* William, Guenther and Arnott, 2011: 19).

Here, it appears Australian government makes *ad hoc* plan which are inconsistent for traditional healers. Though more emphases have been given on the improvement of aboriginal housing for their general well-being rather than to address their trauma, grieving, and heading (Belfrange, 2007; Cummingham and Stanley, 2003). The government has encouraged the development of aboriginal or Torres Strait islander Healing Foundation. This Foundation is investigating intergenerational trauma and their strategy of healing methods, which are traditional and cultural healing practices, which can be: healing centre; family support and sources centres; ceremonies, going back to country, traditional healers; Elder support groups, support group for sexual assault survivors, leadership programme for youth; anger management groups etc.

There has been less emphasis on aboriginal traditional healing in Aboriginal traditional healing in Australia, ageing of older traditional healing for training other healing; mainstream credibility of healing. There is little hope on healing families has been created to help or lead the Australian indigenous healing movement (see William, 2009: 20). Besides, there are few issues remaining unsolved—integrating Western or aboriginal healing modalities, building an evidence based practices for Aboriginal healing and cultural or intellectual property right issues and the main benefits of such aboriginal healing.

III

Traditional Medicine and Traditional Knowledge

Traditional medicine (TM) is well known in most of the world. Most of the people use it in Asian and African countries. Further 70 to 80 per cent of the populations in developing countries use varieties of alternative or complementary medicine. It is the blend of social, cultural, and scientific values prevailing among the indigenous people. WHO has already recognized its importance in commercial and scientific areas (WHO, 2008). Traditional Knowledge (TK) refers, as WHO mention elsewhere, as the sum total of the knowledge, skills and practices based on the theories, beliefs and experiences indigenous to different cultures, whether explicable or not, used in the maintenance of health, as well as in the prevention, diagnosis, improvement or treatment of physical and mental illnesses (WHO, 2002).

The traditional knowledge has assumed a critical dimension in the area of intellectual property rights in developing countries. The phrase "*Traditional Knowledge*" implies the development and transmission of the knowledge from generation to generation within a system, held by local individuals, families, lineages or indigenous communities. These local people or communities have a store-house of knowledge about their geographical flora and fauna. However, the local individuals and communities do not have the means to safeguard their traditional knowledge in the increasing global process of extraction, exploitation and commercialization of the biodiversity of the Third World. It is a stark reality that globalization is threatening the biodiversity, bio-information and creativity of indigenous approaches into proprietary knowledge for the commercial profit of a few. The existing IPR agenda is oriented around the concept of private ownership and individual innovation which encourages the co-modification of traditional knowledge without benefit sharing to indigenous communities (Mishra, 2003).

Traditional knowledge and traditional medicines (WHO, 2008) make a very important contribution to the holders of traditional knowledge in the Committee though their representation is not made mandatory in the Act or Rules Health of a particular community. Most of the Asian and African countries depend on traditional medicine for primary health care *(Ibid.)*. In China, traditional medicine accounts for around 40 per cent of all health care delivered. In Chile, 71 per cent of the population and in Colombia 40 per cent of the population use such medicine. In India, 65 per cent of the population in rural area use *Ayurveda* and medicinal plants to help meet their primary health care needs. Traditional systems of medicine are based on traditional beliefs, norms and practices of old experiences at the household or community level normally passed through oral tradition (Carlos, 2002).

National Policy on Traditional Medicine (1940)

India possesses rich heritage of traditional medicinal practices of *Ayurveda, Unani* and *Siddha* system. The knowledge of these systems is well documented and has been successfully practiced for centuries in our country (Venkataraman and Swarna, 2008). The *National Policy on Traditional Medicine* was introduced in 1940 in the country. National laws and regulations were also issued in 1940, and updated in 1964, 1970 and 1982. The national office, the Department of Medicine and Homoeopathy was established in 1995 as part of the Ministry of Health and Family Welfare. There are a number of expert committees for different forms of traditional medicine; the earliest of which was established in 1962. There are also a number of national research institutes; the first being the Central Council of Indian Medicine, established in 1970. India also has two multivolume national pharmacopoeias, the *Ayurvedic Pharmacopoeia of India* and the *Unani Pharmacopoeia of India.* Both are considered to be legally binding. Regarding national monographs, several sources are used, including a national database on medicinal plants used in Ayurvedic medicine and monographs contained in the national pharmacopoeias. Safety requirements include those required for conventional pharmaceuticals, as well as special requirements of traditional use without demonstrated harmful effects and reference to documented scientific research on similar products. No control mechanism is used for these requirements, as the long standing use of herbal medicines in the *Ayurveda, Unani* and *Siddha* systems demonstrates their safety for human use (WHO, 2005). The demand for protection of traditional medicine arose in the context of bio-piracy and patenting of new products based on traditional knowledge using biotechnology (Venkataraman and Swarna, 2008). Western science has acknowledged the usefulness of traditional medicine for the development and commercialization of new pharmaceutical products.

Traditional Medicine in IPR Perspective

Traditional Medicine (TM) plays a crucial role in health care and serves the health needs of a vast majority of people in developing countries. Access to "modern" health care services and medicine may be limited in developing countries. TM becomes the only affordable treatment available to poor people and in remote communities. World Health Organization (WHO) defines traditional medicine as the sum total of all the knowledge and practices, whether explicable or not, used in diagnosis, prevention and elimination of physical, mental or social imbalance and relying exclusively on practical experience and observations handed down from generation to generation, whether verbally or in writing. Health care providers worldwide including major pharmaceutical giants are turning to incorporate many of these into their mainstream activities. As traditional medicines are largely based on medicinal plants, indigenous to these countries, where the system has been in vogue for several centuries, the effort is on accessing them either directly or through the use of modern tools of breeding and cultivation, including tissue culture, cell culture and transgenic technology. IP issues linked to such endeavours remain unresolved (Mashelkar, 2001).

The protection of Traditional Medicine (TM) under intellectual property rights (IPRs) raises two types of issues. First, to what extent it is feasible to protect, existing IPR system. Certain aspects of TM may be covered by patents or other IPRs. There have also been many proposals to develop *sui generis* systems of protection. Such proposals are based on the logic that if innovators in the formal system of innovation receive a compensation through IPRs, holders of traditional knowledge should be similarly treated. The codification of TM varies significantly. A distinction can be made, particularly in Asia, between the codified systems of 'traditional medicine' and non-codified medicinal knowledge, which includes *'folk', 'tribal'* or *'indigenous'* medicine.

In our country the folk traditions are transferred orally from generation to generation. The 'folk' medicine is based on traditional beliefs, norms and cultural practices, trials and errors, successes and failures at the household level. These are passed through oral tradition and may be called, *'people's health culture'*, home remedies or folk remedies. Healers use rituals as part of their traditional healing methods, which often allow them to monopolize their knowledge, despite disclosure of the photochemical products or techniques used. The codified tradition consists of medical knowledge with sophisticated foundations expressed in thousands of manuscripts covering all branches of medicine. Examples are *Ayurveda, Siddha, Unani* and the *Tibetan* tradition. The grant of patents on non-original innovations (particularly those linked to traditional medicines), which are based on what is already a part of the traditional knowledge of the developing world have been causing a great concern to the developing world (*Ibid.*).

World Intellectual Property Organization (WIPO) has been sensitive to these concerns. In 1998, WIPO put forth an agenda for the future of IPR in the field of traditional medicines which prioritized activities in this area, namely, development of standards for the availability, scope and use of IPRs on traditional medicine in Asian countries, systematic documentation of traditional medicine for protection purposes, regional and interregional information exchange and compilation of the requisite databases etc. Still this agenda needs to be implemented for saving the prevailing knowledge of healing traditions. There are following examples showing that how profit-making originations exploiting their healing traditions.

Amazon Rainforest Plant Patent

Traditional healers and religious leaders from the indigenous tribes of the

Amazon used to collect a plant named *Baniste-riopsiscaapi*, and process it to produce a ceremonial drink—'*ayahausca*', also called '*yage*'. They used *ayahausca* in religious and healing ceremonies. According to tradition, *ayahausca* was prepared and administered only under the guidance of traditional healers.[1] Although the patent claimed to have identified a variety of the species with new and distinctive physical features, particularly the colour of the flower. This plant grew naturally throughout the Amazon basin. By law, plant patents cannot be awarded to plants 'found in an uncultivated state'.

Neem Oil Case

Similarly, the US has been taking undue advantage of the low level of patent awareness and laxity in enforcement of law. The *Neem* tree is used in India in the areas of medicine, toiletries, contraception, timber, fuel and agriculture. Its uses have been developed over many centuries but never patented. Since the mid 1980s, US corporations have taken out over a dozen patents on *Neem*-based materials. When the US Patents Office (USPTO) granted patent for '*Neem oil*' for antiseptic use, then *Council of Scientific and Industrial Research* (CSIR) urged for re-examination of the case, but failed. In this way, collective local knowledge developed by Indian researchers and indigenous communities has been expropriated by outsiders who have added very little to the process (Shiva and Bhar, 1993).

There is a problem on the grant of such patents linked to the indigenous knowledge of the developing world that needs to be addressed jointly by the developing and the developed world. We need to understand that there is a distinction between the patents that are granted based on modern research and patents, which can be categorized as traditional knowledge-based patents. A recent study by an Indian expert group examined randomly selected 762 US patents, which were granted under A61K35/78 and other IPC classes, having a direct relationship with medicinal plants in terms of their full text. Out of these patents, 374 patents were found to be based on traditional knowledge not that all of them were wrong. The Governments in the Third World as well as members of public are rightly concerned about the grant of patents for non-original inventions in the traditional knowledge systems of the developing world. At international level there is significant level of support for opposing the grant of patents on non-original inventions. For example, more than a dozen organizations from around the world to oppose the *Neem* patent and the entire process took five years. Such a process of opposition is understandably expensive and time consuming (Shiva and Bhar, 1993).

The issue of '*protection*' of traditional knowledge needs to be looked at from two perspectives, the 'protection' may be granted to exclude the unauthorized use by third parties of the protected information. On the other hand, the 'protection' also means to preserve traditional knowledge from uses that may erode it or negatively affect the life or culture of the communities that have developed and applied it. Further, the protection also promotes self-respect and self-determination. While recognizing the market-based nature of IPRs, other non-market-based rights could be useful in developing models for a right to protect traditional knowledge, innovations and practices. To date, debate on IPRs and biodiversity has focused on patents and plant breeders' rights. Provisions under undisclosed information or trade secrets could be invoked to protect traditional knowledge not available in the public domain. Geographical indications and trademarks, or *sui generis* analogies, could also be the alternative tools for indigenous and local communities seeking to gain economic benefits from their traditional knowledge. The potential value of geographical indications and trademarks is in protecting plants and germplasms that are specific and unique to geographical regions. They could protect and reward traditions while allowing innovation (Chauhan, 2004)

New experiments are beginning to emerge on benefit-sharing models for indigenous innovation. An experience in India is worth sharing. It relates to a medicine that is based on the active ingredient in a plant, *Trichopuszeylanicus*, found in the tropical forests of south-western India and collected by the *Kani* tribal people. Scientists at the Tropical Botanic Garden and Research Institute (TBGRI) in Kerala learned of the plant, which is claimed to bolster the immune system and provide additional energy, while on an expedition with the *Kani* in 1987. These scientists isolated and tested the ingredient and incorporated it into a compound, which they christened '*Jeevan*', the giver of life. The tonic is now being manufactured by a major Ayurvedic drug company in Kerala. TBGRI agreed to share the licence fee and royalty with the tribal community on a fifty-fifty basis and formed a registered trust with an understanding that the interest accrued from this amount alone can be used for the welfare activities of the *Kani* tribe. It is significant to note that while the issue of material transfer and benefit sharing was discussed and debated after *Convention on Biological Diversity* (CBD), India has already pioneered one of the first models (Chauhan, 2004).

Developing countries need a systematic documentation of traditional medicine for protection purposes, regional and inter-regional information exchange and compilation of the requisite databases etc. To mitigate this problem, the Indian Government has taken steps to create a *Traditional Knowledge Digital Library* (*TKDL*) on traditional medicinal plants and systems, which will also lead to a *Traditional Knowledge Resource Classification* (*TKRC*). Linking this to internationally accepted *International Patent Classification* (*IPC*) System will mean building the bridge between the knowledge contained in an old Sanskrit *Shloka* and the computer screen of a patent examiner in Washington. This will eliminate the problem of the grant of wrong patents since the Indian rights to that knowledge will be known to the examiner. It is right time that India must evolve a viable and effective mechanism to protect the biodiversity, bio-information and creativity of indigenous communities (Chauhan, 2004).

Indian Legal Frame for Protecting Traditional Medicine

Indian Patent Act

The terms of the *Indian Biodiversity Act* in some limited ways may help protect TM, owing to its focus on genetic resources and associated TK. However, since TM is an intricate combination of both tangible and intangible TK resources, the Biodiversity Act alone will not suffice to protect TM. So far as the intangible aspects of TK are considered, the *Indian Patent Act* (as amended in 2002) acknowledges its value and contains provisions that proscribe the patenting of TK. Under Section 3(p) of the *Indian Patent Act*, an invention which in effect is traditional knowledge or which is an aggregation or duplication of known properties of traditionally known component or components is not patentable. This provision, however, does not prevent granting of patent to new products and process based on traditional knowledge. The Act also mandates the disclosure of the source and geographical origin of the biological material in the patent specification when the invention claimed is based on biological material. There is also no reference to the provisions of the *Biological Diversity Act* in this regard at least in cases where the traditional knowledge is based on genetic materials. The Indian Patent Act acknowledges the oral tradition in TK and accordingly allows opposition to a patent application, if the invention claimed in the application is anticipated having regard to the knowledge, oral or otherwise, available within any local or indigenous community in any country [Indian Patent Act, Section 25(k)]. Opposition to patent is also allowed where the complete specification does not disclose or wrongly mentions the source or geographical origin of biological material used for the invention [Indian

Patent Act, Section 25(j)]. Similarly, a patent granted can also be revoked on the above said grounds [Indian Patent Act, Section 64(p) & (q)]. But here again there is no provision to oppose a patent application or revoke a patent granted on the ground that the traditional knowledge is used without the prior informed consent of the community or the patent owner failed to satisfy the terms and conditions including benefit sharing. Thus, the Act while treating the traditional knowledge as public domain property has failed to recognize the customary ownership and Right of the custodians of this knowledge (Gopalakrishnan, 2004). Another legislation that has a very limited application in case of protection of traditional medicine is the *Protection of Plant Varieties and Farmers' Right Act* (PVFA)[2], 2001. The PVFA though primarily intended to protect new plant varieties also include provisions for the registration of existing varieties and payment of compensation and benefit sharing to the community. The law is useful for protection of traditional medicine only if there are medicinal plant varieties. The benefit under this law is mainly targeted to the farming community. To protect the traditional knowledge of farming community the PVFA facilitates the registration of extant variety[3] and farmers' variety under the Act.

As far as the integration of traditional healing or medicine in the Western medicine is concerned, there successful attempts have been made in America, Canada, South Africa and New Zeeland. Illness like trauma, loss of cultural identity, its common effects, substance abuses etc. often addressed through healing modality require concerned culture and their place or land. Though, sometimes aboriginal patient may visit Western clinic for physical injuries and afterwards needs own cultural ceremonies in their community for a life. The main content of such ritual is "high emotional content". Some countries like Canada, South Africa or New Zeeland, have supported for integration of traditional healers with main stream health care system. There are fears also generated for example in Canada that increasing acceptance of traditional healing may result into sea change. The lessons of these countries can be useful for our planning for integration of healers and their medicine in our country for effective utilization of the traditional healers and their medicines.

Note: This chapter was earlier presented in *National Seminar on Law and Policy Interface Vis-à-vis-Tribal Societies of India*, November, 6th and 7th, 2015 Guru Gobind Singh Indraprastha University, Sector-16C, Dwarka, New Delhi-110078. Now it is again revised for *National Seminar on Relevance of Medical Anthropology and Tribal Health care systems in Globalizing World* (REMATH) March 16th to 18th 2018, School of Studies in Anthropology, Pt. Ravishankar Shukla University, Raipur, Chhattisgarh. Recently part of this chapter, was presented in the *Conference on Tribal Identity and Tribal Integration:*

Issues of Nation Building, organized from July 31st–August 1st 2018 by Department of Anthropology, University of Hyderabad. Various suggestions had come during the discussions which have been included. I wish to thank for the constructive criticism about the roles of traditional healers.

NOTES

1. A Plant Patent No. 5,751, issued to Loren Miller on 17 June, 1986 by USPTO claimed rights over a supposed variety of *B. caapi,* which Miller dubbed 'Da Vine'. The challenge to this patent was made by the Centre for International Environment Law (CIEL), on behalf of the *Coordinating Body of Indigenous Organizations of the Amazon Basin* (COICA) and the *Coalition for Amazonian Peoples and Their Environment* (*Amazon Coalition*). COICA is a coordinating body of more than 400 tribes. On re-examination, USPTO revoked this patent on 3 November, 1999. However, the inventor was able to convince the USPTO on 17 April, 2001, the original claims were reconfirmed and the patent rights restored to the innovator.
2. The PVFA is India's *sui generis* legislation for the protection of plant varieties giving effect to Article 27(3(b) of the TRIPS Agreement. The Preamble to the Act outlines some of the basic objectives behind the PVFA. The Act is purportedly for the establishment of an effective system for protection of plant varieties, the Right of farmers and plant breeders, and to encourage the development of new varieties of plants. The PVFA acknowledges the need to protect plant breeders' Right to stimulate investment for research and development. The PVFA was also created for the purpose of facilitating the growth of the seed industry in India, which will ensure the availability of high quality seeds and planting material to farmers.
3. The PVFA defines "extant variety" in Section 2(j), as a variety available in India which is
   (i) Notified under Section 5 of the Seeds Act, 1966; or
   (ii) Farmer's variety; or
   (iii) A variety about which there is common knowledge; or
   (iv) Any other variety which is in public domain.

REFERENCES

Aboriginal and Torres Strait Islander Healing Foundation Development Team. (2009). *Voices from the campfires: Establishing the Aboriginal and Torres Strait Islander Healing Foundation.* Retrieved on March 2018 from http://www.fahcsia.gov.au/sa/indigenous/pubs/healing/voices_campfire/Documents/HealingFoundationReport.pdf.

Aboriginal Healing Foundation (2008). *Active Funding Grants [as at February 2008]*. Retrieved on March 2018 from http://www.ahf.ca/funded-projects.

Adelson, N. and Lipinski, A. (2008). The Community Youth Initiative Project. *Aboriginal Healing in Canada: Studies in Therapeutic Meaning and Practice*. Ed. J.B. Waldram. Ottawa, Aboriginal Healing Foundation: 9-30.

Archibald, L. (2006). *Decolonization and Healing: Indigenous Experiences in the United States, New Zealand, Australia and Greenland*. Ottawa.

Belfrage, M. (2007). "Why 'culturally safe' health care?." *Med J. Aust 186*(10): 537-538.

Carlos, M. Correa (2002). *Protection and Promotion of Traditional Medicine: Implications for Public Health in Developing Countries,* Geneva, South Centre.

Castellano, M.B. (2006). *Final Report of the Aboriginal Healing Foundation: A Healing Journey: Reclaiming Wellness*. Ottawa.

Chansonneuve, D. (2005). *Reclaiming Connections: Understanding Residential School Trauma Among Aboriginal People*. Ottawa.

Chauhan, B.L. (2004). *The Protection of Traditional Knowledge: Problems and Perspectives.*

Dobson, V. (2007). *Arelhe-KenheMerrethene: Arrernte Traditional Healing*, Alice Springs, IAD Press.

Fiske, J.A. (2008). Making the Intangible Manifest: Healing Practices of the Qul-Aun Trauma Program. *Aboriginal Healing in Canada: Studies in Therapeutic Meaning and Practice*. Ed. J.B. Waldram. Ottawa, Aboriginal Healing Foundation: 31-92.

Finke, B. (2009). *The SCF NUKA Model: Customer-Owned, Customer-Driven Health care Facility Design–Primary Care*. Indian Health Summit, Denver. July 2009. http://conferences.thehillgroup.com/healthsummit/Documents/Day2_Presentations/Better%20Facilities%20&%20Better%20Care%20Principles%20of%20Facility%20Design_Bruce%20Finke.pdf.

Fletcher, C. and Denham, A. (2008). Moving Towards Healing: A Nunavut Case Study. *Aboriginal Healing in Canada: Studies in Therapeutic Meaning and Practice*. Ed. J.B. Waldram. Ottawa, Aboriginal Healing Foundation: 93-130.

Gopalakrishnan, N.S. (2004). "TRIPS and Protection of Traditional Knowledge of Genetic Resources: New Challenges to the Patent System", *European Intellectual Property Review*, *27*(1), pp. 11-18.

Hewson, M.G. (1998). "Traditional Healers in Southern Africa." *Annals of Internal Medicine 128*(12 Part 1): 1029-1034.

Horn, M. (2008). *Rethinking employment assistance to strengthen social and economic participation*. The 2008 Economic & Social Outlook Conference, Melbourne. 27 March, 2008, Retrieved on March 2018 from http://www.melbourneinstitute.com/conf2008/Presentations/Session%204B/Horn,%20Michael.pdf.

Iris, M. (1998). "Life in Balance." *Park Ridge Centre Bulletin*, Park Ridge Centre. http://www.parkridgecentre.org/Page126.html.

Jain, Sumeet and Jadhav, Sushrut (2009). "Pills That Shallow Policy: Clinical Ethnography of Mental Health Programme in North India." *Transcultural Psychiatry*, 46, 60. DOI:10.1177/1363461509102287

Lane, P.J., Bopp, M., Bopp, J. and Norris, J. (2002). *Mapping the healing journey: the final report of a First Nation research project on healing in Canadian Aboriginal communities*. Aboriginal peoples collection; APC 21 CA. http://www.fourworlds.ca/pdfs/Mapping.pdf.

Mashelkar, R.A. (2001), "Intellectual Property Rights and the Third World, Special Section: Science in the Third World", *Current Science*, Volume 81, No. 8, 25, p. 959.

Mishra, B.S. (2003). *Huge Commercial Implications of GI in Third World*.

Moran, H. and Fitzpatrick, S. (2008). *Healing For The Stolen Generations: Document prepared in Response to the National Indigenous Healing Forum*. Canberrahttp://www.nsdc.org.au/images/stories/files/healing_stolen_generations_sept_2008%5B3%5D.pdf.

Mrinal, M. (2018). *Troubled Mind: Healing Rituals and Healing,* Fourth Semester, Summer Field Work Report submitted to Amity University, UP (*Unpublished*).

NMHS-2014. *National Mental Health Survey-2014,* NIMHANS, Banglore.

Peter Drahos (1994). "Decentring Communication: The Dark Side of Intellectual Property." In Tom Campbell and Wojciech Sadurski (eds.) *Freedom of Communication.* Aldershot: Dartmouth.

Phillips, G. (2003). *Addictions and Healing in Aboriginal Country*, Canberra.

Ross, R. (2008). *Institutional Colonization and the Delivery of Healing Programmes in First Nations*. Yukon Government, Retrieved on 24 February, 2010 from http://www.correctionsconsultation.yk.ca/implementation/docs/focus_conf/institutional_colonization.pdf.

Sandner, D. (1979). *Navaho Symbols of Healing: A Jungian Exploration of Ritual, Image, and Medicine*, New York, Harcourt Brace Jovanovich.

Shastri, Parth (2016). "Science of the soul: *Dava* and *Dua* Project creates wonders to mental illnesses and how!" *The Times of India City,* Ahmedabad.

Smith, R. (2003). "Learning from indigenous people." *British Medical Journal* 327 (7412): 0.

Smith, P. (2009). *American Indian and Alaska Natives Traditional healing practice in the Indian Health Service*. Indian Health Summit, Denver. July 2009 http://conferences.thehillgroup.com/healthsummit/Documents/Day2_Presentations/Traditional%20Medicine%20in%20the%20Indian%20Health%20System_Phillip%20Smith-Part2.pdf.

Swan, P. and Raphael, B. (1995). *Ways Forward: National Aboriginal and Torres Strait Islander Mental Health Policy National Consultancy Report* http://www.health.gov.au/internet/main/publishing.nsf/Content/mental-pubs-w-wayforw-toc.

Towne, J. (2009). *Innovations in Planned Care for the Indian Health System (IPC): Virtual Site Visit: Whiteriver Service Unit*. Indian Health Summit, Denver. July 2009http://conferences.thehillgroup.com/healthsummit/Documents/

Day2_Presentations/Better%20Facilities%20and%20Better%20Care%20 Principles%20of%20Facility%20Design_%20Jana%20Towne.pdf.

Vandana Shiva and Radha Holla-Bhar (1993). "Intellectual Piracy and the *Neem* Tree", *Ecologist*, Volume 23, No. 6.

Varshney, Vibha (2013). "Troubled Beautiful Minds", *Down to Earth,* 15 August, 2013.

Venkataraman, K. and Swarna, S. Latha (2008). "Intellectual Property Right, Traditional Knowledge and Biodiversity of India", *Journal of Intellectual Property Right, 13* (2008), p. 326.

Yasmeen, Afshan (2016). "India needs to talk about mental Illness." *The Hindu*, October 23, 2016.

WHO (2005). *National Policy on Traditional Medicine and Regulation of Herbal Medicines.* Report of the WHO Global Survey, Geneva.

WHO (2008). *Report on Intellectual Property Right and Access to Medicines: a South East Asia Perspective on Global Issues.* Regional Office for South-East Asia, India.

Waldram, J.B. (Ed.) (2008). *Aboriginal Healing in Canada: Studies in Therapeutic Meaning and Practice.* The Aboriginal Healing Foundation Research Series, Aboriginal Healing Foundation.

Wearne, G. and Muller, S. (2009). *Dilthan Yol\unha: An Evaluation of a Yol\u Healing Place*, January 2009, Wearne Advisors and Associates. Darwin.

Williams, E., Guenther, J. and Arnott, A.(2011). *Traditional healing: a literature review.* Working chapter series 2: Evaluation and policy. No. 2, Co-valuator Network, Retrieved on March 2018 from http://www.covaluator.net/docs/S2.2_traditional_healing_lit_review.pdf

13

Globalization, Mental Health and Ethnography: The Role of Medical Anthropology in Mental Health Research

Khirod Chandra Moharana

Introduction

Humanity is experiencing a surge in incidences of mental illness in recent times. Almost everyday there are reports of new studies which try to estimate the true burden of mental illness. Almost all studies proclaim that for reasons being explored or yet to be explored we are witnessing increasing burden, of mental illness globally. Given this alarming picture of the disease burden, the legitimate question which can be asked is why such increase has happened? Trying to understand the increase in mental illness burden in recent years has two dimensions. The first is about the very time period in which we live today which can be considered as contributing to the increasing burden of mental illness and the second being the acceptance that we have, till now, been incapable of understanding the true nature of mental illness as a result of which proper interventions and treatment has not been possible yet. The chapter dwells on these vital issues related to mental illness and tries to find out an answer by discussing globalization and its effect on individual, and then by arguing that a methodological shift is crucially needed for understanding the origin, diagnosis and treatment of mental illness, thereby minimising the global burden of mental illness. Anthropology's conceptualization of a holistic man and ethnography as a methodology to unfold the intricate links between apparently separate domains of human life such as biological, social and political are discussed in this chapter to strengthen the idea that apart from biomedical interventions what we need more is the recognition that social and political are as important as biological to create and heal illness in human mind.

Present Burden of Mental Illness

There are several studies in recent time which claim that the humanity is experiencing an increasing burden of mental illness. According to the WHO, today there are more than 300 million people globally who live with depression. The corresponding figure for schizophrenia is about 21 million people. The report also provides a very disturbing statistics about the incidences of suicide worldwide. According to the report an average of one person kills himself/herself in every 40 seconds globally (WHO, 2018). A study conducted in 2016 claims that mental, neurological, and substance use (MNS) disorders contribute to a significant proportion of global burden of disease. There was 41 per cent increase in the absolute disability-adjusted life years caused by MNS disorders between 1990 and 2010 (Patel, 2016). The 2016 WHO study of global burden of diseases claims that mental illness accounts for 21.2 per cent of YLDs and 7.1 per cent of DALYs (WHO, 2016). The same year a chapter published in *The Lancet* claims that these figures are underestimated and the true numbers are much higher than estimated by the World Health Organization. The study estimated that the global burden of mental illness accounts for 32.4 per cent of years lived with disability (YLDs) and 13.0 per cent of disability-adjusted life-years (DALYs), instead of the earlier estimates suggesting 21.2 per cent of YLDs and 7.1 per cent of DALYs (Vigo *et al.*, 2016). Citing five reasons for underestimation of global burden of mental illness Daniel Vigo *et al.* argues that the underestimation is responsible for the ongoing apathy of government as well as funding agencies to scale-up mental health interventions globally (Vigo *et al.*, 2016). These digits certainly can throw a light on the enormity of the global mental health problem today. The picture of mental health in India too is distressing. The status of mental health in India is deteriorating as per a study conducted by the National Institute of Mental Health And Neurosciences (NIMHANS) in 2014. The study concluded that at least 13.7 per cent of Indian population suffers from a variety of mental illness and 10.6 per cent of this requires immediate interventions.

Globalization and Mental Illness

The fact that the global burden of mental illness is a recent phenomenon naturally provokes us to question the factors which are typical of these recent decades. Since the last two to three decades there have been enormous changes in the socio-economic, technological and political state of the world. This is often explained with the help of the concept termed as globalization. The term has gathered enormous academic and media attention due to its power to shape almost everything on earth. Globalization can be defined as the increasing flow of trade, finance, culture, ideas, and people brought about by the sophisticated technology of communications and travel and by the worldwide spread of neoliberal capitalism, and it is the local and regional adaptations to and resistances against these flows (Lewellen, 2002).

Can globalization be considered responsible for increasing incidences of mental illness? The crucial mover of globalization is economic liberalization marked by the march of global capitalism. It is a well known fact that capitalism thrives on individualistic competitive values and this value has been accepted as a determinant of success in almost all spheres of our lives. Being competitive is now considered as an essential quality of a successful person of any walk of life. We are now competitive as a student, as a professional, as a not-for-profit organization, as a corporate organization, as a government department and the list goes on. As a result, we are becoming lonely and prone to increasing stress and anxiety day by day.

Mental health is intricately linked with individual and collective identity. Ethnocultural identity plays crucial role in creating conducive environment and social support for persons with mental illness. Globalization has been shaping identity in major ways in which distinct boundaries of ethnocultural groups have been diluted. Migration and advanced communications have led to intermixing of cultures in spite of the apparent resiliance of distinct cultures. This results in a "creolization" of identity and of the cultural idioms through which emotional distress is communicated (Kirmayer and Minas, 2000).

Economic disparities, structural violence and social suffering are some of the factors which are attributed to determining origin of mental illness. Globalization has witnessed increasing economic disparities across the world and it is often associated with violence and social suffering. and resulting violence and as studies have tried to link an increasing sense of competition and loneliness with the process of gloabalisation. Globalization is based on economic liberalization without any type of restrictions on the part of governments. As a result, a new sense of competition arises among the market players catering to the global consumers. The global economy percolates to most aspects of human existence and accordingly competition becomes the central driving force of human life. The nature of this competition is qualitatively different from the type of competition which was observed in the pre-globalization market. Most sectors of our society, namely health, education, welfare, politics etc. are now marred with a naked form of competition where little cultural considerations and norms are followed.

Globalization has converted many impossibilities of yester-years a reality today. We are now granted a communication system which has revolutionalized the way we connect to others. Today we also use very efficient means of travel which has created a sense of global village. These technological and communication revolutions have both positive and negative effects in human lives. The changes due to globalization bring a pressure which is often termed as acculturative stressor (Bhavsar and Bhugra, 2008) and has definite effect on mental health.

There are also many negative consequences due to globalization. There is now an increasing gap between the haves and the have-nots in terms of economy and technology. There are now a few numbers of people who control the world economic and technological know-hows. A large proportion of the world population has now been controlled by a small fraction of the population who enjoy knowledge, technology and resources (Okasha, 2005). This widening gap creates competition, struggle, structural violence and suffering among a large proportion of the world population today.

If we accept that the factors related to globalization have precipitating effect on mental health we are actually challenging the reductionist biomedical approach of psychiatry. The dominant paradigm of mental health research revolves around the "chemical imbalance" theory, which is now being looked critically by many researchers.

Reasons for Increase in Burden of Mental Illness

Is Chemical Imbalance the Reason?

The extraordinary increase in the global burden of mental illness since last several decades has ignited the old debate about the ontological foundation of mental illness. How an upsurge in socio-political and economic changes can trigger onset of mental illness? If the evidences are to be accepted then there has to be a pathway which connects socio-political, economic and other non-biological factors with mental illness. Scholars have argued that the traditional way of reducing everything to biological causes does not solve psychiatric issues and problems. Even the psychiatric claim of discovering magic bullets to mental illness has been questioned. Do the psychiatric medications undo the chemical imbalance those are believed to cause mental illness? In Whitaker's words, do people diagnosed with depression and schizophrenia suffer from a chemical imbalance that is then corrected by the medication (Whitaker, 2010)?

Many researches argue that there is no definite evidence till now which can establish cause-effect relationship between a mental illness and specific biological/chemical factors. Quoting from Steve Hyman's "Initiation and Adaptation: A Paradigm for Understanding Psychotropic Drug Action", Whitaker argues that *prior to treatment, patients diagnosed with schizophrenia, depression, and other psychiatric disorders do not suffer from any known "chemical imbalance". However, once a person is put on a psychiatric medication, which, in one manner or another, throws a wrench into the usual mechanics of a neuronal pathway. His or her brain begins to function, as Hyman observed, abnormally* (Whitaker, 2010).

Causes of mental illness as biological abnormalities have been refuted by scholars like Allan Horwitz. He further argues that:

> *...the symptoms of most psychological dysfunctions are not direct indicators of discrete underlying disease entities....Culture, not nature, influence how most disorders become real both to the people who suffer from them and to those who treat them* (Horwitz, 2010).

Horwitz further claims that there is simply no conclusive biomedical evidence that altered brain chemistry and abnormal brain structures are the causes of mental disorders though a burgeoning psychiatric literature is trying to establish that chemical imbalances are the predominant causes of mental illness. There is a tendency in the psychiatric establishment to emphasize only on biological causes though socio-cultural factors are equally shown to be correlated with mental illness.

The recent advancement in the field of genetics, one would hope, must have developed strong evidences in support of causal factors for mental illness. But the claim that genetic vulnerability as a causal factor has been questioned too. Scholars have argued that there is no laboratory evidence that the serotonin transporter genotype has anything to do with a genetic weakness that increases the risk of depression in either men or women (Risch *et al.*, 2009). Further, all these recent advancements in genetics "have not been able to identify a specific [genetic] marker for any of the current diagnostic categories" (Maj *et al.*, 2002).

Serious and thoughtful psychiatrists have questioned the chemical imbalance theory proclaiming it as an "urban legend" (Pies, 2011). Scholars within the field of psychiatric establishment have questioned the efficacy of the drugs prepared to treat mental illness. Though there are extraordinary developments in the field of neurological sciences, the exact neurological pathway for the origin of mental illness is far from revealed (Gold, 2009). Neither genomics nor neurosciences have identified a biological cause of any psychiatric diagnosis (First, 2002).

Due to this uncertainty regarding our knowledge about the origin of mental illness some scholars hesitate to discuss mental illness as a biological disease or illness. No psychiatric disorder meets the scientific definition of disease as departure from normal bodily structure and function (Szasz, 2001). DSM categories are heuristics and can never be considered as "natural kinds" (Hyman, 2010). However, psychiatrists, as a move to legitimize their field as biological/biomedical try to explain mental illness as neurobiological disorders. The limitations discussed above regarding the unsuitability of mental illness to be considered as biological disease imply that psychiatrists' proclamation that mental illness as neurological disorder are ideological, economic and non-scientific motives (Deacon, 2013).

Do Social factors cause mental illness?

According to a recent Lancet publication on the report by the Lancet Commission on global mental health and sustainable development social determinants influence mental health by acting across distal and proximal levels. Distal levels refer to the upstream social arrangement of the society, and proximal levels refer to the way these arrangements are experienced by individuals and families (Patel *et al.*, 2018). Gender plays crucial role in mental health and it is observed that women are at an increased risk for anxiety and depression whereas the men are at higher risk for substance use disorders (Chandra and Satyanarayana, 2010). Economic conditions also determine the status of mental health in a society. Adverse economic conditions are independently associated with common mental disorders such as psychosis and suicide (Lund *et al.*, 2010). Poverty affects negatively on neurological development and mental health of children (Yoshikawa *et al.*, 2012). Kwok has studied the association between lower socio-economic status at birth and adult mental illness, and argued that there are crucial evidences in support of the argument that social class at birth determines the risk of psychosis during adulthood (Kwok, 2014).

A meta-analysis by Patel and his team explores the link between income inequality and depression. The impact of neo-capitalism and the increasing inequality in income among people can be considered as a strong factor of social comparison and status insecurity, which eventually precipitates in depression. The contemporary global village not only decreases the distance between persons and communities but it also has increased the anxiety and insecurities in people's lives. Today the world is experiencing increased incidences of violence, migration, civil conflicts, war etc. All these have very dangerous effect on mental health of people who experience these. Political upheaval, civil conflicts, religious violence and other traumas have strong effect on mental health of affected people. Researchers have tried to explore pathways depicting the process by which trauma gets translated into mental illness. Using the concept of "social suffering" scholars have argued that adverse socio-political factors have the power of writing negative scripts on human bodies (Kleinman *et al.,* 2003). Social suffering gets embodied with the help of a dialectical interplay between biological and social factors (Kleinman, 1988). Positive socio-political environment creates better mental health in society. Cultural factors such as shared meaning and identity protect mental health and the loss of cultural identity is associated with negative mental health outcomes (Bhugra and Becker, 2005).

The Ontological Uncertainties

With the kind of evidences that we have till today can we be certain about the causes of mental illness the way physical illnesses or diseases claim, for example tuberculosis? Notwithstanding neurological and genetic advancement in recent time mental health research is still way back in terms of causality of mental illness. One would expect similar advancement in the diagnosis and treatment of mental illness as we have marked in the field of neurology and genetics. But the increasing global burden of disease is a testimony to the argument that the developments in the field of neurology and genetics have actually not helped much.

The discipline within medicine which deals with mental illness is psychiatry. The discipline of medicine itself is based on the bio-medical model, which presents illness and disease as organic malfunctions located primarily within the body. Disease is regarded as being a discrete entity, having specific causal origins, which can be objectively identified and treated accordingly. Being a part of medicine, for psychiatry, natural sciences have become the basis for its intellectual foundations and thus biological thinking has been dominating in the field since the nineteenth century. Therefore, the conceptual model of psychiatry maintains that there are distinct boundaries between the 'normal' and the 'abnormal' that can be objectively recognised (diagnosed) and classified as discrete disease entities, applying value neutral scientific reasoning. The emphasis is placed on the idea that the causes of mental disorders are to be found in the disturbances of a biological kind, presenting themselves as specific symptoms for each particular disorder, that should be targeted by somatic treatments (Haslam, 2000). Thus, this standpoint implies that mental illness is not considered to be dependent on socio-cultural aspects and time.

There are some differences in determining the nature of a disorder between psychiatry and other branches of medicine. In medicine diagnosis implies the causal identification of disorder, however in psychiatry diagnosis in most cases involves "assigning a diagnostic label on the basis of the observed and/or reported behaviours and symptoms" (Allen, 1998). Consequently, assigning a psychiatric diagnosis does not necessarily suggest that "the etiology (cause) of the symptoms is known, but only that an individual's symptoms meet the criteria for the particular mental disorder" (*Ibid.*). Both major classifications of mental disorders used internationally—the Diagnostic Statistical Manual (DSM) in its fifth edition now and the WHO's International Classification of Disease (ICD) now in its 10th edition—are based on this kind of reasoning which is called "descriptive categorical approach" (Baltrusaityte, 2010).

These symptom-based intellectual constructions guiding psychiatric practice are far from stable. What constitutes psychiatric knowledge is always under negotiation and subject to revision and transformation (Busfield, 1996). This instability of psychiatric knowledge is reflected in the frequent revisions of diagnostic manuals. For example, the first edition of DSM appeared in 1952. It was revised in 1968, 1979, 1987, and in 1994. The DSM-V, which is used now, was issued in May 2013. Each of the new versions was supposed to provide a more elaborated and refined description of mental disorders since research evidence showed that there are difficulties and inconsistencies among clinicians in deciding on diagnoses (Manning, 2000). Many mental disorders have been deleted and added during each revision of DSM till the recent one. Some of the previous mental disorders during these revisions disappeared from the list (e.g., homosexuality), and at the same time new ones like 'hyperactivity in children', 'excoriation' (skin-picking), and 'female sexual interest/ arousal disorder' were included.

From the above analysis, it is clear that the psychiatrists use a method of diagnosis, which is prone to judgement based on social and cultural factors. Since the precise boundaries and meanings of mental disorder vary over time (and place) and are highly contested, mental disorder seems in fact to be a culturally and socially relative category. Moreover, the frequent revisions of diagnostic manuals, which reflect the changing boundaries of mental disorders, imply that the concept of disorder in psychiatric field is not free from value judgments, despite the declared scientific basis of psychiatric knowledge.

The above discussion substantiates our argument that mental illness is not an objective reality which is independent of social cultural and temporal dimensions. The current revolution in the field of neurology and genetics has not been able to ascertain the biological nature of mental illness. Whitaker has argued that there is no evidence to support the psychiatry's claim that chemical imbalance is at the root cause of mental illness. In other words, the traditional argument that the socio-cultural factors give shape to the underlying biological causes of mental illness has been questioned by both psychiatrists and non-psychiatrists. With increasing evidences of social and other non-biological factors contributing to the burden of mental health conditions simply discard the psychiatric assumptions that there are underlying biological causes of mental illness. Earlier we have discussed that none of the so-called biological evidences considered to be the causes of mental illness are unsubstantiated. Similarly, the claim that social factors are equally responsible for the origin of mental health conditions need further research and evidences. Both psychiatrists and social scientists have argued for a strong role of social and environmental factors in the origin of mental illness but we are far away from arriving at a clear picture about how these factors interact and create mental illness. In other words we are still unsure about the nature of mental illness *per se*.

It is also argued that mental illness is a disorder related to mind, which is different from brain. Brain has a structure and is a biological entity whereas mind is neither material nor biological. The defining characteristic of mind is its "intentionality" (Campbell, 2005). So what is the nature of "mental" illness? Can we explain this in terms of our physical and genetic heritage? Can we conceive "mental" as resulting from our interaction with the "social", "economic" or "environmental"? Does "mental" have its own existence? The psychiatric diagnoses are based on symptoms those are agreed upon not according to any definite biological criteria but on human behaviour and its interpretation. Accordingly, the Diagnostic and Statistical Manuals (DSMs) keeps on adding as well as removing mental disorders. Homosexuality, once included in the DSM is now out of the list. Likewise, the Attention Deficit Hyperactivity Disorder (ADHD) is a relative new entrant to the list of mental disorders. Symptoms or a cluster of symptoms can never be an objective natural entity. Thoughts, emotions, attitude, etc. are a different type of reality separate from the domain of objectivity. Modern psychiatry, based predominantly on symptoms-based diagnosis and believing on "underlying biological causes" of mental illness is thus ontologically uncertain and methodologically invalid.

Rethinking Methodology: Contributions from Ethnography

The uncertainty about the nature of mental illness prevails even today. Researchers across disciplines continue to examine the issues related to the origin, diagnosis and treatment of mental illness. Not only the ontological dimensions of mental illness are relooked but a similar effort was also started with respect to the methodology of mental health research. Many studies revealed that given the ontological reality of mental illness we need to have a different methodology to understand, diagnose and cure from mental illness. Most researchers argue that a dominance of quantitative methods in research has limitations in exploring the complexity of mental illness. The required methodology should be such that the inherent variables in mental health and illness can be explored. For this, qualitative methods can deliver in significant ways.

A quantitative study rarely has the scope to explore variables that may be influencing certain phenomenon. Mental health research based on a biological essence of human existence and experience is blind on the possibilities of interactions between our bodies and non-biological factors. A natural scientific research methodology based on empiricism and experiment is the dominant methods followed in psychiatric research. In this kind of research, it is hardly possible to study the lived experience of illness and suffering. Quantitative methods have certain limitations in exploring the experiential dimensions of human life. Many of the recent studies have claimed that it is in the experiential world of human existence where the proper interplay between biological and non-biological factors happens (Kleinman, 1988).

Ethnography thus comes into picture which is a powerful method to explore the dialectical link between biological factors and social factors to produce mental illness. Research on mental health and illness tends to be more epidemiologically oriented taking mostly a quantitative approach (Patel, 2001; Meltzer *et al.,* 1995). But this approach rarely explores the complexity involved in the nature of mental illness. Ethnography helps in exploring unique social and demographic aspects related to mental illness. It aims to attend to the ways in which experience of mental illness is rooted in social situations and conditioned by cultural factors. Ethnography also allows an open-ended approach required for exploring the unique and complex realities in each case of mental illness in the field.

It is from the analysis of the "lived experience" that one can understand the dynamics of social factors involved in mental illness. The "social" as a component of illness experience cannot be revealed with quantitative studies. The "social suffering" framework which uncovers the complex interactions between biological and social/political factors requires ethnography as a suitable method. The quantitative study rarely helps us to know the intricacies of socio-cultural influence in experiencing mental illness. Paul Farmer argues that graphs and statistics can prove the existence of suffering but they cannot tell us what suffering does to people (Farmer, 1996).

Ethnography helps in understanding both the local and global discourse of any matter. The special insider/outsider position of the ethnographer helps in examining actual interpersonal engagement and the moral processes in a society. Ethnography explores "what really matters" in our social life and accordingly can design suitable interventions to undo the bad effect of complex interacting factors on what matters most in our lives. Values and emotions are embodied and projected into social and inter-personal relations, family life and inter-personal struggles.

Kleinman's concept of "experience" is quite helpful in understanding the contribution of ethnography in mental health research. Experience for him is essentially inter-personal or "inter-subjective". Macro level social, political, and economic processes shape and are shaped by "lived experience" (Kleinman, 1999, 2006). His notion of social and moral experience places the collective and individual in the same analytical space. Experience is always "moral" because it is connected to local world of values, and "what matters most" in a particular society. Engaging with social life as moral experience can help in finding the links among various seemingly unrelated aspects in illness experience.

For Kleinman ethnography is a model for moral engagement. This is because ethnography is "an engagement with others that brings the ethnographer into the ordinary, everyday space of moral processes in a local world" (Kleinman, 2006). He advocates for ethnography as it is a practice which allows an insider-outsider engagement with a world of social experience.

Kleinman argued that despite the possibility by an ethnographer to capture the suffering and pain experienced by a person it is also true that the ethnographer is always an outsider. The ethnographer always faces the limits of language and moral meaning. Describing the difficulty involved in ethnography Kleinman maintains that "she (ethnographer) will come to understand local categories and even perhaps to feel the weight of local obligations, and she will almost certainly at some point get caught up in the give and take of daily life, but, for all that, she is not so fully absorbed by what is most at stake for local stakeholders that their world of experience becomes hers as well (Kleinman, 1995) (*parentheses mine*).

This marginal position of an ethnographer is an advantage so far as enquiring the moral process is concerned. The ethnographer's angle of exposure places her so uncomfortably between distinctive moral worlds and local and global ethical discourses and, what is more, creates such a destabilizing tension between them that she is forced to become, even at times it seems from published accounts against her will, self-reflexively critical of her own positioning and the commitments and problems it leads to as well as attentive to the new and unexpected possibilities that can (and so often do in real life) emerge (Kleinman, 1995). The ethnographer's very marginality enables a comparison of the moral processes specific to the field and the ethnographer's own moral process linked to his or her own moral world. Ethnography allows an understanding of both the local and global ethical discourses and examines how both are rooted in particular forms of "moral experience". This can be regarded as a crucial contribution of ethnography in the context of illness studies.

Ethnography also allows the researcher to engage with the stories and lives of others by listening, witnessing and taking account of what is at stake for people. The lived experience thus collected through ethnography can lead the researcher to understand the process of embodiment. Lived experience of people can through a light on the connection between the medical and non-medical aspects of life. Thus, ethnography allows us to analyse health problems not as separated from social problems.

Apart from the question of ability of "ethnography" to study suffering the crucial matter that draws frequent attention is that the methodology should also have the ability to convey the essence of suffering adequately to the world. Social scientific language lacks its ability to actually study and convey "what suffering does to people". Rather it does symbolic violence when it tries to study suffering (Bourdieu, 1999). Farmer also asserts that the human face of suffering cannot be shown with the help of numbers and quantitative research. "Numbers have lost their ability to shock or even move us." Further, he asks: "where, in the midst of all these numbers, is the human face of suffering? (Farmer, 2006). Thus, the methodology should also have the ability to convey adequately the reality of suffering. Arguing on the failure of social science to adequately account for what suffering does to people Wilkinson asserts that sociological writing should aim to educate a "politics of compassion" (Wilkinson, 2005). The poor and marginalized of the world can have a wider audience if the sociologists/ social anthropologists convey the human face of suffering to the world. Ethnography can be used as a method to achieve this goal.

Ethnography helps in investigating the nature of mental illness, thus trying to minimize the ontological uncertainties around it. The methodology also has amazing potential in designing proper interventions for treatment or healing of mental illness. The broad areas, which have not been discussed above, where ethnography has strong role to play are: relevance of subjectivity in mental health, embodiement of suffering, decoding structural violence, cultural idioms, women's mental health, cultural construction of body etc.

Conclusion: Role of Medical Anthropology

Much of the work after 1990s in the field of psychiatry is not about delving deep in to exploring the true nature of mental illness but a coordinated effort to strengthen the foothold of psychiatry in the field of medicine. Psychiatry has been sidelined from the mainstream subjects of medicine which is reflected from the funding disparities in the field. It has been argued that a miniscule amount of money has been spent for psychiatric research and services compared to the other branches of medicine. This is due to the ongoing ontological uncertainties surrounding mental illness.

Researchers at one extreme argue that mental illness is not an illness at all and it is merely a myth or social construction. On the other hand, many psychiatrists proclaim that mental illness is real and social factors only influence the expression of the underlying biological causes. The debate is not new and has been continuing since Scheff (Scheff, 1966, 1989, 1999) and Szasz (Szasz, 1960, 1974) argued in favour of a social origin and social construction of mental illness. But more crucial than this debate is how the "social" is embodied and expressed in illness. In the context of increasing global burden of mental illness and publications linking mental illness with socio-economic conditions, the question of embodiment of the "social" is of crucial significance now. As discussed earlier, mental illness is linked to the physical, social, psychological, spiritual, economic, and human right issues of an individual. When a person suffers from mental illness all these factors work together to produce the effect. How these factors interact with each other to produce mental illness is a matter of ethnographic study.

Today Medical Anthropology needs to relocate itself from the periphery to the core of mental health research. There are studies which have already recognized the multiple dimensions in the experience of mental illness. The recent report on the Lancet Commission on Global Mental Health and Sustainable Development has rightly recognized the social, biological and environmental factors linked to the origin, diagnosis and treatment of mental illness. Medical Anthropology needs no more evidence to argue that mental health is not "mental" *per se* but an essential condition for human flourishing. The Lancet report and the evidences discussed in this chapter show that mental health is not the outcome of only the mental dimension of human existence but is an outcome of a strong interrelations among various dimensions of human existence. This is how research in mental health can trigger the essential anthropology to reestablish the idea of holism in human affairs.

REFERENCES

Allen, J.J.B. (1998). "DSM IV". In H. Friedman, N. Adler, R. Parke, C. Peterson, R. Rosenthal, R.C. Silver, R. Schwarzer, & D. Speigel (eds) *Encyclopedia of Mental Health* (pp. 29-41). San Diego: Academic Press.

Baltrusaityte, G. (2010). "Psychiatry and the Mental Patient: An Uneasy Relationaship". *Culture and Society: Journal of Social Research, 1*(1), 9-27.

Bhavsar, V. and Bhugra D. (2008). "Globalization: mental health and social economic factors." *Glob Soc. Policy*; *8*:78-396.

Bhugra, D., Becker, M.A. (2005). "Migration, cultural bereavement and cultural identity." *World Psychiatry*; *4*: 18-24.

Busfield, J. (1996). *Men, Women, and Madness: Understanding Gender and Mental Disorder.* London: MacMillan Press Ltd.

Bourdieu, P. (1999). "Understanding." In Bourdieu, P. *et al. The Weight of the World: Social Suffering in Contemporary Society*. Cambridge: Polity Press.

Campbell, N. (2005). *A Brief Introduction to the Philosophy of Mind.* Neil Campbell. Orchard Park: Broadview Press.

Chandra, P.S. and Satyanarayana, V.A. (2010). "Gender disadvantage and common mental disorders in women." *Int Rev Psychiatry*; *22*: 513-24.

Deacon, B.J., (2013). "The biomedical model of mental disorder: A critical analysis of its validity, utility, and effects on psychotherapy research." *Clinical Psychology Review, 33*: 846-861.

Farmer, P. (1996). "On Suffering and Structural Violence: A View from Below." *Daedalus, 125*(1), 261-283.

Farmer, P. (2006). "Never Again? Reflections on Human Values and Human Rights." In G.B. Peterson (ed.), *The Tanner Lectures on Human Values*. Salt Lake City: University of Utah Press.

First, M.B. (2002). "A research agenda for DSM-V: Summary of the white chapters." *Psychiatric Research Report, 18*: 10-13.

Gold, I. (2009). "Reduction in psychiatry." *Canadian Journal of Psychiatry, 54*: 506-512.

Haslam, N. (2000). "Psychiatric Categories as Natural Kinds: Essentialist Thinking About Mental Disorder." *Social Research, 67*(4), 1031-1058.

Horwitz, Allan V. (2002). *Creating Mental Illness.* Chicago: University of Chicago Press.

Hyman, S.E. (2010). "The diagnosis of mental disorders: The problem of reification." *Annual Review of Clinical Psychology, 6*: 155-179.

Kirmayer, L.J. and Minas, I.H. (2000). "The future of cultural psychiatry: An international perspective." *Can J Psychiatr Nurs*; *45*: 438-46.

Kwok, W. (2014). "Is there evidence that social class at birth increases risk of psychosis? A systematic review." *Int J Soc Psychiatry*; *60*: 801-08.

Kleinman, A., Das, V. and Lock, M.M. (eds.) (2003). *Social suffering*. Berkeley: University of California Press.

Kleinman, A. (2006). *What Really Matters: Living a Moral Life Amidst Uncertainty and Danger*. Oxford: Oxford University Press.

Kleinman, A. (1995). *Writing at the Margin: Discourse Between Anthropology and Medicine.* London: University of California Press.

Kleinman, A. (1988). *Rethinking psychiatry: From cultural category to personal experience*. Free Press.

Lewellen, T.C. (2002). *Anthropology of Globalization: Cultural Anthropology Enters the 21st Century*. Bergin & Gervey: Westport Connectiut, London.

Lund, C., Brooke-Sumner, C. and Baingana, F. *et al.* (2018). "Social determinants of mental disorders and the Sustainable Development Goals: A systematic review of reviews." *Lancet Psychiatry*; *5*: 357-69.

Maj, Mario *et al.*, (eds.) (2002). "Preface." *Psychiatric Diagnosis and Classification.* West Sussex: John Wiley & Sons.

Manning, N. (2000). "Psychiatric Diagnosis Under Conditions of Uncertainty: Personality Disorder, Science and Professional Legitimacy". *Sociology of Health and Illness, 22*(5), 621-639.

Meltzer, H., Gill, B., Petticrew, M., *et al.* (1995). *OPCS Surveys of Psychiatric Morbidity in Great Britain*. London: HMSO.

National Mental Health Survey of India (2016). Prevalence, Pattern and Outcome. National Institute of Mental Health and Neuro-Sciences, Bangalore.

Okasha, A. (2005). "Globalization and mental health: A WPA Perspective." *World Psychiatry*; *4*: 1-2.

Patel, V., Burns, J.K., Dhingra, M., Tarver, L., Kohrt, B.A. and Lund, C. (2018). "Income inequality and depression: A systematic review and meta-analysis of the association and a scoping review of mechanisms." *World Psychiatry*; *17*: 76-89.

Patel, V. and Kleinman, A. (2003). "Poverty and Common Mental Disorders in Developing Countries." *Bulletin of World Health Organisation*, *81*(8).

Patel, V., Chisholm, D., Parikh, R., *et al.* (2016). *Addressing the burden of mental, neurological, and substance use disorders: key messages from Disease Control Priorities*, 3rd edition. Lancet; *387*: 1672–85.

Pies, R., Psychiatry's new brain-mind and the legend of the "chemical imbalance" [Electronic version]. *Psychiatric News.* Retrieved on October 31, 2018, from http://www. psychiatrictimes.com/blog/couchincrisis/content/article/10168/1902106

Risch, Neil *et al.* (2009). "Interaction between the Serotonin Transporter Gene (5-HTTLPR), Stressful Life Events, and Risk of Depression." *Journal of the American Medical Association. 301*: (23), June.

Scheff, T.J. (1966, 1989, 1999). *Being Mentally Ill: Sociological Theory.* NewYork: Aldine Transaction.

Szasz, T. (1960, 1974). *The Myth of Mental Illness: Foundations of a Theory of Personal Conduct.* New York: Harper Collins.

Szasz, T. (1961). *The Myth of Mental Illness*. New York: Free Press.

Szasz, T. (2001). *Pharmacracy: Medicine and Politics in America.* Westport, CT: Praeger.

Vigo, D., Thornicroft, G. and Atun, R. (2016). "Estimating the true global burden of mental illness." *Lancet Psychiatry*; *3*: 171-78.

WHO. *Mental Health Atlas 2014*. Geneva: World Health Organization Press, 2015.

WHO. *Depression: key facts*. 2018. http://www.who.int/news-room/factsheets/detail/depression (accessed on Ocobcrt 31, 2018).

WHO. *Schizophrenia.* 2018. http://www.who.int/mental_health/managcment/schizophrenia/en/(accessed on October 31, 2018).

WHO. *Suicide data*. 2018. http://www.who.int/mental_health/prevention/suicide/suicideprevent/en/(accessed on October 31, 2018).

Wilkinson, I. (2005). *Suffering: A Sociological Introduction.* Cambridge: Polity Press.

Yoshikawa, H., Aber, J.L. and Beardslee, W.R. (2012). "The effects of poverty on the mental, emotional, and behavioural health of children and youth: implications for prevention." *Am Psychol*; *67*: 272-84.

PART IV
LIFE COURSE AND GENDER

14

Perceiving Menstrual Health in a Punjabi Village

Srishti Bhatnagar

Menstruation is a regularly occurring physiological process, experienced by nearly all adolescent girls and women (of reproductive age) around the globe. It marks one of the most "important biological differences between females and males; one has been used—in many contexts—"to justify discrimination against women and girls."[1] Though menstruation is a biological reality, culture-bound values and practices shape its meaning and management that tend to separate and often define the experiences of women in contrast to men. Societal adherence to certain cultural and traditional practices has rendered the concept of menstruation a topic of taboo[2] and an eminent part of the culture of silence. In many societies, menstruating women and their menstrual blood are depicted as dangerous or offensive leading to their physical and social exclusion.

With the onset of puberty (menarche), girls begin to face increasing restrictions to their mobility and agency. A society's reaction to menarche affects individual experiences of young girls and often dictates their behaviour to facilitate its own needs. There are over 355 million menstruating women and girls in India, yet maintaining a proper menstrual care becomes a problematic affair for many.

According to UNICEF, a woman spends about 2,100 days menstruating (equivalent to almost six years of her life) and such a recurrent event requires access to appropriate materials and facilities, without which females suffer from poor menstrual hygiene, which further restricts their movement and self-confidence. Good menstrual hygiene is, therefore, crucial for the health, education and dignity of all girls and women.

On the whole, menstrual health has an important bearing on any society's health and prosperity. How one manages their menstrual health greatly affects one's well-being, mobility, identity and agency. Hence, a comprehensive study of cultural perception towards menstruation is imperative to understand a multifaceted issue such as menstrual health.

Menstrual Health and Hygiene

The broader term of 'Menstrual Health' encompasses "menstrual hygiene management practices and the broader systemic factors that link menstruation with health, well-being, gender, education, equity, empowerment and human rights (in particular the human right to water and sanitation)."[3] Menstrual hygiene management (MHM) is an integral component of achieving the Sustainable Development Goals (SDGs), particularly SDG 3 (Good Health and Well-being), SDG 4 (Quality Education), SDG 5 (Gender Equality), SDG 6 (Clean Water and Sanitation), SDG 8 (Decent Work and Economic Growth) and SDG 12 (Responsible Consumption and Production).[4] Improving menstrual hygiene management in India is an important agenda of the 'Swachh Bharat Mission'. According to the 2011 Census, about 89 per cent of the nation's population lives in homes that lack toilets and less than 12 per cent of women have access to 'safe' products for feminine hygiene. The Ministry of Drinking Water and Sanitation has issued 'The Menstrual Hygiene Management Guideline' (2015) outlining the role of government officials, teachers and health care providers to support all adolescent girls and women and to generate awareness regarding menstrual health.[5]

Numerous women across the globe still face significant barriers to a comfortable and dignified experience with menstrual hygiene management (MHM).[6] A wide scale study on menstrual practices by UNICEF and TISS-Mumbai (2015) proved that menstruation taboos still have firm roots in Indian society. India is known for its rich cultural heritage and this cultural diversity is also reflected in beliefs and practices pertaining to menstruation. A massive body of evidence documents the impact of society on molding menstruating bodies to maintain an order. There can be polarizing cultural views on menstruations. For instance, menarche as a symbol of maturity can have variegated reactions. While auspiciously celebrated and rejoiced over in a few cultural traditions such as '*Tuloni Biya*'[7] in Assam or '*rutukkaliyanam*'[8] in Tamil Nadu, menarche is also highly concealed and silenced in other areas such as Nepal, Sri Lanka and many parts of India where a newly menstruating girl goes through ritual and physical seclusion and resides in a separate 'menstrual hut'. Dube in her chapter '*On the Construction of Gender: Hindu Girls in Patrilineal*

India' (1988) considers menarche as "the definite point of departure" and the time interval between menarche and marriage to be the most vulnerable period as the process of transition becomes more evident in terms of behavioural expectations. She discusses the radical changes subjected to a menstruating body in terms of appearance, movements, habits and dispositions, "to be honed into the approved model of beauty, self-restraint and self-abnegation", for the single-minded pursuit of matrimony (Dube, 1988).

Socio-demographic factors such as age at marriage, socio-economic status, educational attainment, occupation, gender relations, family type and size, religion and the like play an important role in determining menstrual health in a given society. Lack of knowledge and indifference towards basic scientific facts readily contribute towards adverse health consequences (Kamaljit *et al.*, 2012). Studies reveal that cultural beliefs about menstruation heavily influence menarcheal expectations associated with concept of ritual purity and "hot and cold" foods, and food avoidance (Chopra and Sharma, 2011). Certain conservative communities, such as those in Lebanon, Nepal, India and Bangladesh, prevent girls from adopting what is generally considered good menstrual hygiene practices (Santina *et al.*, 2013). Baishya and Thakur (2017) worked among the female workers of the unorganized sector in Guwahati and discussed the association of menstrual blood with "demonic spirit".

The discipline of anthropology has significantly contributed to the study of menstruation and the role of culture shaping it. However, many such studies have been subjected to a great deal of criticism. Rayna R. Reiter's (1975) "double male bias" critiques male anthropologists to have neglected the narrative of menstruation of women because of the popular belief that menstruation belongs to the private sphere, a woman's sphere. Many scholars believe that in the current academic climate, menstrual activism presents a subject worthy of anthropological enquiry because unlike the women's health movement to which anthropology has richly contributed, menstrual activism is an attempt not only to redefine the androcentric meanings ascribed to the female body but also to publicly confront and repudiate the menstrual taboo.

Prior research work on menstruation is either purely quantitative or qualitative. The current study ventures a holistic understanding of menstruation and investigates changing behavioural patterns through factors such as space, time, gender, age, relationships and institutions. This chapter attempts to understand the perception of menstruating bodies through a socio-cultural study of menstrual health, beliefs and practices.

Lived experiences of menstruation can be explored through anthropological theories of body which study human body as a social and cultural phenomenon. Phenomenologists Merleau-Ponty (1962), Desjarlais and Throop emphasize the theory of embodiment to understand the lived experience of perception or "bodily aspects of human body and subjectivity" (Desjarlais & Throop, 2014). Foucault contributed immensely on the notions of "disciplining the female body" and presented that "the body is regulated by 'dominant discourses' within the society which prescribes norms for male, but insistently, the female body" (Alsop *et al.*, 2001). In the book titled 'The Second Sex', Beauvoir discusses body through different stages of a woman's life. She describes the ways in which a body of a girl, as an entrant to puberty, becomes to her a source of horror and shame. The lived realities are different for men and women and bodies, when viewed as products, become "primary signifier of gendered identities" (Alsop *et al.*, 2002). Psychoanalytical theories of gender are concerned about what we make of these subjective differences. According to social role theory, men and women become masculine and feminine, respectively, through social conditioning. In this way, the meanings attached to menstruation and menstruating body by a society, 'condition' behaviour of women and men alike. By developing a discourse on lived experiences of women regarding menstruation, the current ethnographic research study strives to find out the awareness and knowledge regarding menstruation; determine the cultural and indigenous ways of managing menstrual health and discover embedded patterns of socio-cultural beliefs and practices and record the associated prescriptive and prohibited norms and rituals.

Methodology

A community-based research study was conducted among the inhabitants of rural Gurdaspur district of Punjab, India in early 2018. The universe of study included two neighbouring village communities of distinct religious affiliations: Hindus of Pindori Mahantan and Gujjar Muslims of Karwal and Rasoolpur.

The stigma attached to menstruation demanded utmost privacy, thereby shaping the methods of research methodology. Ethical considerations led to snowball sampling method to recruit participants of the study. This respondent-driven technique proved to be fruitful in close-knit communities such as these, where word travels fast and the process of data collection gains momentum at a fairly impressive pace.

The cross-sectional sample population consisted of 50 unmarried and ever-married females of ages ranging from 12 years to 85 years. In order to minimize bias and maximize the scope of study, the sample size was kept even-handed, i.e. out of 50 females, 25 belonged to Pindori Mahantan and the other half belonged to hamlets of Karwal and Rasoolpur villages.

A mixed-method approach was adopted to understand the intricacies involved in a comprehensive study of menstrual health and associated socio-cultural aspects. Theoretical orientation of the research methodology is inspired from anthropology of body, gender and health which studies human body as a social and cultural phenomenon in a wide spectrum of temporal and spatial connections. The concept of menstruation can also be viewed as social event(s) and constituent of time using life course theory or perspective.

Both qualitative and quantitative methods of data collection and analysis were employed to provide a thorough account of the culture being investigated. Narratives of menarche (first menstrual bleeding), information on products used for menstrual hygiene management (MHM), pre-pubertal and general awareness regarding menstruation, sources of knowledge transmission, prescriptive and prohibited menstrual behaviour were recorded with informed consent. Use of audio-visual recording devices, written documentation such as jotted notes, diagrammatic representation and any other means was made explicit throughout the course of data collection. Semi-structured interviews using interview schedules clubbed with genealogical method and household census schedules erupted extensive ethnographic and comparative data. To capture the underlying intensity and subjectivity as well as an elaborate detail on the lived experiences of menstruation, individual and face-to-face interviews were conducted, with in-depth information on cultural and traditional belief patterns. Focus group discussions (FGDs), though unavoidable at certain times, aided in analyzing normativity and peculiarities associated with menstrual health beliefs and practices. Quasi-participant and non-participant observation helped in gauging communal as well as personal reactions towards menstruation from varied lengths. Case studies, domain analysis, tabular and pictorial illustrations, statistical tools as well as expanded field notes were utilized for data analysis and interpretation.

The Idea of Menstruation

Perception of menstrual health can be gauged by understanding the existing general knowledge among individuals. From its commencement (menarche) to its cessation (menopause), the process of menstruation gets recorded in a series of events. For instance, experiences of menarche alone can illustrate details about societal outlook on menstruation. This section discusses the visualization of menstruation through lived realities.

Menarche: Introduction to Menstruation

Menarche, the first menstruation, distinctly marks the onset of puberty among girls. The average age at menarche of the sample population (n = 50) is about 13.5 years with a standard deviation of 0.67 estimated by method of recall. Accounts of the first menstrual bleeding can be highly helpful in extracting intensive data on pre-pubertal awareness, sources of knowledge transmission, various learning and coping mechanisms along with physical, social and emotional changes. Contrasting menarcheal encounters with existing understanding and management of menstruation can help in evaluating changing patterns of perception and practice of maintaining menstrual health in time and space.

Menstrual Ideologies

> *"Jis aurat ko hote nahin [menstruation], vo aurat aurat hi nahin hai"*
> [A woman who doesn't menstruate is not considered to be a woman (Period)]
>
> — Pooja, 35, Matric Pass, Pindori Mahantan

The above statement strongly brings out the prevalent notion of menstruation among the women of these Punjabi communities. In-depth interviews generated a consensus of women's opinion (mostly married women) regarding the importance of menstruation, which inadvertently lays in its ability to able the 'female' body to become a 'woman'. As an insurer of fertility, it plays a crucial role in fulfilling the perceived demand of femininity, i.e. attainment of motherhood.

> *"yeh shareer ke liye bahut jaroori hote hain...mathe ki saari garmi nikal jaati hai"*
>
> — Pooja, 35, Matric Pass, Pindori Mahantan

> *"Agar periods nahin ho toh blood clots ho jaaten hain bacchedaani me"*.
>
> — Kiran, 28, Secondary School Graduate, Pindori Mahantan

> *"shareer ki taakat badhate hain"*
>
> — Asha Rani, 50, illiterate, Pindori Mahantan

> *"bleeding nahin hogi toh phir kaise niklega gand?"*
>
> — Motia Devi, 32, Pindori Mahantan

Menstruation is not only an important indicator of fertility but also vital for proper functioning of body, health and temperament. According to them, especially women of Pindori, menstrual discharge is responsible for releasing toxic wastes from their bodies, preventing uterine blood clots and reinstating the humoral balance[9] of the body.

The physiological knowledge regarding menstruation seems to be highly limited. All of unmarried informants (12-25 years) did not know why menstruation happens let alone the biological process underlying it. Not even a single girl belonging to the above age bracket could underline the organ(s) involved during this process. Most of the married women on the other hand knew that they couldn't give birth without regularly menstruating and therefore, could at least mark uterus ("*bacchedaani*") as the primary organ involved.

Most of the females in both the communities had little to no pre-pubertal knowledge. *About 84 per cent of the total sample population admitted to having absolutely no prior information regarding menstruation pre-menarche* while only a small chunk (i.e. 16%) of these females had a certain idea about it. However, it is important to clarify that simply knowing or having heard about it is different from being aware of the process.

Emotional Competency

Menarche is often associated with the feelings of shock, horror, embarrassment, shame, disgust, guilt and resentment. In-depth interviews using open-ended questions concluded that compared to their counterparts, women who claimed to know about menstruation pre-menarche were not scared or horrified when they encountered their first menstrual bleeding. The experience was "just" embarrassing and disgusting but not dreadful because of which they were able to cope up with this 'life-changing' event in a much healthier manner in terms of psychological and emotional ramifications. In other words, awareness and proper knowledge regarding menstruation pre-menarche is essential to ensure effective menstrual health and to provide the rightful opportunity to cope up with a major physiological change occurring inside the body of a female. The consuming silence and suppression of menstruation turn this rather natural and normal experience into a psychological crisis and interferes with the emergence of female identity to a great extent. Therefore, prior pubertal knowledge serves as an important parameter to lead a healthy, ordinary and pacifying menstrual life.

Transmission of Ideas

What, how, when and from whom a girl learns about menstruation and its associated changes often tends to have an impact on her response to event of menarche as well her approach towards the subject matter in general. According to the literature reviewed upon the sources of menstrual knowledge transmission, it is usually the mother who is the primary source of menstrual information. Yet, the most common sources of information among the sample population came out to be the friends and/or peers of the individuals. A girl has a greater tendency of learning about menstruation from a close friend. This way, *menstruation becomes a mechanism of socialization.* This trend is much more prevalent among the Gujjar Muslims of Karwal and Rasoolpur where young adolescent girls and married women avoid talking to their mothers about menstruation. Their friends and close relatives, who themselves are not well-equipped with adequate knowledge of menstrual health, are more likely the ones prescribing advice about preparing and coping up with the practical aspects of menstruation. To a certain degree, this could be a reflection of the nature of the relationship between a mother and daughter.

> *"My own mother doesn't know that I menstruate even now. I don't know if they [menstrual periods] happen to Maangi [her daughter] or not. We just don't talk about such things with our daughter in our culture."*
>
> —Jitoon Bibi, 40 years, Married, Illiterate, Karwal

The mothers admit to not knowing whether their own daughter(s) is menstruating, let alone serve as a source of knowledge. The mother-daughter bond appears to be more formal among the Gujjar Muslim women of Rasoolpur and Karwal. For them, talking about menstruation with their mothers is almost as embarrassing as it would be horrifying with their male relatives. Therefore, if need be, many women prefer to talk about menstruation with their friends and close relatives. Another

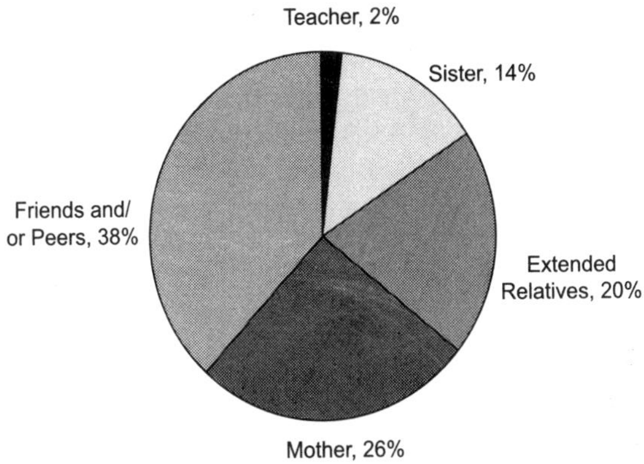

Fig. 14.1: Sources of Menstrual Knowledge Transmission.

common source of information are the mothers, especially among the girls of younger generation of Pindori Mahantan. Many girls reported having no hesitation while talking about menstrual issues with their mothers, who often become the assumed source of imparting such intimate information. In all cases, the transmitters of menstrual knowledge were menstruating females. No male, irrespective of age, relation, profession or status would ever become a source of information regarding menstruation. It would be a highly unfortunate and unfathomable situation should such interaction takes place, for menstruation is (dis)regarded as solely a woman's issue which needs to be tackled by women unless it is a matter of emergency. Thus, *identifying the sources responsible for transmitting menstrual knowledge can aid in understanding interrelationships among people in a given community.* This way *studying menstrual health and beliefs is a significant way of comprehending Kinship system of a society* to a certain extent.

Experiencing Menstruation in Everyday Life

Because menstruation is a recurrent event in a woman's life, it cannot be avoided in conversations and because of the surrounding notions, it is expressed in form of euphemisms such as, "*date*", "*kapade agaye*", "*mahavari*", "*mahina*" etc. Among the women of relatively older generation, "*mahavari*" and "*kapada*" are the common terminologies while "date" and "period" terms are usually referring to menstruation among the females of relatively new generation. While these are direct terms of references, there are more formal and 'safer' euphemistic phrases such as "*jab hum theek nahin hote*" (when we are not okay), "*bimari*" (illness), "*tabyat kharab*" (ill health) to describe menstrual health. These expressions indicate their embodiment of menstruation; women view their bodies as diseased, disordered and unhealthy. Perceived in a perpetual negative light, menstruation is learnt to be viewed as a tabooed concept and as something in need of 'management' as menstrual blood implies disease, social violations, and spiritual corruption.

Practicing Menstruation

Menstruation is a monthly occurrence that requires access to appropriate materials and facilities, without which, females suffer from poor menstrual hygiene, which restricts their movement and self-confidence. This section will elaborate upon the type, use and effect of Menstrual Hygiene Management (MHM) products along with associated practices.

MHM Products

The two types of MHM products known to and/or used by the women of Pindori Mahantan, Karwal and Rasoolpur are home-made cloth and market manufactured sanitary napkins. None of the respondents was aware of other existing options of MHM products. Generally, these cloth pieces are a reproduction of old clothes like bed sheets, pillowcases, towel, old clothes etc. They usually fold a piece of cotton rag (*sooti ka kapda*) thrice in order to make it look like the one shown in Figure 14.2. Cotton is the most useful choice of fabric to maximize absorption and comfort and minimize cost and changing duration. *About 72 per cent of the sample population uses makeshift home-based pads made out of old cotton rags to manage their everyday menstrual hygiene* while almost a quarter of the sample uses commercialized sanitary napkins. The data illustrate that the practice of using the former is much more prevalent than the latter and showcases the existing traditional practices of these areas. Also, while the percentage of home-made cloth users and machine-made sanitary pad users came out to be statistically same among the Hindu women of Pindori Mahantan, about 80 per cent Gujjar Muslim women of Karwal and Rasoolpur use cloths as primary MHM products.

> *"I prefer cloth over pads. Pads are uncomfortable; they often leak and have to be changed more than once a day. It also changes the way I walk. Cloth absorbs more and feels lighter."*
>
> —Tanya, 14, class 9 Student, Pindori Mahantan

Fig. 14.2: A home-made cotton pad

> *"We have always used cloths. We don't know about anything else. We don't talk about such things."*
>
> – Shooma, 17, Married, up to class 5, Rasoolpur

An anthropological investigation strives to learn the rationale behind these choices that needs to be understood within the cultural context of the society in question. Why and why not these products are preferred by a particular set of people reveals the underlying notions and ideologies. Upon further exploration, it was found that familiarity, personal liking, lack of access to or affordability of high-quality commercial sanitary napkins and lack of sufficient awareness can explain the majority's preference towards the former. Another and potentially the most important reason is the fact that the mothers of these primary cloth-users used cloth themselves to manage their menstrual hygiene. *The intimate bond between a mother and her daughter influences the intimate topic of menstruation.*

Prior research studies accuse lack of knowledge and access to sanitary products as main culprits 'forcing' women to use cloth during their menstrual periods. But women are not always "forced" to use cloth. Sometimes, they choose to do so in spite of being aware of other options. Cloths are prevalent for their traditional value and the element of familiarity. Market manufactured pads can be a costly affair when compared to the home-made cost-effective cloths. They are considered to be more comfortable, easy-to-dispose and long-lasting than a sanitary napkin. Many-a-times, young women prefer a combination of these MHM products.

> *"I started using sanitary napkins ("pattis") in the last 3-4 years. I saw them on T.V. and decided to try them. They feel more comfortable and cleaner than cloth rags."*
>
> Maariya, 26, Married, up to class 8, Karwal

Users of sanitary napkins or "*pattis*", "pads", "STs" as some would call them, were either adolescents or younger married women of ages ranging from 18-25 years. None of the older generations use or have used these market-based products. In other words, younger women have a greater tendency to opt for these pads over traditional cloth. Many of them have switched from using cloths to pads. Therefore, *MHM products have the potential to become the index of changing ideology and practice.*

The debate, however, is not between which one of these MHM products is better. There are legitimate concerns revolving around both kinds. For instance, relentless use of sanitary napkins is fast-becoming a potential biohazard while old ratty cloths are more potent to cause serious bacterial diseases. What can be questioned and must be scrutinized is the duration for and the condition in which women are using these products.

Many women use a single multi-folded piece of cotton cloth for the entire day. A few even use the same piece of cloth for the entire period, changing sides of the cloth whenever fully absorbed. Also, since market sanitary pads are a costly affair and become a matter of whim and luxury, one sanitary pad is being used for more than 12 hours, i.e. pads are changed twice a day. This practice can lead to poor menstrual health.[10] Such long hours of direct contact with menstrual blood-absorbed product has a greater tendency of giving rise to certain urinary tract and reproductive tract infections along with other pelvic inflammatory diseases (PID).

A major issue arising out of the surrounding culture of silence is when women reuse old unhygienic ratty cloth to deal with their day-to-day menstrual experiences. Many women do not dispose of their used cloth rags immediately. They wash it, dry it and then reuse it until its exhaustion and then bury it underground in a far away field. They claim to reuse perfectly clean cloth pieces. Yet when divulged on the process of drying, a perturbing issue is developed. Shrouded in an exceedingly overwhelming secrecy and blindsided of normative adherence to rules and restrictions, these cloth rags are not dried up under direct sunlight. Women go to impressive lengths to avoid the wandering eyes of the passerby. The cloths are dried under the shade and are kept in separate dark corners. Consequently, such cloth rags become potent breeding grounds for bacterial growth. Prior studies have shown that such women are at a higher risk of developing bacterial vaginosis.[11] Evidently, an unspoken priority is given to the silent socio-cultural rules. *Women choose to compromise with their health over going against the prescriptive norms.*

The Role of Education

The current study discovered a significant correlation between educational status and use of commercial sanitary napkins. The former acts as an independent variable the latter depends on. That is, *the use of commercial, market-produced sanitary napkins depends on the level of education attained by the individual.* All illiterate women, who make 40 per cent (approx.) of the total sample population, use only cotton cloth rags to manage their menstrual hygiene. In other words, only those women use sanitary napkins who have received some amount of formal education. Majority of these women have either graduated or are graduating from senior secondary school. Another aspect where education directly influences menstrual health is the bathing practice during menstruation. *About 65 per cent of illiterate women do not take bath during menstruation.* Most of these women either belong to Karwal and Rasoolpur or age more than 40 years or both.

Bathing Practice

While majority of women engage in regular bathing practices, a significant percentage of women (and girls), i.e. 38 per cent of the total sample population, do not indulge in regular baths during menstruation. In fact, 32 per cent of women never bathe while menstruating. Some women, especially older Gujjar Muslim women, take bath only on the fourth day of menstruation. They are guilty of not knowing the reason behind this tradition yet nonetheless they feel bounded by this cultural obligation. This presents a serious hygiene issue since these women are much more prone to develop bacterial infections and diseases. Another discerning conclusion drawn from the subjectivities of these numbers is that the 'polluting element' encompassing the notion of menstruation has more to do with symbolic and spiritual causes than it is to do with the actual physical body.

Access to Safe and Sanitary Places

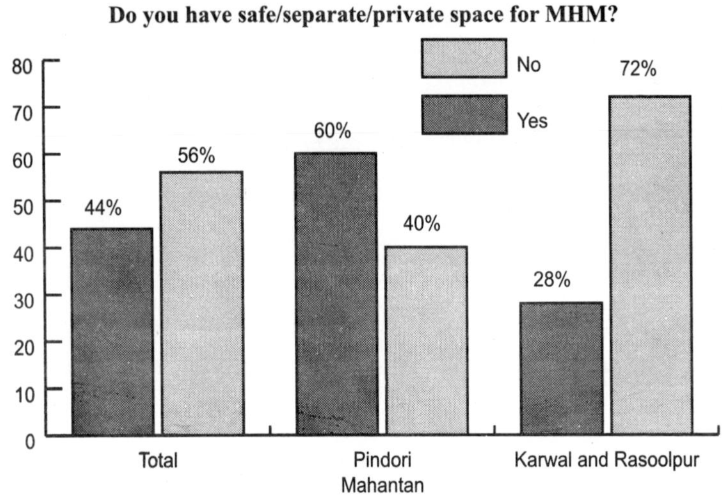

Fig. 14.3: Column graph representing access to safe space for MHM.

When it comes to having abundant access to safe, separate and private spaces for managing their menstrual hygiene, an overwhelming portion of women denied of having such basic and fundamental opportunities. *More than half of the sample population does not feel that they can safely and privately manage their menstrual hygiene.*

Many households in both the areas lack basic sanitation facilities. Women go out, either before sunrise or after sunset (or whenever it is discreet enough), into the farmlands (*khet*) to defecate and manage menstruation. Also, on an average, each household comprises 4-5 family members and more often than not, live together in a highly limited one or two-room space. Suffice to say, a private and personal place to lead a dignified menstrual experience is lacking in this community. This lack of access to essential sanitary facilities is much more prevalent among the Gujjar Muslim women belonging to hamlets of Rasoolpur and Karwal. About 72 per cent of the sample population in these areas believe to be devoid of such basic amenities.

Menstruation in Spaces: Application of Culture

While analysing and evaluating different beliefs and practices regarding menstruation, a prevalent theme in terms of spatial observances came into being. The values attached to physical spaces seem to directly alter menstrual behaviour in a society. This section explains the different ways in which places, inside and outside home govern menstruation.

Hearth and Home

Restricted entry to the kitchen is one of the most widely followed rules of menstruation till date. More specifically, it is access to the household hearth, which is primarily denied to a menstruating body. The symbolic impurity and toxicity of such a body is believed to contaminate the food in question. This age-long traditional belief dictates the mobility of menstruating woman by and large among these communities. Among the Gujjar Muslims, it is believed that a learned man, i.e. an individual, who can read and/or write Urdu, will become sick and suffer from indigestion if a menstruating woman serves his meals. Women, in Rasoolpur and Karwal, faithfully follow this rule because the health of wise men cannot be compromised. This exclusion of women from a space (hearth), which is traditionally a symbol of femininity, is also sometimes thought of as a breakaway from the monotony of life. They expressed their relief from being relieved from their domestic duties. Adhering to this norm is possible for people of Karwal and Rasoolpur because they are members of one large family. Among the Hindu women of Pindori Mahantan, entering and operating the kitchen while menstruating is considered an unfortunate necessity. Many of them feel guilty for consciously feeding germs to their family members, who at the time hold a higher spiritual position. The element of untouchability is more pronounced as it appears. Women are 'restricted' to enter a place which 'belong to them' in their respective communities. Hence, in a way, she is being denied and deprived of performing her prescribed feminine role. So does it mean that a menstruating body is less-feminine in this regard? Or by denying her that "female right", does her concealed period of impurity becomes more enhanced? Also, a woman feels guilty if she 'has' to enter the kitchen or cook for her family. Even if her polluting body is considered offensive and dangerous, the men never seem to take in charge of the kitchen. Patriarchy has a wicked way of making the 'subordinate' feel guilty of not being able to play the role of a subordinate.

Cohabitation

The living arrangements too get affected accordingly. A Gujjar Muslim woman should not sleep in the same room as her husband for it is believed that her 'germs' can make the man ill. Although this tradition is largely abandoned today, a few older, non-literate women still adhere to it. This could also be a cultural way of regulating sexual behaviour of a couple during menstruation.

Bathing Rituals

As established before, many women do not bathe during menstruation. They take a ritual bath of purification once they have stopped menstruating. The strong cultural hold over traditional beliefs does not let them deviate or question the age-old practices in their respective families. Also, more importance is placed upon washing the head than the body. The sacred head wash restores the normative state of purity and spirituality. However, this rule can tolerate a certain amount of deviation. If a menstrual cycle lasts for more than four days, a woman may take a bath on the 4th day to manage her hygiene. This practice is persistent among the Gujjar Muslims.

Dietary Practices

A menstruating woman, to prevent contamination, must not touch any food item having a ritual and spiritual value. 'Cold' food such as curd, rice, milk, radish, sugarcane, onion, garlic etc., should not be consumed during menstruation to avoid stomach-ache and cramps. 'Hot' food items on the other hand can help smoothen the process. A popular home remedy to treat stomach cramps is to drink a hot glass of milk mixed with dry dates (*chhuhare*), almonds (*badam*), *sogi* and purified butter (*ghee*). The heat produced in body will make menstrual blood-flow smooth and pain-free. Also, milk of a menstruating cow is not served to the priests and other men of significance.

Personal Sacred Spaces

All households have assigned spaces that are sacred in nature. Among the Hindus, a menstruating female is not allowed to light or touch '*jyot*' (sacred flame) for her impure state may bring bad luck over her house and family, a chance she is not willing to take. Any misfortune would be blamed on her if she is indulged in this sinful and inauspicious act. She is also condemned to face the Gods and Goddesses placed in their private temples. Sacred, tangible objects such as the religious book of 'Urdu Arbi' (containing phrases from the holy book Qu'ran) must not be touched by a profane and impure menstruating body. Women are not allowed to enter such rooms altogether.

Public Sacred Spaces

Visiting a temple, in case of Hindu women of Pindori Mahantan or a Mosque for Gujjar Muslim women of Karwal and Rasoolpur, during menstruation is morally impermissible. The confounding notions revolving around a menstrual body become more prominent and prevalent outside of the house, in public spaces. Menstruation and the elements of impurity, pollution and even danger become much more pronounced, gain more consciousness and develop more relevance in sacred spaces. Religious institutions in Pindori Mahantan, such as Pindori *Dham*, *Sarovar*, temple of *Bhole Shankar,* shrine of *Peer* or the Masjid in Karwal, or any other religious space prevent religious females from performing her religious duties of a devotee. It is especially in these areas where patriarchal deliberation to control the mobility and agency of a menstruating female body becomes evident, acceptable and embodied. A few interviews revealed that the prevailing Maharaj ji had once told the women of Pindori Mahantan that when they are not 'okay' (common euphemistic expression for indicating menstruation related topics) they shall not visit the *Dham* for it will make the sacred place ritually impure and thus offend the Almighty. When such a revered religious leader dictates women for recognizing the 'requirements' of this period of impurity, a god-fearing society such as this is bound to adhere to these norms and beliefs. Some people, including the Maharaj himself explained this spiritual restriction through the ancient literature of Shastra. However, none of them knew what the scriptures actually say. Believing in the scientific nature of Hindu Dharma which regards menstruation to be an unhygienic situation, the physical bodies are thought to pollute the spiritual atmosphere of the *Dham*.

Ritual and Spiritual Events

Menstrual bloods in particular and menstrual bodies in general symbolize things, which are profane, ritually impure and tainted. Participating in festivals is a joyous occasion yet not everybody enjoys the same right to be a part of it. To be more specific, a menstruating woman is not supposed to be a part of festivals which are ritualistic in nature. To understand the impurity associated with menstruation, the societal behaviour on festive occasions can showcase the pragmatic aspect of such beliefs. The mobility of a menstruating body is highly regulated on such public events.

Ramzan, a month of intense prayer, dawn-to-dusk fasting and nightly feasts is an extremely important event celebrated among Muslims. As a way of physically and spiritually purifying the body and the soul, observant Muslims abstain from eating and drinking all day for the entire month. Yet on such auspicious occasions, an inauspicious menstruating body is not deemed fit to be fasting. She is also not allowed to perform Sunni Namaz, a prayer among Muslims that is performed five times a day, according to the village Maulvi.

"The custom of worshipping and the ritual feeding of virgin girls (*kanya*) on special occasions is widespread in India" (Dube, 1988) and in Pindori Mahantan as well. On *Ashtmi* (the eighth day) and/or *Navmi* (the ninth day) of *Navratri,* the festival of nine nights, the 'privileged' status of a girl in the pre-pubertal phase visibly contrasts sharply with the pubertal and post-pubertal status and helps define the latter with utmost clarity. During other festivals too, women avoid participating in *Puja* or having '*Bhog laga hua khana'* (food with ritual value).

After giving birth, a woman goes through a period of pollution, a customary ritual practice known as '*Sootak'*. This period of observance lasts for about a month and eight days (commonly referred to as *sawa mahina*), where both, the new mother and her new born are refrained from going out of house. It is considered to be ritually impure and ominous as it directly linked to a woman's menstrual conditions followed by childbirth.

Another belief regarding menstruation is known as '*silam'* in which a menstruating woman shall not go near an infant until he/she becomes a month old. Newly born babies begin to cry incessantly and the family has to seek a divine intervention where a religious specialist prescribes certain amulets or potion to the child to restore his/her normal health. However, these incidents have been thought to be untrue by many young mothers in Pindori Mahantan.

Generally, it is believed that merely talking about menstruation can induce menarche earlier than the 'supposed natural timing' among pre-pubescent girls. This could be one of the reasons behind the utter lack of pre-pubescent knowledge of menarche among the women of Pindori Mahantan. Some of them consciously avoid menstruation-related conversation with their pre-pubertal daughters to extend their period of 'childhood innocence'.

Menstruation and Witchcraft

It is an age-old belief that if a woman does not dispose her used '*kapda'* or sanitary napkin properly, and if it comes in contact of someone with bad intentions, especially women who are infertile (for they are always believed to be jealous of other women who have children), she can be cursed with future infertility. As per the principle of contagion, the menstrual blood, which is the known indicator of fertility, can transfer the woman's natural ability to conceive to the infertile woman. Nevertheless, adherence to this notion may at least motivate its followers to dispose of the used MHM products properly in this regard.

Menstruation, Media and Market

Most of the change in MHM products, i.e. from the customary practice of using cloths for managing menstrual hygiene by the previous generations to increasing popularity of commercialized sanitary napkins by the current generation, is attributed to social media, in the form of television, internet in phones, etc. Women who have abandoned their traditional practices for a more seemingly dignified option of using sanitary napkins claim television advertisements to be their greatest source of information.

Yet from a critical perspective, advertisements and 'femcare' companies sell their products using shame as their biggest marketing strategy. This in turn extends and re-enforces the stigma surrounding menstruation. Advertisements play an instrumental role in shaping people's perception. When it comes to the topic of menstruation, they create the fear of staining, leaking, bulging and smelling in us. Although a reflection of society, such media re-instill and further crystallize the existing beliefs regarding the culture of silence surrounding the notion of menstruation.

Understanding the role of market inside the village is important and relevant not only to increase the scope of the current study but also to understand the behaviour of women as customers towards buying these items surrounded by a tabooed ideology, from the sellers, who are mostly men, i.e. with whom the topic of menstruation shall never be discussed.

Easy access to sanitary napkins is highly limited. Girls find it difficult to buy napkins themselves and often send their mothers to buy for them. A prominently patriarchal community such as this has a deep rooted control over the mobility of its women. When every step taken is under constant scrutiny, the actual act of buying sanitary napkins and walking back home with the infamous black polythene bag[12] becomes highly problematic and bothersome. In spite of having two small shops in their vicinity, women usually avoid these overtly embarrassing trips. Also, with no such shops around the villages, girls in Karwal and Rasoolpur have to travel longer distances (and in groups) to buy such products. To avoid the walks of humiliation and the effort of putting themselves out there, girls usually resort to using cloth rags during menstruation. It saves them time, effort and more importantly, from facing daunting situations.

Conclusion

The current study underscores low levels of awareness, interest and many misconceptions regarding the subject of menstruation. Keeping up with the national trend[13], menstruation continues to be shrouded in secrecy and shame among the people of the Punjabi community under study. The body of a menstruating female is considered to be polluting, disordered and utterly undesirable and therefore, is 'kept' ritually and physically secluded. It is the object of patriarchal aversion and scrutiny, all at the same time. The idea of keeping the 'situation' contained, by virtue of adhering to certain norms and restraints, is internalized within the community and as a consequence, the fate of a menstruating girl in terms of her behaviour, agency, mobility and idea of freedom, is decided beforehand. Menstruation is solely a 'woman's issue' that needs to be dealt with within a close-knit circle of women. As a highly private affair, menstruation does not take a public stance among them. Nor is it highly concealed unlike many other communities. However, diluted forms of rules of exclusion, restrictions on diet, operationalization of kitchen, bathing practices etc. associated with menstrual etiquette could be analyzed. A menstruating woman shall not touch anything of ritual and religious value nor is she supposed to cook and/or serve food to other members of her family due avoid upsetting The Almighty and contaminating the food with germs, respectively. As a rule, menstruating women are barred from entering religious institutions and attending ritual and spiritual events. Consequently, the body is looked down upon as impure and contaminated and is thus reduced to a degraded status. The embodiment of these restrictions and prescriptions, however, could interfere with a girl's menstrual health. An overwhelming portion of these girls and women had no prior knowledge of menstruation before menarche, use home-based cloth rags as primary MHM product, do not take regular baths during menstrual periods and deny having a safe and sanitary place to manage their menstrual hygiene. Suffice to say, they do not meet any requirements of proper menstrual health management, as per national guidelines. Taboos or stigma around menstruation may prevent women and girls from seeking or receiving timely medical treatment related to abnormal bleeding or pain, and lack of knowledge around menarche and menstruation may increase anxiety or psychosocial stress, in particular for adolescent girls. Therefore, rather than teaching women to how conceal it, they should be taught how to maintain good menstrual health. Encouraging efforts may be aimed at empowering women to come forward and discuss their menstrual health barring any hesitation, guilt or embarrassment.

NOTES

1. For more information, refer to "The Menstrual Cycle: A Feminist Lifespan Perspective". *Society for Menstrual Cycle Research* [www.menstruationresearch.org 22/1/18 5pm]
2. Kandaul's definition of Taboo (2014). "Taboo is a strong social prohibition or ban relating to any area of human activity or social custom that is sacred or forbidden, based on moral judgment and sometimes even religious."
3. Keith, B. (2016). "Girls' and women's right to menstrual health: Evidence and opportunities", *Outlook on Reproductive Health*. PATH, Seattle, USA.
4. For more information, please visit "Menstrual Hygiene Day" website http://menstrualhygieneday.org/
5. For more information, please see "Menstrual Hygiene Management: National Guidelines". 2015. The Ministry of Drinking Water and Sanitation, Government of India.
6. For more information, refer to "Menstrual Health in India: Country Landscape Analysis". (2016) *FSG*.
7. Tuloni Biya, also known as Shanti Biya, is a rite of passage publically celebrated among the Hindu Assamese to mark the attainment of puberty and transition into womanhood.
8. Rutukkaliyanam is an auspicious rite and a formal ritual observance among Hindu Tamils in which puberty is linked to marriageability.
9. Bodily Humors of hot and cold; the body is believed to be 'hot' during menstruation.
10. According to "Menstrual Hygiene Report" (2008) prepared by UNICEF INDIA, a sanitary pad should not be worn for more than 3-4 hours to prevent poor menstrual health.
11. According to a study conducted in Mumbai (2014), women who use cloth are twice more likely to have 'bacterial vaginosis' compared to women who use nothing during menstruation.
12. Black polythene bags are generally used to carry sanitary napkins clandestinely.
13. According to FSG's Country Landscape Analysis Report (2016), more than 71 per cent of girls in India lack awareness about menstruation before menarche.

REFERENCES

Baishya, J. & Thakur, M. (2017). "I Don't Want Others to Know, I am on My Periods: A Study of Menstruation among Women Workers of the Unorganized Sector in Guwahati." *The Eastern Anthropologist, 70*, 269-283.

Chopra, S. & Sharma, K. (2011). "The development of menstrual-related beliefs and behaviours during adolescence in a semi-rural Haryana (India): A conceptual and empirical formulation." *Anthropologie,* 95-107.

Dube, L. (1988). "On the Constriction of Gender: Hindu Girls in Patrilineal India." *Economic and Political Weekly, 23*(18), 11-19.

Kamaljit, K., *et al.* (2012). "Social Beliefs and Practices associated with Menstrual Hygiene among Adolescent Girls of Amritsar, Punjab, India." *JIMSA,* 25(2), 69-70.

Kaundal, M. & Thakur, B. (2014). "A dialogue on Menstrual Taboo". *Indian Journal of Community Health, 26*(2), 195-196.

Keith, B. (2016). "Girls' and women's right to menstrual health: Evidence and opportunities." O*utlook on Reproductive Health*. PATH, Seattle, USA.

Lennon, K. (2014). "Feminist Perspective on Body." *Stanford Encyclopedia of Philosophy.*

Lorimer, F. (1954). "Culture and Human Fertility: A Study of the Relation of Cultural Conditions to Fertility in Non-Industrial and Transitional Societies." Zurich: UNESCO.

MacCormack, C.P. (1982). "Biological, Cultural and Social Adaptation in Human Fertility and Birth: A Synthesis." In C.P. MacCormack (Ed.), *Ethnography of Fertility and Birth.* London: Academic Press Inc. Ltd., 1-24.

MacCormack, C. (1982). *Ethnography of Fertility and Birth*. London: Academic Press Inc. Ltd.

MacCormack, C. (2016). "Menstrual Health in India–Country Landscape Analysis." *FSG*.

MacCormack, C. (2018). Menstrual Health Management Symposium. http://mhmsymposium.info/Retrieved on July 25.

Menstrual Hygiene Management: National Guidelines. (2015). The Ministry of Drinking Water and Sanitation, Government of India.

Santina, T., Wehbe, N., Ziade, F.M. and Nehme, M. (2013). "Assessment of Beliefs and Practices Relating to Menstrual Hygiene of Adolescent Girls in Lebanon." *International Journal of Health Sciences & Research, 3*(12), 75-88.

Santina, T., Wehbe, N., Ziade, F.M. and Nehme, M. (2008). Sharing simple facts: Useful Information About Menstrual Health and Hygiene, UNICEF and Government of India.

Thakur, H., Aronsson, A., Bansode, S., Lundborg, C.S., Dalvie, S. & Faxelid, E. (2014). "Knowledge, practices, and restrictions related to menstruation among young women from low socio-economic community in Mumbai, India." *Front. Public Health, 2*, 72. doi: 10.3389/fpubh.2014.00072

Williams, L. (2017). "Educating Communities on the Importance of Menstrual Hygiene." *Global Health Council.* [Blog Post] Retrieved on from https://globalhealth.org/educating-communities-on-the-importance-of-menstrual-hygiene/

15

Pathways of Decision-Making in Childbirth: Social Contexts of Biomedical Practice

Priyanka Ghosh and *Mathew George*

Background

Obstetrics is the branch of medicine that deals with pregnancy, labour and puerperium[1] of women. With the help of this branch, medicine redefined childbirth as delivery; removing its socio-economic and cultural context from it. It became a procedure carried out by the obstetricians and no more an activity of women (Rothman, 1978). Labour pain during the initiation of childbirth is an intense and expected pain which is considered as a normal phenomenon. It is often described as the most severe pain by those women who have experienced childbirth (Jangsten *et al.*, 2005). But in medicalized childbirth, absence or presence of analgesia or anesthesia, more specifically, avoiding pain and presence/absence of pain relief medications, are the areas where pregnant women focus their decision-making abilities while preparing and experiencing childbirth (Dillaway and Brubaker, 2006). In North America, there are a lot of childbirth options available, ranging from giving birth in a planned setting with non-medically mandated C-section type of medicalized childbirth to a vaginal birth attended by midwives, which are free from drugs and interventions. Still, all the options are neither equally available to all the women, nor all the choices are equally viewed as responsible (Malacrida and Boulton, 2012).

Exercising Control on Pregnancy

Medical view of childbirth as pathological, where something can go wrong at any time is a powerful and dominant model. Institutional delivery is always quoted as the best possible measure to deal with childbirth complications, as it is the doctor who decides the type of delivery based on nature of complications. But this useful intervention has become a source of exploitation in many countries (Ghosh, 2010). Shanley and other proponents of free-birth believes that medical profession hassled the natural life event of pregnancy and childbirth to disease, creating unwanted complications and thereafter misleadingly claiming to respond and/or guard against them. When choices for pregnant women are determined by the professionals on their behalf, women have lesser control on their own pregnancies, resulting in disembodiment in their own pregnancies. Midwifery care, thus, is often preferred by the women for they have greater control on their own pregnancy as well as they exercise greater agency when it comes to type of care they need to receive and the location where they want to receive the care. The way the women experience pregnancy and childbirth under midwifery care is more of holistic approach, where greater number of in-depth discussions and meetings take place. A report from Canadian Institute of Health Information (CIHI, 2004 b) claims that pregnancies and childbirth attended by midwives involve fewer medical interventions and lower C-section rates (Johnson, 2008). Continuous medical surveillance, as per feminist bioethicists and practitioners, on the weight, diet, behaviour, appearance, activities etc. of women tend to bring them under pressure which increases further during pregnancy through routine ultrasounds and genetic testing to ensure best medical practices for mothers and normal growth for fetuses. The whole range of medical interventions takes place in each case of pregnancy, irrespective of necessity. Thus, disembodiment and alienation of pregnancy and commodification of the foetuses progress further. Privileged women fall more as prey to these continuous surveillance as compared to the women in developing countries and/or disadvantaged population (Johnson, 2008).

Dimensions of Pain Relief Options in Delivery

Epidural anesthesia started as a pain relief during labour in the 1970s and continued as the same for about 20 years and thereafter it became an alternative and preferred form of anesthesia for C-sections. Although it became an easy, convenient and routinely practiced procedure but studies (MacArthur *et al.*, 1990) have shown that epidural had made women suffer from subsequent newly occurring long-term backaches that begun within three months of their delivery and lasted for more than six weeks. This study also showed that this backache also persisted for months or years and even became chronic (MacArthur *et al.,* 1990). Epidural proves to be beneficial for both mothers and the new-born, especially in high-risk cases. But the shortcomings include time, skilled and trained professional, better infrastructure for continuous vigilance, and money. In addition to these, weakness of legs, dizziness, and shivering, prolonged labour in the second stage are the ill-effects associated with the mother who undergoes epidural. Reduced neonatal mortality and better neonatal period are the benefits enjoyed by the new-born whose mothers have received epidural before delivery. Apart from this it acts as a pain relief in labour and proves beneficial for those women who suffer from Preeclampsia (Reynolds, 1989).

Mode of Delivery Based on Maternal Request

In a National Survey of Sweden Antenatal Clinics (1999-2000), it was shown the previous Lower Segment Caesarean Section (LSCS) led to recurrent C-section to the women in their next deliveries, but women's own wishes to opt for C-section was of limited help to explain rise in C-section rates. The study also found that women who wanted to have C-section as the mode of delivery was less interested in making their own decisions than the women who wanted to have normal delivery. Maternal request for C-section was found among the women who were less well educated, lived in small cities, were depressed and worried during their pregnancies for several reasons. Thus, the study concluded that C-section on maternal request is not associated with highly educated urban women rather it is contrary to the stereotype, in context of Sweden. According to Gamble and Creedy (2000) maternal request for C-section could divert the attention away from obstetrician-led influences on the growing rates of C-section. Their belief was based on their study report which said that maternal request for C-section in the absence of complications are quite few (Hildingsson, *et al.,* 2002). According to Emmett *et al.* (2006), review of various studies claim that family factors remain the primary reason due to which women with previous LSCS choose repeat LSCS or Vaginal Birth After Caesarean (VBAC). The studies explored the reasons behind choosing VBAC and/or repeated C-section and concluded that VBAC was chosen to have quick recovery post-delivery while repeated LSCS for convenience and for the opportunity to have concurrent sterilization surgery.

Role of Information in Decision-making Process

The National Institute of Clinical Excellence (NICE) guidelines for C-section (2004) states that decisions regarding mode of childbirth after previous LSCS should involve maternal preferences, priorities and associated risk-based discussions. According to the study by Emmett *et al.* in 2006, women felt that information related to delivery after having previous LSCS was not provided routinely to them by the health professionals. Rather they were available only on request and thus they were not robust. Women believed that more facts and figures-based information could have led them to be more active in decision-making process regarding the choice for mode of delivery. Some women felt that procedural information like induction of labour, monitoring during labour, VBAC success rates etc. could have helped them in getting more involved in the decision-making process. However, the overall study results show that there was a mix of experiences for women regarding their roles in decision-making process about choice of mode of delivery after previous LSCS. As to the contrast of the experience of women stated above, majority of women felt that there was a negotiation involved between the hospital and the pregnant women where the women were allowed to make their own choice about mode of delivery. Some women were even fine with the doctors making the decision all alone, while there were only two women who felt that obstetricians totally ignored their requests. Another qualitative study conducted by Moffat *et al.* in 2006 regarding decision-making about mode of delivery among women with previous LSCS came up with the observation that the process of decision-making evolves during the entire period of pregnancy and is influenced mostly by events occurred in previous pregnancy as well as in the current one. Although the women wanted to be involved in the decision-making process but they lacked confidence in taking the final decision as they believed that they do not possess the necessary skills. Also, their wish regarding the amount of involvement varied widely, i.e. from no wish of getting involved to wanting the decisions to be taken out of their hands.

The process of decision-making in choosing the mode of delivery, ideally, involves the opinion of both the pregnant women, their obstetricians and the medico-legal factors of the institution (hospital/ setting). The mode opted as the final decision must be a negotiated opinion decided between all the three groups. It must not be the imposition of one on the other, rather must be respected and supported by all the groups. Thus, to understand the series of steps in leading to the larger step of decision-making, this chapter examines the pathways of how and when the decision for choosing the mode of delivery is taken and by whom, by interacting with the obstetricians and the women who delivered under them in the recent past.

Methodology

This chapter is taken from a larger study (Ghosh, 2016), for which data were collected during August 2015 to October 2015. Present chapter is based on the pathways of decision-making in the process of opting the mode of delivery. The information related to this was collected by interviewing the recent mothers regarding the process of decision-making related to the mode of delivery in their own deliveries. Further the experiences shared by them were triangulated with the corresponding obstetricians, wherever possible, interviewing them about the same case. Necessary permission and informed consent were obtained from all the respondents. Anonymity was also ensured to the participants. Semi-structured interview guidelines with open-ended questions were the tool used for data collection. The responses were either written or recorded, depending on the consent given by the informants. The data was collected mainly in English. Wherever there were responses in Hindi, they were translated without disturbing the original sense of the data. Further, the collected data was coded and is analysed using thematic analysis.

Nature of Participants

The data pertaining to this chapter emerged from a recent mother of 29 years of age who has delivered in a general hospital with special focus on maternal care, followed by a junior obstetrician of that setting. Additionally, two recent mothers of age 29 and 33 years respectively who delivered in a general hospital were interviewed. Her obstetrician is having practicing experience of 25 years, in the same setting.

The third theme was taken based on the interview of a recent mother of 26 years of age and her obstetrician. Her obstetrician is practicing for 20 years in total. Out of which for the first six years, she practiced abroad and for the remaining 14 years she is practicing in India. It is only for the last three years she is in the current setting, which is run on a public-private partnership mode, before which she was practicing in another private hospital.

Findings

The findings of the study are briefly categorized under three broad themes based on the different contexts that emerged out stating the course of decision-making process followed by these women while opting for the mode of delivery.

Convenience of the Obstetricians

Data show that one of the recent mothers was made to deliver through C-section in the 37th week of her pregnancy, against her wish to deliver normally. As she was not prepared for the issue at that point of time, neither her husband was. So, she wanted to visit the most experienced obstetrician of that hospital. Her family chose the hospital because it was nearest to her house. She wanted to avoid C-section because she was afraid of operation and stitches. She was under good diet, and minimal medication. As recommended by her obstetrician, she undertook morning and evening walks. But, when her obstetrician, who was having experience of 36 years, asked her to deliver through C-section as he (obstetrician) would be out of town for couple of weeks. She said that initially she got tensed on hearing this. According to her, she was having a normal pregnancy and even her obstetrician agreed to that but due to non-medical reason which was beyond her control, she was forced to deliver through C-section. On further probing regarding the final decision regarding the choice for her mode of delivery, she stated that—

> *...any options left? Parents' in-laws, husband and even me; no one wanted to take a chance. For that moment even, I had that weak corner at my heart speaking like what if anything goes wrong?... What I will do then? After going through these many things in my head I went for a yes....*

She went for the C-section without being comfortable with the decision because she and her family members felt that there was no point in changing the doctor at the 11th hour, as her entire pregnancy history was known and handled by this particular obstetrician.

Although it was not possible for the researcher to interview the obstetrician under whom this recent mother (case stated above) delivered her baby, regarding this particular case. But when this issue was discussed with a junior obstetrician practicing for two years in that particular setting where the woman had opted for C-section half-heartedly, she replied that—

> *...suppose you are my patient and I insist you upon something you are bound to do that...it rarely happens that the patients do things outside the doctor's advice....*

Thus, the case suggests that the pregnancy was terminated and the child was born through caesarian before the due date to suit the convenience of the doctor.

This category, as the name suggest, deals with the context in which the ultimate decision is being taken by the obstetrician and the pregnant woman obliges to it, irrespective of her own wish. Here, it was shown that the pregnant woman was going through a normal pregnancy but was forced to deliver her baby, half-heartedly, through C-section. In that case, the woman was afraid of stitches and wanted to deliver normally which could not happen due to non-medical reason from her obstetricians' side.

Women as Passive Patients

Women delivering their babies under mid-wives exercise greater control and agency in their pregnancy and childbirth. Home-births are possible under their surveillance and they are respected as 'subjects' in the experiences of childbirth, rather than as 'passive patients' receiving care in a biomedical setting (Johnson, 2008).

There were two instances found from the primary data that the recent mothers had gone for C-sections where they had a negotiation with their doctors before operation. Both of them were having their second deliveries, with the previous one being Lower Segment Caesarean Section (LSCS) for both. So, in their first visit itself they were told that their mode of delivery will be planned and repeated C-section. They didn't have any problem with the repeat of operation and agreed to what their obstetricians say. Both of them delivered in the same private-tertiary care hospitals. Both of them were of the opinion that they didn't have any problem with any of the modes of delivery, as for them C-section is very common and both of them have had gone through it in their previous deliveries under the same obstetrician under whom they were prepared to deliver for the second time. Shila (one of the recent mothers; name changed), was already having one son and was on her second pregnancy. Both she and her husband wanted a girl child to complete their family and were of opinion that two kids become more responsible and value-oriented. She had her son through C-section due to a non-medical emergency, as her obstetrician was supposed to travel abroad. This time, she also joined maternity exercise classes after her fourth month was over. She reported—

> *I was having no problem with anything. You know, nowadays who soever get pregnant will deliver artificially. Because I was used to with this thing so it didn't bother me. . .*

Although, her mother-in-law wanted that she should be made to give at least a try for vaginal birth. But her obstetrician did not want to take risk because there are chances of rupture of her previous stitches.

Upon interviewing her obstetrician, she replied that it is true that C-section rate has increased because it can save both the mother and the child at emergency situations, which was not possible some years back. She also opined that—

> *After you reach 35, complications grow by 35 per cent, so this is a big reason for rise in C-section rate.*

So, in the subsequent deliveries, the age of the women gets higher and there are changes in their lifestyle also for which she prefers not to opt for Vaginal Birth After Caesarean (VBAC). According to her, the mothers with previous C-section can develop serious problems related to the previous stitches.

Thus, this segment shows that C-section being a common form of operation today, when announced to the women with previous LSCS in their initial check-ups, they passively accept it. This theme clearly demonstrates the situations where the women were made passive in their own pregnancies, given no role to play in the birth of their child other than being submissive to their obstetricians. In both the cases, the women were having previous LSCS and were delivered using repeated C-section because of their previous operations. The women did not have say in the decision and agreed passively to their obstetricians. Their rising age and emergency complications from previous stiches made their obstetricians avoid VBAC.

Delivery Mode Chosen against Patients' Will

One of the interviews showed that a pregnant woman along with her family wanted and demanded caesarean section as the preferred mode of delivery, but their obstetrician made the delivery go normal without operation. The case goes like this—

> One of the recent mothers, who delivered in the hospital, run under public-private partnership mode, demanded caesarean section on the third day of *leaking* of her amniotic fluid. She started leaking in the 39th week of pregnancy but didn't develop with labour for the first two days of leaking. She along with her family became tensed and demanded C-section. But her obstetrician, who has an experience of 20 years, firmly believed and made her patients believe that prime pregnancies often take time to start with labour and thus she can deliver normally without any problem.

Upon interviewing the obstetrician, she opined that when one woman demands C-section, the job of her obstetrician is to get back to root cause of that problem. Thereafter, she should be given adequate pain relief support or psychological counselling to cope with the problem. According to her, it is very essential for a woman to know the benefits and risks of any given mode of delivery. She believes that where things are possible without stitches, she prefers to avoid them at her best. According to her—

> There are some cases where patients point blankly demands for an artificial delivery, you have to get an informed consent and then have to make sure to the patients that they are informed well about all the possible risks involved in a C-section. And then even after that the patient is ready to bear the risk then what to do. But it is very important to know that an operation always have some risks if done without any proper reason. There can be operative risks which involves short and long-term risks. Short-term includes extended hospitalization, blood loss, infection in the absence of prophylactic antibiotics, pain, heavy blood clots in the lower portion of the body etc., and long-term includes surgical pains like pain in the stitches, re-hospitalization, hysterectomy or even it may lead to breathing problems in the new born; the baby might get subjected to use breathing machine and then put into NICU. There are many, I am telling you. For the time being it is like less painful but in a long run you might have to suffer. And then it is like once a caesarian always a caesarean, particularly in the private hospitals. So, the risks tend to increase.

Thus, the case was entirely different as what is known in general. The obstetrician did not go for a C-section in case of her patient who was having her first delivery, rather waited for her labour to start, which usually takes time in first conception. Even after two days of wait when she did not develop labour, the obstetrician induced and delivered normally. So, it is exactly the opposite of the earlier two cases where the obstetricians preferably chose C-section as a mode of delivery.

This third theme talks about the situation where the woman got delivered against her own wishes. This category is different from the first one with respect to the reasons given by their respective obstetrician. In the first case, the obstetrician made the woman opt for C-section because of his convenience which was having no medical basis. While in this case, the obstetrician let the woman opt for vaginal delivery because C-section was not indicated medically. The woman and her family members wanted to opt for C-section due to fear of not developing labour on the third day of leaking. But the obstetrician made them opt for normal delivery making them believe that women, often, in their first conception take time to develop labour.

Conclusion

This study was an attempt to explore and understand various pathways through which the ultimate decision regarding the opted mode of delivery happens. Although the study could not focus on the contexts of public hospital; but tried to capture a brief glimpse of the decision-making process occurring in private and semi-private (PPP types) hospitals. Based on the understanding of various literature, the researcher tried to narrow down the study specifically to the issue regarding how and when the mode of delivery is being decided in a pregnancy case and the final call is taken by whom. Thus, the findings were classified into three categories, namely convenience of the obstetricians, women as passive patients, and delivery mode chosen against patients' will.

Thus, the study concludes that the obstetricians are also social beings and their practices, though carried out in clinical settings and are based on medical knowledge, are not free from socio-cultural constraints. The final call regarding the decision of mode of delivery is being taken by the obstetricians, be it in medical or non-medical grounds. The women are convinced, forced or even made passive and alien in their own pregnancy and childbirth. The process of decision-making regarding opting the mode of delivering a child does not involve the three factors of obstetricians, pregnant women and the settings. The second component often gets missed out in the process. The study has some limitations where the number of respondents interviewed were quite less to describe the entire phenomena of decision-making and researcher has also not focused much on the third component, which needs further research.

This study is not meant to draw generalization on each delivery happening in the country under the purview of biomedicine, rather it is only meant to briefly browse the processes through which the decision is taken to opt for delivery modes in an Indian cosmopolitan setting.

NOTE

1. The period between immediately after childbirth to the return of uterus to its normal size.

REFERENCES

Barnes, Lindsay. (2007). "Women's Experience of Childbirth in Rural Jharkhand." *Economic and Political Weekly, 42*(48), 62-70.

Dillaway, Heather and S.J. Brubaker. (2006). "Intersectionality and Childbirth: How Women from Different Social Locations Discuss Epidural Use." *Race, Gender and Class, 13*(3/4), 16-41.

Emmett, C.L. *et al.* (2006). "Women's experience of decision-making about mode of delivery after a previous caesarean section: the role of health professionals and information about health risks." *British Journal of Obstetrics and Gynaecology, 113*, 1438-1445.

Ghosh, Priyanka. (2016). *Interaction of Biomedicine in Pregnancy and Childbirth.* Unpublished Thesis. Mumbai: Tata Institute of Social Sciences.

Ghosh, S. and K.S. James. (2010). "Levels and trends in Caesarean Births: Cause for Concern?" *Economic and Political Weekly, 46*(5), 19-22.

Hildingsson, Ingegerd *et al.* (2002). "Few women wish to be delivered by Caesarean section." *British Journal of Obstetrics and Gynaecology, 109*, 618-623.

Holmes, Chris. (1979). "Bioethical Decision-making: An Approach to improve the Process." *Medical Car. 17*(11), 1131-1138.

Jangsten, Elisabeth *et al.* (2005). "Women's Perceptions of Pain and Discomfort after Childbirth in Angola." *African Journal of Reproductive Health, 9*(3), 148-158.

Johnson, Candace. (2008). "The Political 'Nature' of Pregnancy and Childbirth." *Canadian Journal of Political Science, 41*(4), 889-913.

MacArthur, C. *et al.* (1990). "Epidural Anaesthesia and Long-term Backache After Childbirth." *British Medical Journal, 301*(6742), 9-12.

Malacrida, Claudia and Tiffany Boulton. (2012). "Women's Perceptions of Childbirth 'Choices': Competing Discourses of Motherhood, Sexuality and Selflessness." *Gender and Society, 26*(5), 748-772.

McCourt, Chris *et al.* (2007). Elective Cesarean Section and decision-making: A Critical Review of the Literature. *Birth, 34(1),* 65-79.

Moffat, M.A. *et al.* (2007). "Decision-making about mode of delivery among pregnant women who have previously had a caesarean section: A qualitative study." *British Journal of Obstetrics and Gynaecology, 114,* 86-93.

Movsas, T.Z. *et al.* (2012). "Does medical insurance type (private *vs.* public) influence the physician's decision to perform caesarean delivery?" *Journal of Medical Ethics, 38*(8), 470-473.

Paterson, C.M and N.J. St. G. Saunders. (1991). "Mode of Delivery after One Caesarean Section: Audit of Current Practice in a Health Region." *British Medical Journal, 303* (6806), 818-821.

Paterson-Brown, Sara. (1998). "Yes, as Long as the Woman is Fully Informed." *British Medical Journal, 317*(7156), 462-463.

Reynolds, P.C. (1991). *Stealing Fire: The Atomic Bomb as an Symbolic Body.* CA: Iconic Anthropology Press.

Rothman, Barbara Katz. (1978). "Childbirth as Negotiated Reality." *Symbolic Interaction, 1*(2), 124-137.

16

Listening to the Body: Health, Experience and Rationality

Gunjan Arora

Introduction

Health, illness, disease and health care have always presented a complex scenario. Initially being assigned entirely to biology, the understanding of health and illness had to do little with culture and social structure. While it is understood that biology/medicine is indispensable to the understanding of the human body and its functions, to the anatomy of the human body and for the study of disease and illness, the target has always been to achieve a disease free body. The whole responsibility was then considered to be of biomedicine and the medical practitioner had a prime role. But it was soon realised that disease and health are not entirely a biological phenomenon, they are the composite outcome of the biological, social, economic and cultural factors (Sujatha, 2014: 5).

Various disciplines like Sociology and Anthropology have had different approaches to study the health and illness. While Sociology adopted a macro-perspective by focusing on the health institutions and prioritized on the social structure and its role in health and illness, the culture-centric approach of medical anthropologists not only brought out the traditional healing practices of the people but also captured the subjective aspect of illness. Studies on the experience of illness and disease, aetiology of the disease, meaning of suffering, coping strategies, or the social adaptations the patient undergoes were produced. The anthropological approach was not only able to capture the lived experience of illness but also articulated as what health or being healthy meant to an individual. This is not to say that the sociological approach did not gather the health and illness at the local level. But the two disciplines have contributed sufficiently on the studies of health and medicine though with diverse approaches.

The present study tried to collect a subjective interpretation provided by the informants of the illness experience they had. And in most cases this experience was having a subordinate status to the biomedical explanation provided by the doctor to them. The hegemony of the biomedical system and its explanation of the disease often overpowers the lived experience of illnesses like body ache, discomfort or pain. An encounter with the medical system often leads to a situation where the subjective experience of illness finds a subordinate status to the expert-centred view of the disease.

The subjective or lived experience of illness is conditioned by cultural factors such as religious values, shared social experiences, livelihood skills and the natural environment as well as sedimented habits (Sujatha, 2014). An individual, while explaining the illness gives a broader, lay view of the condition and attributes it to a number of causing factors. Dipankar Gupta (1988) in his work has shown that a lay person has the tendency to see health condition as part of a broad set of factors that affect the ill persons life and has more than one way of solving the problem. He further says that the health seeking behaviour is essentially pluralistic and humans generally resort to multiple ways to become illness free. In contrast, the biomedical approach may seem to be narrow where certain measurable figures or medical tests aid the clinical diagnosis and a particular nomenclature is assigned to the medical condition of the individual.

The words 'disease' and 'illness' also need a consideration here. Arthur Kleinman (1988) distinguishes between 'disease' and 'illness'. Disease is referred to the biological or psychological problem as diagnosed by the biomedical physician or psychiatrist. Whereas illness has been defined as the innately human experience of symptoms and suffering, how a sick person and the members of the family or wider social network perceive, live with and respond to symptom or disability (1988: 3). He further says that illness is the lived experience of monitoring bodily processes such as abdominal cramps, painful joints or respiratory wheezes. Such illness experience also includes the categorization and explanation of the illness in the most common sensical way which is understandable to the lay self as well as to the social group, the forms of distress caused by those pathophysiological processes (1988: 4).

So, if health and illness are partially biological and partially social, where does the 'body' stand? Because disease and illness is seen to be located in the body as a physical object or physiological state and the medical knowledge consists of the objective representation of the diseased body, for both the person who is sick and the clinician the disease is experienced as present in the body. But for the person who is experiencing pain or illness, the body is not simply a physical object or physiological state, but an essential part of the self (Good, 1994: 116).

Changes in the body that are experienced by individuals are, therefore, embodied experiences that differ in different cultures. For instance, life cycle events in a woman's life like child-birth or menopause are culture-specific bodily experiences. The phenomenon of menopause for example is dealt with differently in Japanese and Western culture. Margaret Lock (1993) argued that the phenomenon of menopause in Western culture includes a constellation of symptoms such as hot flushes, irritability, body ache and depression and people are advised to take medical treatment whereas among Japanese there is no word for menopause and as the menstruation ceases, women are seen to be entering a new prime phase of life as 'good wives and mother'. Japanese women do not report any associated symptoms of illness. Another study by Van Hollen (2003) shows that women in obstetric wards in south Indian government hospitals assign positive value to labour pain and do not take drugs for painless delivery unlike their counterparts in North America. The local constructions of the body are such that women request for inducing labour (which intensifies the labour pain) and the woman's body bearing the pain of the childbirth is considered synonymous with a divine experience which every woman should brave and such local constructions are in steep contrast to their Western counterparts. These local constructions of the body then demand a discussion, especially with respect to health and illness studies. This further problematizes if a discussion is on childbirth, motherhood experiences, menstruation and menopause which have increasingly come under the 'medical gaze' and are unique female experiences.

Listening to the Body

While exploring body and health issues among women in an urban setting during my fieldwork the first encounter was with the concept of Cartesian dualism, as the conceptions of body are not only a theme in medical anthropology and health sciences but also in philosophical sciences. Cartesian dualism that separates mind and body, sees body as subordinate to mind. The body resembles a machine or an object in which the self is located and mind is considered the source of thought through which the self is produced. This philosophical dualism between the mind and body formed the basis of Western epistemology and aided the development of scientific rationality. This also formed the basis of modern medicine which claimed human body as an object compliant to scientific observation and manipulation. This idea on Cartesian dualism prevailed long until 1970s when scholars wrote about body which is evident from the work of Pierre Bourdieu (1977), Bryan Turner (1984), Emily Martin (1989), Featherstone, Hepworth and Turner (1991), Shilling (1993) and others.

In Anthropology, Mary Douglas's (1970) work brought to focus the "two bodies" referring to the social and physical aspects of the body. Douglas differentiates between how we make use of our bodies and how our bodies function. She further emphasized the way, the elements of physiology and anatomy can be taken up to the symbolic domain. In her book *Natural Symbols* (1970/2012) Douglas draws on the work of Marcel Mauss who outlined a systemic anthropology of the body. Mauss in his essay *Techniques of the Body* (1934/1973) sees body as a tool, agent and object all at once and argued that people in different societies know how to use their bodies. Mauss identifies all body functions and techniques and believed that all bodily expressions are learned.

While Douglas's work provided many valuable insights between the relationships and between the physical body and the social body, Michael Foucault (1975/1991) saw the body as the site of discipline, training, domestication and manipulation. These measures produce 'docile bodies' through institutionalized structures such as the prison, the hospital and the school.

Foucault's view may be essentially pessimistic, but his great contribution to Anthropology and other disciplines, was to shift the body from back stage to front and the centre, and to emphasize the operation of power, beyond symbolism, in the production of docile bodies (Synnott and Howes, 1992: 161-62).

In the mid-1980s, Medical Anthropologists Margaret Lock and Nancy Scheper Hughes (1987) problematized the body in another way. They began with an assumption that body is simultaneously a physical and symbolic artefact, is both naturally and culturally produced and is securely anchored in a particular historical moment. In outlining their theoretical approach Scheper and Hughes state—

> The three bodies represent, then, not only three separate and overlapping units of analysis, but also three different theoretical approaches and epistemologies: phenomenology (individual body, the lived self), structuralism and symbolism (the social body), and post-structuralism (the body politic). (p. 8)

But another line of argument proposed by Jackson (1983) is that anthropological analysis of body has been more symbolic and semiotic one which causes it to treat the body as a diminished version of itself. Also if the body tends to be defined as a medium of expression or communication 'it' is not only reduced to the status of a sign, it is also made into an object of purely mental operations, "a thing onto which social patterns are projected" (1983: 329).

Jackson further argues that Douglas speaks body as 'it' and examines how in its role as an image of the society, the body's main scope is to express the relation of the individual to the group. As a result, a Cartesian split is made which detaches the knowing and speaking subject from the unknowing inert body. Also here the society is made to assume the active role of governing, utilizing and charging with significance the physical bodies of individuals. This notion of body as an instrument of mind or of society is fallacious on epistemological grounds as it contradicts our experience of the body as lived reality.

> In anthropological studies of the body, the body is regarded as inert, passive and static. Either body is seen to be neutral and ideographic means of embodying ideas, or is dismembered so that the symbolic value of its various parts in indigenous discourse can be enumerated. There seems to be dearth of studies on the body-as-subject, of a phenomenology of embodied experience, of studies of interactions and exchanges occurring within the field of bodily existence rather than resulting from mechanical rules or innate preprogramming (Jackson, 1983: 329).

In other words, phenomenological approach to body praxis would capture how human bodies are informed by habits and forms of body use are conditioned by our relationship with others. Jackson calls for a grounded view which begins with interactions and movements of people in an organized environment and details on patterns of body praxis which thus arise. Jackson while working with Merleau-Ponty's concept of 'lived body' and Bourdieu's notion of 'habitus' endeavours to move away from the unduly abstract semiotic models, by developing a more grounded mode of analysis which lays emphasis on bodily praxis in the immediate social field and material world.

The feminist scholarship (Butler, 1990; Grosz, 1994; Martin, 1989; Young, 1990) too while challenging the Cartesian dualism have furthered the concept of lived body and a notion of lived experience. This phenomenological approach to body suggests a possibility of wholeness in women's bodily experiences and each woman experience differently within the wider context of social structural forces like caste and class. The feminist scholarship in India has paid little attention to female body, self and reproduction (Chaudhuri, 2004). Especially with issues relating to motherhood experiences, childbirth, menstruation and menopause which were seldom covered as the main focus and concern had and has been maternal mortality rates, declining sex ratios and epidemiological studies. Moreover, among the urban middle class, motherhood, child care and reproduction being less directly governed by official policies are constituted as natural, unproblematic and apolitical sites of privilege (Donner, 2008: 34). Sketching the connections on body and health, the chapter gathers narratives on motherhood and menstruation among the urban middle class.

Notes from the Field

The fieldwork among the urban middle class women working in white collared jobs in Delhi intended to deconstruct the hegemonic codes that regulate or guide the female's body with special reference to the health issues they faced and the consequent health seeking methods they adopted. Being an ethnographic qualitative research, the intention was to gather the narrations of these women around the broad themes of motherhood, menstruation and menopause and the associated illnesses they faced. As a qualitative endeavour, the aim of the whole study was to enter, feel and understand the subjective world of these women. The group was a heterogeneous mix between age group 22-60 years belonging to different parts of Delhi and India but had been residing in Delhi for more than 20-30 years. It was mostly their parents who had shifted to Delhi for better job and educational opportunities. Few were residing in Delhi since birth or had shifted to Delhi after marriage. They belonged to various age groups; had different educational qualifications and were involved in different Departments in the Organization. These women self-identified themselves to be belonging to middle class. While the category of middle class has been economically defined it would be erroneous to label a certain strata of people as middle class only on the basis of income. Their self-identification as belonging to middle class and their self-defined parameters that distinguishes them as middle class were accepted in the study. The education; professional achievement and a respectable job as one of the main indicators, other being having a comfortable life, possessing basic gadgets at home, owning a house or vehicle and focusing and saving for their children's education and future.

The group though a heterogeneous one, had few common concerns with regard to motherhood experiences; menstrual disorders and body pain; work-life balance issues; concern for their children's growth and educational achievements. The study hinges on how do life events of women affect their subjective well-being and how those life experiences impact and inform the female which is reflected on the body. The concern for the body image and being healthy in contemporary times is relevant so as to understand the already created image of a strong, assertive, independent urban working woman.

Their unique body experiences like motherhood, menstruation and menopause have highlighted a few issues about their health, illness and health seeking behaviour. The women interviewed were working in a job that demanded at-least 8-9 hours of deskwork and additional 2-2.5 hours of commuting time daily and were left with little time for themselves. The remaining time was adjusted for family, children's education and social obligations. The weekends were meant for pending household chores and maintenance. Though support from the elderly within the family (parent-in-laws) or parents living at a convenient distance (parents in the natal house) was considered essential, but my informants still felt that they were overworked and had 'tired bodies'. Because of their sedentary mode of work many complained of backpain, leg pain and neck and shoulder pain and other medical conditions like diabetes, thyroid and blood pressure which they had developed were mainly attributed to the kind of work they were doing. This general idea about the overall health condition was the initial explanation during the fieldwork but, later a study of the individual cases reflected the importance of being healthy and taking a rational course for treating themselves was important to them. Interactions amongst themselves during lunch hours and in general revolved around discussing about their household problems, concern for child's education and their health. The discussions highlighted that maintaining a positive-self was of utmost importance to them so that they are able to continue with their job. Maintaining a healthy body and mental peace was essential and body was not seen as separate from self.

A peep into their motherhood experience reflected the importance of becoming a mother and proving ones' fertility within first few years of her marriage. Being a pronatalist society, the importance attached to the procreative role of a woman often lands her in compromising her decision to become a mother or having a career or handling both. The informants agreed that it was important to become a mother as it was not only a gratifying experience for them but it also solidified their status/ position in their conjugal home.

> *I have no choice, I have to become a mother..... if in the next two years I don't conceive, my in-laws family and my natal family would start questioning.... I have no choice (silence)... It's ok..... it's not whether I am prepared or not....(pause).....our society is like that....as if becoming a mother is the ultimate aim of a woman's life...If a woman does not want to become a mother she is made to think as if she is lacking or something is wrong with her......Am I wrong if I need some time to think whether I am ready for this responsibility....* (26 years old informant in research department).

This narration from a single informant also resonated with other informants who felt that it was compulsory for them to procreate and many agreed that motherhood was an uneven and challenging phase of their lives. The main concern that came up during the interviews and group discussions with my informants was the medical check-ups they had to undergo and how they were under constant *medical gaze*. Though the informants of the older age (45-60 years) informed that it was much easier to have a child in earlier times; pregnancy was more of a personal experience and the experience of foetal movements were only for the to-be mother. In contrast, the younger generation (22-44 years) mostly in their reproductive phase said that the desire to become a mother was also guided by other factors like the cost of pregnancy and they recalled that their mothers and mother-in-laws in earlier times considered pregnancy as a normal episode of one's life and so many medical tests were not done to ensure mother or foetal health. These days doctors have made pregnancy an illness and the associated conditions like heartburn, body pain, nausea, swelling in hands or legs during those nine months is seen as a medical condition. The blood tests are done to ensure the optimal level of haemoglobin, vitamin-D or calcium in the body which is a recent phenomenon and women are given calcium and iron tablets throughout their pregnancy. The ultrasounds these days are done more frequently to follow foetal growth. This medicalization of pregnancy and the medical terms used by the doctors baffled many of my informants but they had little choice on how their bodies are objectified during the whole nine months and also in the labour room.

> *You are under constant surveillance of the gynaecologist... What you eat, how you eat, additional supplements, walk and exercise routines, monthly check-ups, costly medical tests have left me exhausted in my first pregnancy...(pause) I decided not to have another baby. It was so difficult to manage baby and work....* (34 years old informant working in administrative department).

The constant surveillance and the technology dependent diagnosis of their condition left them anxious and indecisive on how they were feeling during those nine months. Some also mentioned that how they felt during the nine months was not a concern to their gynaecologist and many thus resorted to alternate home remedies and other alternate Ayurvedic and naturopathic methods to relieve them of their anxiety, body pain and stress. The other alternate systems of medicine like homoeopathy and Ayurvedic which my informants resorted to, as per them had little side effects (unlike the allopathic medicine which they felt that they do not know how the medicine would affect their unborn child) and they felt the homeopathic doctor/Ayurvedic practitioner listened to them carefully and the subjective explanations about their illnesses were taken care of. Few women who were following homeopathy or Ayurveda showed complete faith in the system as the approach in these medical systems was more holistic and the practitioner took detailed journal entries before prescribing any medicine.

This not only indicates that the health-seeking behaviour is essentially pluralistic and a rational, coherent decisions about self were taken by these women, it also highlights that the doctor-patient interaction has profound effect on the patient's illnesses. Though the diagnosis, treatment and the pharmacological combinations given by alternate systems may not be a labelled bottle or *puriya* medicine (which the homoeopathic doctor gives) would not be available easily on the common drugstore, these women complemented allopathy with the other systems available to them. But few dreaded the Ayurvedic medicine for their taste and homoeopathic *puriyas* for being unlabelled and had no choice but to totally depend on the biomedical advice and treatment.

Same was the view regarding menstruation and menopause. Menstruation and menopause being the unique female body experience was also captured during my fieldwork. Though a strictly private experience, the data gathering was initially difficult but gradually in multiple interview sittings it was revealed to me that there were certain established pollution beliefs and taboos associated with it and having a regular menstrual cycle was normal and considered healthy.

The temporary state of ritual impurity during menstruation has been the subject of study and a rich source of symbolic analysis. Bypassing the ritual and symbolic analysis I had questioned women about their body experience of 'those days'. It was revealed that the elderly ladies in my informant's house still asked them to observe certain taboos like not entering the *mandir* in the house or light a lamp in the morning or evening in the *mandir* or even cook in the kitchen. But many informants who were living in nuclear family setup had no choice but to do away with the associated concept of pollution menstruation had. Many managed to give scientific explanation to their family members about their physiological state and negotiated with them to consider it as a natural phenomenon and as a mark of their procreative abilities. It was thus revealed that a bodily process like menstruation became a social experience and not having a regular monthly cycle was a sign inadequacy for some.

Few respondents brought out a different perception and saw menstruation as not polluting but rather a cleansing mechanism of the body and by adopting a scientific explanation the informants considered menstruation as something which is not to be abhorred but just managed and concealed especially in office space. Women found office space as a 'rigid', 'alien' (words used by informants) space in 'those days' and desired the comfort of home space but this could not be possible as they could not take so many leaves from work.

Though being a biological process, a socio-cultural lens if adopted to study this bodily process highlights how the body is self-monitored and how these women attach meanings to these bodily processes. It also gives an insight into the hegemonic codes of the society that guide and regulate the female body. The whole discourse on pollution and taboos (symbolic meanings) on one hand and the pain and discomfort (physiological experiences) on the other hand provide a rich text about the female body which resonates with the female self.

The cessation of the menstruation or menopause is another event that marks the female body. The biomedical explanation explains the changing levels or oestrogen or ovarian dysfunction which is accompanied by a constellation of other related illnesses like hot flushes, irritability, joint pain, back pain, insomnia and sometimes excessive bleeding before complete cessation of the cycle. These symptoms were shared by the informants in the age group of 45-60 years. Though many accepted it another phase of life, free from the monthly 'tension' (*jhanjhat*) many had to recourse to medical treatment and hormonal therapy. But looking at 'local biologies' (Lock and Kaufert, 2001: 494), I found that many informants used naturopathic treatments for menopause related illnesses. For instance, a lady who believed in naturopathy took flax seeds to ease her condition during pre-menopause as it has natural oestrogen. She advised her colleagues in office about natural products to ease any of their conditions from normal cold and cough to menstrual cramps in young women to heavy bleeding in menopausal women. During a group discussion my respondents voiced that they should 'age well' and they used many natural products from their kitchen to cure/prevent illnesses. They all agreed that taking care of one's body should be a prime concern especially for women who go through so many changes in their life. Their bodies which have undergone pregnancy, childbirth, breastfeeding, menstruation, and menopause and have witnessed dual responsibilities of house work and office work are bound to degenerate as this is the law of nature. By accepting ageing and bodily changes, many reflected a positive outlook towards their overall health.

But a glance at the biomedical language provides an insight on how the process of menstruation and menopause are explained in medicine. For menstruation phrases like 'failed production', 'deterioration', 'breakdown of internal lining of the uterus', 'failure of fertilization' and for menopause phrases like 'ovarian dysfunction', 'atrophy', 'senile ovaries', 'decline in sexual powers', 'emotional disturbances' and 'failure of the authority structure in the body' all have negative connotations and reinforce and reflect the cultural fragmentation of the female bodies (Martin, 1989). Though these women were aware of these phrases used by the doctors or what they had read in the print media, many did not allow these negative phrases overpower their personal meanings on health. They accepted it as a different phase in their life and believed that accepting these changes makes it easier for them to handle the situation. Some even attached it to the *karma*, that the amount of pain and distress they had to handle in their health issues were a result of their good or bad deeds they did may be in their past of present life.

The notion of a universal experience and the dominant medical view that menopause as a pathological condition in need of medication has been challenged in cross-cultural studies (Lock and Kaufert, 2001; Chirawatkul and Manderson, 1994). The cross-cultural studies have also shown that menopause is not an event but a gradual process where over a period of time the complete cessation of the menstrual cycle occurs.

Final Inferences

Listening to middle class women's narratives has provided vital clues to the process of defining and normalizing the female body. The physiological and biological understandings of these women and self-monitoring attitude attempts at gaining control over their experience. A more scientific and rational behaviour towards seeking medical help or deciding to go for alternate medical system not only indicates towards medical pluralism but also towards the agency these women have who want to maintain their health. These educated urban women showed heightened awareness about their bodily processes and they negotiated well their body, their personal social relations and their workplace assignments. The patriarchal nature of our society does impinge certain behavioural codes both at the workplace and at home and these women were seen to be negotiating with the codes and rules/norms but at the same time did not totally do away with the traditional norms. For instance becoming a mother is traditionally essential for them but postponing it for few years either for career growth or for giving herself some time for preparing her for the additional responsibility of the child, showed her agentic skills.

Read against these hegemonic discourses a discussion on health and illness among the urban middle class working women has allowed me to know how the sense of being a woman is internalised. A study body as subject has allowed me to bring together the fragmented body (as depicted in biomedicine) towards a whole body experience. Though this experience occurs in a particular socio-cultural context and the meanings produced by my informants about their health and illness is mediated through the structural forces of the society, the phenomenological approach offers a comprehensive look about the body that is visible, tangible and a located entity as also understood by my informants.

These women voiced that the impact of their work, childbirth and menstruation is visible on their tangible bodies especially in later years of their lives as my respondents said that "*we abuse our bodies, do not give it enough sleep and nourishment and only when we get some ailments we start working on the body*". The women in the older age group who complained of backache, knee pain, cervical, spondylitis, thyroid, blood pressure and high cholesterol linked it to the tight schedule, sedentary work and stress they faced all their lives, where their own rest time or health issues were last on the priority list. Their work, gendered roles and their body roles (childbirth, menstruation) sometimes constrained their health seeking behaviour. Demand at both home and work spaces; lack of physical activity because of sedentary work; dividing time for child care and house work; accommodating family life and work; saving for child's future and retirement; their own education and career advancements; family obligations and elderly care; intergenerational dependencies have led these women to make choices and adapt socially as per their abilities and opportunities.

Dropping health care to a lower priority especially during years where childcare and sometimes elderly care took most of the time of my respondents was perceived as beyond their control. Many shared that "*the family situations which do not give us 'me time' are beyond our control and we can't do much about it. Sometimes inadvertently we are the last priority for ourselves.*"

These choices are not made in a vacuum, rather are shaped by the context in which they are made. The choices my respondents made and the constraints they face had a cumulative effect on their physical being. It is well known that both the men's and women's choices and their exposure to stressors and work pressures are different which in turn affect their biological processes and thus leads to differential health outcomes. Though the Office policies and the Government policies in recent years like the provision of Child Care Leave and extension of Maternity Leave ensure that women could fair well on both the fronts, but there is enough individual variability on how my respondents opted for these provisions to address their different needs.

The choices these women made might appear rational in certain context but might not be consistent with their health decisions. Though the women in the present study were very conscious of their health and made changes in eating habits and exercise routines, but this was more visible in the older age group of women who now had lesser care giving tasks at home as their children had grown and had no elderly to take care for. They had joined Community groups like the Laughing group, the Yoga group and even a Walk group near their homes. The group members of these Community groups were either their friends or their neighbours from the Housing society in which they resided or the members of the RWAs of their locality. Many of my respondents who had ailments like high cholesterol, diabetes or heart disease were conscious of their health and felt responsible for themselves and made changes in their eating routine, focused on eating frequently and small meals full of roughage and fruits. Like one women got four small lunch packs for her which included sprouts or fruits, normal *chapatti* and *sabzi* cooked with less oil and salt and lemon water in a bottle as she was advised by her endocrinologist (she had diabetes). She shared "*I never took so much care of myself as I do now*".

Being conscious of one's health does not always indicate that the individual would exercise on that knowledge. The individual's behaviour is shaped by cognitive perceptions and the social context and the actors choose the best rational option available to them. As actors these women might have at some point ignored their health because of family or work responsibilities but this does not amount to say that they were careless. The competing demands/expectations do not work in tandem with the health choices but actors with agency do have a 'substantial decision latitude'(Bird and Reiker, 2008: 148) where they act autonomously and creatively organize their work and their time. But this decision latitude may vary across roles and responsibilities at home. Respondents who were supported by their parents or parent-in-laws still managed to organize their recreational activities during weekends and on holidays and engaged in some form of 'body project' which included going for walk/yoga, joining weekend health clubs or playing badminton and other outdoor games with their spouses or children which they said rejuvenated them for the coming hectic week.

A discussion on constrained choices helps us examine that how the rational actors who have agency, make rational health choices and socially adapt by prioritizing their daily work demands and gendered expectations. Women ascribe meaning to their everyday practices or their life cycle events. They have assigned meanings to events, circumstances and their gendered roles which in a cumulative way affect their female bodies.

REFERENCES

Bird, Chloe, E. and Patricia, P. Reiker (2008). *Gender and Health: The Effects of Constrained Choices and Social Policies*. New York: Cambridge University Press.

Bourdieu, P. (1977). *Outline of a Theory of Practice*. London: Cambridge University Press.

Butler, J. (1990). *Gender Trouble: Feminism and the Subversion of Identity*. New York: Routledge.

Chirawatkul, S. and L. Manderson. (1994). "Perception of Menopause in North East Thailand: Contested Meaning and Practice." *Social Science and Medicine*. Vol. 39, No. 11, pp. 1545-1554.

Donner, Henrike. (2008). *Domestic Goddesses: Maternity, Globalization and Middle Class Identity in Contemporary India*. USA: Ashgate Publishing Company.

Douglas, Mary (1970/2012), *Natural Symbols: Explorations in Cosmology*. London: Routledge.

Featherstone, M., Mike Hepworth and Bryan Turner (1991). *The Body, Social Process and Cultural Theory*. New Delhi: Sage

Foucault, M. (1975/1991). *Discipline and Punish: The Birth of the Prison*. New Delhi: Penguin Books.

Good, Byron, J. (1994). *Medicine Rationality and Experience*. Cambridge: Cambridge University Press.

Gupta, Dipankar. (1988). "For a Sociology of Health and Illness". *International Sociology, 3*(4): 403-13.

Jackson, M. (1983). "Knowledge of the Body." *Man* (New Series) *18*(2): 327-45

Kleinman, Arthur. (1988). *The Illness Narratives: Suffering, Healing and the Human Condition*. USA: Perseus Books Group.

Lock, Margaret. (1993). "Cultivating the Body: Anthropology and Epistemologies of Bodily Practice and Knowledge." *Annual Review of Anthropology. 22*: 133-55.

Lock, M. and Nancy Scheper Hughes. (1987). "The Mindful Body: A Prolegomenon to Future Work in Medical Anthropology." *Medical Anthropology Quarterly*, New Series, Vol. 1 No. 1, pp. 6-41.

Lock, M. (1991). "Contested Meanings of Menopause." *The Lancet, 337*, pp. 1270-1272.

Lock, M. and Patricia Kaufert. (2001). "Menopause, Local Biologies and Cultures of Aging." *American Journal of Human Biology*, Vol. 13, pp. 494-504.

Martin, Emily. (1989). *The Woman in the Body: A Cultural Analysis of Reproduction*. Boston: Beacon Press.

Mauss (1934/1973). "Techniques of the Body." *Economy and Society*, Vol. 2, Issue 1, 70-88.

Shilling, C. (1993). *The Body and Social Theory*. New Delhi: Sage Publications.

Sujatha, V. (2014). *Sociology of Health and Medicine: New Perspectives*. New Delhi: Oxford University Press.

Synnott, A. and David Howes (1992). "From Measurement to Meaning: Anthropologies of the Body." *Anthropos,* 87, pp. 147-166.

Turner, Bryan. (1984). *The Body and Society: Explorations in Social Theory*. Basil: Blackwell.

17

Social Care and Habitus Transformation in the Elderly Indian Immigrants in Belfast (United Kingdom)

Ashwin Tripathi

Introduction

The rapid demographic transitions worldwide provide an opportunity for social scientists to study accounts of families and communities, affected by globally changing family structures, and ageing population. Scholars (Buch, 2015, Lamb, 2000) have raised ageing as one of the emerging social phenomenon. Moreover, with improved technology, better medical families and enhanced global connectivity, the intensity and duration of care has also increased. Families have played a crucial role in providing social care aided through Information and Communication Technologies. Nonetheless, focusing on care in later life is particularly valuable because of the alteration brought in caring model through various new developments. Thus, resulting in diverse and complex social changes.

Demographic and economic transitions amongst Indian migrants, along with cultural globalization, presents challenges to establish family structures and inter-generational relationships. These bonds form an important part of a person's social identity, which is defined at individual, family and societal levels (Paltasingh and Tyagi, 2017). Relationships of mutual help, care and support, influence each other (Tabuchi & Miura, 2015). Indian tradition, from religious scripture to popular precepts, emphasise the moral obligations upon children to revere and respect their parents and provide support and care for them (Croll, 2006). The rightful attitudes and behaviours of children towards parents are very much framed within a context of indebtedness and obligations. Although allusions are made to the mutual responsibilities of both generations, age hierarchies accord precedence and authority to seniority, thus ranking respect for, and support of, the older generation before all other obligations. Therefore, this inter-generational contract, depends upon obedience, nurture, and the subordination of the younger generations. Croll (2006) observes that in popular imagination, a prosperous old age means being surrounded, and supported, by one's children in a multigenerational household. Croll (2006) also notes that reality does not always correspond to this ideal, however.

Divergence from traditional ideals is particularly apparent in the context of globalization, which has led to increased mobility and interaction with diverse cultures. Consequently, there is a tendency for traditional values to be weakened, in association with a shift from traditional Indian "joint families" to "nuclear families" (Bhat & Dhruvarajan, 2009). The joint family is an extended family arrangement in which many generations, related by blood, share the same household. The nuclear family, typical of Western capitalist societies, comprises a household which includes only parents and their children.

In this chapter, I present how care plays an important role in the creation of relationships, bonds and understanding. To date, there has been relatively little research in the anthropology of caring particularly, in Indian contexts (Paltasingh and Tyagi, 2017, Singh, 2016, Rajan, 2017). With different life stages, these relationships are prone to changes. In most cases, the younger generation take responsibility for the elderly, who might also be considered a socio-economic burden (Khan & Raikwar, 2011). This ideology of social obligation, duties and responsibilities, is important as family is the one basic and universal social structure of human society (Patel, 2005). For Patel (2005), the family is the "socio-economic backbone", whilst Croll (2006) describes the family as "a pivotal cornerstone of social organization."

With a tradition of strong kinship bonds and shared cultural values, Indian families maintain the idea of co-operation and caring, even in extended households (Paltasingh & Tyagi, 2012). Care, a universal phenomenon is rooted in all human societies. Russell and Edgar (1998) defined it as "the process of normalizing or optimizing the well-being of dependent individual". Similarly, Noddings (1984) points out that the motive of those who provide care is to remove or alleviate the pain and discomfort of those who they care for. However, a normative set of care is difficult to explain (Swanson, 1991). Gilligan (1982) sets the concept of care, within an ethical framework, emphasising that "care is associated with a sense of morality and duty", which is often innate within families. Keeping in mind these works, the Indian care system can be explained as a social obligation to take care of people related by blood. At the same time, it is a moral and an ethical duty to provide help and to free others from discomfort. This is not always within kinship boundaries. Humans, as social beings will enlarge their social dependency outside the biological kinship.

Responding to the socio-economic and cultural conditions of global diaspora is transforming the cultural and moral ideologies of the middle-generation. These changes are also defined by economic circumstances that tend to elevate the social dependency of older parents upon their middle-generation children, whilst, at the same time, also increasing the economic dependency of adult children, opening possibilities for both negative and positive changes in intergenerational relationships (Hogerbrugge & Silverstein, 2014).

Ethnographic Fieldwork

"*Khayal kar liya karo kabhi, mai Monday ko intezar karugi*" (Are you reminded of me in between the weeks, I will wait for you on Monday), says Anju Aunty over the phone. A 65-year-old widow, Anju moved to Glengormley, on the outskirts of Belfast, from the Indian city of Amritsar, after her marriage. Her son, who lives across the street, rarely speaks with his mother. Anju would wait for me religiously every week in the temple, and often asked me if I ever think of her. Every Monday, she would come to open the temple gate for me, and she would enquire "*kaise ho ap, beta?*" (how are you, dear?).

With my regular visits, we established a rapport. She was a quiet, unassuming lady, who would often take me to a quiet corner. There she would sit comfortably for hours and talk with me. As this became a routine, I began to ask myself: "Who cares for her? Why does she care about me? Why is she living alone when her child lives in a house across the street? Why is her son not talking to her? How is her relationship with her daughter-in-law and grandchildren? How was she connected to her siblings and relatives?

To address the 'Nature of Nurture', in this chapter, I aim to reflect how we understand and define care as practiced within Indian migrant families. This empirical research is conducted from the perspective of care-givers. The ideology of kinship blood-ties and its relationship to social care within Indian families in Northern Ireland has been examined.

The two specific questions I investigate are: (i) How is care defined by middle-aged care-givers as they care for the old and the young?,

(ii) Has care-work in families changed over time? If yes, what are the new ways of caring. In the process of exploring these questions, I have also explored the idea of 'the middle generation' (60-80 years old), which in my research have held a dual position of simultaneously caring for the old (90 years old and above) and the young (30-50 years). Interestingly, the main informants (senior citizens) identified themselves as the middle generation as they do not see themselves as old, because they care for even more elderly people in their family.

To study this intriguing cohort of "Sandwich Generation"[1] and their care giving techniques, the emphasis, in this work, therefore, is on middle-generation perspectives, as they represent an interesting cohort, demographically and socially. This appeared to be an ideal entry point for deepening connections between theory and practice on many levels. Moreover, with enhanced demographic changes, migration and mobility; family studies provide a rich platform to understand the transformative nature of elderly care and ageing. In the caring process, on one hand, they retain traditional values of care-work, but on the other, they are conforming to new notions of care.

The Indian Families and Migrant Care

Old people are not easy to live with. Sorry. One of those...they become like children. They are very demanding. I am not. Well, I think I am not. But ask my daughter. She might have a different opinion. They are hard to keep...look after. And there comes a stage that you do get irritated and even your daughter or son or your daughter-in-law gets frustrated. They say things and they feel it's a burden. But then you do it [care]. You do it.

(Paramjeet, female, 82 years old)

The "One-Caring" and the "Cared-For" (Noddings, 1984), both have to confront their own humanity, as well as their limitations. The family-care dyad is based on these two social actors: one who provides care and the other who receives care. In the above statement, my informant Paramjeet (pseudonym) the one-caring, discusses the complexity of the caring process, demonstrating the limitations of care. Care-work, can be stated as an integration of caring, empathy and ethics. Moreover, her description of elderly care shows that "human beings want to care and to be cared for" (Noddings, 1984:7), implying that care is important in itself. Medical anthropologist Arthur Kleinman (2008, 2009a) reminds us: 'Caring' is part of what makes us human, and also states, it is essential to twenty-first-century medicine (2008, 2009a). Scholars (Paltasingh and Tyagi, 2017, Tabuchi and Miura, 2015) have discussed that the qualitative studies of care-work will allow better understanding of family and intergenerational relationships. Moreover, with enhanced mobility and widespread globalization, these studies have been rapidly increasing among immigrants populations. Their fluid status allows researchers to social changes. Nevertheless, the second and third generations fare—their situation allows a better perspective on the long-term effects of immigration on societies.

What is Care?

Indian tradition, from religious scripture to popular precepts, emphasise the moral obligations upon children to revere, respect their parents and provide support and care for them (Croll, 2006). The rightful attitudes and behaviours of children towards parents are very much framed within a context of indebtedness and obligations. Although allusions are made to the mutual responsibilities of both generations, age hierarchies accord precedence and authority to seniority, thus ranking respect for, and support of, the older generation before all other obligations. Therefore, this intergenerational contract, depends upon obedience, nurture, and the subordination of the younger generations.

Similarly, Croll (2006) observes that in popular imagination, a prosperous old age means being surrounded, and supported, by one's children in a multigenerational household. He also notes that reality does not always correspond to this ideal, however. Divergence from traditional ideals is particularly apparent in the context of globalization, which has led to increased mobility and interaction with diverse cultures. Consequently, there is a tendency for traditional values to be weakened, in association with a shift from traditional Indian "joint families" to "nuclear families" (Bhat & Dhruvarajan, 2009). Care plays an important role in the creation of relationships and bonds within these families, but also improvising itself eventually.

In most cases, the younger generation takes responsibility for the elderly, who might also be considered a socio-economic burden (Khan & Raikwar, 2011). This ideology of social obligation, duties and responsibilities, is important as family is the one basic and universal social structure of human society (Patel, 2005). For Patel (2005), the family is the "socio-economic backbone", whilst Croll (2006) describes the family as "a pivotal cornerstone of social organization." With a tradition of strong kinship bonds and shared cultural values, Indian families maintain the idea of co-operation and caring, even in extended households (Paltasingh & Tyagi, 2012).

While anthropology, demography and population studies have a long history of research, until the past two decades relatively little systematic attention was paid to age-related issues beyond the widespread recognition of the negative stereotyping of old age or of the labelling of conditions associated with old age. The neglect of ageing issues is attributable, in part, to the dearth of theoretical work on how ageing processes affect and are affected by social and behavioural processes. Not to leave, social class, race, gender and other social factors. With medical advancements that prolong human life, old age has taken on a new meaning in societies with the means to provide high-quality medical care. To date, there has been relatively little research in the anthropology of caring particularly, in Indian contexts (Paltasingh and Tyagi, 2017, Singh, 2016, Rajan, 2017), with different life stages, these relationships are prone to changes.

Ageing: An Inevitable Evil

As I sit in this gathering place for middle-aged carers in the Indian Community Centre in Belfast (UK), coming together over sips of Indian *chai*, to share experiences of their daily lives, jokes are exchanged about ages and looks.

> "Would you believe that Roli is 65?" Prem Aunty asks me. When did you come here, Roli?"
> "On 16th July, 1962. Oh God! It has been so many years", Roli Aunty responds.
> "It just feels like yesterday", she continues, as if to herself.

Roli Aunty goes on, addressing me:

> "We are all your grandmothers here."

Some had migrated to Belfast as children with their parents, whilst others had come as a result of marriage. The discussion led them to look back in time, providing them with an opportunity to consider how things have worked out, how families have changed, and how their own way of living has altered. Some showed happiness while others showed resentment, but the sentiment expressed by one respondent was common:

> "We know we are growing old, but this group makes me forget how old I am. Everyone here is so caring."

Ageing, a universal phenomenon, has brought them together in this group, providing them with "family outside family", according to another informant. The caring will typically take the form of emotional and physical support. Most of her family is scattered across the UK. Family has always been the main source of help for older people (Twigg, 1998), however, this group referred themselves as social family, voluntarily formed outside kinship boundaries.

From a universal perspective, care is rooted in all human societies. Russell and Edgar (1998) defined it as "the process of normalizing or optimizing the well-being of dependent individual". Similarly, Noddings (1984) points out that the motive of those who provide care is to remove or alleviate the pain and discomfort of those who they care for. However, a normative set of care is difficult to explain (Swanson, 1991). Gilligan (1982) sets the concept of care, within an ethical framework, emphasising that "care is associated with a sense of morality and duty", which is often innate within families. Keeping in mind these works, the Indian care system can be explained as a social obligation to take care of people related by blood. At the same time, it is a moral and an ethical duty to provide help and to free others from discomfort. This is not always within kinship boundaries. Responding to the socio-economic and cultural conditions of global diaspora is transforming the cultural and moral ideologies of the middle-generation. These changes are also defined by economic circumstances that tend to elevate the social dependency of older parents upon their middle-generation children, whilst, at the same time, also increasing the economic dependency of adult children, opening possibilities for both negative and positive changes in intergenerational relationships (Hogerbrugge & Silverstein, 2014).

In light of these changes, it becomes important to study how people, from both the middle and younger generations, are defining these changed relationships as they experience transformation in their habitus. With asymmetrical care chains, family relationships of care include complex systems of cultural values embedded in a cultural context and are not necessarily unidirectional (Hochschild, 2000). In the construction of family and kinship, the circulation of care between individuals plays a key role (Baldassar and Merla, 2013). The enhanced rates of migration has led many people to not spend old age in their origin country. This allowed me to vividly explore new configurations and analyse multiple understanding of transnational experience.

This led me to investigate the hidden aspects of ageing and care-work. In the subsequent sections, I explore the lived experiences of two of my informants, enabling a better understanding of elderly care by middle-aged carers.

Case Study 1: Social Obligation and Caring Burden

Isha Janeshwar, is a 62-year-old homemaker, who lives in Ballymena. Along with her husband, she runs a clothing business from home. Her inter-generational household comprises her mother-in-law, her husband and their youngest son. For the past 46 years, she has been working as a primary carer for her mother-in-law and still continues to be her main support. For her, caring is a never-ending and agonising process. She shares her decades of experience, during which she has maintained her obligations as a daughter-in-law.

If the responsibility of caring comes as an obligation, where "children", now middle aged carers, have no choice of opting out of the service, it is deemed as a burden, as explained by Isha Aunty. The domination of the *saas* (mother-in-law) and exhausting care-work seem to be never-ending and it is emotionally draining for her. In a joint family, which is seen as the strength of the Indian culture; caring can be defined in various ways. On one hand, it may be seen as a responsibility, obligation or as reciprocity. On the other hand, it can be seen as a way to show affection, love, and well-being. Caring can also be a source of differences, disrespect and problems, however, as in this case.

Isha Aunty had wished to move out of the house that she and her husband shared with her husband's parents, but the unexpected death of her father-in-law gave the couple no choice. Since her husband was the only child of the family, they were expected to take responsibility. Isha Aunty did not feel a "natural sense of care" (Noddings, 1984), but did feel ethically bent to care for her *saas*. Caring for her *saas*, then, can be perceived as one aspect of ethical caring (Noddings, 1984): and yet another household chore for which she is responsible. In this case, Isha Aunty experiences caring as a source of emotional and physical stress. Nevertheless, the restrictive norms of traditional Indian culture result in frequent criticism within the families.

> Care is not just not one activity, especially for elders. They live the life, but you actually make them live that life.

Isha describes how she is responsible for waking up her *saas* in the morning, preparing her breakfast, preparing her prayer service accoutrements and spending time with her. She exclaims, "everything that my mother-in-law does, involves work for me!" Moreover, if one is not able to adhere to these cultural dictations of caring for one's parents, this leads to social stigma (Brijnath, 2014).

Although Isha is upset because of her caring workload, at the same time, she is concerned about the language barrier, her mother-in-law will face, if sent to an old care home. This illustrates the complex nature of care and the fact that there often exists no ideal care solution. The very nature of *seva* (care) is deemed ambiguous and nebulous (Phillips, 2007).

The family core is based around love and care, but at the same time, there are complex emotions at play. Traditionally, in India, older people are revered, while younger people are expected to comply, and to give respect. As Isha Aunty describes her early years of marriage, "the daughter-in-law ought to show appropriate respect." Moreover, *seva* is not always hierarchical, with older people respected and younger people subjugated. This was made clear with another example, in which Isha Aunty confronts how, over the years, she has learnt to take greater control of her life and care for the household. Caring can also be seen as a way (i) to exercise power, (ii) to reveal the decline and decay of ageing bodies, and (iii) symbolically to relocate older people to the peripheries of everyday domesticity (Cohen, 1998; Lamb, 2000). The social expectations include acts such as feeding, cleaning, clothing, sheltering and listening. These underlie the disciplinary transition that ageing bodies and ageing identities must undergo: from doing to accepting; from authoritative to ethereal selves (Brijnath, 2014).

In the above discussed example, 'ageing' as a social phenomenon has multiple meanings. One aspect of this experience can be described in the language of pain, which carers experience. Isha Aunty suffers constant leg and joint pain. She says, "My legs are always sore. I take regular medicine for them." This experience of pain can be seen as an ambivalent juncture of culture, ageing and care (Brijnath, 2014). It is also a process which is neither fixed nor immutable. From caring fatigue to hidden meanings, this particular case study presents a nuanced perspective of Indian caring.

Isha Aunty and her husband, have been saving towards a future in which they will be spending their golden years in an old-age home. Dinesh says, "these days elder-care homes have changed. Their motto is to welcome more old people. Not just because old people do not have any other option, but because they will enjoy these years with similar people." These institutional forms of care operated in the context of social welfare systems (Singh, 1997).

The services provided by elder-care homes, can also be seen as providing relief to primary carers, like Isha Aunty, who have been working endlessly for so many years. Care homes can provide some "time-out" for carers who face a significant physical and emotional burden. This coping mechanism enables some degree of emotional disengagement from their problems. Another informant support the idea of elder care homes.

> Elder-care homes is a necessity here. If both partners are working, they cannot look after their parents. They will visit them sometimes. Some people do not visit at all. But even in India, elder-care homes are becoming common.

Informants like Isha want to keep their mother-in-law at home as long as possible. But at the same time, Isha and her husband have accepted that they will go into an elder-care home. As observed during the interviews, every informant accepted that the stigma surrounding elder-care homes has to change.

The middle-aged generation supported the notion that, "it is about getting care, irrespective of where it is coming from." Another informant concurs, saying: "I believe in getting care and protection, and if the carer comes from outside, what's the harm?" This form of financial care somewhat contradicts the idea of "diminishing obligation", as discussed in the writings of Cohen (1998) and Lamb (2000).

Case Study 2: Silence and Loneliness

'*Khamoshi*' (silence) persists in their house as they enter the twilight of their lives. *Khamosh*, resounds in all its dramatic intensity throughout Bollywood cinematic episodes (Singh, 2016), in which ageing parents are left alone to survive. Ageing may entail not only an erosion of self-reliance and but also a loss of company that cannot be compensated with any social interaction.

Intro of the informant. Balraj's parents decided to move back from Belfast, not to Kenya, but to India. Similar to Isha Aunty's case, Paramjeet Aunty's husband, as the only child of the family, had the sole responsibility of taking care of his parents.

> They did not want to stay here and they went back to India, rather than to Kenya. They spent their last years in India. Although they wanted to be close to us, they did not want to be in Belfast. Our relatives in India took care of them.

Inability to take care of one's parents comes with a huge amount of social stigma. Although the family provided all the necessary resources to their relatives to sustain proper care, Paramjeet and her husband were looked down upon by other family members.

> We never wanted to leave them alone. But there seemed no other choice. At least they were happy in India, even when they were away from us. We would always call them, and the relatives, who were taking care of them. We never allowed money to become a problem.

Caring through money, though not a recent phenomenon, has commonly been used to replace physical forms of care.

Soon Paramjeet's father-in-law passed away. They returned home to India to complete the last rites of passage. During this visit, they asked her mother to come and stay with them in Belfast. This would ensure that she was not alone and that they could care for her. Paramjeet sympathises with her mother-in-law, as she was given no choice to move or not. She was completely dependent upon her son.

> "But you know my father-in-law was a wise man. He always planned for the future. In his will he wrote, 'everything I have will go to my son only if he takes care of his mother'." (Paramjeet)

Paramjeet Aunty makes herself clear, saying that they would have cared for her mother-in-law with or without money. The currency of care has been seen as a way to get care from children, as stated by Brijnath (2014), where institutions prevent parents from transferring everything to their children.

> My mother-in-law had the same problem of loneliness, but there was no other choice. I tried my best to make her comfortable by giving her small household chores to do, along with me in the kitchen. (Paramjeet).

Paramjeet describes her daily chores, the fixed routines of prayer times, bathing times, meal times, siestas, evening walks and bed. In between, there were many hours in which no activities were undertaken and sometimes her mother-in-law would phone people, but most of the time she would just sit or lay on the bed. There were limited opportunities for pleasure. She wouldn't watch TV or spend time with other people outside. Paramjeet used to give small tasks to her mother-in-law like peeling vegetables or sewing to keep her engaged. But the days were long, involving the same mundane routines—slowly waking up and getting dressed, praying, eating and just lying down. Brijnath (2014) observes that many in such situations feel depressed and oscillate from being withdrawn and quiet, to being aggressive and repetitious. For them time becomes a commodity in surplus.

Paramjeet Aunty's domestic experiences ranged from Kenya to Belfast to India. She empathised with her parents-in-law and would herself experience their disengagement and loneliness. Caring from a distance resulted in Paramjeet and Balraj being socially stigmatised. Therefore, she has decided to spend the remainder of her life with her husband, without asking for help from her only daughter who resides in Canada.

This case study explicitly reveals how caring and its effects are experienced irrespective of distance.

Case Study 3: Virtual Caring

Expectations are normal within families. Caring in these families is 'inherently reciprocal' and 'asymmetrical'—the expectation that giving of care be reciprocated, although it may be realised (Baldassar and Merla, 2013) forming a generational contract (Bengtso and Achebaum, 1993). This case study shows how constant negotiation between the two generations results in the development of distinctive ways of caring, which are also influenced by globalization and technological change. Information and communication technology (ICT) and money—are increasingly deployed in the new innovative treads for caring.

Excerpt Interview 1

> **Meena:** We have a father-in-law, who is 92 years old, who we look after. My brother-in-law lives with him, but we would travel almost every weekend and my children feel it is important to visit him. They take turns, even when they are married. My girl came over from London last weekend, only to visit her grand-dad. They will also talk using "face-time", so as we don't lose him to dementia.
>
> **Ashwin:** So, technology has been helpful in facilitating care?
>
> **Meena:** Every week they have decided upon a fixed time with

> my father-in-law. My brother-in-law sets up the computer. My children and great grandchildren can talk to him, more importantly, they can see each other. My son-in-law and grandchildren are English but still they do it. They make Skype calls. Similarly, I am connected with Roli through Whatsapp everyday. She was in Canada last week, although we could not (physically) talk to each other, we talked over text almost everyday.

Excerpt Interview 2

> **Roli:** In the past, not too many girls were working. Now things have changed. For example, during my time, I had to leave my job. One reason was being a woman, we are designed to care. Another reason being my husband was earning more. However, now my daughter and son-in-law are equally earning and they manage their time, instead of putting all of the caring burden on one person.
>
> **Ashwin:** Do you still believe in joint family structures to maintain family ties?
>
> **Roli:** I personally feel, it is time for the parents to get over these things. It's time to move on! They have their own aspirations and goals and they should not be pulled back, because they have to care for their parents. I am 100 per cent sure, if anything happens to me today, my children would be here. What else does one need? They will be more than willing to help financially, but they cannot be with me 24/7. When I cannot do household work, I pay the money to someone else to do it. It is the same way.

The above two excerpts exemplify modern forms of families and their responsibilities. Meena's story is exemplary of the growing usage of ICT in caring for one another. Roli's story supports the notion of personally adapting according to the needs of modern culture, saying, "it's time to move on!". She supports these contemporary means of caring. However, the emotional aspect of caring has not changed.

Meena, 63 years old, works as a committee member in the ICC. She migrated to Belfast with her family in the early 1960s. She grew up in a large extended family network and still believes in maintaining strong family bonds. The family is widely scattered across the UK and India. To overcome distance, they frequently use ICT. They make regular phone-calls to each other, and also use the Face-Time application, as well as Skype calls. It is apparent that Meena and her family members continue to feel a sense of moral obligation which requires them to maintain family relationships even across transnational dimensions. It can be difficult to find time each day to meet these demands, but nevertheless, they continue so to do.

These case studies describe how the middle-aged who anticipate a need for care adapt to changing circumstances. Roli, 65 years old, is adored in the 50+ group for her caring attitude. She is respected for maintaining a caring network, both with families and friends. She does not resent the way children provide care. She accepts that the Western upbringing of the younger generation has transformed Indian caring traditions, and she also accepts the ways that these transformations have affected her. "I have invested so much in my children's education. I would rather see them successful, than close to me and suffer in their lives", she opined, as she exchanged views on the discourses between the two generations. Her views on new lifestyles can be related to the concept of "privileged irresponsibility", as a way of excusing oneself from caring responsibilities because one has other important work to perform (Tronto, 2006:11). In this case, however, it is Roli, who makes the excuses for her children and indeed, pushes them to be independent and thus to give her independence, as is seen in the fact that she asked her unmarried son to move out: something that would not typically happen in traditional Indian families. It is clear then, that it is not just the younger generation that is influenced by Western individualism. Roli, also places value on her own freedom. There are still expectations of mutual care in Roli's family: but Roli only expects and desires financial care: not personal care.

The common theme that emerges in all of the above examples, is of care being both multi-directional and pragmatic. Growing technological development, the emergence of smartphone applications, Skype, email, as well as cheaper travel, is shaping the meaning of care (Baldassar and Merla, 2013). In this new form of caring, children are also providing considerable assistance to their parents and grand-parents, in their use of new communication technologies, resulting in the expansion of family networks.

Although distance remains an issue even in this globalised world, in some cases, distance has helped to maintain good relationships. It has strengthened their family ties and the care has grown stronger. With increasing resources, new ways of caring have emerged and are being accepted in family domains, changing expectations. Money as a social phenomenon (Singh, 2016) now shapes relationships and cultural values, with the major constraint on the younger generation being time.

Ideological Mobility and Habitus Transformation

The above cases, based on different timelines, illustrate how relationships can change within families. This observation of change over time led me to explore the idea of caring with respect to changing habitus (Bourdieu, 1977). Some scholars have argued that the concept of habitus is deterministic, thus, negating any transformation (Alexander, 1995). However, Isha enacts the ideology of family responsibility. In her case, care can also be seen as labour, making them difficult to distinguish. Similarly, care presents itself as both an emotion and a moral obligation. Although Fisher and Tronto (1993), define care as, "neither self-referring nor self-absorbing", we see in the case study that care can be seen as both. It acts as a glue that binds relationships. Thomas (1993) sees care not as a theoretical category, but its existence at the level of everyday familial and political discourse. Thus making family a platform of relationships.

At the same time, Isha Aunty being sandwiched between her mother-in-law and daughter-in-law is quite evident. Moreover, another interesting area is the transformation of habitus from a nuclear family to a joint family (for Isha Aunty). Was the change more difficult for her mother-in-law, than it was for her? Habitat, as we say is accumulated experience; it is a complex social process in which individuals' dispositions established through practice. The three generations of family coming to a different environment, at different times, has affected their socio-cultural norms and how they perceive the 'logic of understanding' (Bourdieu, 1977).

It is evident that each consecutive generation is more adaptable to the changes they face in a new country. In this multi-generational case study; dependency, disability and demand, emerge as key areas within the family care dyad. The hidden costs of the "unsustainable obligation" (Baldassar, 2008), might ultimately lead to the breakdown of these networks, however, leading to the commodified care provided by old-people's care homes. In light of these changes, therefore, it becomes important to study how people, from both the middle and younger generations, are defining these changed relationships as they experience transformation in their habitus.

With asymmetrical care chains, family relationships of care include complex systems of cultural values embedded in a cultural context and are not necessarily unidirectional (Hochschild, 2000). In the construction of family and kinship, the circulation of care between individuals plays a key role (Baldassar and Merla, 2013). In order to understand this, I draw upon Bourdieu's ideas of habitus.

I introduce the concept of habitus to explain the recent care changes by throwing light on the mechanism of social reproduction and care as disposition (Phillips, 2007). Habitus refers to embodied behaviours derived from the unconscious internalisation of the social structure (Bourdieu, 1977). According to habitus theory, individuals internalise their social position, within the social structure, into their unconscious behaviours (Lee & Kramer, 2013). This internalisation of structure explains why agents from different social groups, such as class, gender, and race, show different attitudes and patterns of social behaviour, resulting in different social outcomes—thus resulting in the stable reproduction of social structure (Bourgois & Schonberg, 2007). The early years of childhood are seen as a stage in which habitus is embodied through family interactions, producing dispositions that last a lifetime (King, 2000).

Moreover, the concept of habitus is used to explore the changing ideologies and practices of the middle-generation carers. In so doing, I adopt a conception of habitus as fluid, rather than fixed. Contrary to writers such as Alexander (1995), therefore, I do not see habitus as totally deterministic.

The concept of "cleft habitus" sought to explain the changes in habitus which result from social mobility. According to Lee and Kramer (2013: 31), habitus cleavage or cleft habitus, resulting from a move from one social context to another, leads to "weakening relationships in the home community because the potentially painful process of habitus cleavage makes it difficult to balance the newly acquired with the old habitus."

As I record the lived experiences of middle-generation Indian care-givers in Northern Ireland, I see the dilemmas which result from juggling between their old and new habitus, and, being sandwiched in between. Social mobility, in this case, a result of migration from India to Northern Ireland, has changed both ideas and practices. This process is not easy or painless. The concept of a cleft habitus helps us understand the ways in which individuals interact with changing social circumstances, as they acquire and develop strategies to cope with a new social context by acquiring a new habitus.

Whilst a new habitus is quickly formed for the young generation, and may be difficult or impossible for the old, the middle-generation can acquire a new habitus, but not without considerable effort and struggle. The key informants in this study, the middle-generation, nevertheless do seem to exhibit a fluid habitus as they move from the habitus of the old to the habitus of the young. Schneider and Lang (2014) use the term "multiple habitus" to describe the application of different codes of behaviour to different social contexts, suggesting that the processes of change may be more complex than the old/new binary of "cleft habitus".

This ethnographic study provided me an impression of care and culture as dispositions, in which social structures are unconsciously internalised. The middle-generation occupy a centre-ground, between the encultured traditional norms that they brought from India and those new ways of interacting which are imposed upon them by their new environment. These experiences of caring and habitus transformations gave me an insight into the Indian migrant community in Northern Ireland, allowing me to understand how social actors have been adapting their forms of care-giving to their new social environment.

The notion of a cleft habitus, "presumes that the acquisition of a new habitus necessarily involves moving away from the previous one" (Schneider and Lang, 2014). Amongst the Indian migrants I researched, habitus transformation is not solely based on migration or mobility but is also affected by acculturation to the Western world. The present study of middle-aged carers, as they occupy the niche of both old and young, does not find them alienated from their traditional norms. Rather than "habitus cleavage", the behaviour of these middle-generation Indians may better be seen as "habitus diversification", which Schneider and Lang (2014) describe as frequent bridging and switching between different forms of habitus.

Research Methodology

I explored the field through ethnographic methods of interview and participant-observation. The live engagement through these qualitative methods allowed me to experience activities directly, "to get the feel of the events and have my own perceptions too" (Spradley, 2016).

Being from India myself, I had the "privileged" position of understanding the cultural context and thus communications and interactions were easier. My informants were middle-aged (predominantly females) and originally from Punjab region of North India. The Indian Community Centre (ICC), which hosts a 50+ age group, located on Clifton Street in Belfast, became somewhere that I would regularly visit. The evocative case studies of Isha, Paramjeet, Roli, Meena and Anju Aunty, provided me fascinating qualitative data.

However, I soon realised that the obligations placed on me reflected their traditional ideas of morality. These discourses and obligations were largely organised around *panditji* (priest): the religious discipline which specifies how Hindus should pray and conduct religious services in the temple. My incorporation into these networks allowed a genuinely participatory methodology to be adopted.

As I started my anthropological "rites of passage", I kept field-notes in ethnographic diaries from my ICC visits which were conducted from June to August 2017. From being a participant in group activities, to becoming part of their lunch group, the experience has been particularly intense. Using an autobiographical interview method and auto-ethnographic form of writing, I reflexively incorporated my experiences into the work, creating a dialectic relationship between interview and observation. On listening to my informants, I began to understand that there is no blueprint for caring. Moreover, my experiences were shaped *via* listening and observing, which made me appreciate that the human body should not be seen "as a mere biological or physical unit, but as the body which structures one's situation and experience within the world" (Merleau-Ponty, 1996).

"What goes on inside the family, stays inside the family", says 65 years old, Prem Aunty, letting me know the barriers I had to overcome to make them comfortable sharing family information. With frequent meetings and casual interactions, they allowed me to cross the boundary from being a researcher to a member of the group. I often found myself holding hands, helping them put their feet in shoes, and supporting them while walking. People responded positively to show affection. However, even after becoming close to my informants, "becoming part of the furniture" as Briggs (2003) described it, was impossible. Relationship-wise, crossing the line from researcher to "being a friend" (Tillmann-Healy, 2003) had limitations, with age-difference being an important barrier.

Interviews ranged in duration from a few minutes to several hours. Interviews were recorded when informants consented to this. The only difficulty encountered in the field was establishing initial contact with the ICC group. The priest, Gopal Mishra, was not very keen in providing me with contacts, which I felt was his way of taking care of his people.

My questions ranged from family histories to what is care, family cultures to ideal care. Reliability and validity were ensured by cross-checking of factual data of interview, observational data and discourse analysis. The data compiled presented a complex montage of discourses on care perception, giving and receiving.

The spheres of the research included 50+ age-group activities. During these encounters, I gained insights into the realities of daily life, from the perspective of middle-aged care-givers. As noted above, the 60–80 year old age group do not consider themselves old as they take care of the elderly (80+ years) and this complicated network of relationships amid bodily and social change is explored through shifting negotiations of caring. A processual approach to caring was adopted, considering people as social actors who are actively engaged in shaping "the conditions of their existence" within the cultural, social and historical context in which they live (R. Rosaldo, 1993: 92-103). This approach allowed me to emphasise how meaning and experience emerge in interaction with others and the world, and social relations are negotiated.

Conclusion

This research has provided a close-up picture of a particular generation in a particular small part of the global Indian diaspora. Although limited in scope, the study makes a contribution to an area of anthropology that remains under-researched, particularly in relation to the Indian diaspora. The study draws upon the Bourdieu's (1977) notion of habitus, but deploys Schneider & Lang's (2014) work to show that Indian migrants in Northern Ireland are not culturally divided, in the way Bourdieu's notion of a "cleft habitus" suggests: rather they are creatively adapting their traditions to the new context in which they find themselves through processes of "habitus diversification".

On exploring the different dimensions of "care" within different relationships, the word proves to have a wide range of connotations, aspects and values. It does not remain static. Family care has connotations of responsibility and cultural obligation, whereas institutionalised care is conceived of more in terms of welfare and support. There is no ideal way to define care. Caring within Indian families emerges as both an emotional and a moral obligation. It is "neither self-referring nor self-absorbing" (Fisher and Tronto, 1982). As Isha Aunty says, "one cannot get away from the feelings of duty and responsibility." However, my research suggests a fall in expectations with respect to mutual caring. This is perhaps one reason for the increased acceptance of elder-care homes.

Intriguingly, my key informants, who were all 60-80 years old, identified themselves as 'middle-aged'. Even at this late point in their lives, with people living longer, they found themselves looking after their parents. Due to slow habitus transformation for the older generation, their children are hesitant to put them in elder-care homes, to which they might struggle to adapt, preferring to take the burden on themselves. But with the increased workload, some carers reflect "How much can I give?" It was apparent that compassion fatigue was common within families. On the other hand, despite the family stigma, we do see some children neglecting their parental care responsibilities. In these instances, the parents will often seek to cover-up for their children, because of the stigma attached, to prevent the family getting a bad name.

To conclude, I have asked questions as to how we should perceive and understand contemporary ageing processes, in the face of dramatic demographic, social and cultural transformations of both local and global ageing landscapes. We have captured ageing processes from the ethnographic fieldwork conducted among five immigrant families. To understand the process of care processes transformation, I have relied on Bourdieu's idea of Habitus Transformation. In the process, I explored how spaces define the way care is provided. For example, the care provided in community care centres stand different from the care provided within houses. Moreover, care through social care worker in old care homes is seen as more professional care. This idea of 'space' defining care can be developed further in the future studies of care and its processes.

NOTE

1. The ageing children of ageing parents (Miller, 1981).

REFERENCES

Alexander, J. (1995). *Fin de Siecle Social Theory*. Verso: London.

Ames, M.G., Go, J., Kaye, J.J. and Spasojevic, M., (2010, February). Making love in the network closet: the benefits and work of family videochat." In *Proceedings of the (2010) ACM conference on Computer supported cooperative work,* pp. 145-154, ACM.

Askham, J., Briggs, K., Norman, I. and Redfern, S., (2007). "Care at home for people with dementia: as in a total institution?" *Ageing & Society*, *27*(1), pp. 3-24.

Baldassar, L. (2007). "Transnational families and aged care: the mobility of care and the migrancy of ageing." *Journal of Ethnic and Migration Studies*, *33*(2), pp. 275-297.

Baldassar, L. (2008). "12 Debating Culture across Distance: Transnational Families and the Obligation to Care." *The Family in Question*, p. 269.

Baldassar, L. (2017). "10 Australian migrant families and the transnationalisation of care. Critical Reflections on Migration,'Race'and Multiculturalism: Australia in a Global Context", In Bengtson, V.L. and Achenbaum, W.A. (eds.), (1993). *The Changing contract across generations*. Transaction Publishers.

Baldassar, L. and Merla, L. (eds.), (2013). *Transnational families, migration and the circulation of care: Understanding mobility and absence in family life* (Vol. 29). Routledge.

Baldassar, L., Majella Kilkey, L. Merla, and R. Wilding. (2016). "Transnational families, care and wellbeing." In *Hnadbook of Migration and Health*, edited by Felicity Thomas. Cheltenham & Northampton: Edward Elgar Publishing. pp. 477-97

Bhat, A.K. and Dhruvarajan, R., (2009). *Ageing in India. Sociology of Ageing: A Reader*, p. 334.

Bourdieu, P. (1977a). *Outline of a Theory of Practice*. Cambridge, U.K.: Cambridge University Press.

Bourgois, P. and Schonberg, J., (2007). "Intimate apartheid: Ethnic dimensions of habitus among homeless heroin injectors." *Ethnography*, *8*(1), pp. 7-31.

Briggs, K., Askham, J., Norman, I. and Redfern, S., (2003). "Accomplishing care at home for people with dementia: using observational methodology." *Qualitative Health Research*, *13*(2), pp. 268-280.

Brijnath, B., (2014). *Unforgotten: Love and the culture of dementia care in India* (Vol. 2). Berghahn Books.

Caturvedi, M. and Tivārī, B., (1975). *Practical Hindi-English Dictionary*.

Clifford, J. and Marcus, G.E. (eds.), (1986). *Writing Culture: The Poetics and Politics of Ethnography*. University of California Press.

Cohen, L., (1998). *No ageing in India: Alzheimer's, the bad family, and other modern things*. University of California Press.

Croll, E.J., (2006). "The intergenerational contract in the changing Asian family." *Oxford Development Studies*, *34*(4), pp. 473-491.

Das, V., (2012). *Ordinary Ethics 8: A Companion to Moral Anthropology*, p. 133.

Fassin, D. (ed.), (2012). *A Companion to Moral Anthropology*. John Wiley & Sons.

Geertz, C. (1973). *Interpretation of Cultures*. New York: Basic Books.

Gilligan, C., (1982). *In a Different Voice*. Harvard University Press.

Goulbourne, H., Reynolds, T., Solomos, J. and Zontini, E., (2010). *Transnational Families: Ethnicities, Identities and Social Capital*. Routledge.

Hank, K., (2007). "Proximity and contacts between older parents and their children: A European comparison." *Journal of Marriage and Family*, *69*(1), pp. 157-173.

Hochschild, A.R. (2000). "Global care chains and emotional surplus value." In Hutton, W. and Giddens, A. (2000) (eds), *On the Edge: Living with Global Capitalism*. Jonathan Cape, London, pp. 130-46.

Hogerbrugge, M.J. and Silverstein, M.D., (2014). "Transitions in relationships with older parents: From middle to later years." *Journals of Gerontology Series B: Psychological Sciences and Social Sciences*, *70*(3), pp. 481-495.

Kaufmann, J. and Rabodoarimiadana, A.P., (2003). "Making kin of historians and anthropologists: Fictive kinship in fieldwork methodology." *History in Africa*, *30*, pp. 179-194.

Khan, A.M. and Raikwar, M., (2011). "Relationship between expectations, life satisfaction and diseases amongst elderly from different social groups." *Indian Journal of Gerontology*, *25*(2), pp. 160-176.

King, A., (2000). "Thinking with Bourdieu against Bourdieu: A 'practical' critique of the habitus." *Sociological Theory*, *18*(3), pp. 417-433.

Lamb, S., (2000). *White saris and sweet mangoes: Ageing, gender, and body in North India*. University of California Press.

Lambek, M. (ed.), (2010). *Ordinary Ethics: Anthropology, Language, and Action*. Fordham University Press.

Lee, E.M., & Kramer, R. (2013). "Out with the Old, In with the New? Habitus and Social Mobility at Selective Colleges." *Sociology of Education*, *86*(1), 18-35.

Merla, L., (2010). *Transnational practices of Salvadoran migrants in Australia: an analysis of the factors influencing the capability to care across borders*. Lisbon: University of Lisbon.

Merleau-Ponty, M., (1996). *Phenomenology of Perception*. Motilal Banarsidass Publisher.

Miller, D.A., (1981). "The 'sandwich' generation: Adult children of the ageing." *Social Work*, *26*(5), pp. 419-423.

Nedelcu, M., (2012). "Migrants' new transnational habitus: rethinking migration through a cosmopolitan lens in the digital age." *Journal of Ethnic and Migration Studies*, *38*(9), pp. 1339-1356.

Noddings, N., (1984). *Caring: A Feminist Approach to Ethics*. Berkeley: University of Barkeley.

Paltasingh, T. (2017). "Situating Elderly Role in Family Decision-Making: Indian Scenario." *Indian Journal of Gerontology*, *31*(1).

Paltasingh, T. and Tyagi, R. (2012). "Demographic transition and population ageing: building an inclusive culture." *Social Change*, *42*(3), pp. 391-409.

Patel, T. (ed.), (2005). *The Family in India: Structure and Practice*. Sage.

Phillips, J., (2007). "Care: Key concepts. Polity Key Concept" in *The Social Sciences Series*. UK: Polity Press.

Rajan, S.I. and Balagopal, G. (eds.), (2017). *Elderly Care in India: Societal and State Responses*. Springer.

Reay, D., (2015). "Habitus and the psychosocial: Bourdieu with feelings." *Cambridge Journal of Education*, *45*(1), pp. 9-23.

Robbins, J., (2016). "What is the matter with transcendence? On the place of religion in the new anthropology of ethics." *Journal of the Royal Anthropological Institute*.

Rosaldo, R., (1993). *Culture & Truth: The Remaking of Social Analysis: With a New Introduction*. Beacon Press.

Rosenthal, C.J., Martin-Matthews, A. and Matthews, S.H., (1996). "Caught in the middle? Occupancy in multiple roles and help to parents in a national probability sample of Canadian adults." *The Journals of Gerontology Series B: Psychological Sciences and Social Sciences*, *51*(6), pp. S274-S283.

Russell, A. and Edgar, I.R., (1998). "Research and Practice in the Anthropology of Welfare." *The Anthropology of Welfare*, 1, pp. 1-15.

Schneider, J. and Lang, C., (2014). "Social mobility, habitus and identity formation in the Turkish-German second generation." *New Diversities*, *16* (1), pp. 89-105.

Shah, A.M., (1998). *The Family in India: Critical Essays*. Orient Blackswan.

Singh, S., (1997). *Marriage Money: The Social Shaping of Money in Marriage and Banking*. Allen & Unwin.

Singh, S., (2016). *Money, Migration, and Family: India to Australia*. Springer.

Sokolovsky, J. (2009b). "Ageing, Globalization and Societal Transformations", in J. Sokolovsky (ed.), *The Cultural Context of Ageing: Worldwide Perspectives*, 3rd edn. Westport: Praeger, pp. 175-83.

Spradley, J.P., (2016). *Participant Observation*. Waveland Press.

Stacey, B.G., (1998). "Marriage Money: The Social Shaping of Money in Marriage and Banking" [Book Review]. *Journal of Family Studies*, *4*(2), p. 246.

Swanson, K.M., (1991). "Empirical development of a middle range theory of caring." *Nursing Research*, *40*(3), pp. 161-165.

Tabuchi, M. and Miura, A., (2015). "Young people's reactions change elderly people's generativity and narratives: The effects of intergenerational interaction on the elderly." *Journal of Intergenerational Relationships*, *13*(2), pp. 118-133.

Thomas, C., (1993). "De-constructing concepts of care. *Sociology*, *27* (4), pp. 649-669.

Tillmann-Healy, L.M., (2003). Friendship as method. *Qualitative inquiry*, *9* (5), pp. 729-749.

Tilly, C., (2007). March. Trust networks in transnational migration. In *Sociological Forum* (Vol. 22, No. 1, pp. 3-24). Blackwell Publishing Ltd.

Tronto, J.C., (1993). *Moral boundaries: A political argument for an ethic of care*. Psychology Press.

Tronto, J.C., Noddings, N., Buker, E., Sevenhuijsen, S., Bozalek, V., Gouws, A., Minnaar-Mcdonald, M., Little, D., Walker, M.U., Robinson, F. and Tucker, J.S., (2006). *Socializing Care: Feminist Ethics and Public Issues*. Rowman & Littlefield Publishers.

Twigg, J., (1998). *Informal Care of Older People. The Social Policy of Old Age*. London: Centre for Policy on Ageing, pp. 128-41.

Vatuk, S., (1990). "To be a burden on others. Dependency anxiety among the elderly in India." In O.M. Lynch (Ed.), *Divine Passions: The Social Construction of Emotion in India*, pp. 64-90.

Zontini, E., (2010). "Enabling and constraining aspects of social capital in migrant families: Ethnicity, gender and generation." *Ethnic and Racial Studies*, *33*(5), pp. 816-831.

18

Inside a *Ghosal*: Understanding Occupational Health of Craftsmen in Metal Handicrafts of Assam

Drabita Dutta

Introduction

Cottage industries play a significant role in the industrial sector of Assam. The major cottage industries of the region are the bell and brass, the bamboo and cane and the silk. These industries fall under the purview of rural cottage and small scale industry sector. These industries directly and indirectly employ thousands of artisans, local wholesalers and dealers. The present chapter deals with the artisans working in bell and brass metal industry in Assam. The objective of this chapter is to examine various issues related to occupational health problems faced by these artisans. The bell and brass metal items are crafted by manual labourers who are locally knows as *kahars*. It is the *kahars* who are the centre of the bell and brass metal industry and through their skill and proficiency it is them, who keep the industry afloat.

Around the world, the number of work related accidents and the frequency of occupational injuries is very high. According to International Labour Organisation (ILO), globally, the annual number of fatal occupational injuries is 3,80,000. This is composed mainly of an Asian burden of 2,50,000 deaths (Takala, 2019). Injuries and accidents due to unsafe working environments remain a standout amongst the most preventable medical issues throughout the world. These mishaps often lead to off of wages, perpetual body hårm and huge expenses to the life of the workers (Jovanovic et al., 2004). In the case of the informal sector, occupational health and safety is neglected even more.

Akin to other industries, cottage industries are also characterised with several occupational hazards. The artisans working in the bell and brass metal industry face several occupational health hazards. These hazards are sparsely known to the artisans and to their owners. Such ignorance often leads to the continuity of the harmful effects not only for the workers but to their dependents as well. According to McCormick (1997), a number of workers have been affected by health risks emerging from their occupation resulting in death. In many cases, the hospital expenses have exhausted the worker's savings and pushed their families into destitution. Cases have also been observed where the sole providers of the family have been disfigured due to the lack of safety procedures and gears (McCormick, 1997: 8).

The present chapter is situated in the backdrop of such occupational hazards and its impact on the life of the *kahars* working in the metal industry of Assam. Based on ethnographic study conducted in the two metal clusters of Barpeta District in Assam, I examine the nature of health risks, related factors and barriers associated with occupational health. I also attempt to explore the perspective of the artisans regarding their health and occupational hazards of their work.

Since the past two decades, owing to continuous socio-economic upheavals, the metal craft industry hasn't been performing well in Assam. For this reason, there is a need for a comprehensive and critical analysis of the problems concerning the industry, especially the health related hazards to the *kahars* (*local term used for metal artisans*) employed in the sector. With this aim in view, the current study was conducted to generate an understanding of the nature of occupational health risks and related factors and barriers faced by the artisans in the metal industries of *Sarthebari* and *Sarukhetri* clusters of *Barpeta* District of Assam. The *Sarthebari* cluster is one of the original areas for bell metal craft and the *Sarukhetri* cluster is known for its brass metal craft. Assamese people refer the *Sarthebari* as '*kahar* or '*nogori'*. Villages in Sarukhetri, like *Baniakushi* and *Haldhibari* are famous for their '*sarai slilpo'* (metallurgy).

The study centers around the state of occupational health safety among cottage industry artisans following the model based on one of the eight-dimensional constructs of occupational health hazards of Walton (1973). The chapter explores the key occupational hazards, injuries, and accidents experienced by *kahars* with the intention to come up with recommendations and safety measures in order to make their working environments more safe and secure. The chapter argues that *Kahars* understand the need and importance of personal protective equipment as a measure against mishaps, injuries and illness but fail to use to them due to unavailability of these safety gears. This study attempts to seek the answer of the following interrelated questions. First, what kind of occupational hazards affect the metal artisans of the *kahar* community of Assam? Second, how does work affects health and health affects work? And, finally, what are the impact of occupational hazards upon the artisan's family and the role of government schemes?

This work is situated in medical anthropology of occupational hazards, which I have established in the first section of this chapter. Then I have discussed in length the methodology of collecting data for this work and the analytical tools that I have used to evaluate my findings. Based on the data collected, I have presented the health risks of these artisans and a few observations that can be taken away from this situation. Finally, I have concluded this chapter by advocating for changes in the occupational environment of these artisans.

Occupational Hazards, Political Economy of Health and Medical Anthropology

Occupational hazards were studied by R. Virchow who proposed the political economic approach. He was influenced by Boaz and by the beginning of 1970 his significant contribution to the political economic approach became a part of medical anthropology. Combined with medical anthropology, the political economy of health approach was uniquely positioned to bridge the divide between occupational and community health by reinserting work into the lived experiences of workers, their families, and their communities. However, broad literature aligned to the health and occupational safety focused largely on injury events and how to prevent them. Further, it was Morgan who portrayed the 'political economy of health from a macro analytical, critical and historical point of view for understanding the disease distribution and health services which are again under various economic systems, particularly on the political, economic relations within world economic systems and with the stratified social effects' (Morgan, 1984:132). This view takes account of the economic and political interests as well those which are mostly involved with the administration of health services under the umbrella of a capitalist system. This expansion is regarded as a significant landmark for its differential formation of societal form into a contemporary course. Moreover, macro-economic transformations create economic and social exclusion of large social groups, manifested in their marginal access to economic and social resources, security, housing and health.

Largely due to the unorganized nature of the work and the percentage of the population working independently (self-employed), it becomes difficult to cover such artisans under their safety check-up schemes. In developing countries, small scale mechanics, metalworkers, stone carvers, the nature of their work makes them susceptible to occupational injuries and accidents. The problem of improving safety among these craftsmen is difficult due to informal management structures, lack of regulation and inspection regimes, lack of organizational safety cultures and limited unionization, among others (Clarke, 2005).

Research conducted in the field of occupational health and safety talks about the physical and ecological conditions of the working environment. This encompasses the natural characteristics of the work zone (hazardous airborne synthetic compounds, noises, extreme temperature, humidity and dimensions of lighting), the physical organization of the building comprising the working environment and the outside facilities and their site arrangements. Safety at the work environment has numerous implications on the life of the individual labourers in light of the fact that the labourer is a social being and not a machine that can be utilized for production and neglected there after. In their pursuit of livelihood, workers have to bear varying health hazards, some of which are particular to their very own occupation while others emerge from specialists' themselves or the negligence of associates (Adamson, 2004). According to Tadesse and Admassu (2006), an expected 160 million new instances of occupation-related illnesses occur around the world such as back pain, respiratory diseases; noise induced hearing problems, physical strain, exhaustion, and stress. Artisans working in cottage sector industries are bound to work for extended periods because the returns are not proportionate to the production efforts. These artisans in the informal sector, most often participate in manual labour. Monotonous work routine, carrying heavy weights, and bad body posture, lifting, turning, twisting, pushing and pulling are some of the activities they engage in which causes physical strain and exhaustion prompting injuries and poor health.

Loewenson (1997) have discussed the profitability and management of small scale ventures on one hand and the empowerment of the workers on the other hand. The empowerment of workers in the informal sector, according to him, is based upon advancing their well-being. Walton (1999) found in his study that work-structuring, humanization of work and socio-technical systems are used interchangeably with the quality of work life. A study by Avotri and Walters (1999) explained that sanitation issues which are caused by the open running water, the lack of toilet facilities have the most noteworthy impact in causing malaria fever and the runs, muscular-skeletal torment, drying out, and migraines. Amedofu (2002) in his study, found that commotion actuated hearing loss is distinguished as one amongst the most common occupational health and safety-related risk in the development of small scale industries, as it affects the well-being of the artisans.

This research work especially focuses on the occupational hazards, the long-term impact of occupation related injury on the artisans along with the worker's community. However, from the review of literature, it has been found that academicians generally ignored the relation between poverty along with workplace related hazards. Poverty is one of the causes for the condition of the occupational hazard inside the informal small-scale sector artisans. Hence, the argument of this chapter has stressed that the economically poor, below poverty line artisans are worst affected in workplace-related risks. Another trend observed during the process of literature review was the scarcity of qualitative studies on the occupational hazards in Indian context. Most of the existing studies on occupational hazards, especially in cottage sector industries are focused upon the socio-economic condition of the artisans. The present study combines the socio-economic perspective with occupational hazards to assess the life of the artisans and the threats posed to their health because of their occupation. In the present study, I attempt to understand from a model based on one of the eight-dimensional constructs of Walton, that is, safe and healthy working conditions, studied in the context of health-related issues of metal artisans. Studies conducted on the quality of work-life, especially the recent studies, have considered artisans' involvement in decision-making process as an essential component besides other variables.

According to Walton (1973), most workers are affected by insecurity which arises because of their working conditions. But it is a complicated issue as the responsible factors for the quality of life of the worker at work are very difficult to ascertain (Walton, 1973). In this regard, Walton (1973) proposed to measure the interrelationship between them the parameters that influence the problem. He suggested eight categories to assess Quality of Work Life which are: (i) Adequate and fair compensation; (ii) safe and healthy working conditions; (iii) opportunity to use and develop human capacities; (iv) opportunity to growth and security; (v) social integration in the work organization; (vi) constitution in the work organization; (vii) work and total life span; and (viii) social relevance of work life. The descriptions for each category proposed by Walton (1973, 1975) can be observed as follows:

1. *Adequate and fair compensation*: Payments and issues such as work, obligation and preparation. Parameters such as income share and outcomes, supply-demand relationship, and average population wage indicate that payment fairness exists. It must also satisfy the needs of workers, but must also have no major pay differential from the same role in other enterprises.
2. *Safe and healthy working conditions*: This dimension involves overtime pay, circumstances that minimize the risk of injuries and health concerns for physical conditions and working hours. In order to change working conditions, the factors that can affect the worker, such as visual interference, noise and odours, must be reduced.
3. *Opportunity to use and develop human capacities*: It is an integral component of relevant factors for capacity growth, such as: the provision of autonomy for work, the use of worker skills, process experience, work efficiency and prior planning.
4. *Opportunity to growth and security*: This is related to professional growth and health and career security opportunities. The issues involved are: ability and growth of expertise, incentives for the creation and use of new information and skills.
5. *Social integration in the work organization*: The facets of personal self-esteem and relationships include sense of community, friendship, social inclusion, social mobility, discrimination and the exchange of information.
6. *Constitution in the work organization*: Constitutionalism exists to protect staff from violent acts. This dimension involves the following factors: anonymity, free expression, justice and equality.
7. *Work and total life span*: If the job offers the workers the most versatile experience, this will be expressed positively, just as if it is the other way around, it will suffer negatively.
8. *Social relevance of work life*: The worker continues to increase his self-esteem as the organization seeks changes on issues like social responsibility (adapted from Fernandes, 1996).

Methodological Approach

In the present study, I have used the 'emic' perspective to understand the point of view of the artisans. The field data was collected by using the ethnographic method and analysis was done based on qualitative approach along with narrative analysis. It involved the use of interview guide which was semi-structured in format. Patton (1990) has observed that this method of producing qualitative data amplifies their (data) depth as well as the scope.

The participants of this study were bell- brass metal artisans or *kahars*. These artisans are comprised of master artisans, semi-skilled artisans and other workers. In the two clusters, i.e. *Sarthebari* and *Sarukhetri,* the artisans were selected through random sampling techniques. The participants were all most male artisans between the age group of 16-80 years as the industry is mostly dominated by the men.

The fieldwork was conducted over a four-month time frame; documenting the local metal cluster development, the problems of *kahars* regarding their health status, the low infrastructure of the units, and the lack of hygiene inside the *ghosal* (*local terms specifically used for the bell-brass metal working units*). The in-depth interviews with the *kahars* provided their narratives regarding their work conditions and occupational health risks. An interview guide was used for three reasons: firstly to make sure that all applicable themes were raised; secondly to ensure that the scope and direction of questioning followed the objectives of the study, and thirdly to explore when further information was necessary (Kvale, 1996). The interviews with the *kahars* allowed me sufficient time with each informant and I could ask them follow up my inquisitions about their responses which could not have been possible through the questionnaire method. Thus, I carried on with the in-depth interview with the *kahars* which was balanced with participant observation as I studied the *kahars* at work.

The Metal Industry and its Occupational Hazards among the Kahars of Assam

Handicraft division is a part of the small scale manufacturing industry. A huge section of the Indian population is reliant on this area. Health issues related to handicraft production arise due to uncomfortable body postures (for example neck, shoulders, elbows, wrists/hands, upper back, bring down back, thigh, knees, and lower legs). It is reasoned that the high rate of absenteeism has an effect on the quality and amount of production, the effectiveness of artisans and association, organizational order which makes it all the more crucial for the organization to satisfy the new market requirements.

Metal Craft clusters are prone to inappropriate ventilation, noise pollution, heat, poor lighting which further raises the non-attendance of artisans because of the polluted air from the work environment. Loud noise is produced for extended period of times; workers are also exposed to heaters, poor lighting condition, and consistent weight lifting which are detrimental to their overall health.

In the process of making bell-brass metal articles the production units are found to be still following their traditional management system. These units are locally known as *ghosal*. The procedure of manufacturing any products at *ghosal* is called as '*kah kobowa*' where *kah* means bell metal and '*kobowa*' means hammering the metal or the process of making any articles like, *kahi*, *tal*, *bota*, etc. These working units are household enterprises and usually comprise of five to six people. Sometimes, depending upon the product, like *bati*, *lotas,* the units have three to four people working together. Every *ghosal* (working unit) manufactures a specific type of metal item (which could be a plate, *kahi*, *lota*, *tal* etc.) and specializes in its production. Based on the skill and experience, the artisans are classified into hierarchies. The *oja kahar* (the main or oldest skilled *kahar*) is at the top of the hierarchy. Generally, it is the *oja kahar* who sets up a unit at his own place and arranges all instruments which are used in manufacturing the items. Other *kahars* are known as *gurelia*, *maithnar*, *kaitner*, *kandal* and *garakhiya* (learner). They are the semi-skilled and unskilled artisans who assist the *oja kahar*. They are selected by the *oja kahar* on the basis of their working capability. Thus, in every *ghosal,* the *kahars* can be categorized as the skilled, semi-skilled and unskilled based on their working ability.

These *kahars* receive no formal training. Most of the times, they choose the occupation out of their own interest. They learn the technique right from the childhood, having grown up and taught by other family members engaged in the manufacturing. The process of manufacturing requires great physical labour and technical skill. The tradition is carried forward by the male *kahars* who are collectively known as the *kahar-bahigas* of the family. Women are not entrusted to carry forward the tradition but along with the kids, they do assist in the lighter work.

The artisans in the *ghosal* work under harsh conditions. These harsh conditions vary from weather related challenges such as hot sun, thunder storms, earthquake and floods. Assam is a remarkably calamity prone area and the artisans often bear the brunt of it. The working units are mostly out in open, prepared with the help of bamboo poles and a thatched roof. Inside the unit, the space is limited and artisans work very closely. They are susceptible to contaminants released during the work process, such as exhaust from metal-working. And since these units are home-based, the rest of the family members and general populace is also vulnerable to the effects. These artisans and their families are economically deprived and not in the financial situation to meet medical expenses in the case of injuries and other health effects. For most of the artisans, fulfilling basic requirements such as heat regulation is out of means. They continue to work in extremely hot environment which brings down not only their health but also their work productivity. Heat regulation alone can prevent several medical visits for a lot of *kahars*.

Srinivas and Pallen (2004:2) take note that even though workers do move towards becoming acclimatized (to extreme heat), the vast majority of these workers, because of the combined impact of lack of healthy sustenance and presentation, experience the ill effects of cerebral pain, issues related to overheating, and dizziness. Their report goes ahead to take note of the toxic gases which are spread in environment because of their exchanges, regularly impact lives of both the mechanics and metalworkers (Srinivas and Pallen, 2004:9). In the *ghosals* of Barpeta, the artisans are accustomed to working in harsh conditions but it negatively impacts their health and work. Price (2004) has shown in his study that exposure to extreme heat may cause heat stroke in small scale cluster artisans and heat exhaustion which may also expand the risk of acute cardiovascular diseases. Contact to heat throughout work has also been reported to cause reduced reproductive ability in men and rise in risks of non-melanoma skin cancer (Fartasch, Diepgen, Schmitt and Drexler, 2012). Such health risks are applicable in the case of the *kahars* working in the *ghosals*.

Health and the Socio-economic Challenges of the Kahars

According to Walton's quality of life model, safe and healthy workplace includes the use of proper working methods, the use of protective clothing and appliances, medical care, first aid and avoidance of hazardous materials. Workplace safety and health is ensured by establishing and implementing standards; training and education are provided; partnership is established and the safety and health of the workplace is continuously improved. Defense against maladministration and illness in and outside work promotes good health and the working environment. However, in the metal clusters of Barpeta, an absolute absence of these factors is observed. The occupational hazards and resulting health complications are not taken seriously neither by the artisans nor the government authorities.

The artisans working in the metal clusters work tirelessly during the peak demand season which is from February to July and from September to mid-January. In the earlier times, the artisans used to work from 5 a.m. in the morning till the midnight. However, recently, the artisans have brought flexibility to their work schedules and they work for about eleven to twelve hours a day, from six in the morning till five in the evening. Though shorter than earlier schedule, the hours are still long and impose many health complications upon the artisans.

The *ghosals* are poorly constructed and artisans spend most of their working hours inside it. The *oja kahars* normally sit near the furnaces inside the *ghosal* and these structures do not have appropriate ventilation. The lack of appropriate ventilation in the workshop makes the artisans susceptible to fibres and dust which is produced during the cleaning process of the metal articles. This often builds the risk of respiratory illness in the artisans. During the process of manufacturing, the *kahars* have to work with fire, engage in cutting, cleaning of items and most of this is carried out in the closed space which has no ventilation. The contamination risk is accelerated by the presence of microbes and parasites as these working units are mostly unhygienic in nature.

Another significant observation shows that, apart from such exposures, the *kahars* are subjected to extreme noise. This noise exceeds beyond the suggested maximum noise levels of 85 dB (A) for an eight–hour working day (ILO/WHO, 2013). This noise was present in all the production units where metal clanged all day. This slowly led to severe hearing impairments at an early age of fifty among the *kahars*. It was observed that being subjected to constant noise all day raised the anxiety levels in the majority of the *kahars* I interviewed. They expressed that it was a major trouble for them but there was nothing they could do about it as noise making was a major of their occupation.

According to a 52 year old respondent:

> "*The noise level within units is too high for us and at working times it is even difficult to hear our colleagues when they call us. Maximum of our colleagues have started developing hearing problems as a result. However, there is nothing we can do about it as we do not have earplugs.*"

Studies have indicated that negative health impacts have risen in the cottage industries. These impacts are often chronic/long term impacts rooted in repetitive exposure. Chronic diseases are complicated to diagnose and generally, the symptoms are barely visible until severe internal damage has occurred. In the case of contact to small amounts of spray-solvents throughout a lifetime by artisans may produce skin damage (dermatitis), chronic liver, kidney failure, brain damage etc. Earlier, *kahars* used to work for an indefinite amount of time from early morning till evening and because of the continuous work near the fireplace, they faced many problems particularly with vision. This was exacerbated by the fact that they do not wear any protective gears for their eyes. Problems such as allergic conjunctivitis, corneal abrasion problems, cataract etc. were often found in the artisans.

During the fieldwork, I further observed that these small units were poorly equipped. Artisans did not have all the required tools and equipment that are used in making articles. It caused more injuries and health risks to them. Additionally, the artisans did not have proper seating space and ergonomic instruments which resulted into poor body postures while working. Physical strain due to poor body postures was a common element in the working units. The artisans often worked while sitting on the mud floor or concrete floors. Sometimes, they used short wooden stools while working for longer durations which boosted their lower-back problems and injuries.

A 48-year-old respondent, whose views were shared by others observed:

> "*We have to make our seats out of solid mud floor, stones, and wooden stool and so on. This is the only way we can sit while working; some of us have experienced pain in our lower back. Now I feel difficulty in bending down while working*".

One remarkable character of the *kahars'* occupation was the lack of personal protective equipment (PPE). It was found that in many cases, the *kahars* lacked gloves, eye goggles, safety boots, and protective clothes. For example, not a single *kahar* was seen using any goggles to protect their eyes from gas flames. In fact, it was observed that in many cases, the proper PPE was not used. One of the informant explained that they are not aware of the any dangers on working without protection for face or eyes besides from generation wise they never used any personal protective gear. Nor anyone suggests them to wear goggles or other means of eye protection. For example, a 35-year-old respondent who has been working on units without eye goggles, protective gear and hand gloves said that he realizes it was hazardous however felt it was normal to work without the PPEs. In his words,

> "*We know that working before the fire with naked eyes can cause injuries, but you see, we have been like this since long and everything is fine. Although we do sustain some injuries and accidents, it is part of our daily work and it is very common to bear burns from fire and cuts from the metals as we work.*"

It has been observed that the constructions of *ghosals* were not planned properly moreover maximum numbers of *ghosal* does not have enough ventilation. They lack sanitary facilities, potable water, and sufficient dumping facility. Waste disposal has become a problem as many units in the area dispose of the hazardous waste without properly treating them which negatively impacts the unit's environment. The *kahars* are also at the risk of being exposed to the extreme climatic conditions and weather risks like frequent occurrences of flood or thunderstorm or heavy rain from the month of April to September. Cleanliness and hygiene issues are present in the clusters. Used water packets made of plastic, unused pieces of spare parts and other waste materials choke the open drains which run through the area. During rainy season, these choked drains become the breeding ground for mosquitoes besides the unpleasant smell coming from them.

A few informants explained that their injuries or sickness is not covered by social security and medical insurance schemes. Due to this reason, when old age or sickness sets in, many of these enterprises are shut down. It is so because most of these enterprises are household-based and mainly function outside the main institutional structure, they are rarely supervised. The artisan do not have enough earnings for getting their *ghosal* registered with the government offices. They did not have sufficient money or knowledge to follow the safety guidelines prescribed by the government for the occupational health safety in small-scale industry. There was a lack of essential medical aid kit and personnel with the knowledge of simple first-aid skills. This was compounded with the lack of medical services in the vicinity of the working units which many a times, cost the life of the artisans in the case of major accidents. The importance of medical-aid equipment and provisions for the availability of personnel with basic skills in medical aid at the workplace has been stressed by several other studies as well (Erickson, 1996; Alli, 2008).

During the Eleventh Five Year Plan, the Government of India announced few conventional plans in the central sector for holistic growth and development of handicrafts sector in the country. Two of them are:

- Rajiv Gandhi Shilpi Swasthya Bima Yojana—the first-ever health insurance initiative for the artisans in the country, covering the artisan, spouse, and two children.

- Bima Yojana for Handicrafts Artisans.

However, these schemes failed to work successfully at the ground level. The *Kahars* and other artisans are not aware of these schemes and have never received any help through these schemes. Most of the *kahars* have not even heard the name of these schemes. The *Sarthebari* town has only one government C.H.C. hospital and *Haldhibari* village has one government health sub-centre. C.H.C. only provides the nominal facility of health care without having major operation facilities for treatment. In the case of any serious medical condition, the patient's family members have to travel from *Sarthebari* to Nalbari District Civil Hospital or Guwahati Medical College for proper treatment. For this, they have to hire private cars or call 108 for emergency ambulance services. The Nalbari District town and Guwahati city is about 25 km and 60 km away from the *Sarukhatri* region respectively. In case, the villagers choose to go to Nalbari or Guwahati, the damaged and unrepaired roads cause major hindrance. In the case of any emergency, people often lose their lives on the way to the hospital. *Kahars* and other villagers normally prefer homoeopathy treatment or some herbal remedies which are available in every household for normal fever. For minor sickness, a few respondent informed, that they believe in *jhar phunk* (curative magic) which they sometimes avail for their kids. This is because they believe that children mostly get sick due to evil's eye. To cure the evil's eye (*kaali nazar*), *pani-jhara* or amulet oil and rice is used as an antidote. For generations, problems like twisted ankle pain, backbone pain etc. are relied on *jhar phunk* for cure.

The findings from the field data points towards the fact that the enclosed structures like those used by the auxiliary part units are not planned to be used as units and so do not have enough ventilation. The *kahars* are also at risk of being exposed to the extreme climate conditions and the hazardous substance generated during the work. They lack sanitary facilities, potable water, and sufficient refuse dumping facility. Waste disposal has turned into a problem as many units in the area dispose their waste without treating them and it further worsens the environment of the units. At the same time, production units are not concerned with hygiene of the artisans and other workers. It has been observed that all units are barely covered from above. They are made up of tin shade roof with bamboo stakes and few of them have thatched roofs with wooden posts and earthen open space floor for working. They do not maintain cleanliness, and due to this reason many artisans within the unit suffer from viral fever, dengue, and yellow fever. The medical facilities available in Sarthebari area are not well organized with only one C.H.C. and a very few chemist shops.

Conclusion and Recommendations

In Assam, it has been observed that the metal craft clusters and the working units are characterised with long working hours, poor housekeeping, lack of public utility areas, ventilation and lighting, poor work postures and work methods, exposure to chemicals and deficiency of personal protective equipment (PPE). The health risks are even more in the metal industry. During the peak seasons, the artisans carry on with their work for longer durations without any care for personal safety. Most of the artisans working in these clusters are young people because with increasing age, artisans begin to lose the strength required to work in these harsh conditions. This is enhanced by the fact that artisans often develop health complications while working in the industry and slowly become incapable of continuing with the work.

The industry is dominated by the men and most of them are not educated beyond the basic levels (Primary and H.S.L.C.). They do not have enough knowledge and awareness regarding the long-term effects of the occupational hazards. Their physical environment and the nature of work continue to affect them over the course of their lifetime. The entailed risks such as uncomfortable sitting posture, lifting of heavy objects and lack of safety gears negatively impact their body and work. It was observed during the study that maximum number of *Kahars* and their family members who belong to economically deprived background suffer from more workplace-related illness than any other workers.

Cleanliness facilities (toilets, water, seepage, transfer of waste) are not accessible over the area, demonstrating the potential for its development in this community at an aggregate level. The level of noise, dust, residue and heat inside the working unit is often spilled outside the *ghosal* and impacts the rest of the members of the household. It also affects the artisans who might be working outside the *ghosal* who are not engaged with heating and hammering segment. Work environments are dreary and inadequately ventilated. The artisans experience ill effects of skin diseases, eye strains and other eye issues pertaining to excessive stress and gloom, and respiratory problems. Their general weakness and sick health increases the likelihood of long-term health complications. A significant number of *kahars* were seen to engage in self-treatment of their sickness by utilizing over the counter drugs, and substance abuse like tobacco chewing. *Kahars* spend a high percentage of (their) expenditure on food and do not leave enough wages for other expenditures like education; medical treatment and housing. But, they can be seen spending a good amount of money on smoking, tobacco, betel nut and betel leaf. Such products are consumed as a result of occupation-related stress. While a large number of *kahars* have suffered visual impairment because of their work, still buying eye-safety equipment is considered a costly affair.

To overcome the health risks and challenges ridding the lives of the metal artisans of Assam, it is important to understand their working conditions and the way they carry out their work. Along with this, it is important to understand the *kahar*'s perception about their occupation and awareness about the health risks of their occupation. According to Okuga et al. (2012) in Kenya, awareness of occupational accidents and hazards is the first step in promoting workplace safety. It is relevant in the case of the metal artisans of Assam as well. It is seen that the majority of the artisans are not alert that there are risks and hazards connected with their work which can result in long-term chronic health complications. The *kahars* only recognize the short-term injuries and sickness resulting from their work. The work processes undertaken by these artisans involves physical hazards such as cuts, burns, hearing impairment resulting from loud noises and eye injuries due to excessive UV-radiation and respiratory dysfunctions due to inhaling of nauseous metal fumes and spray paints. There is also a risk of psychosocial hazards which may occur due to pressures at workplace and physical weakness about which the artisans are unaware.

Awareness programmes and local group discussions are necessary for improving the health condition among *kahars*. There must be various provisions of safety equipments like face masks, medical aid facility, hand gloves, and suitable uniform for the safety of *kahars*. There must be suitable lighting at the place of the units so that eye injury can be avoided. These artisans should be provided with earplugs to protect them from loud noise produced during the manufacturing. Medical health check-ups should be carried out by the government for the artisans from time to time. If significant occupational health risk issues are experienced, suitable actions should be taken by the government authorities.

A few researchers have done their research in managing the informal sector in the area of health and safety improvement and reassurance. Moreover, appropriate recommendations along with the suitable help, informal sector workers can move from a circumstance of negligible survival to a more stranded economic position upgrading their assurance to monetary development and social reconciliation, as well as additionally taking an interest in the change of their working and living conditions. Keeping in mind the main goal is to increase their productivity also it is important to create actions which effectively stick together with administrations to empower small scale ventures to increment both their livelihoods and administrations to help workers in securing their well-being and improving their working conditions. Again as Walton has mentioned, the unsafe and hazardous working condition generally cause both the owners and staff issues unhealthy. The workers may have little benefits in the short term, but it does affect productivity in the medium and longer term. Necessary investment must also be made in order to ensure safe and secure working conditions.

Through the examination of the occupational health hazards in the metal craft cluster of Assam, the chapter recommends that policy modifications are required to develop minimum safety standards and the dissemination of information. It is advised to set up a comprehensive Occupation Safety and Health Insurance Scheme for *kahars* in this cluster to counter the effect of occupation related mishaps and injuries. This study suggests the requirement of training in all dimensions for the artisans, about Occupational Health and Safety issues at the workplace. This will help in checking hazards and risks associated with the nature of their work. Health and Safety plans concerning training and education regarding the hazards, are suitable as safety measures, and can create safer alternatives. This will require training of local health care officials in the diagnosis and treatment of occupational hazards in the metal craft cluster of Assam.

REFERENCES

Adamson, M. (2004). "A Healthy and Safe Workplace in Zambia." *African Newsletter on Occupational Health and Safety, 14* (2), 42-45.

Alli, B.O. (2008). *Fundamental Principles of Occupational Health and Safety.* (2nd Ed). Geneva, Switzerland: International Labour Office.

Amedofu, G.K. (2002). "Hearing Impairment among Workers in Gold Mining in Ghana." *African Newsletter on Occupational Health and Safety. 12*(3), 65-68.

Clarke, E. (2005). "Do Occupational Health Services really exist in Ghana? A special focus on the Agricultural and Informal Sectors." Ghana Health Services, Accra, Ghana.

Erickson, P.A. (1996). *Practical Guide to Occupational Health and Safety,* California, Academic Press.

Fartasch, M., Diepgen, T.L., Schmitt, J., and Drexler, H. (2012). "The Relationship between Occupational Sun Exposure and Non-melanoma Skin Cancer: Clinical Basics, Epidemiology, Occupational Disease Evaluation, and Prevention." *DtschArztebl International, 109*, 715-720.

Fernandes, E.C. (1996). "Qualidade de vida no trabalho: comomedir para melhorar." *Salvador: Casa da Qualidade.*

Forastieri, Valentina. (2002). Occupational Health Services at the workplace, Multidisciplinary Team for Central America Safe Work Program on Safety, Health and the Environment International Labour Organization (ILO)

J. Jovanovic, M. Aranđelović & M. Jovanović (2004). "Multidisciplinary Aspects of Occupational Accidents and Injury." *Work and Living Environmental Protection, 2*(4), 325-333

Kvale, S. (1996). *Interviews: An Introduction to Qualitative Research Interviewing.* Thousand Oaks, CA: Sage.

Loewenson, R. (1995). "Occupational health in small-scale industries in Africa." *African Newsletter on Occupational Health and Safety, 2*, 35-37

McCormick, D. (1997). Enterprises Clusters in Africa: On the way to industrialization. Discussion Chapter 366.

Morgan, L. M. (1984). "Dependency theory in the political economy of health: An anthropological critique." *Medical Anthropology Quarterly, 1*(2):131-154.

Okuga, M., Mayega R.W., & Bazeyo, W. (2012). "Small-Scale Industrial Welders in Jinja Municipality, Uganda: Awareness of Occupational Hazards and use of Safety Measures." *African Newsletter on Occupational Health and Safety, 22*(2), 35-36.

Patton, M. Q. (1990). *Qualitative Evaluation and Research Methods.* Newbury Park, CA: Sage.

Price, A.E. (2004). "Heart Disease and Work." *Annual Occupational Hygiene, 90*, 1077-1084.

Srinivas, H. & Pallen D. (2004). (Eds). *Promoting Workplace Safety: Environmental Health and Workplace Practices for Micro-Enterprises.* The Environmental Colours of Micro-finance, Global Development Research Center.

Tadesse & Admassu. (2006). Occupational Health and Safety: Ethiopia Public Health Training Initiative. University of Gondar, 1-6.

Takala, Jukka. (2019). "Burden of Injury due to Occupational Exposures", In U. Bültmann, J. Siegrist (eds.*), Handbook of Disability, Work and Health.* Cham, Switzerland: Springer.

Virchow, R. (1879). *Gesammelte Ahandlungen aus dem Gebeit der Oeffentlichen Medizin under Seuchenlehre.* Vol. 1. Berlin: Hirschwald.

Walton, R. (1973). "Quality of work life activities: A research agenda." *Professional Psychology, 11*(3), 484-493.

Walton, R.E. (1999). "Quality of work life: what is it?" *Sloan Management Review, 15*(1), 11-21.

WHO. (1976): Meeting on Organization of Health Care in Small Industries, July 22-27, 1975, *World Health Organization*, Geneva, Document: OCW 76.2.

PART V
MEDICAL PLURALISM AND POLICY ISSUES

19

From Politics of Tradition to Economies of Care: Medical Pluralism in Indian Context

Avanee Khatri and *A.K. Sinha*

Medical pluralism, is a long contested topic in the discipline of medical anthropology in which multiple “differentially designed and conceived medical systems” co-exist in a single culture or state (Janzen, 1978), is increasingly the norm worldwide (Frankel and Lewis, 1989). Global migrations have resulted in the “export” of many traditional medicine (TM) systems and practices into a diverse Diaspora outside of their nations of origin. Immigrant influxes between global South states and the global North (Cant and Sharma, 1999; Jennings, 2005) have brought “both a demand for, and, crucially, practitioners of a range of alternatives to biomedicine” (Green, Bradby, Chan, and Lee, 2006).

For a long time biomedical model of health was the dominant perspective on health: medical anthropologists and sociologists who worked in the field of health used Durkheimian (or Parsonian) functional perspective. Attempts have been made by Marxists and others to examine class inequalities in health both outside and in India, abandoning the biomedical model of health (Yadavendu, 2001). The challenge to the functional perspective has come from those medical anthropologists and others who stress that the concept of health as socially constructed. In the field of medicine, basic ethical conflicts are reflected in the struggle for control over knowledge, its use or misuse by professionals/healers, and the role of the state in ensuring equity in health (Qader, 2003). Thus, the subject of health is contextualized and made subjective. This leads to overlapping and multiple perspectives (Walt, 2000). But, often there has been the tendency of limiting pluralistic medical configuration of medical systems to the technologically less-developed world (Good, 1987). However, with all the technological brilliance and advances of biomedicine, studies have shown that the health seeking behaviour of people in Western societies suggests an increasing mutual understanding and cooperation among a variety of contemporary alternative therapy systems.

Western societies are increasingly becoming societies of medical pluralism. The lack of adequate cooperation between modern biomedicine and traditional medicine is partly as a result of what Good (1987) termed "two widespread fallacies" about health beliefs and behaviour about other societies outside the Western world. The first fallacy is what Polgar (1962 cited by Good, 1987) referred to as the "empty vessel fallacy"; this refers to the situation whereby a society (territory) and its people are assumed to lack systematic beliefs and a therapy system until the arrival of biomedicine from Western societies. The second fallacy is "the fallacy of separate capsule" noted by Scrimshaw (1979 cited by Good, 1987). On the contrary, the second fallacy recognizes the pre-existence of indigenous medical resources and theories of disease, but maintains that these indigenous medical systems are inferior and not a viable option or alternative to Western medical practices. These fallacies give the tendency to health professionals and governments to view traditional medicine as archaic and not relevant to modern societies; yet the evidence remains that traditional medicine remains a major resource used by people in the developing world to cope with their health problems.

The need for multiple health options is necessary considering the Indian health landscape, the land of nearly 1.2 billion people and the second most populous country in the world. As the country is divided into 29 States and 7 Union Territories, the State Government has the onus to take care of the health of people in the State. Since India is a developing country where a large section of population is below poverty line, health and hygiene are not up to the mark. The plight of the least advantaged is increased because of the poor public health systems. The government hospitals and health care centres do not completely address to the needs of the poor (Kavitha, 2012).

On the other hand, the private health care institutions charge exorbitant amount of money, which automatically renders them beyond the reach of many. However, the private health care sector in India is flourishing at the cost of the public.

According to some critics, the national policy of the country lacks specific measures to achieve the stated goals. For instance, there is no proper integration of the health care services with the wider socio-economic and social development. There is lack of nutritional support and sanitation and there is poor participation of the people and government officials at the local level. The Central Government adopts the strategy of improving the health systems through five-year plans. It co-operates with the State Governments for that purpose and for sponsoring major health programmes.

The Central and State Governments share the expenditure they meet in providing health care to the people. In mid-1990s, the Government spent 6 per cent of the GDP on health, which is one of the highest levels of expenditure in the developing nations. The Central and State Governments set the goals and strategies in consultation with the Central Council of Health and Family Welfare. The Ministry of Health and Family Welfare monitors the workings of the Central Government and provides technical and administrative services along with medical education.

According to a World Bank study, the per capita spending on health in India is around Rs. 320 per year with a significant input of 75 per cent from private households. The State Governments contribute 15.2 per cent, the Central Government 5.2 per cent, third party employers 3.3 per cent and the municipal government and foreign donors provide about 1.3 per cent to the total spending, of which 58.7 per cent goes to primary health care (curative, preventive and promotional) and 38.8 per cent is spent on the secondary and tertiary ones (Kavitha, 2012) (www.health careindia.net).

Medical Pluralism in India

Health care in India presents a complex scenario that is shaped significantly by colonial, post-colonial history and politics, and is enhanced by a vibrating and thriving medical pluralism. The global trends in health seeking behaviour of citizens provide enough evidence of pluralistic choices being exercised for fulfilling different health needs. The era of integrative medicine and health care appears to have commenced. Politicians, policy-makers, medical institutions and the education sector need to recognize this reality of "Integrative health care in the 21st century". India has adopted the approach of pluralistic system of medicine with Western medical system commonly known as allopathy, and AYUSH systems being the recognized systems of medicine. The AYUSH system incorporates Ayurveda, Unani, Siddha, Sowa Rigpa, Homoeopathy along with Yoga and Naturopathy as the drugless therapies. A few decades from now, single knowledge system based medical hospitals, clinics and even medical colleges, will become relics and even AYUSH systems will not be any exception. The best way ahead seems to be for AYUSH systems and modern medicine to collaborate on sound footing of scientific evidence base, in the best interest of public health. Strengthening AYUSH sector in education, research, services, industry and public health is critical to prepare the country for its journey towards integrative health care (Ministry of AYUSH, 2015).

In addition to AYUSH (Ayurveda, Yoga & Naturopathy, Unani, Siddha & Homoeopathy) which represents the tradition of codified, textual health knowledge systems other than the allopathic system, Local Health Traditions (LHT) represent the practices and knowledge of the common people and folk practitioners who follow an oral tradition of learning and passing on of the knowledge. To some extent, the recent concern about inclusion of AYUSH is the product of the realization of inadequacy, unaffordability, inaccessibility and contradictions of 'scientific medicine'. But this has also a potential for uncritical and disinterested acceptance of AYUSH. There is also a need for empirical examination of beliefs held by people in areas not much touched by modernity. The new ideas require to be situated in the current debate on processes and power in health policy in the developing countries.

Is AYUSH the Answer for Health Disparities in India?

The development of biopsychosocial model of health has renewed interest in alternative or complementary care approaches. If the goal is to treat the "whole person" the evidence-based scientific medicine may be combined with the alternative approaches including acupressure, acupuncture, massage, chiropractice, herbal therapies, homoeopathy, yoga, meditation etc. (Grochowski, 2014). In the West both pull factors and push factors have attracted patients towards alternative systems of medicine. The pull factors include stress on the idea that complementary treatments are "more natural, effective, relaxing, sensible and that one could take an active part in it." The push factors include "specific failure of orthodox medicine to bring them relief", "adverse side-effects of orthodox medicine"; and "poor communication between patients and orthodox medicine practitioners". Easy availability and their cost-effectiveness also explain the movement of people from orthodox to alternative therapies (Vincent and Furnham, 2001, Sharma, 2013). Studying the Kung approach to healing in Africa, Katz (2001) avers that most diseases are self-limiting and they heal on their own. In the cultures of developing world people may, however, believe that the traditional healing practices such as dance cure the disease. At the level of patients similar factors may be at work in India. But that does not explain state's interest in AYUSH. There are two reasons for promotion of AYUSH in India. One reason is the failure of the modern medicine to ensure universal health, and the other is the promise of health by integrating well-established traditional practices and the indigenous medical knowledge system. The collective outcome of state, medicine, and business has failed to provide required services to all classes, regions, ethnic groups, men and women. The cost of modern medicine for most people is exorbitant. There are new afflictions impossible to cure life style diseases. And the relationship between doctor and patients is very unequal and disempowering to people. In remote areas people are going for medical pluralism due to inadequate facilities of modern medicine. This is the context when people are looking for alternatives. Obviously, the alternatives will not come from the vacuum or from a completely alien world as the alternatives will have to be supported by pre-existing social representations (Sharma, 2013).

AYUSH system provides a ray of hope. Governments get attracted to AYUSH for a number of reasons: supplementing manpower at the lower levels for services and campaigns, low cost, consistency with the value system of people, and effects of pressure groups (vested interests). Using the distinction made between *sociology of* medicine and *sociology in* medicine by Robert Strauss (Hafferty and Castellani, 2007), it may be said that poor development of *sociology of* medicine in India, which could offer a sociological critique of medical practices making them sociologically more reflective could be another reason. *Sociology in* medicine (though practiced by those working in sociology departments) has remained in supportive role and has not been able to look for reflexive interventions (Sharma, 2013).

Government is using AYUSH to meet the unmet needs in different fields of medical services. To quote from the Twelfth Five Year Plan (Planning Commission, 2013, p. 30):

> AYUSH doctors, wherever feasible, would be given SBA, RCH and IMNCI training and their services will be used in meeting unmet needs. This will increase the availability of trained human resource for better outreach of child and maternal health services.

Medical Pluralism and the Hierarchy of Health Systems

As the process of globalization continues to spread the products and practices of capitalism, science, and the "developed" world to all corners of the globe, many expected an increasingly homogenous world as a result. This, of course, is not exactly what has happened (Tsing, 2002). Instead, we find the growth of pluralism and creolization, wherein people incorporate global products and practices into their everyday lives in unique and novel ways such that the global becomes blended with the traditional and the local. In Indian context, and elsewhere around the world with colonial histories, the process or creolization has resulted in the blending of languages, religion, food, and other traditions. Despite contention, resistance, and friction, this ongoing process continues with the increase in global flows of ideas, goods, and people (Wilk, 2006, Tsing, 2005, Reeser, 2014).

This blending or pluralism can be seen in any number of cultural settings and activities, but has been especially prevalent (and increasingly documented) in the arena of health and health care. Crandon-Malamud offers a very simple definition of medical pluralism: "The concept of medical pluralism refers to an environment in which there is more than one medical tradition" (Crandon, 1986). This definition, however, obscures the complexity of the concept, as well as the fact that a region, culture, or community scarcely exists, except perhaps the most isolated locations, that does not have some form of medical pluralism at play in their health system. With the implementation of the State system, and the increasing influence of globalization, societies today experience an array of medical systems that coexist in time and space, although not always complementary or equally, thus making medical pluralism the norm around the globe (Baer, 2003).

Medical pluralism exists, most simply, because the means through which various cultures have addressed health and illness have varied through time and place around the globe, and innumerable distinct medical systems have arisen in various cultural contexts. Some well-known examples of alternative medical systems include Traditional Chinese Medicine, developed and utilized through much of East Asia, Ayurveda, an ancient medical system of the Indian subcontinent, not to mention the numerous traditional medicines and other ethnomedicines that exist around the globe. Ethnomedicine have been defined as medical or healing systems of any particular group that is different than Western biomedicine (Ericson, 2008). However, biomedicine can also be seen as an ethnomedicine, having developed out of the specific Western scientific worldview, and out of a uniquely Western culture (Leatherman, 1998, Erickson, 2008).

The importance of alternative medicines has long been recognized by anthropology; however, they have not always held equal status as Western scientific biomedicine. Ngokwey (1988) characterizes much of anthropological research on non-Western medical systems as rooted in evolutionism that posits Western science and biomedicine at the top. Thus, non-Western medical systems are categorized as based on religion or the supernatural and somehow less rational. Early anthropological investigations into indigenous and traditional medical systems were typically guided by an assumption that such systems were largely alike and homogenous in practice, belief, and behaviour (Cosminsky, 1983). They were also held to be separate from biomedicine; thus, early examinations of medical pluralism typically sought to develop a typology of systems, so as to be able to classify a health system and place it in the popular hierarchy of medical systems, which has historically held biomedicine (or Western medicine) at the top (Reeser, 2014).

One example of such a hierarchical ordering is that of anthropologist Frederick Dunn (1976), who created three main categories for health systems: local, regional, and cosmopolitan. A local system is of the smallest scale, and is common in rural and indigenous communities, and contains "folk" or indigenous health systems. A regional system is present in larger geographical areas, and includes the like of Ayurvedic, Siddha system of south India, Traditional Chinese Medical systems etc. Finally, the cosmopolitan system is present on a global scale, and consists of the multiple aspects of biomedicine. If perceived as bounded systems, Dunn's categories are adequate for most health systems around the globe. However, as noted above, health systems vary greatly by context, and within any given context, multiple medical systems exert influence on each other in unique ways (Belliard and Ramirez-Johnson, 2005). Further, as will be seen, this type of categorization does not represent the way people blend and utilize multiple systems concurrently in their daily lives.

A similar typological system has been proposed to explain medical pluralism, and consists of the popular sector, the folk sector, and the professional sector (Kleinman, 1980, Chrisman and Kleinman, 1983). In this typology, the popular sector includes the self (for self-treatment), families, friends, and others in the social network of the sick person. The folk sector includes informal healers, including shamans, midwives, herbalists, bonesetters, and the like. The professional sector includes health systems that have been professionalized, including not only biomedicine, but also systems such as Ayurveda, Homoeopathy, Traditional Chinese Medicine and the like who have diversified and increased their patient base over the years. This typology remains popular across disciplines, and reflects a more patient-centred view of health systems. Such typologies, however, remain limited in their ability to explain not only how people negotiate health care options, but why, and what factors play a role in the decision-making process.

Scholars have also begun to more carefully consider power and inequality when analyzing health systems (Brodwin, 1996; Baer, 2003), which has brought to the fore analyses of how and why biomedicine has become a dominant system around the globe. Anthropologist Charles Leslie (1980) details how nations around the world have aimed to standardize their medical systems so they are all linked to national and international standards and practices through biomedicine. "Efforts to increase the scope and to improve the quality of health care have sought to eliminate or severely restrict 'irregular practices', so that ideally local medical systems will simply become extensions of a nationally and internationally standardized medical system" (1980). He notes that as of 1980, only China had incorporated a traditional medical system (Chinese Medicine) into the state sanctioned system. However, in China, as is the norm elsewhere, numerous traditional practices remained unsanctioned and outside the system, all the while maintaining high rates of utilization, epitomizing a medically plural context. Leslie's is but one example of how biomedicine remains on top of the medical hierarchy around the globe.

Thirty years later, this hierarchy has remained, and perhaps become more deeply entrenched, as Baer explains: "Medical pluralism in the modern world is characterized by a pattern in which biomedicine exerts dominance over alternative medical systems" (2003). However, this dominance has always remained contested, such that medical pluralism has become the norm in people's lives (Goldstein, 2004).

Hans Baer (2003) expands on the idea that medical pluralism reflects the hierarchy present in the society being examined. "Patterns of hierarchy may be based upon class, caste, racial, ethnic, religious, and gender distinctions. Medical pluralism flourishes in all class-divided societies and tends to mirror the wider sphere of class and social relationships." Thus, in a context with high rates of poverty, and where biomedicine rests atop the medical hierarchy, it can be surmised that those ranks of poor not only have limited access to the biomedical system, they rely more heavily on other alternative systems that fit into the popular and folk typologies (Frankenberg, 1981, Reeser, 2014). Thus, medical pluralism remains vital, in part; to fill the gaps in health care that biomedicine is unable to reach.

An examination of specific examples of medical pluralism can reveal the hegemonic position that biomedicine has achieved for itself, even in contexts where alternative systems also thrive. Broom and colleagues (2009) examine the experiences of cancer clinicians in post-colonial India, where despite a State-sanctioned medically plural system, biomedicine remains at the top. In India, "traditional medicine and systems of knowledge may on the one hand be celebrated as indigenous forms of knowledge to be cherished and actively promoted by the State, and yet, in many Indian contexts, biomedicine has achieved hegemonic status, framing illness and determining institutional credibility" (Broom *et al.*, 2009). They further explain the role of the State in shaping the medically plural nation: by choosing what traditions and even what aspects of those traditions are to be sanctioned, they in turn marginalize other traditional systems while helping to shape those aspects of medicine that in general should be protected or discouraged (*Ibid.*). Still, as Baer notes, biomedicine has never had complete dominance over other medical systems, explaining: "The State must periodically make concessions to subordinate social groups in the interests of maintaining social order and economic productivity" (Baer, 2003). The concessions of the State then, occasionally lend legitimacy, if not legal rights, to alternative health systems; however, biomedicine has continued to maintain its spot atop the medical hierarchy.

Deeply entrenched feelings of the superiority of biomedicine exist among practitioners as well as the State and other institutions. Broom and colleagues (2009) report that when asked about their experience with alternative medical systems, clinicians tended to tell horror stories or recall negative experiences. They concluded that the plural system in India was accepted as reflecting the variety of contemporary Indian identities; however, the traditional systems were not perceived to be working in harmony with biomedicine, and were thus somehow at fault or even ineffectual. Further, clinicians viewed patients that utilized alternative systems as uneducated and/or backwards, while, in fact, many such patients are either from more traditional rural villages or economically marginalized. "Medical pluralism, while reflecting important richness in cultural knowledge and practice, emerged as inextricably linked to forms of social inequality and suffering" (Broom *et al.*, 2009). While the plural health care system in India reflects the complexity of social life there, it also reveals the economic inequality and associated restraints that also exist. "This intermingling of identity, culture and medicine necessarily shapes hierarchies and dynamics between professional groups and systems of medicine" (Broom *et al.*, 2009). In this critical view, they conclude that the push for pluralistic medical systems in developing contexts ignores the larger social/structural problems that affect health, health care, and access to that care. In addition, by promoting a pluralistic system, the State is able to trump their inclusion and acceptance of tradition while at the same time, valorize their efforts to modernize through the biomedical system. Thus, by promoting pluralism, the official recognition of alternative medicines satisfies the need for access to care, but masks very real social and economic constraints to access that still exist (Reeser, 2014).

Discussion

Dimensions of health inequalities operating in India are mostly identified by the inequalities associated with access barriers to health care facilities. Health inequalities emerge for a number of reasons—one of the major ones being due to inadequate public health financing and public provisioning of health care. The need for public funding in health cannot be over-emphasised given that there are large positive externalities associated with such spending. The presence of such positive externalities means that if left to the market, there is a strong likelihood that the wider positive external effects would be ignored. Therefore, lack of adequate public provision of health care is likely to result in health care being socially underprovided as well as the poor being denied access to adequate health care. In other words, public health provisioning is necessary both from efficiency as well as equity point of view.

The inequities arising from inadequate provisioning of health care facilities in turn are aggravated by the existing disparities based on place of residence (rural-urban), caste, occupation, gender, religion, education entitlements and socio-economic status (Mitra, 2014). The politics of tradition by integration of traditional systems of medicine now termed as AYUSH is considered to be the answer for the growing health inequalities but can they actually cater to economies of care in political as well as medical concept is the biggest question that needs an answer.

Also, as pointed out in the present chapter it would not be wrong to say that while the process of professionalization of indigenous practitioners has been widely documented, it is often seen as a straightforward manifestation of competition with or mimicry of biomedical arrangements (Lambert, 2017). The role of the state and attention to forms of governance as constitutive of medical pluralism (the character of medical plurality) is particularly crucial, not simply as a means to understand the effects of political formations in shaping both the character of and access to elite and subaltern therapies, but also for conceptual reasons as discussed in this chapter. Similarly, recent move in India to valorise non-codified medical traditions through mainstreaming AYUSH practitioners into primary health care provides an apposite illustration with focus on "revitalization" of "local health traditions" (LHTs). On the one hand, the terminology of "revitalisation" demonstrates continuity with prevailing modernist assumptions that such traditions are always-already disappearing. On the other, the recognition of a role for non-codified therapeutic modalities that would once have been designated as "folk medicine" signals an important shift in Statist views from a position of neglect to a revivalist advocacy. While few details are provided in policy documents as to the nature and content of these "local health traditions" (LHTs), the only specified activities refer to the utilisation by local communities and primary health workers of medicinal plants and to the "validation" and testing of these natural resources, indicating that the "LHTs" envisaged as having potential for providing state-sanctioned care are those that entail the use of medicinal substances. Initiatives have been started by non-governmental organisations to promote local medicinal plant use and to "validate" and offer accreditation to particular kinds of indigenous practitioner. The substantialisation of medicine to "medicines" clearly reflects broader processes of commodisation (Bode, 2006) and an eagerness on the part of the Indian Government to profit from the country's bioresources. Social scientists have begun to study these processes of "pharmaceuticalisation" but their consequences with regard to the nature and configuration of therapeutic practices, the social distribution of therapy and patterns of access to treatment have been largely overlooked (Banerjee, 2010; Dabhai, 2012; Lambert, 2017; Venkat, 2012). Also, within the space of a decade, a new category—the now-capitalised Local Health Traditions ("LHTs")—has been established, with a restricted referent of herbal medicinal treatment that nonetheless reaches back historically to retrospectively reconstitute of existing vernacular forms an entirely new medical object. While it might seem inappropriate to deny approbation to initiatives that offer some scope for (re)valorising subaltern therapeutics through some measure of official recognition, anthropologists are uniquely positioned to provide critical reflection on the nature of these moves as simultaneously constituting intra-cultural narratives that shape medical pluralism (the character of medical plurality), to point up distinctions between, for example, local health traditions and "LHTs" and to highlight the displacements and exclusions that the creation of such new designations inevitably entail (Lambert, 2017). Moreover, the promise of AYUSH policy as the answer to the growing health inequalities in India and the stance of medical pluralism in India need to be viewed with a broader lens to unleash its full potential.

REFERENCES

Baer, Hans A. (2003). "Contributions to a Critical Analysis of Medical Pluralism: An Examination of the Work of Libbet Crandon-Malamud." In Joan D. Koss-Chioino, Thomas Leatherman, and Christine Greenway, (eds.) Medical Pluralism in the Andes. pp. 42-60. New York: Routledge.

Banerjee, M. (2010). "Gunis' 'mission' for 'rashtriya' legitimacy: When subaltern medical practices confront the state". Chapter presented at workshop *Situating Subalternity in South Asian Medicine*, Centre for the Study of Social Systems, Delhi, February.

Beliard, Joan Carlos, and Johnny Ramirez-Johnson. (2005). "Medical Pluralism in the Life of a Mexican Immigrant Woman." *Hispanic Journal of Behavioural Sciences, 27*(3): 267-285.

Bode, M. (2006). "Taking traditional knowledge to the market: The commodization of Indian medicine." *Anthropology and Medicine, 13*(3): 225-236.

Brodwin, Paul. (1996). *Medicine and Morality in Haiti: the Contest for Healing Power*. Cambridge: Cambridge University Press.

Broom, Alex, Assa Doron, and Philip Tovey. (2009). "The Inequalities of Medical Pluralism: Hierarchies of Health, the Politics of Tradition and the Economies of Care in Indian Oncology." *Social Science and Medicine, 69*: 698-706.

Cant, S., and U. Sharma. (1999). *A new medical pluralism? Alternative medicine, doctors, patients and the state.* New York, NY: Routledge.

Chrisman, Noel J., and Arthur Kleinman. (1983). "Popular Health Care, Social Networks, and Cultural Meanings: The Orientation of Medical Anthropology." In *Handbook of Health, Health Care, and Health Professions,* David Mechanic, (ed.) pp. 69-79. New York: Free Press.

Cosminsky, Sheila. (1983). "Medical Pluralism in Mesoamerica." In *Heritage of Conquest: Thirty Years Later,* Carl-Kendall, John Hawkins, and Laurel Bossen, (eds.) pp. 159-173. Albuquerque, NM: University of New Mexico Press.

Crandon, Libbet. (1986). "Medical Dialogue and the Political Economy of Medical Pluralism: A Case from Highland Bolivia." *American Ethnologist, 13*(3): 463-476.

Dabhai, B. (2012). "Certification of folk practitioners by panchayats". Chapter presented at workshop on *Integrating Traditional South Asian Medicine into Modern Health Care Systems*, Jawarharlal Nehru University, Delhi, October.

Dunn, Frederick. (1976). "Traditional Asian Medicine and Cosmopolitan Medicine in Adaptive Systems." In *Asian Medical Systems: A Comparative Study*. Charles Leslie, (ed.) pp. 133-158. Berkeley, Ca: University of California Press.

Erickson, Pamela I. (2008). *Ethnomedicine*. Long Grove, IL: Waveland Press, Inc.

Frankel, S., and G. Lewis, G. (1989). *A continuing trial of treatment: Medical pluralism in Papua New Guinea.* Dordrecht, The Netherlands: Kluwer Academic.

Frankenberg, Ronald. (1981). "Allopathic medicine, profession, and capitalist ideology in India." *Social Science and Medicine, 15*(2): 115-125.

Green, G., H. Bradby, A. Chan, and M. Lee. (2006). "We are not completely Westernised: Dual medical systems and pathways to health care among Chinese migrant women in England." *Social Science & Medicine, 62*: 1498-1509.

Good, C.M. *et al.* (1979). "The interface of dual systems of health care in the developing world: toward health initiatives in Africa." *Social Science and Medicine, 13*, 141-154.

Good, C.M. (1987). *Ethnomedical systems in Africa: patterns of traditional medicine in rural and urban Kenya*. New York: Guilford Press. 354.

Goldstein, Michael, S. (2004). "The Persistence and Resurgence of Medical Pluralism. *Journal of Health Politics, Policy and Law, 29*(4-5): 925-945.

Grochowski, Janet, R. (2014). *Families and Health*. Sage Publications: Los Angeles.

Hafferty, Frederic W. and Castellani Brian. (2007). "Medical Sociology." In Bryant, Clifton D. and Dennis L. Peck (eds.), *21st Century Sociology: A Reference Handbook*, Sage Publications, UK.

Janzen, J. (1978). *The quest for therapy in lower Zaire*. Berkeley, CA: University of California Press.

Jennings, M. (2005). "Chinese medicine and medical pluralism in Dar es Salaam: Globalization or glocalisation?" *International Relations, 19*: 457-473.

Katz, Richard (2001). "The Kung Approach to Healing", in Matcha, Duane A. (ed.), *Readings in Medical Sociology*, Allyn and Bacon, Boston, pp. 318-331.

Kavitha. R. (2012). "Health care industry in India." *International Journal of Scientific and Research Publications, 8* (2)

Kleinman, Arthur. (1980). *Patients and Healers in the Context of Culture. An Exploration of the Borderland between Anthropology, Medicine and Psychiatry*. Berkeley, CA: University of California Press.

Lambert, H. (2017). "Health care, hierarchy and the intracultural politics of recognition: Medical pluralism and its narratives as ethnographic objects." *L'Uomo, 2017*(1): 157-176.

Leatherman, Thomas (1998). "Changing Biocultural Perspectives on Health in the Andes." *Social Science and Medicine, 47*(8): 1031-1041.

Mitra, Sona. (2014). Major dimensions of inequalities in India: Health care. Centre for budget and government accountability. www.cbgaindia.org.

Ngokwey, Ndolamb (1988). "Pluralistic Etiological Systems in Their Social Context: A Brazilian Case Study." *Social Science and Medicine,* 26(8): 793-802.

Planning Commission. (2013). *Twelfth Five Year Plan (2012–2017): Social Sectors*, Volume III. Planning Commission: New Delhi.

Qader, Imrana. (2003). "Ethics and Medical Care in a Globalising World: Some Reflections." In Sen, Kasturi (ed.), *Restructuring Health Services: Changing Contexts & Comparative Perspectives*, pp. 53-64, Zed Books: London.

Reeser, Douglas Car. (2014). *Medical pluralism in a neoliberal state: health and deservingness of in southern Belize*. http://scholarcommons.usf.edu/etd/5295

Sharma, A.K. (2013). Alternative Systems of Health Care and National Health Mission: Treading with Care. Paper presented at the eleventh conference of IASSH organized by School of Public Health, SRM University, Tamil Nadu.

Tsing, Anna. (2002). "The Global Situation." In Jonathan Xavier Inda and Renato Rosaldo, (eds.) *The Anthropology of Globalization: A Reader,* pp. 453-485. Malden, MA: Blackwell Publishers.

Tsing, Anna. (2005). *Friction: an Ethnography of Global Connection*. Princeton, NJ: Princeton University Press.

Venkat, P. (2012). "A new approach to quality and safety research on LHT". paper presented at workshop Integrating traditional South Asian medicine into modern health care systems, Jawarharlal Nehru University, Delhi, October.

Vincent, Charles and Furnham, Adrian (2001), "Why do Patients Turn to Complementary Medicine? An Empirical Study", in Matcha, Duane A. (ed.), *Readings in Medical Sociology*, Allyn and Bacon, Boston, pp. 309-318.

Walt, Gill. (2002). *Health Policy: An Introduction to Process and Power*. Zed Books, London.

Wilk, Richard R. (2006). *Home Cooking in the Global Village: Caribbean Food from Buccaneers to Ecotourists*. New York: Berg.

Yadavendu, Vijay Kumar. (2001). "Social Construction of Health: Changing Paradigms." *Economic and Political Weekly*, pp. 2784-2795. www.healthcareindia.net

20

Medical Pluralism, Continuity and Change in Himachal Pradesh

Gurinder Kaur and *Sukhbir Singh*

Background

Multiple systems of therapy and healing are employed by people for their own illnesses and those of significant others. These multiple systems of medicine are distinguished by their history, ideology and present day politics, in addition to their methods of treatment/healing. In consequence, they often are considered to be contrasting and competing by both the users of these systems and the providers. However, this contrast moves in a universe of ambiguity. It is more the complementarity that emerges when actual implementation of healing strategies is chosen, wherein people often combine different forms of medicine to treat their illnesses. These systems may be incompatible in terms of their basic working principles, but for the people who use them in a complementary way the incompatibility dies nit matter. Also as observed by Das (2016), practitioners of alternative medicine also at times prescribe allopathic medicines for minor ailments like cough or cold or other seasonal illnesses. Therefore, incompatibility may exist in theory but in practice it is more complementarity and contrast. The 'either/or' dichotomy does not describe well the everyday reality of the people dealing with an illness, although aetiological theories of the disease, methods of diagnosis, prognosis and implementation of healing rituals and acts differ widely.

This holds true for village based communities and urban centres. Very few societies have only one system of medical prevention (Brodwin, 1996). People's choices are pragmatic, being based upon their needs, their worldview and availability of multiple systems of healing and therapy. Thus, in their quest for healing the people combine methods which could be even competing to one another in their approach.

This chapter attempts to locate the plurality of healing systems in the world of people in a single village of Bhatgarh located in hilly terrain of Sirmaur district in the northern state of Himachal Pradesh, India. It explores the continuity, hybridity and change in the perception and choices of healing systems in the village over a decade.

Subjective understanding of health, illness and healing for the people of this village undulated between the causes attributed to two explanatory systems: one rooted in the local religious realm and the other in the modern understanding on which national and global policies on health and health care are based and which are transforming the local village society.

This chapter theorises on·Paul Brodwin's (Brodwin, 1996) work on medicine and mortality in Haiti: the contest for healing power, where he presents a comprehensive account on how the concept of medical pluralism underwent change in anthropology and why this change necessitated a differing approach towards this concept. He provided a larger understanding about the concept by locating the extended history, politics, ideology and religiosity of it in the town of Jeanty in Haiti. He refers to medical pluralism as "social organisation of healing practitioners, who often occupy different religious, ideological, 'ethnic' or class [and caste] positions in their communities. It also refers to the cultural organization of their practice... how people choose between competing therapies. In the widest context, medical pluralism alludes to the way that competing medical discourses mediate between bodily experience, the local moral order, and supra-local institutions and ideologies" (Brodwin, 1996: 14).

Medical pluralism had had a privileged place in anthropology, particularly medical anthropology, which began to change in the 1990s. Prior to this many significant academic works (Leslie, 1980; Lieban, 1977; Good and Good, 1980; Kleinman, 1980; Beals, 1976; Nichter, 1989) find frequent reference on this topic of research. These studies presented an account of medicine/healing/therapy at temporal and spatial intersection. They focused upon causation, diagnosis, treatment perspective and explanations of people utilising these systems. Most often these studies located medical pluralism in the contrast between biomedicine and traditional systems of medicine. The early studies on medical pluralism treated multiple systems of medicine as reified structures which competed with each other, especially between the traditional (local) medical systems and Western biomedicine (Crandon, 1986). All medical systems can then be conceived of as pluralistic structures in which cosmopolitan medicine is one component which functions in competitive and complementary relationships to numerous "alternative therapies" (Leslie, 1980).

Reification failed to acknowledge the heterogeneity within these systems and the competition between ideas, theories and methods of treatment within them rather focused on the same between them, especially with respect to biomedicine. Medical pluralism can exist within a given medical/healing system or between them (Minocha, 1980). The heterogeneity within traditional systems of healing/medicine was studied in terms of typology, diversity and complexity of urban *curanderos* in Latin America by Press (1971) focusing on the factors that influenced the choice of a particular curer/healer in an urban setting. The pattern of such studies acknowledged the heterogeneity within the systems of medicine but also contrasted them based upon the traditional-modern dichotomy. The theme of medical pluralism was one central focus if not the only focus of these studies, which located various systems of healing and their performativity in the ambit of medical pluralism.

The trend saw a change in approach in which influence of institutional and structural forces and global factors were also taken into account to study and analyse medical pluralism. However, with this changing trend, the focus on medical pluralism declined as it was "eclipsed by newer theoretical concerns. Academic interest shifted to the body as a site of coercion and resistance, the political economy of health and health services, the hegemonic power of biomedicine, and the hermeneutic construction of clinical realities.... Medical pluralism dropped out as central topic in its own right" (Brodwin, 1996: 15).

The critique in epistemological approach towards medical pluralism in anthropology was put forth by Comaroff as early as 1980. She argued that accounts on beliefs and perceptions about health, illness and healing, "utilitarian models" of making choice for therapies or providing an account on hierarchy or strategies of resort to curers[1] could not "yield more than descriptive accounts...of behaviours" (Comaroff, 1980: 638).

Keeping in focus the changing journey of medical pluralism in anthropology, this chapter attempts to understand and analyse medical pluralism as embedded in the everyday life experiences of the people, as impacted by the larger global and local dominant ideologies and as influenced by the dominant discourse of the present and the past in form of continuity and change reflected through entrenching of health and illness "...in the informal logic of everyday life, animated through specific healing activities, and articulated with overarching material and ideological forces" (Brodwin, 1996: 15).

For the people, the categorical distinction between traditional *vs.* modern is blurred by pragmatic use of competing medical traditions/

systems for negotiating the crisis generated by an illness. There is a constant interaction between the people and medical system and in each interaction there is affirmation as well as challenges and change. Health, illness, plural medical systems are reflective of interactions between larger social domains of caste, class, global and national policies on health in the rural society of a village. Approaching medical pluralism from this perspective opens up the space for understanding the "systematic attempts to counter affliction [illness, which] tend to merge thought and action; hence, they frequently make accessible to observation those patterns of meaning which are otherwise obscure in context of cultural transformation" (Comaroff, 1980: 637) and to "…comprehend the relationship between forms of subjective experience and the structural features of changing context…" (Comaroff, 1980: 638).

Medical pluralism in any given society cannot exist in isolation as a reified structure. The dichotomy between biomedicine and Indian medicine or Western medicine and traditional medicine was understood as an outside influence contrasted with an already existing inside system in a society. Medical pluralism is not merely co-existence of multiple systems of therapy/healing. It reflects an interconnection between structural and institutional forces with implications for those who live with the impact, influence and use of these systems.

Globalization and Health Care Programmes

Globalization "reshapes geography and radically increases the speed of interaction…cultural dimensions of globalization enter the local context through multiple stranded homes of people, images and ideas[2] and contribute redefinitions of identity and suffering. As a result, globalization is not something out there it is in here" (Janes, 2004: 463).

In the field of health care, there has been a long-standing debate about the impact of globalization on health policies, planning and implementation at the national level. Dependent upon other nations and international institutions, it has impacted the way national policies have addressed local health care needs. The major critique of impact of globalization on health of populations has been that by catering to fulfil international requirements, particularly the developing countries relying on aid from developed nations and international institutions, have had to curtail their ability to meet health needs of their own populations in their local contexts, realities and requirements (Kleinman, 1996; Farmer *et al.*, 2013; Pfeiffer and Chapman, 2013).

In the global domains of health care policies and programmes, two contradictory yet almost parallel approaches existed since the 1960s and 1970s. The first was the Alma Ata declaration[3] of 1978 (Alma Ata is the present day Almaty in Kazakhstan, previously part of the Soviet Union). It endorsed the WHO definition of health as a human right as recognised that people have the right to accessible health care (Farmer *et al.*, 2013). It was a momentous attempt at the international level with the motto of 'Health for all'.[4] The Alma Ata declaration promoted strengthening of rural health care primarily through Primary Health Care (PHC) and considered health as a social and economic indicator.[5]

The second approach of the structural adjustment programme (SAPs), particularly in low and middle income countries[6] was markedly different from this. Eventually, under the impact of international funding institutions (IFI) like the World Bank, UNICEF and WHO, the focus shifted from the vertical-horizontal debate[7] of PHC towards selective PHC (SPHC[8]). Entanglement with SAP made health more of a commodity than right of every individual and hence began the reign of neoliberal era and shift of authority to deal with health issues from WHO to World Bank and UNICEF (Farmer *et al.*, 2013; Janes, 2004).

The 21st century saw the advent and proliferation of major public and private funding agencies particularly from the US working for health care in the Third World (Farmer *et al.*, 2013). This beginning also saw the acceptance and signing of Millennium Development Goals (MDGs) developed and promoted by the UN which were to be achieved by 2015 and now have gotten extended to Sustainable Development Goals (SDGs). They consist of 17 goals, 169 targets of which goal 3 is directly related to health with the focus on 'good health and well-being' and the rest of the 16 goals also impact health directly or indirectly.

With these different phases and waves in health policies and programmes at international level, the national level health policies and programmes in India also fluctuated accordingly. The health system of independent India carried forward the legacy of the colonial past. In the colonial past, the main concern was for the health of the colonial cadre rather than health of the general public. Post-independence, this needed to be rectified. Health of the people was associated with health of the nation, it was a mark of nationalism. This beginning consists of cumulative yet contradictory efforts of nationalist elites, modernists, bureaucrats that ultimately shaped the 'political culture of health in India' (Amrith, 2007).[9] The Bhore Committee Report of 1946 is still considered the benchmark in the field of public health in India. This depicts an influence of external global forces in defining the agenda of health policies and programmes that began in the pre-colonial period and extended into the early years of independent India.

India acknowledged the relevance of health for all as a right as propounded by WHO in 1948, that focused on strengthening primary health care in rural areas. The impact of debates at the global level about the choice between vertical PHC or horizontal PHC was felt in Indian health policy and its implications were strong for the grassroots level as well. For example, the malaria control programme of the 1950s is a classic case of vertical PHC focusing only on malaria eradication, and the polio eradication programme is a more recent example of the influence of international concerns and policies on national agendas.

In these cases, the focus was on only one disease and its subsequent impact on overall health care. However, "it seems that global consensus on the eradication or elimination of certain diseases, such as small pox or polio, which represent global threats under this conception of global public goods, may well have been reached at the cost of other diseases that are of greater local importance" (Das, 2015: 183).

The problem lay within the institutional framework of health care where lack of proper infrastructure and manpower has been identified as the main factors impacting these programmes. The second important initiative in the Indian health care system, though more of demographic concern, was the population control strategy with the setting up of a separate Ministry of Family Planning in 1966. Pulse polio campaigns, specific immunisation days, focus on HIV/AIDS, role of non-state organisations like the Melinda and Bill Gates Foundation, USAID in specific health care initiatives, all coincided with international global health initiatives. With the signing of MDGs by 191 countries, including India in 2000, the focus was once again defined by the international agenda on health care. As part of its commitment to these goals, India initiated a flagship programme of National Rural Health Mission (NRHM)[10] in 2005. This programme also reflects the influence of internal commitments and requirements at the national level. Thus, the existence of particular medical systems and their forms of existence in given time and space "...is not uniform and it shaped by the unique historical and cultural traditions of each country" (Whitaker, 2003: 349).

With this background, this chapter intends to locate the tensions and concurrence between health systems at the grassroots level not as a debate between traditionalism and modernity or as a critique of state policies on health care, but as experienced and lived by people in a village located in the hilly terrain in one of the federal states of India.

The Locale

The chapter refers to global as something inhere and not out somewhere (Janes, 2004). It presents the experiences of people from the mofussil village of Bhatgarh located at an altitude of 1520 metres in the district of Sirmaur, Himachal Pradesh, India. The study was first conducted in September-October 2005, before NRHM as a government programme on health was formally launched in the area, and in the second phase the site was re-visited in September-October 2017 after a decade of implementation of NRHM in health care in the region. The basic methods of data collection included semi-structured questionnaire and interview guides.

The observations and analyses of the study pertain to continuity and change in the health care system of Bhatgarh village. Continuity and change, tradition and progress, are not viewed as opposing processes but as overlapping and embedded in collective histories of the local development processes at the village level and changes in the health sector at national and international levels. According to the 2011 Census of India, Bhatgarh is a small village comprising 108 households. The total population of the village is 854 with 431 males and 423 females.

The village represents a typical village community with close-knit relations amongst households, practicing village exogamy and caste endogamy in marriage. The dominant caste in the village is Rajput followed by Koli and Mochi. The Rajputs are the dominant caste in terms of social hierarchy, landholding and population. It is a village in the panchayat of Bhatgarh which has a total of five villages under its jurisdiction as part of the Panchyati Raj Institution in India. The village is a collection of *pucca* (cemented) houses which are clustered on a hill slope with a partially paved narrow passage that connects the village to the road below. The village is connected to other villages and the nearest towns of Renukaji and Dadahu with an unpaved but jeepable road. The condition of this road has not changed since the first time fieldwork was conducted here.

The people of the village rely mainly on subsistence farming but also sell their produce in the vegetable market in the town of Dadahu located at a distance of about 17 km. Visits to the town are mainly for this purpose or for visiting the civil hospital for various ailments and for a few young people to attend the degree college in the town. Visits to Renukaji, located at a distance of about 15 km, are to visit and pray at the main temple of Renukaji mata and Lord Parshuram. The nearest dispensary is located at a distance of 7 km from the village downhill in another village named Galja. This is a government Ayurvedic dispensary. Sub-centre[11] is now located within the village, whereas earlier the sub centre was located in the village of Channa at a distance of 2 km. The ASHA worker, who lives in Galja village, is a key link between the community and the state health care system, visits twice a month. The village has its own small temple in the name of Lord Parshuram. The main source of water is through taps and hand pumps and under the Government of India's Swachh Bharat Mission, toilets were under construction in the village at the time of fieldwork.

Changes which may seem as a natural progression from one stage of life to another but with a sense of deep connection to us as researchers were significant. A woman who happened to be very closely associated with us at the time of our field visit in 2005 had passed away and her daughter who used to accompany us on our visits then had gotten married. The anticipation of meeting them again gave rise to feelings of missing out on 10 years of life and its progression in this village. Many young men are now migrating out from the village to plain areas of the state or other locales in the country in search of work and the infrastructure of houses had changed over time. *Kutcha* (mud) houses were now very few compared to then. Mobile phones especially smart phones, TV with cable/dish connections were a common sight, two well-constructed shops supplying basic grocery instead of one earlier makeshift shop in 2005 had come up in the village.

The village has one school, which had been upgraded to high school in the last ten years. Mid-day meal was provided in the school. Children from this village and other nearby villages attended this school. Degree college for higher education is located in the town of Dadahu. Lord Parshuram is the village *devta* (patron god) as well as the protector of the entire area along with *Renuka mata* (mother of Lord Parshuram). People's everyday life is entangled with esoterism of religion, religious beliefs and practices, with direct underpinning for the understandings about health and illness. This does not, however, entail that one may draw a strict boundary/ separation between what is traditional and what identifies as modern. The esoterism of activities extended over a range of practices like use of religious practices or home remedies for ensuring health of the people of the village. At the same time people also acknowledged and voiced their expectations, demands and concerns from the state for connectivity of their village to town, infrastructural requirements in terms of roads, health facilities, schools, availability of medical personnel. This reflects the political economy as associated with medical pluralism in the village.

Thus "An understanding of the political economy of medical traditions in pluralistic environment, however, reveals something about the social composition and dynamics of social change within that environment and hence the non-medical significance of medical traditions" (Crandon, 1986: 473) and not just reducing this merely to the debates of traditional and modern.

Juxtaposing the Paradoxes: Medical Pluralism in the Village

Biomedicine in and around Bhatgarh

The political history of biomedicine, not in terms of its genesis but in terms of its spread and implications, is characterized by its relentless spread since pre-colonial times and up until the present-day focus on global health. As part of this process, use of biomedicine in the village and for that matter in the surrounding villages and the area in general has become a routinised part of everyday life of the people. In this chapter, the theorisations, and the intended or unintended consequences of these theorisations are examined not for their deeper nuances but rather for their implications as lived and real experiences of the people.

Biomedicine is as much a part of everyday experience as is religion and religious rituals associated with health and illness. Biomedicine is not understood as something foreign or outside their routine. It co-exists with other forms of medicine categorised as indigenous or religious healing systems. In a study in Jeanty, this co-existence has been identified as the 'paradox of biomedicine' (Brodwin, 1996).

Biomedicine in Jeanty, "...is undeniably metropolitan import, and it arrives with the full weight of foreign power and cultural catches... it does not threaten to replace the work of midwives, herbalists, and religious healers with its own set of reductionist and culturally foreign interventions. Despite its origins, biomedicine does not exist as bounded health care sector in isolation from other forms of therapy, and it has not subdivided the local healing system" (Brodwin, 1996).

This observation holds true in Bhatgarh village. In the decade between 2005 and 2017, the referral hospital at Dadahu was upgraded to a civil hospital. Also, owing to a special focus on improving maternal and child health and controlling the maternal mortality rate (MMR) and infant mortality rate (IMR) as part of the effort to achieve the Millennium Development Goals (MDGs), one prime focus of National Rural Health Mission (NRHM), introduced in 2005, was to increase institutionalised deliveries.[12] This particular intervention and the changes that it has brought about in these ten years present a stark contrast between then and now. In 2005, the village had its local midwife, who performed most deliveries of pregnant women then. She was trained through apprenticeship by her mother-in-law and her maternal grandmother. Apart from the familial training she had received one-time training at the then referral hospital in Dadahu and was provided with a learning kit to ensure safe and clean delivery at home. Complicated deliveries she would refer to the referral hospital at Dadahu.

With the implementation of NRHM community health workers were mobilised at the grassroots level particularly the Accredited Social Health Activist (ASHA), and institutional deliveries have replaced deliveries at home by the traditional *dai* (midwife). The data from the civil hospital (the former referral hospital) also revealed an increase in institutional deliveries, corroborated by the staff members as well. However, a discussion with village women revealed that home deliveries still take place in the village though in a few cases only. The change in this pattern has been attributed to the visits and work of ASHA[13] *behanji* (sister) in the village.

Another major change attributed to NRHM with significant impact on maternal and child health was introduction of 108 ambulance service. The ambulance was often seen travelling on the connecting road between the civil hospital, Dadahu and the villages in the upper reaches. The service of this ambulance is not limited to maternal health, but it has become an important tool for facilitating and encouraging delivery in the hospital. However, narrow and unpaved roads and landslides in monsoon seasons hamper easy outreach of this service to people in the villages. What needs to be emphasised is not just the development of an institutional apparatus *vis-à-vis* commitment to the international agenda of achieving MDGs and SDGs, but to ensure development of allied sectors as well which have direct bearing on accessibility of health care, especially road connectivity which has shown almost no change in the decade between 2005 and 2017. Along with lack of smooth connectivity, the human resource crunch in the government health sector in India is well documented. However, in case of Bhatgarh, there has been an improvement on this front since the implementation of NRHM with availability of community health workers and doctors in village based health facilities. Health is thus not only a matter of availability alone but also accessibility.[14]

Change was also observed in the Ayurvedic dispensary located at Galja about 5 km from Bhatgrah, while going downhill towards Renukaji or Dadahu. The infrastructural changes as well as availability of medicine in the dispensary have shown marked changes in the decade after the implementation of NRHM. The only doctor at the dispensary at Galja concurs with this observation: *"NRHM ke āne se bhaut farak paḍa hai, ye sarï building aur samān NRHM ke āne ke bād hi āyā hai"* (A lot of things have changed after NRHM, this infrastructure was built after NRHM was implemented).

In 2005, when the first field visit was conducted, the infrastructure of the same Ayurvedic dispensary was dependent on the state and the local village Panchayat. It was a single-room dispensary in a building provided by the village panchayat. There was no sitting place for the attendants, one stool for the patient, one almirah for storing documents and a small wooden cabinet for medicines. Whereas now the dispensary was a three-room building, with a well maintained room for dispensing medicine, a separate room for the doctor, sitting arrangements for the attendants, and a separate pantry. The supply of water and electricity was regular unlike earlier in 2005. These infrastructural changes were attributed to NRHM which provided adequate funding to build up the health care facility. Also, since people of the village as well as the area in general had always had faith in Ayurvedic medicine, the upgrading of the dispensary was a boon for them.

The doctor now had a blood pressure apparatus and stethoscope which had been missing paraphernalia earlier. This also reflects the efforts of the statc to promote indigenous medical systems. This has been the case with Ayurvedic, Unani, Siddha and Homoeopathy (AYUSH). Though, similar improvements cannot be generalised for other parts of the country. The reason for the comparative success of the Ayurvedic system in terms of consultation and use by the local people would also be attributed to the faith that people of this region in general have in Ayurvedic medicine or medicinal herbs. It is an embedded part of the pluralist medical cosmology of this area.

The diffusion and acceptance of biomedicine was not in opposition to another state sponsored system of medicine or in opposition to religious and other esoteric beliefs and practices of the people. This diffusion and acceptance was based on demands made by these very people. "The everyday talk about illness was filled with reference to infections, X-ray and injections" (Brodwin, 1996). In terms of Foucaultian theory, this refers to how govermentality and knowledge production create and change discourse over time with certain concepts developing or having developed around scientific knowledge becoming part of the everyday language of the people.

At the same time acceptance of biomedicine by the people and its infusion into their everyday life does not absolve the power imbalance[15] associated between it and other medical systems and it does not replace or diminish the legitimacy of other systems of medicine be they state sponsored or otherwise. Even though biomedicine can bring about profound changes, it cannot be considered as an autonomous system. Rather, it is a system that is formed and impacted by "broader societal variables including culturally informed values and constraints, specific local and global objectives, economic disparities, and inconsistent or non-existent regulations" (Lock and Nguyen, 2010: 5). Therefore, the power imbalance reflects an enmeshment of biomedicine with medical realities, social and political ideologies and interests that have direct impact and consequences for the people.

The Non-biomedical Counterpart in Medical Pluralism

People of the village have an array of other non-biomedical options available to them. These showed continuity of existence from 2005 to 2017. They include the midwife from the neighbouring village of Lathiana and knowledge of locally growing herbs in the hills. This knowledge was not the domain of any specialist serving a particular function or position/ role in the village. Rather this repertoire of knowledge was diffused among the villagers particularly the elderly. This knowledge about locally growing herbs on hills was part of the local social and ecological cosmology of the village. It includes knowledge about the herbs' preparation and usages, commonly termed as home remedies in the literature on medical pluralism. Knowledge about these herbs and their usage is considered part of the village legacy. It is not considered as something extraordinary or in the domain of esoterism where it is limited to only a select few people. It is collective legacy and part of the normal, everyday life of the people. This knowledge, though considered significant and a legacy of the hills, is not something extraordinary for the people of the village. This was also observed by Brodwin (1996) in his study where practiced knowledge of plants to treat certain illnesses was not hidden or 'guarded by high state professionals'.

For any seasonal ailment, be it cough, cold, fever or an occasional imbalance in the perceived normality of the body function like upset stomach or nausea or even for minor injuries and for snake bite, locally available herbs are used for healing. Even though these herbs have been and still are used, when seen in the plane of biomedicine and other technological changes occurring over time, these very herbs introduce a 'discourse of nostalgia' (Macphee, 2004). Nostalgia relegates the very symbols of development like schools, mobile phones, agricultural pesticides and fertilizers, to an ambiguous zone. These symbols become objects of ambiguity with no white or black definition attributed to them. Whereas the arrival of modern technologies like biomedicine and ambulance service has made life easier, at the same time mobiles and pesticides have become causes of social tensions and poor health:

> *Gaon kī āj kī pīḍī buhut achhī hai lekin vishwās kam hotā jā rahā hai āj ki pīḍī kā. Pehle bare buzurg dete the to vishwās hotā thā, ab to kītnāshak ne hī bimārīyā badhā dī hai.*
> (The local village herbs are good but faith in their effects is decreasing in today's generation. Earlier the elders used to give these so faith was there in them but now the use of pesticides has itself started causing diseases).

The reliance and use of locally available herbs used for seasonal physical ailments or minor injuries include *kachûr* and *ajwāin* particularly for stomach ache, *kāḍhā* (concoction) *haldī kā lep* (layering the wound with paste of turmeric in *desī ghī* (saturated oil). *Haldī kā dûdh*[16] (milk mixed with turmeric). There was a very specific herb locally known as *shivali* which was used in case of snake bite. Snakes have been closely associated with Lord Shiva in Hindu mythology and hence the local name of the herb used for snake bite reflects this association.

Across this area, these herbs have maintained the legitimacy that they have had through many generations of people. They are a reality which is not only part of everyday life but signifies its continuity over long periods of time. Continuous use tends to legitimise the knowledge about presence, identification, relevance, use and effectiveness of certain herbs for certain ailments. This legitimation of knowledge sets the foundation for the institutionalisation of the non-biomedical system within the pluralistic medical milieu in the given geographical space. Yet simultaneously "The pluralistic situation goes with conditions of rapid social change, indeed pluralism itself is an accelerating factor.... Pluralism encourages both skepticism and innovation and is thus inherently subversive of taken for granted reality..." (Berger and Luckman, 1966: 143).

This remark holds out to be supportive of the changes in terms of not only acceptance and everydayness associated with biomedicine or demand for developmental changes in terms of connectivity or the health care but also the nostalgia associated with the earlier times when things had not been penetrated by various forms of development.

Another form of continuity was in the realm of the supernatural, "… any disease even one with a known and accepted biomedical diagnosis can be sent upon its victim…" (Brodwin, 1996) through supernatural forces, be it the effect of evil eye, black magic, planetary positions or anger of the village *devtā*. Certain aches like sudden aches or pain in the body were attributed to the realm of the supernatural. The only remedy for these was *jhāḍā*[17] from the temple priest of the village.

The causes ranged from curse of the village *devtā* to effect of evil eye. Apart from these *jhāḍā* was preferred for sudden aches befalling the body, jaundice, snake bite, spider bite and *budrī mata* (chicken pox). Of these *budrī mātā* was associated with sacredness of the goddess rather than curse of the supernatural or ill intent of another human out of jealousy particularly. This is similar to folkloristic traditions in Rajasthan associated with certain illnesses, which here refer to *budrī mātā* particularly. As part of the popular culture, "in its predictable, ultimately harmless form the sickness *mātā* is indeed regarded as a benign manifestation of the goddess but the patient must be protected against the dangerous consequences of its (her) potential virulence" (Lambert, 1997: 257). Since *budrī mātā* was considered to be a communicable disease, the person (usually children) afflicted by it were confined to a separate room in the house and only sweetened foods like porridge or boiled rice were given to them. Special *pūjā* (prayer) is performed in the village temple to ensure the goddess manifested in form of pox leaves the body without causing any harm. Diseases or discomfort afflicting particularly children can be caused by the evil eye, even though these can "locate in their bodies but also manifest disruptive social relation" (Ayora-Diaz, 1998: 179).

During the fieldwork of 2005 we were introduced to the concept of *bāṇ*. It is the sudden attack of extreme pain anywhere in the body. In a study among the Hmong community in Kansas City, US regarding continuity and change in their medical culture owing to their migration, interaction and mingling with other ethnic groups brought changes in certain aspects, yet there were "…certain continuities…regarding illness causation, patterns of response and treatment… [and even though]… Biomedicine was part of the diversity,… in some cases it is thought to be potentially dangerous" (Capps, 1994: 161, 169). This observation holds true for Bhatgarh village community for the problems caused by *bāṇ*, where people believed that *bāṇ kā koī ilāj nahī hai, sirf jhāḍ hai* (there is no other treatment/healing for *bāṇ* other than whiffing and blowing).

The method of countering the impact of effect caused by *bāṇ* through *jhāḍā* involved calculations using astrological charts. For all the issues, the act of *jhāḍā* required a minimum three sittings and the *jhāḍā* was performed using a broom made of peacock feathers or tongs of iron. The movement of these is from head towards the feet. A plausible explanation for this procedure is that "*jhāḍā* itself constitutes an attempt to symbolically sweep away contamination of a serious ailment…" and a broom made of peacock feathers or the iron tong or a charm or an amulet symbolises a "vehicle of transference through which the ailment is removed from the sick person" (Lambert, 1997). No biomedical treatment was sought for *budrī mātā* or *bāṇ*.

Conclusion

There are two strains of argument that emerge, rather than the reductionist dichotomy between modern biomedicine and indigenous medicine or creating a rigid hierarchy between their usages. What is more pertinent is the patronage of the state by sponsoring or supporting systems of medicine, which may be either modern and traditional. Biomedicine and AYUSH, particularly Ayurvedic medicine, both are part of the state sponsored agenda but with differing weight given to each. Caution must be exercised because the state-sponsored patronage of the two systems of medicine is not equitable. Studies have shown that between the two systems, biomedicine gains more weight. Herein lies the history of biomedicine and the construction of the post-colonial idea of the Indian nation-state, which was modernist in approach with lip service to indigenous systems of medicine like Ayurveda[18] (Amrith, 2007; Gandhi, 1947; Das, 1995). As remarked by Banerji (1981: 112) "political leadership…vigorously expanded the Western system of medicine which was much more in tune with their class interests…indigenous system of medicine were never taken seriously."

A second element is the demands by the village community itself for provisions of symbols of modernity, and their preference for and acceptance of biomedicine. In their minds, this is connected with the demand for infrastructural development in terms of road connectivity particularly, but at the same time they maintain their beliefs and reliance on religion for dealing with matters of health and illness. In addition, they consider objects of modernity like mobile technology and use of pesticides in agriculture as causing harm to health. The preference for non-biomedical systems of healing, also those other than the state sponsored 'alternative' systems like AYUSH, are embedded in the local cosmology where everyday life is interlocked with ecology, nature and religion. Attempting to establish any sort of hierarchy to the co-existence of multiple systems of medicine and healing would be thus reductionist in approach. The changes and continuities over the decade show the complexities involved in understanding the concept of medical pluralism. The co-existence of these multiple systems of medicines is not based on premise of being a phase in transition wherein one system would replace or over-shadow the other system over a period of time. It is more about how people understand the precarity of their lives embedded in their local cosmologies of understanding health and illness. The lives of people living in any remote corner of the world are equally influenced by the policies developed in the echelons of the global and national. At the same time, notions of health and illness are equally embedded in the moral life of the people. As Brodwin (1996: 1) observes, "When people fall ill, their search for effective treatment opens up a realm of complicated moral concerns.... They ally themselves with a...source of healing power... [yet at the same time] these religious idioms of suffering and healing mediate between the local world of isolated rural communities and the national and global forces that are transforming...society".

To conclude, "...community, in contemporary contexts, is defined as much by the structures of modernity, including bureaucratic law, as by a customary innate order" (Das, 1995: 50). She terms this as the double articulation of tradition and modernity in any Indian society and cautions against using tradition and modernity as critiques of one another. These remarks hold to be true in context of the present study where the distinction between traditional and modern in terms of health and illness cannot be put in closed boxes but rather emerges as a paradoxical mix for people who live with these notions as embedded in their lives.

NOTES

1. A study by Alan Beals published in 1976 on the same subject is based on a hierarchical cause and effect of choices that people make when seeking treatment from particular healers.
2. Arjun Appadurai [12] identifies five scapes instrumental in global flow: (i) ethnoscapes, (ii) mediascapes, (iii) technoscapes, (iv) finascapes, (v) ideoscapes. These scapes complicate the matter of global cultural economy beyond scientific understanding of centre-periphery relations. For details see Appadurai (1980).
3. WHO and UNICEF were the major organisations involved in this declaration

(Banerji, 1999). It also included representatives from 134 countries and 67 international organisations. The gathering committed to the pledge to achieve the universal primary health care by the year 2000. It was held in one of the states of former USSR and US was also participatory to it, even though the two world powers of the time differed in their ideologies and approach to health care particularly the PHC.

4. The instruments/goals of Alma Ata deceleration were "immunization, reproductive health care, contraception, sanitation, and the promotion of safe motherhood" (Janes, 2004: 457).
5. The focus on PHC got mired into debates and controversies about vertical and horizontal programmes and issue of large scale funding from respective state governments towards health care. The critics of the declaration considered it as overambitious and away from the ground realties.
6. "...SAPs refer to the country-specific agreements negotiated by the IFIs with local ministries of finance that have produced a cascade of profound political economic and social changes in the Third World" (Pfeiffer and Chapman, 2010: 150), in terms of focus on privatisation, less government involvement, reduction in government subsidies, lower wages, disinvestment in government enterprises, reduced barriers and taxes on foreign investment etc.
7. Vertical refers to focus on specific health programmes with top-down approach. It is usually the international organisations like the World Bank, WHO or UNICEF which device specific health programmes and which are carried forward by the signatory countries of these programmes. For example, the universal immunisation programme (UIP). Horizontal on the other hand are more focused on area specific problems related to health focusing on primary health care and community participation.
8. The SPHC focused on GOBI (Growth monitoring, oral rehydration therapy, breastfeeding, immunization).
9. As noted by Amrith (2007), by the 1930s, the nationalists, elites and modernists associated with the Congress had started deliberating about the idea of national health, critiquing the neglect of public health by the colonial government.
10. The NRHM has been renamed as National Health Mission (NHM) in 2014. Continuing on its previous goals and objectives NHM aims to focus on rural as well as urban parameters on health. The urban component was missing in NRHM and is at a nascent stage under NHM and is yet to be devised and implemented fully. The major focus of the programme is to strengthen health parameters in rural and urban centres of India. Its primary area of intervention include reproductive and child health, maternal health, neonatal health and adolescent health (RMNCH+A) and communicable, and non-communicable diseases. As per the latest NRHM policy framework the federal states were to contribute 25 per cent of the cost of the programme on health services according to their requirements by integrating vertical and horizontal health programmes and policies. The rest would be the share of the Central Government.

11. A sub-centre is the first point of contact between the community and the state health services. It provides basic health services to the people and ideally acts as a point of connect between the community and the primary health centre (PHC).
12. In India, in the academic and policy parlance the deliveries conducted at any medical facility, private or government, supported by medical professionals is termed as institutional delivery. It is considered as an important parameter in improving maternal and child health and reducing mortality rates as well.
13. The ASHA is often a woman and as a mark of respect by the village community is addressed as *behanji*, meaning sister.
14. As per the Comptroller and Auditor General (CAG) of India report of 2016, "deficiencies in fund flow management, planning and monitoring, community participation, convergence, infrastructure development and capacity building, procurement and supply of medicines... etc." have been observed and reported. The audit found that substantial amount allocated by Central and State Governments towards NRHM remained unspent and the number of health facilities like sub-centres, primary health centres and community health centres was less and there was a substantial gap in the human resource of doctors and paramedical staff as well.
15. It is equally hegemonic in approach and its representatives (doctors especially) are viewed by the villagers as outsider, as 'the other' with the technical know-how about what ails them and what causes it.
16. Some of these concoctions are commonly used in households across the country and not just limited to the village.
17. Lambert (1997: 259) defines "*jhāḍā*, literally 'sweeping'... whiffing/sweeping and blowing....is commonly sought for a wide range of ailments including migraine, toothache, boils of ear and nose, scorpion sting, snake bite, typhoid-type fevers,...effects of evil eye (*nazar)* in children and spirit possession."
18. However, the recent resurgence political patronage and marketing of indigenous system of medicine particularly Ayurveda and Yoga have started gaining fraction in the Western world and have become symbols of national identify and nationalism in India.

REFERENCES

Amrith, S. (2007). "Political Culture of Health in India: A Historical Perspective." *Economic and Political Weekly, 42*(2): 114-121.

Appadurai, A. (1990). "Disjuncture and difference in the global cultural economy." *Theory, Culture and Society*, *7*(2-3), 295-310.

Ayora-Diaz, S.I. (1998). "Globalization, Rationality and Medicine: Local Medicine's Struggle for Recognition in Highland Chiapas, Mexico." *Urban Anthropology and Studies of Cultural Systems and World Economic Development, 27*(2): 165-195.

Beals, A.R. (1976). "Strategies of Resort to Curers in South India." In: C. Leslie (Ed.): *Asian medical system: A comparative study*. Berkeley: University of California Press.

Berger, P.L. & Luckman, T. (1966). *The Social Construct of Reality: A Treatise in Sociology of Knowledge*. London: Penguin Books.

Brodwin, P. (1996). *Medicine and Morality in Haiti: The Contest for Healing Power*. Cambridge: Cambridge University Press.

Capps, L.L. (1994). "Change and Continuity in the Medical Culture of the Hmong in Kansas City." *Medical Anthropology Quarterly*, *8*(2): 161-177.

Comaroff, J. (1980). "Healing and the cultural order: The case of the Barolong boo Ratshidi of Southern Africa." *American Ethnologist*, *7*(4): 637-657.

Comptroller and Auditor General of India. (2016). *Report of Comptroller and Auditor General of India on performance audit of reproductive and child health under National Health Mission*. New Delhi: Ministry of Health and Family Welfare, Government of India.

Crandon, L. (1986). "Medical dialogue and the political economy of medical pluralism: A case from rural highland Bolivia." *American Ethnologist*, *13*(3): 463-476.

Das, V. (1995). *Critical Events*. New Delhi: Oxford University Press.

Das V. (2015). *Affliction: Health, Disease, Poverty*. Delhi: Orient Black Swan.

Farmer, P., Kleinman, A., Kim, J.Y., & Basilico, M. (2013). *Reimagining Global Health: An Introduction*. Berkley: University of California Press.

Gandhi, M.K. (1947). *India of My Dreams*. Ahmedabad: Navjivan Mudranalaya.

Good, B. & Good, M.J. (1980). "The meaning of symptoms: A cultural hermeneutic model for clinical practice." In: L. Eisenberg and A. Kleinman (eds): *The relevance of social science for medicine*. Boston: Reidel Publications.

Janes, C.R. (2004). "Going global in century XXI: Medical anthropology and the new primary health care." *Human Organisation, 63*(4): 457-71.

Kleinman, A., Das, V., & Lock, M. (1996). *Social Suffering*. Berkeley: University of California Press.

Kleinman, A. (1980). *Patients and Healers in the Context of Culture: An Exploration of the Borderland between Anthropology, Medicine, and Psychiatry*. Berkeley: University of California Press.

Lambert, H. (1997). "Illness, inauspiciousness and modes of healing in Rajasthan." *Contributions to Indian Sociology, 31* (2): 253-271.

Leslie, C. (1980). "Medical pluralism in world perspective." *Social Science and Medicine*. Part B: *Medical Anthropology, 14* (4): 191-195.

Lieban, R.W. (1977). "The field of medical anthropology." In: D. Landy (ed): *Culture, Disease and Healing: Studies in Medical Anthropology*. New York: Macmillan Publishing Co. Inc.

Lock, M. & Nguyen, Vinh-Kim. (2010). *An Anthropology of Biomedicine*. West Sussex, Wiley-Blackwell.

Macphee, M. (2004). "The Weight of the past in the Experience of Health: Time, Embodiment, and Cultural Change in Morocco." *Ethos*, *32*(3): 374-396.

Ministry of Health and Family Welfare. (2014). *Framework for implementation: Natoional Health Mission 2012-2017*. New Delhi: Ministry of Health and Family Welfare, Government of India. Accessed from ww.nhm.gov.in/images/pdf/NHM/Nhm_Framework_for_Implementation_08-01-2014.

Minocha, A.A. (1980). "*Medical pluralism and health services in India." Social Science and Medicine*. Part B: *Medical Anthropology, 14* (4): 217-223.

Nichter, M. (1989). *Anthropology and international health: South Asian case studies*. Netherland: Kluwer Academic Publishers.

Pfeiffer, J., & Chapman, R. (2010). "Anthropological perspectives on structural adjustment and public health." *Annual Review of Anthropology, 39*, 149-165.

Press, I. (1971). "The urban curandero." *American Anthropologist, 73* (3): 741-756.

Whitaker, E.D. (2003). "The idea of health: History, medical pluralism, and the management of the body in Emilia-Romagna, Italy." *Medical Anthropology Quarterly, 17*(3): 348-75.

21

Health care at the Margins: An Account of Women Health Workers in North India

Ravin Srivastava

Background

This research materialised on the sidelines of The National NCD Monitoring Survey (NNMS) 2017-18 which was conducted by the Indian Council for Medical Research (ICMR) and National Centre for Disease Informatics and Research (NCDIR), Bengaluru to assess the Non-Communicable Disease (NCD) Targets and Indicators. The project was made possible by 10 implementing agencies which conduced the survey across 27 States and Union Territories of India, covering 300 rural and 300 urban Primary Sampling Units (PSUs).[1]

During the course of the exhaustive survey 2017-18 in the seven north Indian states it became immensely clear that the health care schemes rolled out by the government would largely be ineffective were it not for the unstinting support of the *didis*—Aanganwadi workers (AWW) and Accredited Social Health Activists (ASHA).

Universe of Study

This study was carried out in both rural and urban areas in the North Indian states of Jammu & Kashmir, Uttarakhand, Punjab, Chandigarh, Haryana and Delhi. These areas or PSUs were chosen by random sampling methods by the Indian Council for Medical Research (ICMR) and National Centre for Disease Informatics and Research (NCDIR), and the survey team had no role in the selection.

Our survey team covered a total of 26 PSUs in the region. The chief languages spoken in the region include Hindi, Punjabi and Urdu.

In urban areas, a census enumeration block (CEB) map was provided to us to demarcate the PSU from surrounding areas. In rural areas, entire villages were to be included in the survey. In case of villages with very large population, the village was divided into segments, two of which were chosen by random sampling techniques for inclusion in the survey.

The foremost duty of the survey teams, on arriving at a PSU, was to contact the village Sarpanch or Counsellor in urban areas and inform her/him about the survey. Thereafter, we were put in contact with the health workers: Aanganwadi Workers (AWW) and Accredited Social Health Activist (ASHA), who provided us with the necessary assistance.

These health workers became an integral part of the survey, helping us map of PSUs, list the households and convincing unwilling individuals to participate in the survey. Their familiarity with the area, the language and the social status that they enjoy proved to be an asset for us.

This ethnographic account briefly traces how the institution of the AWW and ASHA came to be established, including the roles and responsibilities entrusted upon these health workers. Further it examines the support that these health workers provided to us during the course of the survey; their role in making health care accessible at the grassroots level and margins of society; and how they are overcoming barriers of religion and gender while discharging their duties. An effort has also been made to understand the hardships that they face in discharging their duties. Certain inefficiencies on their part have also been highlighted. In doing so, the present chapter tries to delve into the efficacy of the health care decentralisation policy of the Government of India.

Methodology

Ethnography is a mode of knowing that privileges experience (Das and Poole, 2004). The present chapter is based on my interaction with a total of 30 women health workers across the seven states of North India, viz. Jammu & Kashmir, Himachal Pradesh, Uttarakhand, Punjab, Haryana, Chandigarh and Delhi. These women were working in the capacity of AWW/ASHA/MPW (Multipurpose worker). They belonged to the 25-55 age group. Interactions were unstructured. Perceptions of the community were also recorded. Field notes and data were analysed for recurring themes which have been discussed below.

Certain instances of the lives of some of these health workers have been highlighted which serve as the backbone of the chapter. Subsequently, the various themes that came up in my interaction with these women have been discussed. Ideally, it took four to five days for the survey team to wrap up fieldwork in a PSU. These few days allowed for a strong rapport formation between the researcher and the subject. A lot of these interactions took place over tea or lunch, in an environment conducive for openness.

Results

AWW and ASHA–A Brief Historical Context

Hailing from a quaint rural community in Kapurthala, Punjab, Dolly is an ASHA worker. Driving in and out between her in-laws' and parents' villages, Dolly is the champion of health care delivery in the community. From vaccinating infants, organizing health camps to educating the common folk about health issues, she has dedicated her life entirely to the well-being of the people of the community. It was only later that I was told of the tragic life that the 40-something woman has endured—losing first her husband and then her only son, all within a span of a few months.

Nevertheless, Dolly is undeterred in working actively towards the cause dearest to her. Shunting in and out on her scooty, she is bringing health to people's doorsteps. Held in great regard, she is a mother/daughter/sister/counsel/friend to the community.

While we may not even have provided such people with a regular salary, their efforts continue to make small differences in numerous lives.

The Aanganwadi Worker

The institution of the *Aanganwadi Worker (AWW)* was introduced by the Central Government in 1975 as part of the Integrated Child Development Services (ICDS). These services, aimed at the overall development (health, education and nutrition) of the child, were to be delivered by the Aanganwadi and other health workers. An Aanganwadi worker is a woman of the village, preferably in the age group of 18-42 years having higher secondary level of education (Passed class 12). For a population of 1000, one Aanganwadi worker is provided in rural and semi-urban areas. Apart from the responsibilities of the ICDS Scheme, the AWW is also responsible of making home visits in the village; listing births-deaths, differently-abled individuals; organising Pulse Polio Immunisation; assisting ANM (Auxiliary Nurse/Midwife) in administration and maintenance of records. An Aanganwadi Centre—a courtyard play centre—located within the village or a slum is the focal point for delivery of all the services under ICDS programme in an integrated manner to children and women.

The Alma Ata Declaration of 1978 reaffirmed that health is a "fundamental human right" and that "the attainment of the highest possible level of health is a most important world-wide social goal whose realization requires the action of many other social and economic sectors in addition to the health sector" (WHO, 1978). It called for governments to provide adequate health care to people so that the gross inequalities in health between developed and developing countries could be reduced. It set the year 2000 as a deadline for governments, civil society groups, and international health organizations to attain a level of health that will permit people to lead a socially and economically productive life.

Under the National Rural Health Mission (NRHM), 2005, the role of the Aanganwadi Worker was further underscored in delivering health care in a nation where still a large proportion of the population lives in rural areas. NRHM aimed at providing accessible, accountable, effective and reliable primary health care in rural areas. A cadre of Accredited Social Health Activist (ASHA) was to be created to strengthen the health infrastructure.

The Accredited Social Health Activist (ASHA)

ASHAs, commonly referred to as ASHA workers, were created at village level to act as a social change agent to generate demand for health care services, through awareness generation and behaviour change communication among the community (Prinja, 2014). ASHA is a resident of the village—a woman preferably in the 25-49 years age group having formal education up to class eight. For a population of 1000 individuals, one ASHA is provided. This rule can be relaxed in areas with difficult terrain such as mountains and deserts to one ASHA per habitation. The introduction of the ASHA worker programme is a core strategy of the Indian Government in its efforts to meet the 5th Millennium Development Goal (MDG) of reducing the under-five mortality rate by two-thirds between 1990 and 2015 (Rao, 2014). The responsibilities of the ASHA include facilitating community access to health and health services. She is also required to counsel women regarding such issues as importance of safe delivery, breastfeeding, immunisation, birth control measures. She is trained to provide remedy for minor ailments such as diarrhoea, fevers and basic first-aid. She is also assigned the task of creating awareness about important determinants of health such as nutrition, sanitation and hygiene and timely utilisation of health and family welfare services. The ASHA works closely with the AWW.

Penetrating the Margins—Decentralisation of Health Care in India

Decentralisation has improved the functioning of health services to some extent in India (Kaur *et al.*, 2012). Decentralisation entails the transfer of authority from the centre to the local governments. This is achieved by attempting to effectively penetrate the 'margins' of state. Das and Poole (2004) have identified three ways in which the state's margins may be imagined: first, as peripheries or territories in which the state has yet to penetrate; second, as "spaces, forms, and practices through which the state is continually both experienced and undone through the illegibility of its own practices, documents, and words"; and, finally, as the "space between bodies, law, and discipline. The socio-cultural complexity of human life affects to a large extent, health habits and practices of a community. The rigidity of these acts as a barrier in the adoption of innovation" (Rizvi, 1991). Certain aspects of health such as immunization or sterilisation may not find acceptance in certain communities owing to social pressures. At this point, the role of the health workers is crucial. AWW and ASHA are responsible for educating people of their localities about the importance of these well-thought policies and make them comprehend that these are for their own welfare. In other words, they ensure that the government health services permeate into "peripheries or territories in which the state has yet to penetrate." In doing so, the AWW and ASHA become the flag-bearers of India's health programme, particularly in rural areas.

These schemes present a vital opportunity to improve maternal health services through supporting communities to access minor treatments, reducing the pressure on the health system, bringing in-depth health knowledge of the village and facilitating community participation in health programmes (Saprii *et al.,* 2015). National community health worker (CHW) programmes are receiving renewed attention as mechanisms to help overcome health worker shortages, retain health workers in underserved areas, and provide culturally appropriate primary health care (Tulenko *et al.,* 2013; Schneider *et al.,* 2016; WHO, 2016). No longer seen as stop-gap or a temporary solution, they are now considered as part of long-term investments for responsive and community-oriented health systems (Naimoli *et al.,* 2015; Schneider & Lehmann, 2016).

On the first day of the survey, we were required to contact the local community leaders: Sarpanch/Counsellor/MLA, informing them that their village or block had been chosen for the survey. The next step was getting in touch with the AWWs or ASHAs in-charge of the area, who were to aid us in mapping the selected area and listing all the households (unit consisting of individuals eating from a common kitchen). Our movement plan in every state was conveyed to the concerned medical officers in advance to facilitate smooth implementation of the survey. On day two of the survey, 20 households were randomly chosen from this list and interviews, anthropometric and biochemical measurements of the selected individuals were taken. This process was completed over the next three days. After the mapping and listing of households, the assistance of the health workers was required only in certain challenging situations, as discussed below.

Social Capital—Driving the Community Health Worker Programme Forward

The concept of social capital partly explains how the involvement of community health workers has been instrumental in making health care more accessible. Bourdieu (1986) defines Social Capital as the capital of social connections, mutual acquaintance and social recognition. Putnam, Leonardi & Nanenetti (1993:167) define social capital as those "features of social organization, such as trust, norms, and networks that can improve the efficiency of society by facilitating coordinated actions." The health workers have come to represent government authority and are seen as friends who are working for the welfare of the community. Addressing a person as *didi* or elder sister itself is a signifier of familiarity and trust. It indicates an informal relationship which one would associate with ease of approachability.

The Putnam definition points to the role of social capital as a catalyst of coordination/cooperation, an essential device to achieve better (social and/or economic) outcomes (Rocco and Suhrcke, 2012). Coordination entails a range of potential benefits: it may help reduce transaction costs, overcome difficulties due to incomplete or asymmetric information and establish efficient transactions in the presence of incomplete contracts (Alesina & La Ferrara, 2002). This resonates with another instance that occurred in Dolly's village in Kapurthala. The survey team had set up camp, to measure fasting blood sugar levels of the participating individuals, in the primary school by 8 AM. Surrounded by mustard and sugarcane fields, we waited for participants to arrive in the biting cold. Only two of the twenty participants had arrived by 8.30 AM. Disappointed, we called up the health workers, asking for their assistance. As the sun tore through the mist, the gates of the school were swung open, and there Dolly was, with a wave of people. The wave of people were the participants. Our camp turned out to be a success and we achieved a 100 per cent response from the village.

It has been shown that having a high degree of social cohesion contributes measurably to economic growth and investment, to good governance, health and social security (Stanley, 2003, Maxwell, 1996). When accompanied by *didis,* we were warmly welcomed and long detailed conversations about the family health history ensued.

It is noteworthy how female health workers make access to health care easy for other women. Being women themselves, they know the kind of problems other women could be suffering from. They are required to make regular home visits in which they enquire about births or deaths, ailments and disabilities that people, especially women, might be facing. Being from within the community they have forged social connections throughout their lives and their work is socially recognised. This enables them to "improve the efficiency of society by facilitating coordinated actions", which suggests to their role in counselling people and mobilizing them to access health and health-related services. In this sense, AWW and ASHA become the primary sources of contact that rural women have with health care, and provide the only chance they have of meaningful, long term care relationships (Ward, 1988). These health workers are often viewed as educators and link-workers (Saprii *et al.,* 2015), wherein they link people with health care facilities. It might be argued that social capital cannot be overlooked by policy-makers when considering the most effective ways of improving health conditions (Rocco and Suhrcke, 2012).

There was a striking observation as far as people's participation in the survey was concerned. In urban areas there was a marked decline in participation. PSUs like Chandigarh, Mohali, Jalandhar, and Ludhiana reported an abysmal number of consenting adults. In one instance, we were even subjected to heated comments by a woman in a Delhi PSU. In another instance a woman Madhu, selected for the interview, herself answered the doorbell and told us that Madhu was not at home at that time. Such instances might be correlated with the absence of a figure like the AWW and ASHA, or due to the lack of authority that they enjoy in urban areas. Nevertheless, this indifference might be attributed to a whole range of other variables too.

During the course of the survey we faced the most unlikely of challenges: Rumours. There was word in the air that a group of young women and men were travelling across the states posing as government health workers and spreading the HIV virus, through means of infected needles, apparently being used to prick participants' fingers to obtain blood to determine blood sugar levels. Enhanced internet connectivity had made this information into a viral message that was being circulated across the region and had found more weight in the rural areas. This information hindered our progress in at least four PSUs. Alarmed rural folk often turned us back from their doorsteps. In Barara, Haryana our interview in one of the households was interrupted by a concerned neighbour; we were asked to leave thereafter. Had it not been for the Aanganwadi and ASHA workers our sample size would have greatly suffered.

Language proved to be a barrier at a lot of places. In rural communities of Punjab and Haryana, the Punjabi dialect spoken is very different from the vernacular that is popular in the media. The sounds, tempo, and pronunciations present as a major challenge in the course of the research. Moreover, from the street signs to health guidelines, most of the information is inscribed in Gurumukhi. Here the Aanganwadi Workers or ASHA become a medium of communication between the researcher and the natives, apart from providing a sense of ease and comfort for the natives to open up. Hence, rapport building becomes an easy exercise. The Aanganwadi Workers hence become a voice to the grievances and challenges that people face in rural as well as urban communities.

The Dark Side

Taking the social capital concept forward, it is very often the social connections only which help an individual secure the office of a health worker. As per rules laid down by the Health Ministry, the appointment of an AWW or ASHA must be made by a committee consisting of female representatives of the Panchayat Samiti, Block Development Officer, and Medical Officer at the Primary Health Centre (PHC). This committee is supposed to look into the applications and give points to candidates on certain suitability parameters. In some cases Focus Group Discussion or personal interviews of the candidates may be conducted. At the end, the candidate with the maximum points is selected. However, the reality is very different in many places. Bribing to secure the office is quite common. Bribes of as much as Rs. 25,000-50,000 are often shelled out by those desirous of becoming AWWs. The job security, in spite of the low wages, is what entices women to pay huge bribes for this job (Although AWW do not enjoy the status of a government employee, their employment is not terminated until there are not any serious lapses on their part). 'Contacts' with influential decision-making bodies in villages can also be instrumental in securing the office since they have representation in the selection committee too. As such, the entire selection procedure often becomes a mere charade.

The position of an ASHA, however, is not sought after as she is entitled only to 'performance based incentives', rather than a fixed salary.

One might argue that being a resident of the village, or to say an 'insider', an AWW or ASHA may be looked at as a respected, familiar figure, irrespective of how she secured the office. But that is not always the case.

A System in Peril

Paramjeet recounts an incident that occurred two years ago when a newly-wedded woman in her village in Haryana was diagnosed with a complicated pregnancy. Paramjeet along with the other health workers in the village took it upon themselves to provide her with vitamin supplements, moral support and the best care possible. Paramjeet herself accompanied her to Chandigarh for her delivery. But neither the mother nor the child could be saved. Paramjeet laments how even the best possible intentions can sometimes result in something catastrophic. She feels helpless and at the same time guilty of whatever happened.

A large proportion of people still lack an awareness of health issues, health services and education. To make matters worse, the health infrastructure is underdeveloped and there is a paucity of health care specialists. As a result, violence against doctors and health workers is on the rise. Paramjeet found herself in the eye of the storm when despite her best efforts neither the mother nor the child could be saved. Blaming the Aanganwadi and health workers, the family of the deceased have shown hostility towards them and eventually shunned all forms of government health care. A law or a health scheme is not of much use if the target population lacks awareness of their rights and the services that they are entitled to.

It was observed that these health workers have become a vent for people's anger and frustration against the ruling regime. Even I experienced this 'displacement' when a middle-aged gentleman in Jalandhar gave me a small talk on what the government should actually be doing. The brief talk was generously garnished with unparliamentary language directed towards the government, and apologies to me. Much the same way, health workers also face such instances of anger displacement regularly.

However, it would be wrong to say that hostility towards health workers is completely unfounded. At many PSUs there was an attitude of shrugging off responsibility by health workers. In a Delhi PSU, in spite of prior information about the survey, we were greeted with a locked Aanganwadi centre. Apparently, the AWW of the area was running a personal errand for which she had taken off early that day. It was only when we directly contacted the Medical Superintendant at the dispensary that we were able to get in touch with other health workers of the area. While reprimanding the concerned AWW for the lax, she arranged for other workers to fill in her stead. In another incident, the health worker assigned to us repeatedly made pleas that she be relieved as she had been up since quite early that day. While parting she asked us to speak well of her, for the assistance she had provided, before the senior medical officers.

Very often records such as those of birth-death, immunisation and daily activities are not properly maintained. In a slum area in North Delhi, animosity between AWW of adjoining blocks was noticed. The AWW of the block designated for the survey could not be contacted. The other health workers did not have any information of her whereabouts. Her indifference was attributed to her seniority, being in the profession for over 20 years. When she was finally located, it was discovered that her registers were incomplete. This entire conundrum cost the survey team valuable time. This territorial nature of work is common in other states too, where every AWW's area is clearly demarcated and nobody dares to trespass into another's. In rural areas, these boundaries are less rigid.

There have been cases of hoarding medical supplies by ASHA and appropriation of grants meant for the Aanganwadi Centre by AWW, as I was told by one health worker. This, however, is beyond the scope of this chapter.[2]

The Precarious Position of Women Health Workers

By the final few weeks of the project, the survey team had picked up quite a speed. Reaching Patiala a day in advance, on a Sunday, a meeting with the Village Sarpanch was fixed. It was heartening to see a woman Sarpanch leading the village. An Aanganwadi worker and an ASHA worker were called who gladly provided us assistance even on a holiday. Jasvir accompanied me to every household of the village that day helping me record important demographic information. It was only then when I was told that for all the hard work that these women put in they are only paid a pittance.

ASHA workers do not draw a monthly salary unlike the Aanganwadi workers. They are paid according to the number of individuals that they immunise or vaccinate. In other words, their pay is a function of the number of live births occurring in the village. This system of payment is oblivious to many of their contributions.

It is interesting to note that sometimes the responsibilities of these health workers stretches beyond the realm of health care. They are expected to register people for AADHAR cards or Voter ID cards. Their presence is mandated at every event organised by the government in the village or *tehsil,* for which they do not receive any extra payment.

In September of 2018, AWW from across India participated in a rally in Delhi asking the Central Government to heed to their call for better wages. Another demand was to be identified as government employees rather than voluntary social workers. AWW and ASHA provide invaluable health services. Aanganwadi centres are still, for a large proportion of children in the country, their first tryst with health and pre-school education.

Later, as a 'Diwali Gift' to the AWW and ASHA, the Central Government announced a hike in remuneration. While AWW's honorarium has been hiked by Rs. 1500, there has been an increase of Rs. 1,250 per month for mini-AWW. For ASHA, the doubling of routine incentives given by the Union Government was announced, along with an insurance cover. Performance-based incentives were also announced. The other demand of being recognised as government employees was not addressed.

Leaders of Aanganwadi Workers' Unions expressed dissatisfaction at this hike, terming it as meagre.

Against All Odds: Women Health Workers and their Service to the Community

Nadira is the Multipurpose Worker at the Primary Health Centre in Poonch, Jammu & Kashmir. Although trained in Medical Laboratory Technology, her responsibilities stretch much beyond the confines of a microscope. She has keenly participated in the Pulse Polio Campaigns in the district, reaching even the remotest of homes in the hilly and rugged terrain. An outspoken woman, she has given voice to various issues that women face in the community. Her proactiveness and boldness are an inspiration for many women in the community.

Many women are taking to the job of a health worker for the self-reliance and respect that it brings to them. The remuneration they receive, however meagre, gives them a sense of being the makers of their own destinies. Then there are also those who wish to do their bit for the people. "Feels good to be working for the welfare of my sisters", iterates Amrinder, another ASHA from Kapurthala. Her words echo a sense of kinship within the community.

An increasing number of women and men look up to them as role models and leaders. Nadira very proudly recollected how she once drove the entire woman staff of the Primary Health Centre up the perilous Mughal Road to the *Peer Ki Gali* pass for a picnic. Her quirky personality has made her a favourite in every household of the village.

These women also play the role of teachers who are actively educating the community; pillars of strength during illness and agony; change-makers, marching to their own beat.

It is ironic how these health workers who have nursed millions out of disease and distress are themselves not immune from these. It is imperative to impart recognition to their contributions. This recognition would certainly have a bearing on the country's health care programme.

It is vital to address the inefficiencies that are being reported. Appropriate measures such as reducing the workload of a population of 1000 individuals on a single AWW and providing monthly monetary incentives for ASHA would attract more women to join this workforce, giving them an opportunity to be independent.

A feedback mechanism for these health workers to cite the challenges and grievances that they face could also be put in place. These measures would go a long way in realising the ideals enshrined in the constitution—that of equality, socialism and liberty.

Conclusion

Services provided by AWW and ASHA represent a key resource which, if channelised properly, could forward India's health programme. The knowledge and familiarity with the community that they possess is an asset for the same. While they have an important role to play in the delivery of basic health facilities in often remote, margins of society, a better health infrastructure is an essential complement to this goal. It is also important to address the specific challenges that these women face while discharging their duties, whether logistic or as far as emoluments are concerned. Favourable employment condition is a prerequisite to a productive workforce.

Achievement of the highest possible level of health care also requires coordination from social and economic sectors, not merely the health sector.

To sum up, in the words of the British poet Lord Alfred Tennyson (Wages, 1870),

> "*Nay, but she aim'd not at glory,*
> *no lover of glory she;*
> *Give her the glory of going on, and still to be.*"
> (all names have been changed)

Acknowledgements

1. National Centre for Disease Informatics and Research (NCDIR), Bengaluru.
2. National Centre for Disease Control (NCDC), Delhi.

NOTES

1. As part of the survey, 20 households were selected from each PSU by Random Sampling Method. In each of these households, one adult (18-69 years of age) and all adolescents (15-17 years of age) were selected to participate in the survey. They were interviewed on the risk factors of the NCDs such as tobacco and alcohol consumption, salt intake, dietary intake and physical activity. This information was obtained using standard questionnaires by Medical Social Workers. Apart from this, anthropometric measurements such as BMI (Body Mass Index), Waist Circumference and Fasting Blood sugar levels and Urine samples were also collected by Lab Technicians/Fieldworkers. Primary and Secondary Health care Facilities were also surveyed for their preparedness in managing NCDs.
   Non-Communicable Diseases or NCDs refer to chronic diseases such as Diabetes, Cardiovascular Diseases, Cancer and Chronic Obstructive Pulmonary Diseases (COPD), which are a result of a combination of genetic, lifestyle and environmental factors.
   Each of the 10 implementing agencies was entrusted with the responsibility of recruiting a team consisting of an equal number of Medical Social Workers and Field Workers/Lab Technicians, and a Research Associate. The team from the National Centre for Disease Control (NCDC), Delhi, of which I was a part, carried out the survey in seven states of North India—Jammu & Kashmir, Himachal Pradesh, Uttarakhand, Punjab, Haryana, Chandigarh and Delhi.
   The results of the survey are under analysis and will be released shortly.
2. For a detailed discussion on the topic see Drèze, J. (2016).

REFERENCES

A Handbook for Nutrition Trainers of Anganwadi Workers. (1984). New Delhi: National Institute of Public Cooperation and Child Development.

Alesina, A., La Ferrara, E. (2002). "Who trusts others?" *Journal of Public Economics*, *85*(2): 207-234.

Asad, T. (2004). "Where Are the Margins of the State?" In V. Das & D. Poole (Authors), *Anthropology in the Margins of the State* (pp. 279-288). New Delhi: Oxford University Press.

Bourdieu, P. (1986). "The Forms of Capital." In Richardson, J.G. (ed.) *Handbook of Theory and Research in the Sociology of Education*. New York: Greenwald Press (pp. 241-258).

Das, V., & Poole, D. (2004). *Anthropology in the Margins of the State*. New Delhi: Oxford University Press.

Drèze, J. (2016). *Social Policy*. New Delhi: Orient Black Swan.

Joshi, S. & Mathews, G. (2012). "Health care through community participation: role of ASHAs." *Economic and Political Weekly*. *47*(10), 70.

Kaur, M., Prinja, S., Singh, P., & Kumar, R. (2012). "Decentralization of health services in India: Barriers and facilitating factors." *WHO South-East Asia Journal of Public Health, 1*(1), 94. doi:10.4103/2224-3151.206920.

Maxwell, J. (1996). "Social Dimensions of Economic Growth." *The Eric John Hanson Memorial Lecture Series, VIII*.

Ministry of Health and Family Welfare, Government of India. (2005). *National Health Mission–Vision Document*. Retrieved from https://nhm.gov.in/images/pdf/guidelines/nrhm-guidelines/mission_document.pdf

Ministry of Women and Child Welfare, Government of India. (2013). *Role Delineation of Frontline Workers—A Framework for Convergence of Health and ICDS*. Retrieved from https://icds-wcd.nic.in/icdsimg/Role07114.pdf

Mukherjee, P. & Saraswati, L.R. (2011, January). "Levels and Patterns of Social Cohesion and Its Relationship with Development in India: A Woman's Perspective Approach." *International Conference on Social Cohesion and Development*.

Naimoli, J.F., Perry, H.B., Townsend, J.W., Frymus, D.E., & Mccaffery, J.A. (2015). "Strategic partnering to improve community health worker programming and performance: Features of a community-health system integrated approach." *Human Resources for Health, 13*(1). doi:10.1186/s12960-015-0041-3.

National Health Systems Resource Centre (2011). *ASHA Which Way Forward: Evaluation of ASHA Programme 2010-11*. New Delhi. Retrieved from http://nhsrcindia.org/index.php?option=com_

Park, K. (2011). *Park's Textbook of Preventive and Social Medicine* (21st ed.). Jabalpur: Banarasidas Bhanot.

Prinja, S., Jeet, G., Verma, R., Kumar, D., Bahuguna, P., Kaur, M., & Kumar, R. (2014). "Economic Analysis of Delivering Primary Health Care Services through Community Health Workers in 3 North Indian States." *PLoS ONE, 9*(3). doi:10.1371/journal.pone.0091781.

Primary health care report of the International Conference on Primary Health Care Alma-Ata, USSR, 6-12 September 1978. (1978). Geneva: WHO.

Putnam, R.D., Leonardi, R. & Nanenetti, R. (1993). *Making Democracy Work: Civic Traditions in Modern Italy*. Princeton, NJ: Princeton University Press.

Rao, T. (2014). "The Impact of a Community Health Worker Programme on Childhood Immunization: Evidence from India's 'ASHA' Workers." *SSRN Electronic Journal*. doi:10.2139/ssrn.2444391.

Rocco, L. & Suhrcke, M. (2012). *Is Social Capital Good for Health? A European perspective*. Copenhagen: WHO Regional Office for Europe.

Saprii, L., Richards, E., Kokho, P., and Theobald, S. (2015). "Community health workers in rural India: Analysing the opportunities and challenges of Accredited Social Health Activists (ASHAs) face in realising their multiple roles." *Human Resources for Health, 13*(1). doi:10.1186/s12960-015-0094-3.

Schneider, H. & Lehmann, U. (2016). From Community Health Workers to Community Health Systems: Time to Widen the Horizon? *Health Systems & Reform, 2*(2), 112-118. doi:10.1080/23288604.2016.1166307.

Schneider, H., Okello, D., & Lehmann, U. (2016). "The global pendulum swing towards community health workers in low- and middle-income countries: A scoping review of trends, geographical distribution and programmatic orientations, 2005 to 2014." *Human Resources for Health*, 14(1). doi:10.1186/s12960-016-0163-2.

Scott, K., George, A., & Ved, R. (2019). "Taking stock of 10 years of published research on the ASHA programme: Examining India's national community health worker programme from a health systems perspective." *Health Research Policy and Systems*. doi:10.1186/s12961-019-0427-0.

Scott, K., & Shanker, S. (2010). "Tying their hands? Institutional obstacles to the success of the ASHA community health worker programme in rural north India." *AIDS Care, 22* (Sup. 2), 1606-1612. doi:10.1080/09540121.2010.507751.

Stanley, D. (2003). "What Do We Know About Social Cohesion: The Research Perspective of the Federal Government's Social Cohesion Research Network." *The Canadian Journal of Sociology, 28*(1).

Tennyson, A. (1870). "Wages." In *Holy Grail and Other Poems*. London: Straham and Co.

Tulenko, K., Møgedal, S., Afzal, M.M., Frymus, D., Oshin, A., Pate, M., Zodpey, S. (2013). "Community health workers for universal health-care coverage: From fragmentation to synergy." *Bulletin of the World Health Organization, 91*(11), 847-852. doi:10.2471/blt.13.118745.

Ward, K.S. (1988). *Women, and Health in Rural India: An Anthropological Perspective*. (Published Honors Thesis) Oberlin College, Ohio.

World Health Organization. (2016). *Global Strategy on Human Resources for Health Workforce 2030-Draft for the 69th World Health Assembly*. Geneva: WHO.

22

Institutional Response to Tribal Health in India: A Public Policy Perspective within the Paradigm of 'Anthropology of Empathy'

Prashant Khattri and *P.C. Joshi*

Introduction

Economic development seems to be the buzz word in the contemporary global scenario. Developing countries are in the race of projecting their image in terms of better economic growth in order to attract investments from the developed world, especially America. The development model to which this kind of economic growth subscribes is the outcome of the post-cold-war era that established the hegemony and thus necessary dependence on the market for economic growth. The Indian growth story, picks up its pace after liberalization and the economic governance started aiming at the magical double digit growth figures. The methodology adopted for this kind of growth was large-scale industrialization that was based upon harnessing and exploiting natural resources and energy. Industrialization, however, was not new to the Indian growth story as it can be traced back to the post-Independence era where the Nehruvian developmental model occupied the central stage, but a clear difference between the post-Independence and post-liberalization era is evident in terms of greater de-regulation and market orientation in the post-liberalization phase.

This developmental model had a direct bearing on the Indian society as a whole. Being a highly heterogeneous society, in terms of socio-cultural and economic dimension, the outcome of this model has been differential in nature. People who were well-equipped to harvest the fruits of this model were the ones who could gain the most out of it. This was determined by the economic and political capital of different groups which made them fit such a model. In this backdrop, people who suffered the most were the 'tribal' groups of India. For them, the developmental model worked as a double-edged sword. On the one hand, they were not well-equipped to take full advantage of the opportunities that came in with this model and, on the other hand, they became victims of the large-scale exploitation of the natural resources for industrial manufacturing that happen to be in the areas inhabited by such tribal groups. This exemplifies the fact that such a model of development would be dependent solely on the perspective of an economic growth which is not inclusive and has excluded a very large section of the Indian population that make up roughly 8 per cent of the entire population.

This calls for redefining development in terms of "expansion of substantive human freedoms." In other words, development should not only be measured in terms of Gross Domestic Product (GDP) and economic growth but also in terms of the enhancement of human capabilities, freedom to choose and expand and enrichment of the overall quality of life. This model can be successful only when there is substantial investment and focus on the various social dimensions that may be helpful in defining substantive human freedoms. It has been argued that for an inclusive growth and development, it is necessary to invest in certain important social variables that make inclusive development possible. Two such important variables identified and exemplified by Dreze and Sen (2002) are education and health. It is in this context that health gets synchronized with the larger developmental narrative. Health is considered to be of prime importance *vis-à-vis* economic development. The dimension of health is important in the context of a freedom-centred model of development. Being healthy can expand the capabilities and capacities of an individual for better utilization of economic opportunities, which has been exemplified in the context of China. Comparing the growth stories of India and China, Dreze and Sen (2002) have highlighted that it was pre-reform focus on social sectors like health and education in China that had contributed immensely towards the post-reform utilization of economic opportunities. This, in turn has, to a very large extent, made the post-reform economic opportunities available to a very large section of people who had the skills and necessary motivations to utilize these opportunities. On the other hand, "*India's failure to have an adequate public policy in education and health matters can be...of profound significance in assessing the limited success of Indian development efforts over the last half a century*" (Dreze and Sen, 2002: 40). However, in the post-reform China (late 1970s), due to the rapid expansion of private economy, public services in health care have received a major setback. The Indian story, in the post-liberalization era is not very different from the Chinese experience in the health sector. The discourse in the field of modern health care has not always been devoid of larger political systems. Whether it is biological or chemical warfare, swine-flu, bird-flu and related country specific quarantine or the notion of public health, the modern health care model has always been influenced and, in turn, influences the political-economy of a geographical space in which it is negotiated. The contemporary debate on health care practices has evolved from being "person-centred" to the one that has far-reaching consequences for the larger cultural, political and social systems. The functional metamorphosis in the so-called 'modern health care system' has occurred from being healthcare oriented to the one that is market-driven and embedded in the ideology of consumerism. The hegemony of corporate pharmaceutical companies, branded drugs and patent laws has raised some serious questions on the naïve health-care dimension of modern medicine. The debate on branded and generic drugs situates the larger issue of monopoly and affordability within the framework of dichotomous understanding of politicizing modern medicine. It has also created a space for a critical understanding of health and its institutionalization. However, the Indian healthcare scenario is not limited to modern medicine, but rather it extends to include AYUSH and other alternative systems within its fold. Nonetheless, the larger narrative of private economy, profit maximization and rapid institutionalization of health care services have, to a large extent, restricted the free-flow of the advantages of these health care systems to the grass-root level (Khattri and Joshi, 2015).

Viewed alternatively, health is one of the important indicators of development. If the development of a country depends upon the sound health of its citizens, then good health, in turn, is an indicator of development. In the context of the state being a primary health provider as it projects itself to be a welfare state, health become more of a political issue. This has important consequences for how health outcomes are projected in terms of statistical figures. It also has important bearings on the conceptualization of the health care delivery system which may become more mechanistic rather than humanistic. It is in this context that the present chapter tries to argue that there has been a transformation in the way the State plays its role *vis-à-vis* public health which has important consequences for tribal health. The chapter is based upon visiting and re-visiting some of the important policy documents related to health in general and tribal health in particular. The author through policy documents tries to understand how the state is responding to the health care needs of the marginalized sections of Indian society.

Modern State and the Post-Modern Society: Contextualizing Health and State

The discourse of modernity led to simplification and reduction of our histories. A Eurocentric scientific model of health and medicine emerged out of this modern discourse that ignored the inter-flow and the fact that various health care systems had been mutually informed by each other. For example rhinoplasty as discussed in the *Susrut Samhita* in the Indian tradition was studied and adopted by the European physicians and surgeons during the eighteenth century. During the sixteenth and seventeenth century different medical systems came in contact with each other due to trade between countries and mutually informed each other. In this context V. Sujatha (2014: 146) writes, "these early medical interactions and experiments are insightful events in themselves to understand cultural assimilation. It was by no means a one-sided or linear process, rather one of mutual curiosity and learning."

For long, in the Indian Subcontinent, indigenous health providers like *vaidyas* and *hakims* were patronized by kings and kingdoms. It was only in the eighteenth century that Western medicine was introduced in India (Sujatha, 2014). This led to a head-on collision between two different health care systems—indigenous on the one hand and Western on the other. This led to certain changes in the way indigenous systems were practiced. Practitioners started charging consultation fee (earlier they used to get grains and land in return for their services) and started advertising their remedies for various ailments. Kings who patronized native medicine tried to protect and preserve the indigenous system. The Maratha ruler of Tanjore started a health research and training institute called 'Dhanvantari Mahal' where Ayurvedic, Siddha, Unani and Allopathic physicians were called to conduct research on medicine. Many Indian and European texts were compiled and put up in the library to make indigenous practitioners aware of the new kind of medical system.

From mid-nineteenth century onwards, the colonial rulers started cancelling various grants and concessions that were given to the indigenous practitioners by kings. There was also a shift of political power from the kings towards the colonial rulers that led to a withdrawal of state patronage and the indigenous medical system was now only supported by some private patrons. Medical schools were opened by the colonial government where allopathic courses on medicine were taught. This was also the time when the evolutionary paradigm of looking at society and culture dominated and acted as a legitimizing force for colonization. This established modern, Western medicine as the only legitimate and standard medical system driven by science and knowledge. The European model of society and culture was considered to be at the epitome of the evolutionary ladder. Medicine was but one part of this monolithic cultural model.

It can be gauged from the above discussion that the plurality of medical systems metamorphosed into a single homogeneous and hegemonic health care system patronized by the colonial masters and later by the Indian state. This happened despite the fact that the larger society still subscribed to plural medical models of disease causation and treatment regimens. The Indian state played a crucial role in making modern medicine the ideal form to which other systems have to conform to prove their legitimacy and importance. Shamshad Khan, while tracing such an attempt, takes us to 1939, when the United Provinces Indian Medicine Bill was passed by the United Provinces Legislative Assembly. During the discussion, modern medicine was idealized. The colonial outlook overpowered the minds of people and Western standards acted as the reference, overshadowing other alternative systems and their ethos (Khan, 2006).

More recently, The National Medical Commission Bill, 2017, addresses the issue of medical pluralism in a very different way that may eventually lead to medical homogenization. It has been proposed that various medical bodies dealing with Indian and other systems of medicine like homoeopathy should sit together with National Medical Commission Board and propose a 'bridge course' that may help practitioners from medical systems other than Allopathy to prescribe some forms of 'modern medicine.' This may be seen as being against the spirit of medical pluralism and what to talk about tribal systems of medicine getting some recognition or acceptance within the larger hegemonic system governed by Allopathy (Mazumder, 2018).

Health Conditions among the Tribal Groups in India

The tribal population in India constitutes a little more than 8 per cent of the total population. It is not a homogeneous group. Different tribal groups are present at different locations in India speaking different languages and having varied social-cultural and politico-economic co-ordinates. They are also one of the most marginalized and vulnerable sections of Indian society. Recognizing this fact, the Constitution of India has made several protective and developmental provisions for safeguarding the interests of these groups.

As far as health is concerned, the Xaxa Committee Report, 2014, on the status of Scheduled Tribes in India, has made some revealing observations. It is stated in the report that, "At the state level there is data on fertility and mortality, but there is no data generated for the Scheduled Tribes, which is important for targeted approach of planning and programme implementation. This could also be one of the important factors for poor results from interventions in tribal areas and there is no way to monitor or evaluate the programme" (pp. 197). The National Family Health Survey, conducted by the Ministry of Health and Family Welfare, GoI during 2015-16 reveals that the Scheduled Tribe population in India has a higher prevalence of Infant Mortality Rate, Under Five Mortality Rate and percentage of women between 15-49 years of age suffering from anaemia when compared to the rest of the population. On the indicator of nutritional status of under-five children they scored lower than the rest of the population.

The Xaxa Committee Report also highlights that there has not been any concerted effort on the part of various agencies in India to look into the kinds of diseases and disease pattern that is prevalent among the Scheduled Tribes. There are only discrete studies done by some agencies like the ICMR (Indian Council for Medical Research) and some Central and State funded agencies. This leads to only some broad generalizations about the disease pattern among the ST population. The report has categorized diseases prevalent among the ST population into three categories, viz. (a) diseases of underdevelopment that include malnutrition, communicable diseases and maternal and child health problems, (b) diseases that are common to ST population like the sickle cell anaemia and G-6 PD deficiency, and (c) diseases of modernity that include hypertension, alcoholism, stress etc.

Beyond health indicators, the ST population also scores low on various other indicators that are important for health. This includes general sanitation and the availability of clean drinking water. The Census 2011 data reveals that only 11 per cent of ST households have access to tap water and around 3 per cent have access to tap water from treated sources.

Institutional Response towards Tribal Health

This scenario has elicited some special response towards the health needs of the tribes by the biggest player in this sector in terms of investment—

the Government of India. The Ministry of Health and Family Welfare is dedicated towards the goal of a healthy India. There are also some special provisions made by the Health Ministry to cater to the special needs of the tribes. To begin with, the population norms for setting up of primary health care infrastructures have been relaxed for tribal areas. This has been done keeping in mind the special needs of better infrastructural facilities required in the far-flung regions—hill and forest areas—which holds a large tribal population. Having said this, the ground realities project a different picture. As mentioned in the latest report (2017-18) of the Ministry of Tribal Affairs, Government of India, it is contended that, "At all India level, there is a shortfall of 6503 Sub-Centres (SCs), 1240 Primary Health Centres (PHCs) and 273 Community Health Centres (CHCs) in tribal areas as on 31st March, 2017 as compared to requirements. Further, there is a huge shortfall in the number of Sub-Centres in Madhya Pradesh (1806), Rajasthan (1239), Maharashtra (945), Karnataka (822) and Odisha (309)" (pp. 32). The report also mentions that there is a shortfall of doctors at PHCs in tribal areas of Chhattisgarh, Madhya Pradesh and Odisha. Besides this, there is also a shortfall of health workers at the SCs and PHCs. This suggests that even after having a policy of treating tribal areas as special areas needing special care and help, the actual ground reality is far from being realized completely.

The Indian health care sector is a mix of both public and private players. As far as accessibility and affordability of medical services are concerned, it is the public sector which shares the maximum burden. However, recently, the private sector has also been roped in to expand the government's base of health care providers in the form of public-private partnership. A case in point here is the 'Arogyashri' scheme launched by the Andhra Pradesh government where this PPP model is followed. The rationale behind such models is that since the governmental infrastructure and health-care service are inadequate in terms of the demands that it needs to cater, and a majority of super-speciality is positioned in the hands of private players, therefore such model would be useful in bridging the gap between technological innovations and health-care availability. However, such health-care models prove to be far from effective as they are based on the neo-liberal ideology in health care which treats patients as consumers of health care, the only difference being that the consumer in this sector knows little about the services and its nuances due to a hierarchical model of the modern medical system (Prasad and Raghavendra, 2012).

As already stated above, that one of the reasons for the implementation of such models pertain to the lack of adequate health care provisions in

the government sector. Shortcomings in the health sector are also echoed in the draft XII Five Year Plan document that identifies some important areas that need adequate attention in future, viz. availability of health care, quality and affordability. It is contended that, public and private sector taken together, fall short of the desired number of personnel in the health sector. Rural areas are the worst sufferers. As far as quality of health care is concerned, there is a shortage of qualified doctors. Regulatory standards are also not up to the mark and are poorly enforced. "*Affordability of health care is a serious problem for the vast majority of the population, especially in tertiary care. The lack of extensive and adequately funded public health services pushes large numbers of people to incur heavy out of pocket expenditures on services purchased from the private sector. Out of pocket expenditures arise even in public sector hospitals, since lack of medicines means that patients have to buy them. This results in a very high financial burden on families in case of severe illness. A large fraction of the out of pocket expenditure arises from outpatient care and purchase of medicines, which are mostly not covered even by the existing insurance schemes. In any case, the percentage of population covered by health insurance is small*" (Twelfth Five Year Plan document: Volume III, p. 1). Another issue that is of great relevance here is the share of GDP that is spent on the health sector. Public expenditure on health was 0.93 per cent of the GDP in 2007-08. In 2011-12 it rose to 1.04 per cent and according to the XII Plan public expenditure needs to be much more than the present level. The Twelfth Plan outlines an inclusive agenda for health care that envisages special attention to marginalized groups like SC, ST, Particularly Vulnerable Tribal Groups, De-notified Tribes, Nomadic Tribes etc. Some special services like counselling of mental health patients in conflict ridden areas and supply of artificial appendages to differently abled also form part of the inclusive agenda on health care. For the first time, the Twelfth Five Year Plan document incorporated the idea of Universal Health Care/Universal Health Coverage. This has been defined as, "*Ensuring equitable access for all Indian citizens in any part of the country, regardless of income level, social status, gender, caste or religion, to affordable, accountable and appropriate, assured quality health services (promotive, preventive, curative and rehabilitative) as well as services addressing wider determinants of health delivered to individuals and populations, with the Government being the guarantor and enabler, although not necessarily the only provider of health and related services*" (Twelfth Five Year Plan Document: Volume III, p. 10).

On a more pragmatic level, it has been argued that the Indian

health care is dependent largely on three kinds of health providers or practitioners viz., medical doctors trained in modern medicine, doctors trained in alternative system of medicine and untrained and unqualified health providers who do not come out of any formal structure of medical system. It is contended that the first two kinds of health practitioners cater to the needs of merely 20-25 per cent of the people and, on the other hand, the rest 80-75 per cent of the population are at the mercy of unqualified health providers. The reason for such a skewed distribution can be found ranging from unaffordable cost of treatment to inaccessibility of such health practitioners (Joshi and Kalla, 2004 and Prasad, 2007). Also on another plane most of the so-called unqualified health providers come from within the cultural matrix of the people to whom they cater and therefore are easily accessible. They also provide remedies and solution to health problems which are in-sync with the larger worldviews of the entire community.

Tribal Health Care and National Health Policies in India

India has witnessed the formulation of three National Health Policies (NHP) at different times separated by big gaps. The first policy came up in 1983, then, the second in 2002, and the third policy document came up in 2017. It is really interesting to read these policy documents *vis-à-vis* tribal health. The NHP of 1983 documents the need for starting nutrition programmes for pregnant women, nursing mothers and children especially in the tribal, hilly and backward areas. In the policy document tribal health is also dealt with within the heading, "Need for providing primary health care with special emphasis on the preventive, promotive and rehabilitative aspects." Within this, it was realized that priority should be given to people residing in tribal, hilly and backward regions of the country. The policy document also talks about the 'exploitation' of the services of the private medical practitioners, more specifically, those that belong to traditional and other systems of medicine.

The NHP of 2002 is unique in the way that it talks about the importance of Information, Education and Communication (IEC). It is realized within the policy document that there has to be maximum dissemination of information to the population groups that cannot be reached only through mass media. Other forms of communication like the inter-personal, folk and traditional media should be used to disseminate information. This will lead to directed behavioural changes including health behaviours among various groups of population.

The NHP 2017 recognizes that tribal population in India constitutes around 100 million people and hence deserves special attention. It also recognizes that tribal population does have some special health needs. The policy also calls for validation of tribal medicine. The NHP of 2017 lays focus on developing a mechanism of certification. It is envisaged within the policy that a mechanism needs to be developed through which the prior knowledge of 'traditional community health care provider' can be certified. However, the policy does not spell out clearly that what purpose will this certification solve? Also, the mechanism of certification is not spelled out in the policy document. The certification issue has been dealt with under the section on 'mainstreaming the potential of AYUSH.' This makes the 'traditional community health care provider' an ambiguous entity. A question arises in this context that is it the mechanism by which the government wants to integrate AYUSH with the local and tribal health care traditions? The Anthropological perspective on health and health care systems has informed us that there are innumerable kinds of health care systems that are prevalent among the various tribal groups in India. These systems are based on their own understanding of illness and health and prescribe different treatment regimens based on their specific understandings. Such health care systems do not find mention in the policy document.

In Anthropological parlance, tradition has been understood in at least two ways, viz. the Great Tradition and the Little Tradition. The Great Tradition is the one that is associated with the great ancient texts, while the Little Tradition is the one that is related with the oral tradition of various tribal groups in India. It is, therefore, contended that when the policy document is using the term traditional community health care provider, then it largely means the health care providers of the different AYUSH systems and hence leaving a bigger chunk of tribal health care providers unaccounted for.

Tribal Health and the Draft National Tribal Policy, 2006

It is one of the greatest ironies in one of the biggest democracies in the world that despite having tribal populations of over 80 million we still do not have a National Tribal Policy. The Government of India is still in the stage of drafting a tribal policy. However, in the name of the tribal policy what we do have is the Draft National Tribal Policy (DNTP) of 2006. This draft is actually dealing with the tribal health under a separate section. It first recognizes that tribal groups in India do have some special health needs as they are vulnerable to various kinds of diseases. Also, the draft recognizes that tribal population lags behind on many of the health indicators like under-five mortality and morbidity, women health, general mortality and morbidity, etc.

Thus, the policy states calls for some special provisions that needs to be made to address the specific needs of the tribal groups. The draft says that there should be a synthesis of the Indian systems of medicine like the Ayurveda and Siddha with the tribal system and also with modern medicine. However, the point remains that how this synthesis is going to be achieved. There have been no concerted efforts on the part of the policy-makers to come up with a strategy under which this synthesis can be achieved. The other issue is, does this synthesis mean assimilation of different systems or does it mean an integration? Anthropological experiences in the context of cultural contact between the tribal and the non-tribal groups have led them to believe that it was assimilation more than integration that has occurred. It was Jawaharlal Nehru who was of the opinion that the tribal groups in India should develop but at the same time they should also retain their culture and social values. In the preface to the *Philosophy of NEFA* written by Verrier Elwin, Nehru formulated the tribal Panchsheel under which he opined that the policy of integration should be adopted in the context of tribal development. However, studies mostly in Central India have shown that tribal identity was getting assimilated into the larger regional and state identities. This has happened with many of the tribal languages and other cultural attributes. Within this backdrop, the issue of synthesis should always be seen from a critical perspective.

It is also contended by the authors that although the DNTP is talking about a synthesis of the Indian system with the tribal system but what is meant by the term 'system of medicine' needs to be looked at more closely. In anthropological writings, systems have been understood in terms of consisting of different parts that combine together into a functional unity to maintain the society as a whole. The tribal system of medicine, therefore, would not only constitute the knowledge of medicinal plants and other herbs that are used in treating different conditions but essentially means the entire tribal cosmology related to health and illness. This would include different kinds of health specialists and their own understanding of disease causation and treatment regimens. Different systems of medicines might be based upon different etiologies of disease causation. Foster has identified two different kinds of disease causation theories that are prevalent, viz. the personalistic and the naturalistic. The personalistic theory identifies the cause of disease and ill-health in certain malevolent and benevolent spirits and forces. The naturalistic theory, on the other hand, identifies natural causes of illness. Ayurveda and Siddha are based on naturalistic disease causation theory, on the other hand, most of the tribal worldview about illness and disease are based on the personalistic theory. Does the DNTP intend to integrate these systems of medicines?

Further, the DNTP outlines some administrative provisions, in an attempt to address the health issues among the tribal groups. Within the provisions of the PESA Act, 1996, the draft states that at the level of the sub-centre, the Gram Sabha would have the power to control the para-medical staff, again at the level of Primary Health Centres (PHCs), the intermediate *panchayat* would have control over the medical and para-medical staff of the PHCs. Going further, the policy states that at the level of the Community Health Centres (CHCs) the *zilla panchayat* would have control over the medical and para-medical staff. Two practical issues rather questions emerge from looking at these provisions viz., (1) These provisions are made under the PESA Act, giving the impression that all those areas not covered under the PESA that is the Fifth Schedule Areas will not be covered by these provisions, and (2) The draft policy talks only about tribal groups concentrated in the areas under Fifth Schedule and it is really silent on the tribal groups that are part of the areas under the Sixth Schedule of the Indian Constitution. These areas are in the North-East India and are inhabited by sizeable number of tribal populations. One of the reasons for the non-inclusion of these areas in the draft policy could be the greater autonomy that has been accorded to these areas under the Constitution. However, this approach to tribal health seems to be a more administrative and its effects and influences can only be gauged after such policies come into effect.

Do We Need a Tribal Health Policy?: Looking Tribal Health Care System from 'Strength's Perspective'

There is no National Tribal Policy in India till date. What we have in the name of the tribal policy is a draft that was prepared by the Ministry of Tribal Affairs in the year 2006. The Hon'ble Minister of State for Tribal Affairs, in a reply to a question in Rajya Sabha in 2016 stated that the National Tribal Policy is still at the stage of being formulated in the wake of changes that were made in laws related to tribes over a period of time.[1] In this context, it is really futile to expect a National Tribal Health Policy. Such a need also does not figure in various policy documents related with health in general.

K. Sujatha Rao (1998), while writing on the policy dimension of health care services in tribal areas of Andhra Pradesh, states that the need of the hour is to formulate a health policy for the tribe that is in sync with the epidemiology and levels of social development in tribal areas. It is further reiterated that the strategies and approaches that are adopted for disease control in non-tribal areas cannot be automatically extended to the tribal areas. The reason behind this being poor communication, acute poverty, low literacy and social and cultural variations. She further says that a tribal health project was formulated for the tribal areas in Andhra Pradesh but this plan or project had its own shortcomings. Three areas that the policy addressed inadequately were related to physical access to state health care services, quality of care provided and lack of information of the availability of such services to the public at large. Rao (1998) recommends that there is a need to bring about changes in the behaviour and attitudes of people related to health. This again has to be done not at the level of the individual but at the level of community.

The issue of community engagement as an important factor in health care has been brought-up in the context of health care in New Zealand. Tariana Turia (2003) puts before us a case in which there is a separate tribal health policy for the Maori tribes in New Zealand. This policy essentially recognizes the role of community in not only seeking health but, more importantly, in understanding the meaning of the health condition at the level of the community, or more precisely, the kin group or the Therapy Management Group (TMG). Turin calls this strategy *vis-à-vis* tribal health as a breakthrough in dealing with tribal health issues. This strategy has been developed by the Maori health workers. The central idea in this policy is related to *Whanau Ora*. This is basically the extended family group among the Maori. The extended family is the source of their identity, support, security and strength. It is envisaged within the strategy that the health workers should consider individual patients as part of their extended family. Turin gives a specific example to illustrate the said point. It has been argued that there was a case of building epidemic for Type-II diabetes. The health workers were unable to handle it by subscribing to the 'individualistic approach'. It was, however, realized that if the extended family group is brought into the picture and the issues related to the disease are routed through this group then there is a higher level of acceptance and compliance to the treatment regimen. The extended family becomes the therapy management group that understands all the aspects of the disease and takes responsibility for the patient. This has been projected as a paradigm shift in the health care policy from being individualistic to the one that recognizes the entire group involved in the therapy management.

Such cases can be replicated in the context of India and a more community-centric approach can be formulated. This calls for understanding the tribal health care systems and accordingly make plans and policies that best suit their needs. It is also contended by the authors that a need-based approach must be shunned for giving way to a strength-based approach. Tribal health systems need to be studied in order to understand various strengths that are already part of the system and then use those strengths to bring about a change in their status of health. This calls for not only understanding tribal medicine but the entire health care system. Seen from the strengths perspective, the community dimension of tribal health is an important part. Anthropological studies on tribal societies have shown that such societies have strong kinship and community bonds. If culture is visualized as a system of meaning then this meaning is constructed at a collective level. Health being more a cultural issue, the construction of meaning of ill-health and the cause of it becomes a collective issue. This has to be dealt at the level of the collectivity rather than at the individual level.

Anthropological research on tribal health has largely produced an understanding that projects tribal worldview about their health as a magico-religious worldview. However, Anthropologists have argued that it does not mean that since tribal worldview does not subscribe to the hegemonic modern bio-medical worldview of health, it should be shunned and declared null and void. P.C. Joshi (2004) has dealt with this issue in the context of health policies for tribes in India in greater details. He argues that tribal health care system is part of the larger belief system that defines tribal cosmology. In case we assume that this belief needs to be shunned then we must also provide them with effective and guaranteed alternative. He also argues further that we cannot totally disregard tribal belief and magico-religious approach to their health as it definitely has some psycho-social dimension to it. The significance of magico-religious practices lie in reducing anxiety, neurosis, phobias, stress and other psychopathological conditions. Besides this, the ritual performances related to treatment and diagnosis has a mass therapeutic effect that cannot be overlooked.

> "One of the great strength of tribal system of medicine is the involvement of group in therapy. The role and responsibilities of kins, affines, lineage-mates and the villagers who form the therapy management group in health seeking and helping in

therapeutic outcomes is a remarkable property of these systems. It is the lack of social milieu that has made hospitals and health centres alien places where the approach is individualistic and atomistic" (Joshi, 2004: 406).

Addressing Tribal Health Policy from the Perspective of the 'Anthropology of Empathy'

A running thread that binds the discussion so far in the chapter corresponds to the perspective that can be labelled as the 'Anthropology of Empathy'. This perspective emanates from reading the 'Anthropology of the Good' (Robbins, 2013). Joel Robbins has given a call for the 'anthropology of the good'. He is of the view that there occurred a paradigm shift in anthropology during the 1990s in terms of how the anthropological subject was defined. This shift is from viewing the subject as savage to the one who is seen as vulnerable. This vulnerability was due to the fact that the subject was living in poverty, malnutrition, under the conditions of violence and oppression. This kind of a shift gave a new opportunity for relating with the 'other' that occupied the centre stage of anthropological discourse. The relation between the self and the other came to be based upon empathy towards humanity as a whole. The common experiences of agony and distress became a bridge between the self and the other. This empathic turn in anthropology shunned the conception of the other as exotic and instead called for seeing the underlying sameness in the otherwise manifestation of the differences. This kind of a shift corresponds to the structuralist ideas in anthropology that are based upon the sameness of different cultures.

Within the anthropological discourse, the idea of human universal has a long history. The evolutionary paradigm talked about the psychic unity of mankind, but the major problem with this paradigm was that it promoted racism as it was believed that certain cultures have already climbed the ladder of development and progress. Contrary to the evolutionary idea, the relativist view of human universal helped in shedding the racist ideology. It propagated the line of thought that 'no culture is good or bad'. However, it also led to a particularistic view of cultures. It emphasized that every culture should be seen and understood in their own specific context. At the best we can be sympathetic to the 'other' but this line of thought made it difficult to empathize with the 'other'. With Robbins calling for the 'anthropology of the good', emphasis has shifted more towards the notion of 'empathy.' Similar to this line of thinking Dipankar Gupta (2000: 12) writes, "Belief in a common humanity begins with an act of faith. Facts as they present themselves impress us with their obvious diacritics. The temptation to stop here is great....The popular mind loves to separate the world on a perennial basis and a detailed account of pure difference feeds into that mindset straight away. All differences are made to appear as if they are naturally ordained. This is why when the specialist insists only on recording details of strangeness then the work falls in line with popular constructions of reality. Prejudices get a certain respectability, for now an academic work can be cited in its favour. Consequently, humanity takes a little beating....Look a little closer and these same diacritics which were so startlingly different at first sight assume a new meaning. These 'trophy facts' now come through as evidence of the universal human mind straining to make the most of specific histories and contingencies. The facts then lose their otherness. The call of the hour cannot be just for sympathy; that is easily done—it is no challenge at all. Sympathy and benevolence are attitudes of superiority. But to be able to empathize and stride alongside others requires an immersion in imagination....Only then will we realize that we share the same failings, the same talents, and the same drive to make the best of a given situation." This argument is actually based upon a more fundamental conflict in Anthropology and that is between the culturological and structural studies. The culturological studies focus on the cultural differences whereas the structural studies try to look for the underlying similarities. The empathy originates from seeing 'us' in 'them'.

Translating this paradigm into public policy related to tribal health means that we need to look into the tribal health and the health care system not from the point of view of sympathy but from an empathic viewpoint. Again this calls for looking beyond the culturological lens to understand the tribal health and its health care systems. It further means that instead of only looking at the values that differentiate the tribal cosmologies from the modern scientific medicine, we need to go deeper and understand the structural facts that define tribal health care systems. More often the culturological viewpoint juxtaposes the tribal health with the bio-medical system in which the former is viewed as magico-religious and the latter more scientific. Within this culturological view, only the tribal knowledge of herbs and medicinal plants is given importance and are considered as worthy of being emulated and adopted within the fold of larger health care. This level of acceptance of the 'tribal medicine' can still be viewed from the hegemonic and hierarchical lens or in other words it reflects the larger hegemonic way in which we incorporate the 'little' or the 'small' into the larger dominant scheme of things. In the

Indian context particularly, the Great Tradition is actually an extension and compilation of the already existing Little Tradition. This is a salient feature of the primary or indigenous civilization like India. The Great Tradition actually emerges from the universalization of the materials that form part of the Little Tradition.

Incorporating the structural dimensions of tribal health care systems into the public policy then becomes the hallmark and the major appeal of this approach. Visualizing 'us' in 'them' and more importantly transcending this 'we' and 'they' dichotomy informs us that systems originate in order to help us deal with the crisis of existence. Within this perspective tribal health care systems are built to deal with the existential crisis of the human species. This needs to be realized that besides having the 'content', the health system also consists of the 'capacity'. It is this capacity that needs to be factored in while thinking of health policy in tribal context. The example of the tribal health policy for the Maori in New Zealand is the case in point. It demonstrates the capacity of the extended family in a treatment regimen over the individualistic framework that is thought to be associated with the 'modern medicine' or the 'modern medical system'. It has, however, been argued that the individualistic paradigm most commonly associated with the modern medicine is actually 'Western' in origin and content. McKim Marriott (1955) argues that individualism is a Western trait and it has nothing to do with the modern system of medicine. This suggests that the modern biomedicine gets laden with the Western cultural practices and thoughts. It, therefore, supports the case for indigenizing medical practices. This gives another ground for empathic outlook and space for the flow of treatment regimens across different kinds of medical systems. It is, therefore, argued here that the tribal health care systems should be seen from the perspective of the capacity that they hold and not merely from the perspective of being irrational and non-scientific. Within this perspective, Bonaventura de Sousa Santos (2016), a Portuguese sociologist, has argued that there can be no social justice without global cognitive justice. Within the global context, nations are classified hierarchically on the basis of forms of knowledge. The Western form of knowledge based upon science and experimentation is considered as the most valid form of knowledge and the indigenous or traditional knowledge is not considered worthy of any attentions. Within the global context, the global North regards its culture as the most superior due to its rootedness in science. The global South is regarded as being inferior. Modern or bio-medicine then is placed over and above other systems of medicines. Not only the content is degraded by labelling it as non-scientific but the capacity of other systems of medicines is also doubted. Santos has argued that within the paradigm of modernity there are two forms of knowledge that can be recognized viz. knowledge as emancipation and knowledge as regulation. However, the latter form of knowledge has cannibalized the former. The paradigm of modernity and scientism has propagated the belief that there is no 'real knowledge' in the colonized countries except various beliefs, opinions, intuitions and subjective understandings. This is a very 'reductionist' and 'essentialist' understanding of knowledge that is based on the objectification of the orient and therefore reduces the orient to mere 'object of study' devoid of any legitimate form of knowledge. Against this backdrop, the chapter tries to give agency to the 'epistemologies of the south', by contextualizing institutional response to tribal health in India within the structural and relational framework of knowledge related to health and larger well-being. An attempt has been made to de-essentialize knowledge that appreciates content in the context of capacity. Scientism has led to an over-emphasis on the content and 'method' of knowledge accumulation and has neglected the 'capacity' dimension. A call for empathy is a call for a relational understanding that is against discrete and compartmentalized notions of knowledge and disciplines.

Sudhir Kakar (1982), one of the leading psycho-analysts, has for long argued that in the case of mental illness, the indigenous, local or regional systems of healing have the similar capacity as the psychoanalysis practiced and transported from the West. Besides Kakar (1982), it was also Claude Lévi-Strauss (1963) who demonstrated the similarity between shamanistic healing and psychoanalysis. It is here that Lévi-Strauss argued that the form of the myth may be different between the one used in psychoanalysis and shamanism but the underlying structure of the myths are same. Myths in the case of psychoanalysis are more personal and individualistic but in case of shamanism myths are more collective in nature. This similarity demonstrates the capacity of the healing in different systems. The reason that the modern medicine does not recognize the capacity of the indigenous healing practices is the underlying over-emphasis on one kind of idioms propagated by science at the cost of neglecting the indigenous idioms on which indigenous healing practices are based.

Strengthening the above argument in favour of the realization of the capacity of the indigenous systems of health and healing and the necessity of incorporating not only the medicinal aspect of the folk medicine but also the structural aspect like the role of the healer, the larger social network and importance of communistic over individualistic healing practices that is exemplified in the importance given not only to the patient but also to the therapy management group, is the Marxist understanding of health. The Marxist understanding of health raises a very fundamental question that "can the improvement in health be delinked from the fundamental changes in social order?" This question arises from another basic observation which suggests that increasing cost of health care do not coincide with improved health. On the contrary, it has been suggested that there are evidence of decreasing returns despite escalating cost of health care. Within this context Waitzkin (1981: 334) writes that "modern medicine's *effectiveness* in improving health is very hard to prove." During the 1970s, many studies had reiterated the point that technological advances in modern medicine do not correlate with improved measures of health (Waitzkin, 1981). On the contrary studies suggested that improvement in health correlated well with social changes like socio-economic development, better sanitation, environmental conditions and nutrition. Such conclusions are drawn from studies on infectious diseases that are thought to be most responsive to medical treatment. In one such study Edward Kass (1971) tried to link the mortality rate due to bacterial infections with the development of medicine and diagnostic technologies. Based on his empirical findings Kass (1971) came to the conclusion that a major decline in mortality rates associated with infectious diseases came much before the development of diagnostic technology for that particular disease and the medicine required to treat the disease. This observation was true for bacterial as well as for viral diseases. Kass (1971) writes, "This decline in the rate of certain disorders, correlated roughly with improving socio-economic circumstances, is merely the most important happening in the history of the health of man, yet we have only the vaguest and most general notions about how it happened and by what mechanisms socio-economic improvement and decreased rates of certain diseases run in parallel" (Kass, 1971: 111). This does not suggest however that advances in modern medicine are futile but to a very great extent this conclusion drives the point home that "the most impressive improvements in these diseases have not occurred because of modern medicine" (Waitzkin, 1981: 336). Waitzkin (1981) further elaborates on this by quoting Cochrane and he writes, "A.L. Cochrane, an eminent public health expert, has concluded, the twentieth century has been a "straightforward story of the ineffectiveness of medical therapy historically", as contrasted to the "layman's uncritical belief in the ability of the medical professional at least to help if not to cure" (Cochrane, 1972: 8).

Despite the above realization, there has been a continuous increase in the expenditure on modern medical treatments. In countries like India, the out of pocket expenditure on health has increased many folds and the health sector is largely governed by the private players. This emphasis on medical advancements and increase in expenditure can be seen from the perspective of a metamorphosis that happened during the 20th century in which the goals of medicine shifted from 'caring' to 'curing'. A more 'engineered' perspective on health and medicine gained ground at the cost of a more holistic care-oriented perspective that took care not only of the bio-medical dimension but also of the socio-cultural dimensions. Within the 'caring' model an emphasis was put on the physical as well as the emotional dimensions affected by disease. This was a more 'nurturant' approach towards ill-health. It is within this context that the empathic turn in anthropology *vis-à-vis* tribal health and public policy wants to drive home the point that integration of the tribal health care system as a whole with all its healers and relational dimensions will provide a holistic approach to tackle illness. However, within the modern scientific value systems 'tribal' systems of health care are seen as magico-religious, faith based, illogical, irrational and superstitious.

Despite this, within the empathic framework, cognitive justice paradigm and Nietzsche's call for "Re-evaluation of all values", there is a growing body of scholars who advocate for the integration of the tribal systems of health care within the primary health care. Ajit Dalal (2016) puts forth the argument that there are two schools of thoughts dealing with the question of integration of indigenous healing systems with modern medicine. The first school is based on the assumption that there lies a fundamental difference between the two systems of medicines in terms of their ontologies, epistemologies, etiologies and treatment regimens and therefore, no integration is possible between the two. The second school does not deny differences between the two systems of medicines but at the same time visualizes many possibilities for integration and thus the emergence of a unified health care delivery system that is more grounded to the needs, aspirations and worldviews of the people. Dalal (2016: 104) writes, "Apart from providing curative services, rural health centres should also be the nucleus of all-round socio-economic-spiritual development. To achieve this dream, it is important that social workers, school teachers, religious leaders and even faith healers are closely associated with the activities of the health centres."

Conclusion

Unfortunately, these dimensions of tribal health care system do not form the part of the National health policies. As is evident from the above discussion, tribal health gets a very passing reference in the otherwise bulky health policies governed largely by the bio-medical discourse on health. The approach of the state towards tribal health is more administrative and managerial in nature. It is largely driven by exhausting the allocated funding that is received in the name of providing health care. The overall approach of the Government can be visualized in terms of having more contact with the tribes which in turn is aimed at providing medical facilities by giving incentives to both the health-seekers and health-providers for their services in the tribal areas. However, the ground reality is an anti-thesis to what is desired. The health policy is largely driven by the capitalist model that has its base in bio-medicine. It has been argued that most of the major institutes and authorities that are dealing with public health in India have reiterated time and again that public sector spending on health care in India needs to be enhanced (Mishra and Agrawal, 2017). However, the NITI Ayog seems to be on another page *vis-à-vis* public spending on health care. The Ayog has been emphasizing on the role of private sector in primary health care. The National Health Policy, 2017 is largely driven by the Public Private Partnership approach. This calls for a greater say of the private sector in providing health care. At the policy level, it has been argued that the government is trying to shed its responsibilities *vis-à-vis* public health. The government has been recommending the state governments to rely more on the Public Private Partnership and Corporate Social Responsibility model to generate funds for public health concerns (Mishra and Agrawal, 2017).

In contrast to the larger approach of the National Health Policy, 2017, the Xaxa Committee report on Scheduled Tribes has recommended a larger and important role of the government in addressing health issues of tribes. The report recommends for the redesigning of the primary and secondary health care services in Scheduled Areas. The report recommends for a separate Tribal Health Plan. It also calls for investment in opening up new government medical colleges in the Scheduled Areas that cater to the special needs of the tribes. It also suggests for a separate Medical Education for Tribal Areas (META) that should have components like knowledge and sensitivity towards tribal culture and language, methods of communication, training and management of health teams etc. This approach is based more upon recognizing indigenous knowledge and tribal systems of health care rather than totally neglecting them. It is also based on bridging the gap between the bio-medical health system and tribal ways of life. Addressing tribal health also requires more and specific data regarding their health status which is missing at present. This calls for generating specific data on health indicators.

NOTE

1. http://pib.nic.in/newsite/PrintRelease.aspx?relid=148227

REFERENCES

Annual Report. 2017-18. Ministry of Tribal Affairs. Government of India.

Bonaventura de Sousa Santos. (2016). *Epistemologies of the South: Justice Against Epistemicide*, Routledge, New York.

Cochrane, A.L. (1972). *Effectiveness and Efficiency: Random Reflections on Health Care*, Nuffield Hospital Trust, London.

Dalal, A.K. (2016). *Cultural Psychology of Health in India: Well-being, Medicine and Traditional Health Care*, Sage, New Delhi.

Dreze, J. and Sen, A. (2002). *India: Development and Participation*, Oxford University Press, New Delhi.

Gupta, D. (2000). *Interrogating Caste: Understanding Hierarchy and Difference in Indian Society*, Penguin, Gurgaon.

Joshi, P.C. (2004). "Issues in Tribal Health and Medicines." In Kalla, A.K. and Joshi, P.C.(eds.). *Tribal Health and Medicine*, Concept, New Delhi.

Kakar, S. (1982). *Shamans, Mystics and Doctors: A Psychological Inquiry into India and its Healing Traditions*, Oxford University Press, New Delhi.

Kalla, A.K. and Joshi, P.C. (eds.). (2004). *Tribal Health and Medicine*, Concept, New Delhi.

Kass, Edward H. (1971). "Infectious Diseases and Social Change." *Journal of Infectious Disease, 123*: 110-114.

Khan, S. (2006). "Systems of Medicine and Nationalist Discourse in India: Towards 'New Horizons' in Medical Anthropology and History." *Social Science and Medicine, 62*: 2786-97.

Khattri, P. and Joshi, P.C. (2015). "Biomedicalization and Gandhi's Vision of Health: Observations from Sevagram." *Economic and Political Weekly*, Volume L, No. 10, pp 53-58.

Levi-Strauss, C. (1963). *Structural Anthropology*, Basic Books, New York.

Marriot, M. (1955). "Western Medicine in a Village of Northern India." In Benjamin, D. Paul (ed.). *Health, Culture and Community*, Russell Sage Foundation, New York.

Mazumder, P. (2018). "National Medical Commission Bill, 2017: A Shattered Hope." *Economic and Political Weekly*, Volume LIII, No. 5, pp. 12-15.

Mishra, P. and Agrawal, A. (2017). *Public Health in India: Gaps in Intent, Policy and Practice*, Issue Brief No. 7, The Hindu Centre for Politics and Public Policy.

Prasad, N.P. (2007). "Medicine, Power and Social Legitimacy: A Socio-Historical Appraisal of Health Systems in Contemporary India." *Economic and Political Weekly*, Volume 42, No. 34, pp. 3491-3498.

Prasad, N.P. and Raghavendra, P. (2012). "Health Care Models in the Era of Medical Neo-Liberalism: A Study of Aarogyasri in Andhra Pradesh." *Economic and Political Weekly*. Volume XLVII, No. 43, pp. 118-126.

Report of the High Level Committee on Socio-Economic, Health and Educational Status of Tribal Communities of India (2014). Ministry of Tribal Affairs, Government of India.

Robbins, J. (2013). "Beyond the Suffering Subject: Towards an Anthropology of the Good." *Journal of the Royal Anthropological Institute* (N.S.) *19*: 447-62.

Sujatha, Rao, K. (1998). "Health Care Services in Tribal Areas of Andhra Pradesh: A Public Policy Perspective." *Economic and Political Weekly*, Volume 33, No. 9, pp. 481-486.

Sujatha, V. (2014). *Sociology of Health and Medicine: New Perspectives*, Oxford University Press, New Delhi.

The Draft National Tribal Policy, 2006. Ministry of Tribal Affairs, Government of India.

The National Health Policy, 1983. Ministry of Health and Family Welfare, Government of India.

The National Health Policy, 2002. Ministry of Health and Family Welfare, Government of India.

The National Health Policy, 2017. Ministry of Health and Family Welfare, Government of India.

Turia, T. (2003). "Tribal Health Policy in New Zealand." *British Medical Journal*. Volume 327, No. 7412, p. 456.

Twelfth Five Year Plan (2012-2017), Volume III: Social Sector. 2013. Planning Commission, Government of India, Sage, New Delhi.

Waitzkin, H. (1981). "A Marxist Analysis of the Health Care Systems of Advanced Capitalist Societies." In Leon Eisenberg and Arthur Kleinman (ed.). *The Relevance of Social Science for Medicine*. D. Reidel Publishing Company, Holland.

Index